Knowledge in Ancient Philosophy

The Philosophy of Knowledge: A History

General Editor, Stephen Hetherington

'*The Philosophy of Knowledge: A History* is a tremendous achievement. Its four volumes cover the entire scope of Western epistemology, from the ancient world through the medieval and modern periods to the contemporary scene, with essays on the most influential figures in each of these periods. The result is a splendid overview on how fundamental questions about knowledge have been thought about over the millennia. These volumes will be the standard resource for all those interested in the history epistemology for decades to come.'

Richard Foley, Professor of Philosophy, New York University, USA

'This series of four volumes gives a reader the opportunity to take a fascinating voyage through the history of epistemology with an emphasis on the evolution of various theories of knowledge. The authors who contribute to the volumes are experts in their fields and the chapters in each volume are uniformly excellent.'

Richard Fumerton, F. Wendell Miller Professor of Philosophy,
University of Iowa, USA

'This ambitious fourfold work aims to provide an overview of Western epistemology, from the Greeks through contributions on the contemporary scene . . . An invaluable resource on epistemological topics and on the development of Western thought about them.'

Ernest Sosa, Board of Governors Professor of Philosophy,
Rutgers University, USA

The Philosophy of Knowledge: A History presents the history of one of Western philosophy's greatest challenges: understanding the nature of knowledge. Divided chronologically, these four volumes follow conceptions of knowledge that have been proposed, defended, replaced, and proposed anew by ancient, medieval, modern, and contemporary philosophers.

Each volume is centred around two key questions. What conceptions of knowledge have been offered? Which ones have shaped epistemology in particular and philosophy in general? Together, these volumes trace the historical development of knowledge for the first time.

Volume I *Knowledge in Ancient Philosophy*, edited by Nicholas D. Smith

Volume II *Knowledge in Medieval Philosophy*, edited by Henrik Lagerlund

Volume III *Knowledge in Modern Philosophy*, edited by Stephen Gaukroger

Volume IV *Knowledge in Contemporary Philosophy*, edited by
Stephen Hetherington and Markos Valaris

The Philosophy of Knowledge: A History

Volume I

Knowledge in Ancient Philosophy

Edited by Nicholas D. Smith

BLOOMSBURY ACADEMIC

LONDON · NEW YORK · OXFORD · NEW DELHI · SYDNEY

BLOOMSBURY ACADEMIC
Bloomsbury Publishing Plc
50 Bedford Square, London, WC1B 3DP, UK
1385 Broadway, New York, NY 10018, USA
29 Earlsfort Terrace, Dublin 2, Ireland

BLOOMSBURY, BLOOMSBURY ACADEMIC and the Diana logo
are trademarks of Bloomsbury Publishing Plc

First published in Great Britain 2019
Paperback edition published 2024

Copyright © Nicholas D. Smith and Contributors, 2024

Nicholas D. Smith has asserted his right under the Copyright,
Designs and Patents Act, 1988, to be identified as Editor of this work.

Cover image © The Yellow Books, 1887 (oil on canvas), Gogh, Vincent van
(1853–90)/Private Collection/Bridgeman Images

All rights reserved. No part of this publication may be reproduced or
transmitted in any form or by any means, electronic or mechanical,
including photocopying, recording, or any information storage or retrieval
system, without prior permission in writing from the publishers.

Bloomsbury Publishing Plc does not have any control over, or responsibility for,
any third-party websites referred to or in this book. All internet addresses given
in this book were correct at the time of going to press. The author and publisher
regret any inconvenience caused if addresses have changed or sites have
ceased to exist, but can accept no responsibility for any such changes.

A catalogue record for this book is available from the British Library.

A catalog record for this book is available from the Library of Congress.

ISBN: PB: 978-1-3504-4660-1

Typeset by Jones Ltd, London
Printed and bound in Great Britain

To find out more about our authors and books visit www.bloomsbury.com
and sign up for our newsletters.

Contents

List of Contributors	vi
General Editor's Preface	vii
Ancient Epistemology: Introduction *Nicholas D. Smith*	1
1 '*Sophia*' and '*Epistēmē*' in the Archaic and Classical Periods *David Wolfsdorf*	11
2 Presocratic Epistemology *Daniel W. Graham*	31
3 Epistemology in the Sophists *Noboru Notomi*	49
4 Socratic Epistemology *José Lourenço and Nicholas D. Smith*	67
5 Epistemology in Plato's Middle Dialogues *Naomi Reshotko*	85
6 Plato's Later Epistemology *Hugh H. Benson*	107
7 Aristotle on Understanding and Practical Wisdom *Corinne Gartner*	125
8 Aristotle: From Perception to Understanding *Keith McPartland*	145
9 Epicurean Epistemology *Pierre-Marie Morel*	169
10 Stoic Epistemology *Marcelo Boeri*	187
11 Ancient Scepticism *Paul Woodruff*	205
12 Epistemologies in Neoplatonism *Péter Lautner*	223
13 Roman Epistemology *Walter Englert*	241
Index	261

Contributors

Hugh H. Benson (University of Oklahoma, USA)

Marcelo Boeri (Pontificia Universidad de Chile, Chile)

Walter Englert (Reed College, USA)

Corinne Gartner (Wellesley College, USA)

Daniel W. Graham (Brigham Young University, USA)

Péter Lautner (Pázmány Péter Catholic University, Budapest)

José Lourenço (Federal University of Santa Maria, Brazil)

Keith McPartland (Williams College, USA)

Pierre-Marie Morel (Université Paris 1 – Panthéon-Sorbonne, France)

Noburu Notomi (University of Tokyo, Japan)

Naomi Reshotko (University of Denver, USA)

Nicholas D. Smith (Lewis & Clark College, USA)

David Wolfsdorf (Temple University, USA)

Paul Woodruff (University of Texas at Austin, USA)

General Editor's Preface

Stephen Hetherington

The Philosophy of Knowledge: Introduction to a History

Welcome to philosophy – to part of it, at any rate. A powerful and pivotal part of it, though: *epistemology*. Welcome to this survey – a tour, across four volumes – of a significant segment of epistemology's history. Western philosophy began in ancient Greece, before travelling far afield, still prospering. And whatever it is now is at least partly a consequence of whatever it has been. Within these four volumes, we meet much of whatever epistemology has been and is.

Why is this form of historical engagement philosophically important? Why is it important *now* to have some understanding of what epistemology has *been*? One reason is the possibility of current epistemology's being more similar to some or all of its former selves than it might at first seem to be, in productive and destructive ways. We should not merely be reinventing the epistemological wheel; nor should we repeat past epistemological mistakes – design flaws in earlier epistemological conveyances. To know epistemology's history is to know better what contemporary epistemology could be and perhaps should be – and what it need not be and perhaps ought not to be.

Epistemology is usually said to be the philosophy of knowledge and of kindred phenomena. But what makes it *the* philosophy of such matters? Well, epistemology has long been a collective endeavour – a gathering of individual efforts, by a plethora of epistemologists over oh-so-many years – to understand the nature of knowledge and those kindred phenomena. (Some of those efforts even ask whether there *is* a phenomenon of knowledge in the first place.)

How does that collective endeavour take shape? A first – a partial – answer is that epistemology is ineliminably *theoretical*. It is one theory, another theory, yet more theories, and so on. And so it is theories linking with, and departing from, other theories. It is theories living, developing, dying, reproducing, influencing, succeeding, failing. It is new themes replacing old ones. It is old themes replacing new ones.

viii   *General Editor's Preface*

And these four volumes will introduce you to such theories – competing conceptions of knowledge and those kindred phenomena, conceptions from across the ages. Volume I introduces us to theories from parts of the ancient world, the fount of all Western epistemology. Volumes II and III trace theories of knowledge as these arose over the following two millennia, late into the nineteenth century. Volume IV then tells a tale of the past century or so – while gesturing also at how epistemology might continue into at least the near future, taking us there from here. Not all of epistemology's past or present theorists and theories appear in these pages; but many do. The result is a grand story of sweeping intellectual vistas with striking conceptual foundations and ramifications. It is living philosophy. It is here, with you right now.

Ancient Epistemology: Introduction

Nicholas D. Smith

This volume offers thirteen chapters intended to provide at least glimpses of the main figures and schools of thought pertinent to the history of ancient epistemology. The volume thus covers thinkers from early in the Archaic Age of Greece through the work of the Roman philosophers of the first centuries BCE and CE – roughly, 700 years. Readers who go through any of the chapters included herein will quickly recognize that ancient interest in epistemology had a number of features that distinguish the field from what we are most likely to find in most contemporary discussions.

It is sometimes said that ancient philosophy was more interested in how philosophy could provide appropriate guidance in the practical concerns of living, and less concerned with conceptual analysis for its own sake. The following chapters provide significant evidence for such a claim, as every one of them includes some indication of how and why the ancient Greeks and Romans supposed that living a successfully philosophical life had to include some idea about our capacities as human beings to know – or, at any rate, to generate reliable beliefs about the world and our proper place in it. But the focus was mostly ethical and practical, and epistemological success or failure was characterized in practical terms, and not simply in veridical terms. Nor was there the same kind of attention as we find in contemporary debates on what might be called justification or warrant – that is, on what distinguishes knowledge from other forms of true belief. In some cases, what we find instead is that ancient authors tended more to distinguish knowledge from (mere) belief, rather than try to position it as a species of belief, where justification or warrant would be the main indicators of success or failure in one's epistemic mission.

1. Wisdom and skill

Several chapters (see especially 1, 4, 6, and 8) are careful to mention that ancient Greek has a bewilderingly diverse epistemic vocabulary. Moreover, even when some author or school clearly focuses on the subject of epistemology, it is often misleading (at best) to think of their primary focus as being anything we should even call 'knowledge' (see, especially, Chapters 7 and 8, both of which discuss the epistemology of Aristotle). Such discussions generally show us that we should try not to come to ancient philosophy or philosophers with our own primary epistemological terminology as defaults when we attempt to comprehend their works.

Perhaps the clearest example of why we should try to resist applying our own terminology when attempting to understand the ancients comes from the ways in which the Greeks explain what arguably becomes the primary word for ancient epistemology (and from which we actually get our own word, 'epistemology'), '*epistēmē*'. As David Wolfsdorf argues at length in Chapter 1, '*epistēmē*' in the earliest Greek contexts is used in a way that renders it interchangeable with '*sophia*', which Wolfsdorf notes is commonly translated as 'wisdom'. But Wolfsdorf also argues that '*sophia*' should probably be understood in its earliest appearances as denoting something more like 'skill' than anything as lofty as 'wisdom.' Either way, however, we are immediately confronted with something very unlike contemporary epistemology. No one these days would assume that the possession of (our conception of) knowledge was tantamount to the possession of something like *wisdom*, or even obviously anything like a skill.[1]

Knowledge, for us, is a cognitive state that consists in a true belief about some specific information, but which is distinguished from beliefs that have the same content but lack the same degree of justification or warrant. It is, at best, difficult to find anything like this conception in ancient Greek philosophy. For one thing, the content of knowledge (as we conceive of it) can be something so trivial as to be essentially worthless in any of life's meaningful pursuits. Here are some examples given by Ernest Sosa (2001: 49):

> Suppose you enter your dentist's waiting room and find all the magazines missing. Deprived of reading matter, you're sure to doze off, but you need no sleep. Are you then rationally bound to reach for the telephone book in pursuit of truth? Were you not to do so, you would forfeit a chance to pluck some desired goods within easy reach.

Ancient Epistemology: Introduction 3

If random telephone numbers do not elicit a wide enough yawn, consider a randomly selected cubic foot of the Sahara. Here is a trove of facts, of the form *grain x is so many millimeters in direction D from grain y*, than which few can be of less interest. Or take some bit of trivia known to me at the moment: that it was sunny in Rhode Island at noon on October 21, 1999. I confess that I will not rue my loss of this information, nor do I care either *that* or *how early* it will be gone. (Emphases in the original)

For the Greeks, '*epistēmē*' would generally be applied to whole fields of endeavour. Here is how Wolfsdorf puts it in his chapter: 'More precisely the knowledge or understanding that *epistēmē* consists in is a field or domain rather than an isolated fact' (p. 16 in Chapter 1). In this way of thinking, then, one who had *epistēmē* might be reasonably supposed to be in possession of some specific items of information – but even here, notice, *not just any sort of information* would suffice for knowledge. There may be many kinds and immense quantities of information to which the Greeks would recognize no application of *epistēmē*. To take one of Sosa's specific examples of completely trivial and valueless truth that one might know, Greeks might suppose that there could be *epistēmē* of meteorology,[2] but one would not likely ever find an example where a Greek would claim to have *epistēmē* of some completely trivial fact such as that it rained during the Panathenaic Games of a certain year. Similarly, though the Greeks mostly did treat geometry as an example of *epistēmē*, they did not generally count it a candidate for knowledge that, in a pile of sand, 'grain x is so many millimeters in direction D from grain y'. For the Greeks, if some information had no place in the kind of 'body of knowledge' that might constitute something like 'wisdom', then even if one could generate extremely reliable and justified beliefs about such information, it would not be an example of anything that would likely fall within the purview of epistemology, as they conceived it. So, it seems that we should conceive of the Greeks *epistēmē* as something like 'understanding'[3]; but then, we might wonder, didn't the Greeks even think about what *we* think is the main focus of epistemology, namely, *knowledge*?

2. Knowledge

In Chapters 2 and 3, Dan Graham and Noboru Notomi explain how the early Presocratic nature philosophers and Sophists began systematically to question the authority of older religious and intellectual traditions, while also proposing bold and highly controversial new theses about the nature of the cosmos, reality, and truth. The Presocratics, in Graham's account, proposed new naturalistic explanations of phenomena that had been the intellectual province of myth. One aspect of the traditional accounts they opposed was a very pessimistic view of the human epistemic condition: in this view, only gods could achieve any real comprehension of the world. Human epistemic capacity was mostly regarded as paltry. But some of the Presocratics sought to amend this view, and began to propose theories that allowed (mere) mortals to hope to learn more about the world through empirical observation and theorizing. Using (mere) human cognitive capacities, then, we might come to know important truths about our world and ourselves. But this optimistic picture is then paradoxically both amplified by but also problematized in the works of the Sophists. On the one hand, our access to truth, it might be supposed, is radically enhanced if we accept the Sophistical view that truth is whatever human beings may find persuasive. On the other hand, in this same view, what may be true to one cognitive agent will not be true for another, in which case knowledge of truth must either be equally relativized or else abandoned as (once again) available only to something like a god's-eye view of the world.

It was partly in reaction to the epistemic optimism of the naturalistic speculations of the Presocratics, but also to the relativism and anthropocentrism of the Sophists that we find Socrates (discussed by Lourenço and Smith in Chapter 4) attempting to mediate between the old religious strains of epistemic pessimism and the new optimism of the intellectual movements coming out of the Archaic and early Classical periods of Greek thought. As tradition had insisted, Socrates contrasted human epistemic capacities to those of divinity and counted the former as radically deficient. Socrates thus comes to make it his 'divine mission' to expose the pretence of wisdom that he finds so ubiquitous among his human peers. This is Socrates' famous 'agnoiology' – his interest in professing, exposing, and explaining human ignorance. But Lourenço and Smith also find notes of optimism here, as well: Socrates' agnoiology also includes ways in which we can remediate our ignorance and improve upon it.

Socratic agnoiology might be taken as expressing profound doubt about our chances of achieving *epistēmē* or *sophia* of the most ambitious kinds discussed in the previous section. But as Lourenço and Smith also note, Socrates is no global sceptic: they cite Plato's *Euthydemus* 293b where Socrates acknowledges that he knows many things, just 'small' things (*smikra*). The verb for 'know' that is used in his claim here is *epistamai* – hence Socrates here quite explicitly recognizes that one actually can, in his view, have *epistēmē* of *smikra* – which is just what seemed to be ruled out by the more comprehensive treatments of *epistēmē* that seem to require us to treat it differently from our 'knowledge'. Other Socratic claims of knowledge, though rare, can be found in Plato's dialogues, but none seem to involve the kind of *understanding* that other ancient epistemological discussions seem to require. Moreover, as Lourenço and Smith acknowledge, the kinds of knowledge that Socrates does recognize as humanly possible do not seem to be the sort that even Socrates seems to focus on as those that might constitute *sophia*/wisdom. For this sort of knowledge, they say, Socrates thinks we do best to look at skills (or crafts).

3. Epistemology of power and process

By the time we get to Plato's middle and later periods, epistemology has not only become one of the main philosophical concerns, but Plato's own epistemological thinking has become both more sophisticated, and perhaps also somewhat more tentative and exploratory. The complexities of Plato's more mature epistemological views are explored in the chapters by Naomi Reshotko and Hugh H. Benson (Chapters 5 and 6, respectively). Although it is safe to say that the earlier conception of *sophia* as skill remains evident in Plato's mature works, it is also clear that questions of cognitive capacity (or power) and cognitive process have become more significant. Plato explores several possibilities for answers to the questions, 'Can human beings ever know anything?' and 'If so, how can they do that?' In a way that is clearly more (if still guardedly) optimistic about the possibility of human knowledge, Plato's 'method of hypothesis' now appears as a way for human beings to conquer their ignorance. The same can be said for a theory that also appears in Plato –apparently for the first time – in his *Meno* (or possibly *Phaedo*)[4] – of the so-called 'theory of recollection', which, if anything, offers even greater reason for optimism. The former seems to offer a path to knowledge by way of a methodology of intellectual inquiry. The latter provides human beings with all the knowledge they could ever hope to have – provided that they find some way to remember it. In neither case does Plato characterize what is needed for epistemic success as likely to come easily. But in each case, a path to knowledge is opened.

Plato's new focus on methodology and a metaphysics of what can be known leads him to think more deeply about cognitive capacities and processes, and this new focus becomes especially clear in Book V of the *Republic*, where he characterizes knowledge, opinion, and ignorance as cognitive *dunameis* ('powers' or 'capacities'). As Reshotko notes, it seems a mistake to understand what Plato is doing here in terms of our 'propositional attitudes' since the putative objects of these powers or capacities do not seem to be propositions or anything like them, but are, rather, Plato's Forms. It would seem, accordingly, that Plato is here more interested in what we might call 'knowing what F is' where F is a characteristic metaphysically grounded in some Form, rather than anything like our own 'knowing that *p* [some fact or information] is true'. This same suspicion is perhaps made more vivid in the famous similes of light (sun, divided line, and cave) where we are asked to consider the relative merits of cognitions involving Forms and their images in sensible things, or worse, in shadows or reflections of sensible things.

As Benson goes on to show, Plato's epistemology provides discussions of many topics that seem much more familiar to contemporary epistemology than the chapters on earlier figures and works. His argument in Chapter 6, however, runs contrary to certain stereotypes of Plato as a kind of radical rationalist: Benson finds abundant evidence in three of Plato's latest dialogues for accepting the possibility of empirical knowledge. As he notes, all reference to Forms seems to go missing in Plato's *Theaetetus*, and the models for knowledge and examples of it all seem to imply the possibility of empirical knowledge – including what some scholars think is ruled out in the 'two-worlds' of the *Republic*, for example, knowledge of sensibles. Here again, Plato's attention to the kind of knowledge found in craft (*technē*) returns strongly. Even as Plato repeats the same kinds of things he said about knowledge in his earlier works (i.e. that it must display stability, clarity, precision, purity, truth, and being), we find Plato freely applying the highest epistemic honours quite inclusively. As Benson puts it, 'Music, medicine, farming, sailing, generalship, house-building, ship-building, building in general, commerce, arithmetic, measuring, weighing – in both the popular and philosophical varieties, and dialectic are all explicitly described as kinds of knowledge (*epistēmai*)' (p. 120 in Chapter 6). So knowledge may still need to be regarded as skill, here in later Plato, but it is also surely true that such skills would not be possible without knowledge of facts or information in our sense.

4. Aristotle and understanding

It is probable that Aristotle is at once the most epistemically optimistic of the ancient philosophers, but also the one whose requirements for the aspirational ideal of epistemology are the most demanding. Indeed, both chapters on Aristotle

(7 and 8, by Corinne Gartner and Keith McPartland, respectively) emphasize just how demanding his epistemology is. Both consider Aristotle's treatment of *epistēmē* to be best understood as 'understanding' or 'scientific understanding' and explicitly reject the idea that what Aristotle is talking about is comparable to our own concept of knowledge. In Aristotle, *epistēmē* in the strictest sense (what he calls *epistēmē haplōs*, which Gartner and McPartland both translate as 'unqualified understanding') applies only to topics that cannot be otherwise and are thus presumably logically necessary (*Posterior Analytics* 71b15). As McPartland puts it, 'Understanding, therefore, involves both objective necessity and subjective certainty' (p. 145 in Chapter 8). But this immediately raises a problem: can there be understanding when it comes to ethics, politics, and what we would call the 'natural sciences'? Gartner's chapter takes up the first two of these possibilities (ethics and politics), noting at the outset that Aristotle even explicitly stipulates that there is such a thing as the 'political science' (*politikē epistēmē*). The problem is that whatever such understanding might be, it is obviously closely associated with what Aristotle calls 'practical wisdom', which by its nature applies to contingent particularities. There seems, thus, to be a distinct epistemology for the fields of ethics and politics. Gartner and McPartland agree that the way to account for this may be found in the location of practical reasoning in a distinct 'part of the soul' than the one associated with scientific reasoning (understanding).

McPartland's chapter explores the relationships between understanding and other cognitive achievements that Aristotle regards as lesser, but still epistemically significant ones, which include what McPartland thinks we should count as knowledge in something more like our sense. One can have knowledge without understanding; but one cannot have understanding without knowledge. In McPartland's account, the epistemology provided by Aristotle is broadly naturalist and externalist. As familiar as such an approach may seem, however, McPartland warns that we should not forget just how far Aristotle deviates from the concerns of contemporary epistemologists. So, for a few examples, 'some of the central concerns that drive modern or contemporary epistemologists receive little treatment by Aristotle. He never, to my knowledge, undertakes a general discussion of justification or warrant. His treatment of scepticism is brief and can look like it simply misses the point' (pp. 147–8 in Chapter 8).

The net effect of the distinction between Aristotle's conceptions of understanding and knowledge, accordingly, is that what *we* call 'science' belongs to the epistemological domain of knowledge, rather than understanding; what is often translated as 'science' in Aristotle's treatment, however, belongs to a different domain, and Aristotle is clear that what occupies this other domain is a superior epistemic achievement.

5. Epistemology in service of an ethical goal

As much as Aristotle is often characterized as the great ancient empiricist, Pierre-Marie Morel and Marcelo Boeri (in Chapters 9 and 10, respectively) show plainly how the true ancient empiricists were the Epicureans and Stoics. Morel finds that the Epicureans qualify as 'rational empiricists', who recognize a role for reason in accordance with experience, and can thus articulate a broadly 'scientific' worldview that can also ultimately support their primary goal, which is an ethical one: the achievement of *ataraxia*, absence of disturbance. Given the primacy of their empiricism – and especially their belief that perception is always true in some sense – our susceptibility to false belief requires explanation in Epicurean philosophy. Morel locates this in our capacity for what the Epicureans call 'preconception' from which the inerrant perceptions generate conceptions which may then be compared and on the basis of which potentially faulty judgements or theories reached.

Boeri reminds us not only of the thoroughgoing materialism of the Stoics, but also of their claim that 'there is nothing in our souls before our perceptual experience has taken place' (p. 191 in Chapter 10). Boeri contrasts this to Plato's earlier theory (discussed in Naomi Reshotko's Chapter 5) of knowledge as recollection. In spite of this sharp departure from Plato's 'rationalism', Boeri recognizes that the Stoics continue to accept Plato's distinction between knowledge and opinion as involving distinct processes (rather than treating the former as a species of the latter). Like the Epicureans, the Stoics find our original conceptual apparatus to derive directly from perception, via the formation of 'preconceptions' which Boeri explicates as the spontaneously generated concepts that derive from individual perceptions: 'What the Stoics presumably thought is that one can have the concept of horse because one has previously seen a horse' (p. 193). We then add depth and complexity to these first cognitive states by comparing them to others, via memory, and then deploy such conceptions in the making of judgements.

As with the Epicureans and Stoics, the epistemology of the ancient sceptics was intended to serve the same basic ethical goal of freedom from disturbance in the soul. But unlike the Epicureans and Stoics, who each in their own different ways thought that this goal could be achieved through scientific knowledge, the sceptics contended that the goal of tranquillity could only be reached via a suspension of belief (*epochē*) – at least as far as that was possible. Knowledge or understanding, in their view, was not something available to human beings, and the uncertainties and fallibilities of human cognitive capacities were therefore sure to create the kind of psychic disturbance that a humanly wise agent would best avoid. They opposed rationalism and also empiricism, as both would lead us into the error of belief. Accordingly, they advocated strategies of creating opposing reasons on every topic. The goal of such arguments was the opposite of any attempt to *convince* the audience; rather, as Paul Woodruff puts it in Chapter 11 on the sceptics, 'Their arguments then need not be watertight, so long as they make their audience feel like relaxing into *epochē*' (p. 211). Woodruff follows how the sceptics and Stoics actually supported one another through their 200 years of disputing each other, the former seeking to debunk the theories of the latter, and the latter seeking to shore up their doctrines against sceptical attacks. In these debates, the epistemic optimism of the Stoics (shared by the Epicureans) is set against the extreme epistemic pessimism of the sceptics.

6. The last ancient epistemologies

The Neoplatonists (covered in Péter Lautner's Chapter 12) sought to return to Platonic rationalism (and to the epistemic optimism inherent in it), providing even an account of perception that explained its efficacy in terms of innate cognitive content, probably reminiscent of Plato's 'Theory of Recollection'. The Platonists (as they call themselves) thus rejected the empiricism of later antiquity, and also the scepticism that opposed it. So, too, the Platonists rejected the materialism of the Epicureans and Stoics, once again insisting on the immateriality of the soul.

The Romans, however – discussed by Walter Englert in Chapter 13 – mostly defended or expanded upon trends initiated by their Greek predecessors, and return us again to the theories rejected by the Neoplatonists. Englert shows the extent to which Lucretius, for example, both clarifies and adds depth to the Epicureanism that he follows. Cicero, however, brings Academic Scepticism to his Roman readers, and offers a continuation of the sceptics' debates against Stoic views. One hundred years later, Seneca defends Stoicism to the Roman audience. It would not be fair to these later thinkers to say that they merely repeated the efforts of their Greek forebears. Englert puts the point well: 'They also demonstrated mastery of the epistemological doctrines of their schools and showed how epistemology could buttress the arguments they were making about how best to live one's life' (p. 257). So here, at the end of ancient epistemology, we continue to see the importance of epistemology in its service to practical and ethical concerns.

Notes

1   I am aware, of course, of the epistemological works of the general editor of this four-volume series, Stephen Hetherington (2011), who has strongly emphasized what we normally call 'know-how' in his own works. My point is made by the very fact that, in doing so, Hetherington's work is recognized as taking a very different approach to epistemology than is common among contemporaries. In my view, Hetherington's work has much more in common with the epistemological works of the ancients than does most contemporary analytical epistemology.
2   See Aristotle's work on this topic, for example.
3   See Chapters 1, 7, and 8 in this volume.
4   This will obviously depend on how we determine the relative dates of authorship for the different dialogues, which continues to be a matter of controversy among scholars. While this is plainly not the place to engage in such debate, I will simply report that most scholars have taken the *Meno* to have been written before the *Phaedo*, and these are the two places where we might sensibly look for the first expressions of the 'method of hypothesis' and the 'theory of recollection' in Plato's works. Whether there were 'inklings' or 'anticipations' of these ideas in earlier works may also be reasonably debated.

References

Hetherington, S. (2011), *How to Know: A Practicalist Conception of Knowing*, Malden, MA: Wiley-Blackwell.
Sosa, Ernest (2001), 'For the Love of Truth?', in Linda Zagzebski and Abrol Fairweather (eds), *Virtue Epistemology: Essays on Epistemic Virtue and Responsibility*, Oxford: Oxford University Press.

1

'*Sophia*' and '*Epistēmē*' in the Archaic and Classical Periods

David Wolfsdorf

1. Introduction

My aim here is to discuss the philosophical use of the terms '*sophia*' and '*epistēmē*' in relation to one another from their earliest occurrences through Aristotle. I begin with pre-philosophical use for this will help to explain the philosophers' employment and adaptation of the terms.

2. Pre-philosophical uses of '*sophiē*'

In philosophical contexts the originally Ionic noun '*sophiē*', later Attic '*sophia*', is standardly translated as 'wisdom', the adjective '*sophos*' as 'wise'. But this will not do for the earliest, pre-philosophical use (cf. Snell 1924: 1–20; Gauthier and Jolif 1959: 479–89; Gladigow 1965; Meier 1970). In eighth- and seventh-century poetry '*sophiē*' means 'skill', '*sophos*' 'skilled' or 'skilful'.[1] As we will see, wisdom is skill; but in the early poets the skills denoted by these terms are not forms of wisdom.

Formal semanticists have noted that 'skill', 'skilful', and 'skilled' are semantically incomplete terms in the sense that a person who has skill or is skilful isn't skilful *simpliciter*, but in a particular domain. Compare 'citizen', which is semantically incomplete in a distinct, but related way: one is not a citizen *simpliciter*, but of a particular political body.

There are various theories of such semantic incompleteness. In the case of 'skilful' one view is that in its so-called logical, as opposed to surface grammatical, form the predicate contains a domain variable whose value is supplied by context (be it linguistic or extralinguistic). So the logical form of '*x* is skilful' may be represented as:

SKILFUL(s)(x)   where the variable s stands for a domain of skill.

For example, a father may say of his artistic son and musical daughter: 'He is skilful and she is too.' Here the first instance of 'skilful' takes art for the domain of *s*, the second music.

In its earliest uses '*sophiē*' and '*sophos*' range over such domains of skill as carpentry, navigation, and charioteering. Consider the following examples from Homer, Archilochos, and Alcman:

> Just as a carpenter's line makes ship's timber straight
> when the hand of a craftsman applies it, one who, inspired by Athena,
> knows well all facets of the skill (*sophiē*) –
> just so tensely poised the fighting in that battle stood. (Homer, *Iliad* 15.410–13)[2]
> [G]ood with a trident and a skilful pilot (*kubernētēs sophos*). (Archilochos, fr. 211 West)
> Castor and illustrious Polydeuces, skilful charioteers (*hippotai sophoi*), tamers of swift colts. (Alcman, fr. 2A.3–4 Snell)

From about the sixth century, we find instances of '*sophiē*' that denote poetic skill, for instance, in the following verses of Solon (640–558): 'One man earns his living by his hands in the works of Athena and the master of many crafts Hephaestus; another, through his learning in the gifts of the Olympian Muses, knows the measure of the lovely skill (*himertēs sophiēs*)' (fr. 13.49–52). A number of editors have suggested that the noun is so used in the following fragment of Sappho (c. 630–570): 'I do not imagine that any girl who has looked on the sun's light will have such skill (*sophia*) at any future time' (fr. 60 Snell). Certainly by the fifth century '*sophiē*' is frequently used to denote poetic skill (cf. Barmeyer 1968: 155–62), for example, in Pindar: 'May you may plant your feet on high so long as you live, and may I may consort with victors for all my days and be foremost in skill (*sophiē*) among the Hellenes in every land' (*Olympic Ode* 1.115–17).

Also in the sixth century we first find '*sophiē*' used to denote personal or social skills. Particularly fascinating examples occur in the Theognidea. For instance, the following two passages liken quality of character to coins and accordingly the skills required to discern and control character and quality:

> Deception of gold or silver, Cyrnus, is easily endured;
> and it is easy for a skilful (*sophos*) man to disclose.
> But if it has escaped notice that the mind of a friend is false

and that his heart holds deceit,

god has made this most deceptive for mortals. (1.120)

Cunning men know gold and silver in the fire.

And wine has exposed the mind of a man,

when he has drunk too much, when he has taken drink beyond measure,

so that it puts to shame one who before was *sophos*. (1.502)

To my ear 'skilful' sounds slightly awkward as a rendition of '*sophos*' in the second passage. 'Self-controlled' or 'discerning' is more natural. Nonetheless the author is evidently conceptualizing self-control or discernment as a skill, an ability to govern one's social conduct.

It may be questioned whether the sixth-century use of '*sophiē*' to denote personal or social skill is in fact a semantic development. An alternative view is that '*sophiē*' always included these domains, but that the extant record merely happens to lack evidence of such employment.

The following considerations encourage the thesis that the use of '*sophiē*' to denote personal and social skill is a genuine semantic development. One is a sort of argument from silence. In the earliest Archaic poetry, which is replete with references to personal and social skills, '*sophiē*' and '*sophos*' are never so used. For instance, Homer never describes Nestor, Odysseus, or Aeneas as '*sophos*'.

A second consideration relates to the passages of the Theognidea just cited: there '*sophiē*' appears to be deliberately transposed from a non-social to a social domain. Compare the following use of '*sophos*' from a late-sixth- or early-fifth-century Boeotian grave stele:

The children created this memorial for their deceased father Gathon,

a man *sophos* in guest-friendship (*xsenian*) and horsemanship (*hiposunan*). (*SEG* XV.316)

Here the conjunction of a non-social skill horsemanship and guest-friendship a social skill appears deliberately and poetically zeugmatic. Loosely related are the following sixth-century verses in which Anacreon employs equestrian skill as a metaphor for sexual skill:

Thracian filly, why so sharply shy away?

Do you think I know nothing *sophon*?

Be assured, I'd put your bit on smartly,

hold the reins and run you round the limits of the course.

But for now you graze the meadows, frisk and play,

for want of any experienced riding man. (fr. 88 Snell)[3]

Assume, then, that the semantic development did occur. Possibly, one factor contributing to the development was the increasingly common use of '*sophiē*' to denote poetic skill. Some aspects of ancient poetry are relatively technical; others, particularly those pertaining to the content of poetry, involve personal and social thought. Given the prevalent use of '*sophiē*' to denote poetic skill, the ubiquitous coincidence of these two aspects may have contributed to the semantic shift precisely through their association.

Phrases such as 'wise carpenter' and 'wise charioteer' are odd or nonsensical. Not so 'wise poet'. The reason is that poetry can express personal or social thought that satisfies the following two conditions:

G The thought is ethical or moral or at least constitutes or promotes human goodness;

H The thought consists in a deep understanding of humanity.

I am suggesting then that wisdom is precisely this: personal or social skill that satisfies conditions G and H.

A word on the disjunction in G. Consider the peculiarity of: 'He is wise, but unethical' or 'She is wise, but immoral'. So wisdom is ethical or moral. However, what we call 'ethics' as it relates to ancient Greek philosophy is eudaimonistic. Eudaimonia is a life that goes well for the agent. It is an open question whether or to what extent such a life is good for others. For instance, consider Thrasymachus' question in *Republic* I: Is justness an excellence (*aretē*)? Again it is an open question whether, in case such a life is in some way good for others, it more precisely involves respect for the autonomy of others and recognition of their equal worth. But if for character or action to be ethical or moral it must be concerned with the welfare of, respect the autonomy of, or recognize the equal worth of others, and if 'wisdom' is an ethical or moral term, then it is doubtful that Greek eudaimonism is ethical or moral and so whether '*sophiē*' can ever strictly be rendered as 'wisdom'.

Granted this, I will conveniently and stipulatively employ the terms 'wisdom' and 'wise' in what I will call a 'relativistic' sense. By 'relativistic' I mean to acknowledge the variety of conceptions of human goodness and good human lives among philosophers and across cultures and to admit a sense of 'wisdom' as the skill that, in addition to satisfying condition H, constitutes human goodness or promotes good human life, however such goodness is conceived. According to this relativistic sense a self-regarding and self-benefitting skill may be constitutive of wisdom. For example, if, as some have argued, Epicureanism is psychologically egoistic, then the skill required to pursue and maintain Epicurus' hedonistic eudaimonia is a case in point.

Regarding condition H, the following inference does not appear to be valid: 'She is ethical or moral or is a good person or aims to promotes good human life, therefore she is wise.' The reason the inference fails, I am suggesting, is that one may be ethical or moral or at least aim to promote good human life, yet lack a deep understanding of humanity. Such depth of understanding is then required for wisdom. Moreover I underscore that condition H involves no commitment to the universality or fixity of human nature or the human condition. Rather, consistently with the relativeness of conceptions of human goodness and the human condition, H permits such understanding to be culturally and historically local.

Given the extension of the domain of '*sophiē*' to personal and social skill, from about the sixth century it becomes possible to use the noun and adjective in ways that are, according to this relativistic sense, aptly rendered as 'wisdom' and 'wise'. Possibly the following verses of Solon contain an early example (fr. 27.16): 'In the ninth age [= 63–69 years old] a man is still capable, but his tongue and his *sophiē* are weaker as far as great acts of excellence are concerned.'

More certain is an instance of the adjective in the Scopas Ode of Simonides (556–468) where the poet describes Pittacus of Mytilene as a '*sophos* man'. Although Simonides is also critical of Pittacus, the topic is human goodness and Pittacus' judgement of its nature:

> For a man it is certainly hard to be truly good: perfect in hands, feet, and mind, built without a flaw. Only a god could have that prize; but a mere man, he cannot help being bad when some overwhelming disaster knocks him down. Any man is good when life treats him well, and bad when it treats him badly; and the best of us are those the gods love most. But for me the saying of Pittacus doesn't ring true either – even if he was a *sophos* man. He says 'being good is hard'. (fr. 37.1)[4]

3. Pre-philosophical uses of '*epistēmē*'

The verb '*epistamai*' and cognates such as the adverb '*epistamenōs*' occur in the earliest Greek literature. The verb can be used with a direct object in which case it means 'to know or understand something', as well as with an infinitive meaning 'to know how to do something'. The noun '*epistēmē*' is constructed by adding to the verbal root the common nominalizing suffix '-*ma*' (or here '-*mē*').

This suffix often serves to denote a result or product, in this case the knowledge or understanding gained from a process of coming to know or understand. More precisely the knowledge or understanding that *epistēmē* consists in is a field or domain rather than an isolated fact. Compare the knowledge of medicine with the knowledge that Coriscus has pneumonia. At any rate I assume that knowledge of facts and knowledge of a field are interdependent. I return to this point below.

The noun '*epistēmē*' is first attested only in the first half of the fifth century (cf. Snell 1924: 81–96; Schaerer 1930: 1–21), in Bacchylides' tenth epinician ode:

> Each man seeks a different path on which to walk to attain conspicuous glory; and among men the forms of knowledge (*epistamai* [the noun here is plural]) are countless. One man is skilled (*sophos*) if he has a share of honour from the Graces and blooms with golden hope, or if he is knowledgeable in the prophetic art; another aims his artful bow at boys; others swell their spirits with fields and herds of cattle. (10.37–45)

Unfortunately we lack a date for this poem. A *terminus ante quem* is Bacchylides' death; unfortunately this is also unclear, although c. 450 is generally accepted.

An instance of '*epistēmē*' occurs in the Hippocratic treatise *Places in Man*:

> The man who knows (*epistatai*) medicine least depends on luck. But whether with or without luck, his actions would succeed. For all medicine has advanced, and its finest established techniques seem to have very little need of luck. For luck is autocratic and ungovernable; and it is not wont to come in response to one's desire. But knowledge (*epistēmē*) is governable and brings success when one who knows (*epistamenos*) desires to use it. (46.1)

In her recent edition of the treatise, Elizabeth Craik (1998: 25–9) argues for an early-fifth-century date. She also argues for a Western Greek origin for the treatise (29). Bacchylides himself was from Keos in the Cyclades. If Craik's claims are correct, then assuming that Bacchylides and the Hippocratic author did not independently coin '*epistēmē*', the term would have been available across a large portion of Greece in the fifth century in both poetic and prosaic contexts.

Even so through the second half of the fifth century '*epistēmē*' remains a rare term in prose and poetry. The word does not occur in Herodotus (484–25), Antiphon (480–11), or Andocides (440–390). Nor does it occur in Aeschylus (525–456) or Aristophanes (446–386). It occurs three times in Sophocles (496–406): once each in *Antigone* (c. 441), *Oedipus Rex* (c. 430), and *Philoctetes* (409). Especially remarkable, the word occurs only once in Euripides (480–406), in a fragment of his lost *Meleager* (fr. 422), which is dated to 418 or later. (Contrast eleven occurrences of '*sophia*' and hundreds of occurrences of '*sophos*' in Euripides.) The one author in whom '*epistēmē*' occurs with some frequency, precisely fourteen times, is Thucydides (460–395). These occurrences are then datable to the period in which Thucydides wrote his history: 431–11.

With the exception of philosophical usage, discussed below, there are no other instances of '*epistēmē*' in the fifth century. In sum, '*epistēmē*', formed from a common verb using a common nominalizing suffix, was first employed in the first half of the fifth century and throughout the century remained a rare noun.

A note now on the pre-philosophical relation between '*sophiē*' and '*epistēmē*'. Semantically '*epistēmē*' and '*sophiē*' (as it was used by the sixth century) appear to be interchangeable. Compare the uses of '*epistēmē*' and '*sophos*' in the Bacchylides passage cited above: 'among men the forms of knowledge (*epistamai*) are countless. One man is skilled (*sophos*) if he …' In the following passage of the Theognidea, '*sophiē*' is the object of the participle '*epistamenos*' (1.563–5): 'It is well to be a guest at a feast and sit beside a good man who knows (*epistamenon*) all *sophiē*. You should mark him whenever he says anything *sophon* so that you may learn and go home with much gained.' Recall also the verse from Solon cited above: '[he] knows (*epistamenos*) the measure of the lovely skill (*sophiē*)'.

Finally, observe that the interchangeability of '*epistēmē*' and '*sophiē*' encourages the view that knowledge is skill.

4. Philosophical uses of '*sophiē/a*' in the fifth century

The first extant philosophical uses of '*sophiē*' occur in a fragment of Xenophanes (c. 570–475), which contrasts the rewards bestowed on successful athletes with those owed to the author himself on account of his political skill:

> Even if [an athlete] won [in chariot racing], he would get all [these public rewards] but would not merit [them] as I do: for better than the strength of men and horses is our skill (*sophiē*). But most vain is the present custom: it is wrong to prefer strength to noble skill (*agatha sophiē*). For neither if there is a good boxer among the people, nor a pentathlete, nor a wrestler, nor even one swift of foot, the first most honoured in feats of strength in contests, would the city be one whit better governed. Small is the delight that would come to a city if someone won a contest by the banks of the Pisa, for this does not fatten the coffers of a city. (B2.11–22)[5]

Xenophanes' late-sixth- or early-fifth-century usage is consistent with non-philosophical use of the Archaic period, although this appears to be the first time politics is explicitly specified as the domain of *sophiē*. The deployment of '*sophiē*' in connection with politics is significant insofar as political skill and leadership are viewed as consummate human achievements – a view Xenophanes is evidently endorsing.

The most important early philosophical instances of '*sophiē*' and '*sophos*' occur in Heraclitus (535–475) who employs them several times in relation to the divinity responsible for the organization of the cosmos (B32, 82, 83, 108; cf. B50, 112, 118, 129) – for instance, (B41): '*To sophon* is one thing: knowing (*epistasthai*) the thought that pilots all things through all.'[6] Heraclitus' peculiar use of the definite description '*to sophon*' (literally 'the skilful [thing]') rather than the general term '*sophiē*' apparently serves to underscore his idea that only one thing deserves the title of '*sophon*'. In other words strictly speaking there is only one skill.

Other fragments confirm that the divinity that pilots the cosmos is itself *sophos*, for instance, (B32): 'One thing alone said to be the skilful (*to sophon*) would and would not be called by the name "Zeus".'

So, Heraclitus maintains that there is a crucial relation between the excellent state of soul (*psychē*) a human being may achieve and that of the divinity responsible for piloting the cosmos.[7] Consider also Heraclitus' claim that sound thinking (*sōphronein*), which he asserts to be 'the greatest excellence (*aretē*) and *sophiē*', consists in acting 'on the basis of an understanding of the nature of things' (B112). Compare this with Empedocles' characterization of the pinnacle of *sophiē* as consisting in an understanding of each thing:

> Do not let it compel you to accept the blossoms of illustrious honour from mortals by boldly saying more than is pious, and then to sit on the heights of *sophiē*. But come, behold each thing by every means it is clear, not holding any view more reliable than hearing, nor resounding hearing beyond the clarifications of tongue; nor from any of the other organs, by which there is a passageway to understanding, withhold trust, but understand each thing in the way it is clear. (B3.6–13)[8]

And consider Empedocles' praise of Pythagoras whom he regards as an exemplar of such *sophiē* (B129): 'There was a man among them of extraordinary knowledge, who had earned the greatest wealth of mind, the master of every sort of especially skilful works (*sophōn ergon*). For whenever he reached out with all his mind, easily he beheld each of all existing things, for ten or even twenty generations of men.'

In sum, Heraclitus and then Empedocles express ideas here that in various guises play a central role in much subsequent Greek philosophy. The crux of these ideas is that there is a kind of *sophiē* that supersedes all others. This master skill consists in some form of cosmological understanding; and a human being fully realizes his potential, best serves himself and presumably also others by acquiring and then acting on the basis of it (cf. *Dissoi Logoi* 8.2; Democritus B59). When used to denote such a skill '*sophiē*' is reasonably translated as 'wisdom' in the relativistic sense.[9]

Note however that '*sophiē*' is not a common, let alone preferred epistemological term among the major fifth-century philosophers. For instance, neither the noun nor the adjective occurs in the fragments of Parmenides, Zeno, Melissus, Philolaus, or Diogenes of Apollonia. There might be an instance of '*sophia*' in Anaxagoras (B21b), but it is debatable whether the term is part of a quotation or rather Plutarch's paraphrase from the first century CE.

The complete absence of '*sophiē*' and '*sophos*' among these philosophers most likely owes to the paucity of their fragments.[10] However, especially towards the late fifth century and beginning of the fourth century we find '*sophiē/a*' or '*sophos*' in several philosophers or philosophical texts including: Gorgias, Antiphon, Democritus, Critias (assuming he is the author of the *Sisyphus* fragment), the *Dissoi Logoi*, and *Anonymus Iamblichi*.[11] In some of these instances, the term is not specifically used to convey 'wisdom', but rather to denote skill in some other domain, for instance (Cri. B25.34; cf. Antiphon B49.12): 'He beheld the heavenly vault wherein dwell the lightnings and awesome claps of thunder, and the starry face of heaven, beautiful adornment of that skilful (*sophos*) carpenter Time.'[12] But in many cases, especially those in Democritus, the *Dissoi Logoi*, and *Anonymus Iamblichi*, 'wisdom', be it purely personal or political, is the conveyed sense. For instance, in the *Dissoi Logoi* (6.3, 7.3–4), which is dated to c. 404–395, '*sophia*' is used in contrast to '*technē*' (craft, art, skill), where the latter is explicitly used to denote various manual and what might be called 'technical' skills such as smithery, cobbling, carpentry, music, archery, and horsemanship. (Observe the resemblance between this range of skills and those to which '*sophiē*' seems limited in its earliest Archaic usage.) Compare Democritus who contrasts *sophiē* with medical *technē*: 'Medicine (*iatrikē* [*technē*]) heals the illnesses of the body, *sophiē* removes passions from the soul' (B31, cf. B59).

In short, by the end of the fifth century, at least within certain philosophical contexts, the terms '*sophiē/a*' and '*sophos*' could be used without modification in the sense of 'wisdom'.

Linguistically speaking, such instances arguably indicate the emergence in the late fifth century of a hyponym that is also a polyseme. A hyponym is a word whose semantic field is included within that of another word, namely, its hypernym. For example, 'robin', 'sparrow', and 'falcon' are hyponyms of 'bird', which is in turn the hypernym of the former three words. Polysemy is verbal ambiguity in which two or more senses of a single word form are closely related, for example, 'healthy' in 'healthy body' and 'healthy diet'; the former instance denotes a condition constitutive of and the latter causative of health. A hyponym that is also a polyseme then is a hyponym using the same word form as the hypernym. A common example is 'drink' for 'alcoholic drink', as when one comes home after a long day at the office and says: 'I need a drink.' Examples more germane to a philosophical context are 'ethical' and 'moral'. For example, in the phrase 'an ethical or moral judgement', 'ethical' and 'moral' may be used in opposition to 'non-ethical' and 'non-moral' as well as to 'unethical' and 'immoral'. In the latter cases, 'ethical' and 'moral' are hyponyms of 'ethical' and 'moral' in the former cases. In the case of '*sophiē/a*' I am suggesting that by the end of the fifth century an independent sense of '*sophiē/a*' had developed, namely, 'wisdom', as hyponym of '*sophiē/a*' in the broad sense of 'skill'. Among other reasons, the suggestion is encouraged by the fact that in passages such as those of Democritus and the *Dissoi Logoi* '*sophiē/a*' is used in contrast to familiar skills, which are there called '*technai*' (plural of '*technē*').

5. Philosophical uses of '*epistēmē*' to Aristotle

I turn now to philosophical uses of '*epistēmē*' from the fifth century to Aristotle. Among fifth-century philosophers the verb '*epistamai*' or a derived participle occurs five times (Heraclitus B19, B41; Gorgias B11a.3; Democritus B169, 173). The noun occurs in a fragment (B181) of Democritus (c. 460–370) and so towards the end of the fifth, if not in the early fourth century.

The rarity of the noun among fifth-century philosophers is therefore consistent with that in non-philosophical fifth-century texts. Consequently it is a striking fact that '*epistēmē*' is by far Plato's preferred knowledge term, occurring almost 600 times in his corpus. Compare this with the fact that '*sophia*' occurs about 225 times and '*phronēsis*' about 170. It is then extraordinary that a rare noun – indeed in philosophical Greek with perhaps not a single instance in the fifth century outside of the Socratic circle – is so abundant in Plato.

In considering this fact note that Antisthenes (445–365), Plato's older Socratic contemporary by about twenty years, wrote a work in four books entitled *On Opinion and Knowledge* (*Peri doxēs kai epistēmēs*). While there is little reason to believe that Antisthenes entitled the work himself, there is no reason to doubt that he centrally used '*epistēmē*' within it. In addition it is noteworthy that '*epistēmē*' occurs four times in the meagre fragments of the Socratic Aeschines (8.49, 56; 9.10; 17.1 Dittmar), as well as thirty-four times in Xenophon.

Given the prevalence of '*epistēmē*' among the Socratics, it seems likely that Socrates himself employed the term in his philosophical discussions. The following consideration may further support this conjecture. Socrates strikingly abandoned the cosmological or natural-philosophical inquiry of his contemporaries. Insofar as figures such as Heraclitus and Empedocles used '*sophiē*' to denote a master skill requiring cosmological and natural-philosophical understanding for the full realization of human potential, Socrates, in advancing an expressly non-cosmological, non-natural-philosophical ethical-political enterprise, may have deliberately preferred the novel and non-Ionian term '*epistēmē*'.

Unfortunately, the dearth of textual evidence severely impedes our grasp of how Antisthenes or Aeschines, let alone Socrates himself, understood *epistēmē*. A glimpse may be afforded by the way Plato's Socrates, in a famous intellectual autobiographical passage in *Phaedo*, characterizes his predecessors' interests in cognition: 'Do we think with our blood or air or fire or none of these? And does the brain provide our senses of hearing and sight and smell, from which come memory and opinion (*doxa*), and from memory and opinion that has attained a state of rest comes *epistēmē*?' (96b). So a condition of *epistēmē*, in contrast to opinion, is stability.

The question then is what constitutes the stability of *epistēmē*. Evidence from the following two claims attributed to Antisthenes suggests that at least he held that the stability of *epistēmē* depends on reasons confirming the thing known:

> Wisdom (*phronēsis*) is the most secure wall; it neither crumbles nor betrays us. (134 *SSR*)

> We must construct walls through our own indestructible reasonings (*analutois logismois*). (134 *SSR*)

In light of Antisthenes' position (cf. Brancacci 2005), it is also plausible that Socrates himself viewed *epistēmē* as opinion that is *elenchus*-proof.

Plato's conception of *epistēmē* is, to this extent, consistent with Antisthenes'.[13] According to one of at least two distinct, albeit interrelated conceptions of *epistēmē* that Plato advances in his corpus (cf. Wolfsdorf 2013), *epistēmē* is a kind of judgement. In *Meno* (98a) Plato precisely analyses such judgement as true opinion (*doxa*) with a reasoning (*logismos*) of the cause or explanation (*aitia*). The idea here is that one who achieves an epistemic judgement grasps the reasons that both justify the truth and explain the content of the judgement. Given the aetiological condition *epistēmē* so conceived is arguably best rendered as 'understanding' or at least as 'explanatory knowledge'.

Plato also uses '*epistēmē*' to denote a field of knowledge, for example, medicine or geometry. Recall the distinction and example cited earlier of knowledge of medicine versus knowledge that Coriscus has pneumonia. As I suggested, knowledge of facts and knowledge of a field are interdependent. This is because in order to acquire the aetiological reasoning that makes judgement not merely true, but epistemic, one needs to acquire the body of knowledge constituting the pertinent field. In terms of cognitive development then knowledge of individual facts and knowledge of the pertinent field arise in tandem.

The aetiological condition on *epistēmē* seems to answer to two closely related epistemic conditions or perhaps ideals, both of which might be characterized as conditions of power. One has to do with the stability of the cognitive state. Because the possessor of *epistēmē* has compelling reasons for what he knows, his cognitive state cannot be destabilized. The other has to do with the depth of insight that the cognitive state affords. Insofar as the possessor of *epistēmē* has explanatory reasons for what he knows, he grasps why that which he knows is as it is.

Given that *epistēmē* is skill, acts of epistemic judgement are exercises of skill. But the aetiological condition intellectualizes *epistēmē*, and so the skill in question. This intellectualization in turn has the potential to cognitively demote conventionally recognized skills. We see the inception of this demotion in some of Plato's late dialogues.

In *Statesman*, the Eleatic Stranger distinguishes between *epistēmē* that is practical (*praktikē*) and *epistēmē* that is purely cognitive (*gnōstikē*):

> We must divide the various sorts of knowledge (*epistēmai* [plural of '*epistēmē*']) ... Isn't it the case that arithmetic and some other sorts of skills (*technai*) that are akin to it don't involve any actions (*praxeis*), but simply provide cognition (*gnōnai*)? ... Whereas for their part the sort of *epistēmē* involved in carpentry and manufacture ... use it to complete those material objects they cause to come into being from not having been before? ... Then divide all forms of *epistēmē* in this way; call the one sort 'practical' (*praktikē*) *epistēmē* and the other solely 'cognitive' (*gnōstikē*). (258b-e)

A related distinction occurs in Plato's *Philebus* where Socrates divides so-called workman's (*dēmiourgikē*) *epistēmē* and mathematical (*mathēmatikē*) *epistēmē* (55c-d), and further distinguishes popular (*tōn pollōn*) and philosophical (*tōn philosophountōn*) forms of each (e.g. 56d, 57d). The popular forms are applied and therefore practical; the philosophical forms are unapplied and therefore wholly cognitive.

The aim of the analysis is not merely to categorize kinds of *epistēmē* by species and subspecies, but to determine the 'purest' (*katharōtaton*) form of *epistēmē*. Socrates argues that the greater the extent that an *epistēmē* depends on mathematics, the purer that *epistēmē* is. And among mathematical *epistēmai* themselves, the philosophical forms, because wholly cognitive, are purer than the popular forms (58c).

In advancing this position, Socrates speaks of three conditions of epistemic purity: exactness (*akribeia*), clarity (*saphēneia*), and truth (*alētheia*). Accordingly, and at least among the forms of *epistēmē* canvassed, the most exact, clear, and truthful unapplied mathematical *epistēmē* is *epistēmē* in its purest form. The exactness of an *epistēmē* is a function of its aetiological or explanatory priority. For example, the principles of geometry depend on the principles of arithmetic, so arithmetic is more exact than geometry. Epistemic clarity relates to the nature of the objects of *epistēmē*. Sensible objects are mutable. They both come into being and cease to be and admit contrary non-substantial attributes; for example, in the course of a day a stone may be warmed and then cooled. In short, the character of sensible objects is complex, variable, and circumstantially dependent. In contrast, intelligible objects are much less so or not at all. Consequently *epistēmē* pertaining to the former is less precise and its application more stochastic than that pertaining to the latter. Finally insofar as the natures of sensible particulars depend on intelligible objects, a central thesis of Platonism, the latter are more metaphysically fundamental and so *epistēmē* pertaining to such objects is 'truer' in the sense of 'relating to more fundamental aspects of reality'. (On this use of '*alēthes*' and 'true', cf. Wolfsdorf [2014].)

In *Posterior Analytics* and his ethical treatises, Aristotle advances Plato's intellectualization of *epistēmē* and in doing so further demotes practical knowledge and segregates it from purely cognitive knowledge. Aristotle maintains that *epistēmē* is 'contemplative' (*theōrētikē*). This entails that the objects of *epistēmē* are purely intelligible and so immutable and that the function of *epistēmē* is purely theoretical (cf. *Posterior Analytics* 88b30–89a11). Consequently – and assuming that the practical/theoretical distinction can in

24 *Knowledge in Ancient Philosophy*

fact be sustained – for Aristotle, at least in certain texts, no *epistēmē* is practical. Practical cognition precisely concerns mutable sensible objects.

Furthermore, Aristotle distinguishes two forms of practical cognition (*Eudemian Ethics* 1140a1-b30). One, whose perfect realization he calls 'technē', is exercised in the production of things external to the action itself. Aristotle's paradigm case is the builder constructing a house. The other, whose perfect realization he calls 'phronēsis', is exercised in activity that is an end in itself. Here, ethical action is paradigmatic (but cf. also the example of musical performance at *Magna Moralia* 1197a9–10).

Consequently and remarkably, for Aristotle the sort of practical skill that in conjunction with excellences of character (*aretai ēthikai*) enables one to thrive as a citizen or political leader is not a form of *epistēmē* at all. Contrast the view of Socrates who would not have distinguished 'phronēsis' from 'epistēmē' – indeed, Plato doesn't. Moreover, Socrates seems to have thought that the sort of *epistēmē* or *phronēsis* that a citizen or civic leader requires is a *technē*. But again, for Aristotle, in certain texts, a *technē* is not a form of *epistēmē*.

6. Philosophical uses of 'sophia' in the fourth century

While 'epistēmē' is Plato's preferred knowledge term, he uses 'sophia' and 'epistēmē' (among several other terms such as 'phronēsis') interchangeably. A signal example occurs in the following passage from *Theaetetus*:

> (So:) Now isn't it true that to learn is to become more *sophos* about what one is learning? (Th:) How could it be otherwise? (So:) And men who are *sophoi* [plural of 'sophos'] are *sophoi* due to *sophia*? (Th:) Yes. (So:) And does this differ in any way from *epistēmē*? (Th:) Does what differ? (So:) *Sophia*. Isn't it the very things that men are knowledgeable (*epistēmones*) about that they are also *sophoi* about? (Th:) Well, yes. (So:) Then are *epistēmē* and *sophia* the same thing? (Th:) Yes. (145d-e)

Many other examples might be cited. For instance, consider the following two from *Apology* and *Hippias Major*:

> And I say this not to cast dishonour upon such *epistēmē*, if anyone is *sophos* in such matters. (*Ap.* 19c)

> (So:) And knowing (*epistamenoi*) these things that they know (*epistantai*), are they ignorant or *sophoi*? (Hi:) *Sophoi* of course in these very things. (*Hp. Mi.* 365e-366a)[14]

In contrast, Aristotle explicitly distinguishes *sophia* as a kind of *epistēmē* (cf. *Eudemian Ethics* 1411a16; *Metaphysics* 982a4–983a23). Precisely Aristotle maintains that *sophia* is *epistēmē* of 'primary principles and causes' (*prōtai archai kai aitiai*) (cf. *Metaphysics* 982b9–10). To appreciate this description, let's briefly return to the theory of *epistēmē* itself.

The theory of *epistēmē* that Aristotle develops in *Posterior Analytics* follows Plato in maintaining that *epistēmē* requires an aetiological account: 'We think we know (*epistasthai*) each thing in an unqualified way when we think we cognize, of the *aitia* of the thing [known], that it is the *aitia* of that thing' (71b9–12).[15] But one of the points of departure for Aristotle's discussion is a problem arising from this very requirement. What is the cognitive status of the aetiological account? If it is epistemic, then by definition it too requires an aetiological account and a regress ensues. If it is not epistemic, then in virtue of what is it stable? If it is unstable, then given the stability condition the possibility of *epistēmē* is undermined (72b5–23).

Aristotle attempts to resolve this problem by appealing to the function of a cognitive faculty he calls '*nous*', often translated as 'intuition' or 'understanding' (99b15–100b4). *Nous* operates through induction (*epagōgē*) on the basis of experience and thereby generates universal principles (*archai*)[16] that, among other things, have true content, are cognitively immediate, and with respect to the domain of *epistēmē* in question are primary (71b21–23). Given these attributes, noetic principles are both cognitively secure and suited to playing an aetiological role in the constitution of *epistēmē*. Precisely Aristotle conceives of the relation between the noetic principles and facts known as demonstrative: a fact known is one that is validly deduced from noetic principles.

Returning now to Aristotle's claim that *sophia* is *epistēmē* of primary principles and causes – the epistemological concept of primary principles and causes depends on the metaphysical idea that reality is structured in such a way that some entities are fundamental, while others are dependent on the former. Some of the latter entities may in turn be relatively fundamental in relation to other entities that are dependent on them, and so on. This sort of structured view of reality has a long pedigree in Greek philosophy, arguably extending to its inception. It is also typically wedded to the view that the structure is hierarchical in the evaluative sense that the more fundamental an entity is the more value it has. Plato's distinction between Forms and the sensible individuals that depend on and so 'participate' in them is one familiar example.

Aristotle's interest in an *epistēmē* of primary principles and causes arises in an epistemological context. He recognizes that each domain of *epistēmē*, for

26 *Knowledge in Ancient Philosophy*

example, geometry or biology, has its own principles and therefore explanatory grounds. But he wonders whether there exists a primary *epistēmē* whose principles explain the principles of all other *epistēmai*. Since such an *epistēmē* would explain the most fundamental and valuable features of reality, it would be the most exalted form of *epistēmē*.

The various inquiries comprising Aristotle's *Metaphysics* are attempts to determine the *epistēmē* that answers to this description. For example, in *Metaphysics* Gamma Aristotle examines the idea that the *epistēmē* in question is of being qua being, and in Lambda that it is theology. Elsewhere in *Metaphysics*, Aristotle examines conceptions of the knowledge of primary principles proposed by his predecessors as well as some of his Academic contemporaries.[17] For Plato, the first principle is the superordinate Form, the Form of the Good, apprehension of which is required for full realization of ethical life and political leadership. In sharp contrast, Aristotle denies that there is a Form of the Good and that, even if there were one, apprehension of it would be of any practical value (*Nicomachean Ethics* 1096a11–1097a14). Recall that, for Aristotle, what we need for ethical and political success is *phronēsis* and excellences of character, neither of which is or consists of *epistēmē*, let alone *sophia*.

However, Aristotle maintains that the pursuit and exercise of *sophia* and *epistēmē* more broadly constitute a form of eudaimonia that is superior to a flourishing ethical and political life (*Nicomachean Ethics* 1177a12–1179a32). In partitioning the epistemological bases of ethical-political and theoretical life, Aristotle strikingly breaks with Plato who maintains the dependence of ethical and political knowledge on the knowledge of mathematics, Forms and above all the Form of the Good. Plato's position in turn diverges from that of Socrates, who, recall, holds that ethical-political flourishing does not depend on cosmological or natural-philosophical, let alone mathematical or metaphysical knowledge.

Several of Plato's fourth-century associates share his view that ethical and political knowledge depends on cosmological, mathematical, or metaphysical knowledge. For example, the Pythagorean philosopher Archytas (c. 428–347) claims that logistic (*logistikē*), which he conceives as the foundational mathematical skill, is 'far superior to the other *technai* in regard to *sophia*' (fr. 4.1). Carl Huffman (2010: 235) offers the following helpful comment on this claim:

Logistic was viewed as the science of number which underlies the practical application of mathematical calculation (*logismos*) to human life. The second part of Fragment 3 argues that such calculation is the basis of all human society. Therefore, I suggest that, in Fragment 4, it is this sort of wisdom in which logistic far surpasses the other [*technai*]. It is the wisdom that allows us to live a good life ... [and] that will also turn out to be crucial to the functioning of the state.

Plato's student Philip of Opus advances a distinct, but related position. Philip is generally regarded as the author of the short dialogue *Epinomis* that serves as an appendix to a passage in the twelfth book of Plato's *Laws*. The *Laws* passage concerns the education that the Nocturnal Council, the supreme political body of the envisioned city-state, is to receive. Cleinias, the principal speaker of *Epinomis*, ultimately proposes that the Council members must learn astronomy. He understands this study of the celestial bodies to include the mathematical *epistēmai* of arithmetic, geometry, and stereometry, and explicitly claims that it is the supreme *sophia* (990a, cf. 992d).

Plato's, Archytas', and Philip of Opus' conceptions of the *sophia* requisite for ethical and political success are, in various ways, akin to those of Heraclitus and Empedocles insofar as all of these philosophers maintain that personal or political success requires an understanding of broader or more fundamental aspects of nature, the cosmos, and reality.[18] In the Hellenistic period, both the Epicureans and Stoics, albeit in radically different ways, likewise maintain that cosmological understanding is requisite for success in practical life.

In contrast, Socrates and Aristotle, in their own divergent ways, maintain the epistemological independence of ethics. The Socratic position is in turn developed in one direction by various non-Platonic Socratics such as the Cyrenaics as well as by the Cynics – namely, according to the view that human flourishing and the *sophia* on which it depends has no need of cosmological, natural-philosophical, mathematical, or metaphysical knowledge – while the Aristotelian position is, until Plotinus, unique in taking the supreme form of human life, which involves the exercise of *sophia*, to be non-ethical and non-political.

Notes

1 I assume the semantic distinction between 'skilled' and 'skilful' is that the former denotes the condition of having acquired skill and the latter of possessing skill.
2 Translation adapted from Lombardo (1997). Unless otherwise noted, as here, translations are my own.
3 Translation adapted from West (1993).
4 Translation adapted from West (1993).

5 Translation adapted from Graham (2010).

6 I emphasize that *to sophon* is here explicitly identified as a kind of knowing (cf. B50).

7 That Heraclitus views *sophiē* precisely as a state of the *psychē* is confirmed by the following fragment: 'A dry *psychē* is most *sophos* and best' (B65).

8 Translation adapted from Barnes (1987).

9 For instance, Heraclitus endorses aristocratic, not democratic or egalitarian, values. Consequently he does not view *sophiē* as a form of ethical, in the sense of 'moral', knowledge.

10 I strongly suspect that Protagoras used the term '*sophiē*' to characterize his teaching. Cf. Plt. *Tht.* 166d-167d and *Prt.* 316c-317c.

11 Grg. B8a; B11.1, 4, 6; B11a.16, 25; Ant. B49.12; Dem. B31, B47, B59, B197, B216, B247; Cri. B25.12, 34; B29; *Anon Iambl.* 1; *Dis. Log.* 6–8 passim.

12 Translation adapted from Dillon and Gergel (2003).

13 On the other hand, Antisthenes rejected Platonic Forms and so the Platonic view that *epistēmē* requires their apprehension.

14 There is, however, at least one passage in the Platonic corpus where *sophia* itself is distinguished from other kinds of *epistēmē*. At *Republic* 428b, Socrates observes that there are various kinds of *epistēmē* in the polis and he asks, 'Are we then to call our state wise (*sophē*) and good in counsel because of the *epistēmē* of carpenters?' So, here it is clear that *epistēmē* is not equivalent to *sophia*, but that the latter is a type of the former.

15 I note, without endorsing, a common practice among translators of rendering Aristotle's use of '*epistēmē*' as 'science' or 'scientific knowledge'.

16 Aristotle recognizes that in some fields, particularly in the natural sciences, noetic principles may be general rather than universal, in other words may 'hold only for the most part'. Cf. *An. post.* 96a8-10.

17 In this context, it is interesting to note that, in a treatise *On Phronēsis*, Xenocrates, the third scholarch of the Academy, drew the following complex distinction between *sophia* and *phronēsis*. Similarly to Aristotle, Xenocrates characterizes *sophia* as '*epistēmē* of first causes and intelligible being (*noētēs ousias*)'. In contrast to Aristotle, Xenocrates distinguishes two kinds of *phronēsis*: theoretical and practical. Moreover, he describes theoretical *phronēsis* as 'human (*anthrōpina*) *sophia*' (fr. 177 Isnarde-Parente-Dorandi). In that case, Xenocrates must distinguish between two kinds of *sophia*: divine and human – although precisely how the two differ is unclear. Cf. Isnarde-Parente and Dorandi (2012: 192, 331–2) and Dillon (2003: 150–1).

18 Another conception of *sophia* involving the dependence of ethical on cosmological and metaphysical knowledge occurs in Pseudo-Archytas' *On Sophia*; on which, cf. Horky (2016).

References

Barmeyer, E. (1968), *Die Musen. Ein Beitrag zur Inspirationstheorie*, Munich: W. Fink.

Barnes, J. (1987), *Early Greek Philosophy*, London: Penguin.

Brancacci, A. (2005), '*Epistēmē* and *Phronēsis* in Antisthenes', *Methexis*, 18: 7–28.

Craik, E. M. (1998), *Hippocrates Places in Man*, Oxford: Clarendon Press.

Dillon, J. (2003), *The Heirs of Plato*, Oxford: Oxford University Press.

Dillon, J. and Gergel, T. (2003), *The Greek Sophists*, London: Penguin.

Gauthier, R. A. and Jolif, J. Y. (1959), *L'Éthique à Nicomaque*, Tome II Commentaire, Louvain: Publications Universitaires.

Gladigow, B. (1965), *Sophia und Kosmos*, Hildesheim: Georg Olms.

Graham, D. W. (2010), *The Texts of Early Greek Philosophy*, Part 1, Cambridge: Cambridge University Press.

Horky, P. S. (2016), 'Pseudo-Archytas' Protreptics? *On Wisdom* in its Contexts', *Comm. Hum. Litt.*, 20: 114–33.

Huffman, C. (2010), *Archytas of Tarentum: Pythagorean, Philosopher, and Mathematician King*, Cambridge: Cambridge University Press.

Isnarde-Parente, M. and Dorandi, T. (2012), *Senocrate e Ermodoro Testimonianze e Frammenti*, Pisa: Edizioni della Normale.

Lombardo, S. (1997), *Homer Iliad*, Indianapolis: Hackett.

Meier, F. (1970), *Der Sophos Begriff. Zur Bedeutung, Wertung und Rolle des Begriffes von Homer bis Euripides*, Munich: W. Blasaditsch.

Schaerer, R. (1930), *Epistēmē et Technē. Étude sur les Notions de Connaissance et D'Art d'Homère a Platon*, Paris: Macon.

Snell, B. (1924), *Die Ausdrücke für den Begriff des Wissens in der Vorplatonischen Philosophie*, Berlin: Weidmann.

West, M. L. (1993), *Greek Lyric Poetry*, Oxford: Oxford University Press.

Wolfsdorf, D. (2013), 'Plato's Epistemology', in F. Sheffield and J. Warren (eds), *The Routledge Companion to Ancient Philosophy*, New York: Routledge.

Wolfsdorf, D. (2014), 'Plato on Truth-Aptness and Truth-Value', *Methexis*, 27: 135–56.

2

Presocratic Epistemology

Daniel W. Graham

1. Introduction

What do we know about the world? How do we know it? This question lies in the background of most early Greek philosophy. Gradually it becomes an object of inquiry, the theory of knowledge, epistemology.[1]

2. Divine and human knowledge

The world out of which Presocratic philosophy was born was one inhabited by numerous gods, daimons, satyrs, and nymphs. Divine beings were thought to be everywhere and to influence all human events. There were patterns of life that the discerning mortal should follow as to when to sow and when to reap, but even so, '[t]he mind of aegis-bearing Zeus is ever different, / and hard for mortal men to discern' (Hesiod *Works and Days* 483–4).[2] While humans could gain skill and knowledge in various professions, such as agriculture, seafaring, or metallurgy, success in life was, in the end, not up to the individual. Their fate depended on conditions outside their control. As the early poet Semonides puts it:

> My son, loud-thundering Zeus controls the end
> Of all things that are, and disposes them as he will.
> Men have no understanding (*noos*), but like grazing cattle
> We live day to day, knowing nothing
> Of how the god will bring it to an end. (fr. 1.1–5)

The poet Theognis says:

> No man, Cyrnus, controls his own success or failure,
> but the gods are givers of both . . .

> We men make vain plans, knowing nothing;
> the gods accomplish everything according to their own will. (133–4; 141–2)

From earliest times of recorded Greek culture, the civilization is infected by an epistemic pessimism. Humans can know a great deal about their environment, but they cannot control their own destinies. In particular, humans lack knowledge of what the future holds. This the gods have, and accordingly, the divine knowledge is far superior to mortal knowledge.

Furthermore, human memory is short. Events that happened before living memory are inaccessible, or at best knowable through hearsay and tradition. Here the Muses, daughters of Mnemosyne, 'Memory', can help out. In a sort of visionary encounter, the Muses appeared to Hesiod as he was tending sheep on Mt. Helicon. They told him, somewhat ominously, '[W]e know how to speak falsehoods that sound like truths, / and we know how, when we will, to utter truths' (*Theogony* 27–8). Thereupon, they 'breathed into me divine voice' and made him a poet, teaching him to sing of the origins of the gods, theogony. Similarly Homer, when he wishes to tell about the warriors who came to wage war against Troy, invokes the Muses: 'For you, who are goddesses … know all things, / and we have heard only the rumour (*kleos*) of it and know nothing' (*Iliad* 2.485–6, trans. Lattimore). Homer then goes on to give a roll call of all the captains, the number of men and ships they led, and what cities they came from, for 280 lines, the so-called Catalogue of Ships. The Muses offer a treasury of knowledge of events that are forgotten or only dimly remembered.

When something goes wrong that humans are powerless to correct, the gods offer knowledge to manage the problem. At the beginning of the *Iliad*, Apollo the Far-shooter looses his arrows at the Greeks, killing the animals and men in a plague (1.61). 'Come', says Achilles, 'let us ask some holy man, some prophet, / even an interpreter of dreams, since a dream / also comes from Zeus, who can tell us why Phoebus Apollo is so angry' (1.62–4, trans. Lattimore). They turn to Calchas, the best of the bird-watchers (he interprets flights of birds) (1.69), who warns them that Apollo is angry because the Greeks carried off his priest's daughter and would not take a ransom from the priest. What is crucial here is that catastrophes like plagues occur because of some offense humans commit against the gods. The way to end the disaster is to placate the gods; and there are seers who can learn the will of the gods by interpreting the signs they send, whether through dreams or flights of birds or the entrails of sacrificial victims.

In general, the big divide in knowledge is between divine and human: the gods know everything, at least everything that is knowable, while humans know very little, and in particular, are ignorant of their own fates. The attempt to know more than one is allotted is hubris, and is severely punished by the gods.

3. Human knowledge in Ionia

In the sixth century BC a circle of men in Miletus, a prominent city on the Aegean coast of Anatolia, pioneered a new style of inquiry that came to be known as Inquiry into Nature (Aristotle *Metaphysics* I.3; Plato *Phaedo* 96a). Shunning religious explanations, they looked for naturalistic accounts of cosmic events, and indeed offered speculative accounts of how the cosmos itself arose – by purely natural processes. In place of theogony, they offered cosmogony. Thales offered the first known naturalistic theories, followed by Anaximander and then Anaximenes, all in the sixth century BC. Our records of the early theories are sketchy at best; we can say that Thales offered the first attempt to derive all things from a single source, water; Anaximander offered the first cosmogony; and Anaximenes offered the first theory of 'chemistry', with seven basic substances: fire, air, wind, cloud, water, earth, stones, ranked from the most rare to the most dense, with rarefaction and compression as mechanisms of elemental change. Each thinker offers an imaginative reconstruction of the world, based on presumed natural principles, and designed to explain the origin and function of the world and the things in it, including the shape and geography of the world, weather phenomena, and the rise of living things.

At this stage we get a radical new approach to knowledge. The Milesians offer a quasi-scientific account of the origin and function of the world. This approach rejects (tacitly) traditional accounts and in their place presupposes regular natural processes that are knowable through observation and inference and are sufficient in principle to account for all natural events, even portentous ones such as thunder and lightning (traditionally ascribed to the thunderbolts of Zeus), earthquakes (the workings of Poseidon, god of the sea), and eclipses. But on what grounds can the Milesians claim knowledge of remote and obscure events such as these? The first generation of cosmologists offers no explicit justification.

The Milesians make use of speculative theories. Given that the world is composed of certain stuffs, which are related to each other in certain ways and have certain properties, they must have started out from a certain primeval chaos and formed in certain ways. The early thinkers prominently use studies of polar opposites and analogies to develop their models and theories (Lloyd

1966). Some analogies are naturalistic: the earth floats like a raft, or log; some are political: the seasons are like a war in which one side prevails, then another (Anaximander); some are mechanical: one element when it is compressed changes its character, like wool when it is compacted into felt (Anaximenes). In some sense the Milesians are trying to use everyday knowledge to account for unusual phenomena. For instance, Thales says that the earth is like a raft floating on a vast sea; when the waters are stirred up by the winds, they become choppy; a raft floating on the surface will shake; and that shows how an earthquake happens (A14, A15).[3] Anaximenes points out that after a rain the earth dries out and cracks; this cracking process is what happens on a larger scale in an earthquake (A21).

What is perhaps most striking about Milesian theories in their epistemological context is their optimism. All we need, the Milesians seem to assume, are astute observations and insightful analogies, and we can explain everything about the world and its origins. We can, in principle, see the world as a closed natural system in which every event is explained by some simple process that we are familiar with. We do not need to appeal to gods or fate or anything outside the realm of nature itself as revealed through everyday experience.

Thinkers of the next generation do raise scruples about the possibility of human knowledge. Alcmaeon of Croton (early fifth century BC) prefaces his book of philosophy by saying, 'Concerning the unevident and the perishable, only the gods have a clear grasp; for men it is allotted to make inferences' (B1). Here Alcmaeon seems to nod to the archaic distinction between divine and human knowledge. What is new, however, is the determination to press forward in gathering evidence and making inferences in a purely human way. We must, he implies, make the most of the tools at our disposal to understand the world around us. He goes on to develop his own natural philosophy and medical theory.

Xenophanes, an exile from Ionia, lived as a wandering poet in Sicily and southern Italy, in his long life extending from the sixth to the early fifth century BC. Like Alcmaeon, he acknowledges the limits of human knowledge, yet pursues that knowledge anyway. He states:

> Not from the beginning have the gods revealed all things to mortals,
> but in time by seeking they come upon what is better. (B18)

Here Xenophanes implies (but does not say) that the gods have revealed some things; but humans are capable of making discoveries in those areas where the gods are silent. We observe the divide between divine and human knowledge, but see the latter realm as an area capable of expansion. There is, however, a more sceptical side to Xenophanes:

> Now the plain truth (*to saphēs*) no man has seen nor will any know
> concerning the gods and what I have said concerning all things.
> For even if he should completely succeed in describing things as they come to pass,
> nonetheless he himself does not know; opinion (*dokos*) is wrought over all. (B34)

Here Xenophanes alludes to his own constructive theory concerning the gods and all things, that is, his cosmological speculations. He has developed a theory in the style of the Milesians, but he does not advance it as an indubitable explanation. On the contrary, he notes that even if anyone (including himself) should get things just right, he would not know, nor, by implication, will any hearer of the truth. What we have is not certainty but opinion.

Why bother inquiring then? At one point he says, 'Let these things be believed as being like true things' (B35). We cannot guarantee that we have or ever will hit on the truth. But we can hit on what is better (B18). He seems to think that progress is possible through human techniques. Indeed, he goes beyond his predecessors in transgressing the boundary between divine and human knowledge: he offers critique of Greek religious dogmas:

> Homer and Hesiod have attributed to the gods all things
> that are blameworthy and disgraceful for men:
> stealing, committing adultery, deceiving each other. (B11)

He calls out the great mythographers for depicting the gods as subject to human sins. He goes on to criticize the assumption of anthropomorphism in Greek religion (B14, B15, B16). Here we see the possibility that a new theology offers a *better* understanding of deity: the gods should be morally superior to mortals. The world should be a place in which order and reason prevail.

Perhaps he may have in mind also the possibility of discovering better ways of controlling nature and improving our lives. If so, he becomes a kind of proto-pragmatist, looking not for truth, which is beyond our ken, but for power to change things. In any case, Xenophanes makes a quantum leap from a sort of naive epistemic optimism to reflective epistemic optimism, informed by an awareness of human limits, but hopeful of progress nonetheless, and sceptical of religious answers to human questions.

With Heraclitus we get a highly original, indeed highly idiosyncratic, critic of Ionian practices as well as traditional religion. Writing around the end of the

36   *Knowledge in Ancient Philosophy*

sixth century in Ephesus, a city of Ionia, he adopts a misanthropic stance with special scorn for certain authorities:

> The teacher of the multitude is Hesiod; they believe he has the greatest knowledge – who did not comprehend day and night: for they are one (B57).

> What intelligence or understand do they [the people] have? They follow popular bards and treat the crowd as their instructor, not realizing that the many are base, while the few are noble. (B104)

> Homer deserves to be thrown out of the contests and beaten with a stick, and Archilochus [a poet] likewise. (B42)

Heraclitus looks down on the common man and sees the poets, especially Homer and Hesiod, as a bad influence – much as Xenophanes does. Yet Xenophanes himself does not escape his criticism:

> Learning many things does not teach understanding. Else it would have taught Hesiod and Pythagoras, as well as Xenophanes and Hecataeus. (B40)

Here we find that collecting information (*polumathiē*) is not sufficient for wisdom. Two religious gurus, Hesiod and Pythagoras, fail to provide understanding, as well as two secular researchers, Xenophanes and the historian-ethnographer Hecataeus of Miletus.

So is Heraclitus opposed to research? He says, 'Men who are curious should be acquainted with many things' (B35). And indeed he has good things to say about sense perception: 'The things of which there is sight, hearing, experience, I prefer' (B35). 'The eyes are more accurate witnesses than the ears' (B101a). Yet that is not enough: 'Poor witnesses for men are they eyes and ears of those who have barbarian souls' (B107). Just as a barbarian, that is, a non-Greek speaker, can hear Greek speech without comprehending its meaning, so a perceiver can perceive the world without comprehending its significance. Beside the distrust of common people, Heraclitus offers some hope: 'All men have a share in self-knowledge and thinking' (B116); 'Thinking is common to all' (B113).

What then makes the difference between the epistemic barbarian and the native speaker? 'Wisdom is one thing: to know the will (*gnomē*) that steers all things through all' (B41). 'Having harkened not to me but to the Word (*logos*), you should agree that wisdom is knowing that all things are one' (B50). Heraclitus begins his book with a general statement of his theme, method, and project:

> Of this Word's being forever do men prove to be uncomprehending, both before they hear and once they have heard it. For although all things happen according to this Word, they are like the inexperienced experiencing words and deeds such

as a I explain when I distinguish each thing according to its nature and show how it is. Other men are unaware of what they do when they are awake just as they are forgetful of what they do when they are asleep. (B1)

Heraclitus goes on to say, 'Although this Word is common, the many live as if they had a private understanding' (B2). Here Heraclitus announces that he will explain the secrets of the universe, but predicts that most of his readers will not understand. This Word, this message, is available to all, but people are oblivious to it. Clearly he holds that there is a pattern to the cosmos, that it is hiding in plain sight, but people are blind to it. They are deaf to it, for they do not speak the right language (B34).

What then is the pattern? 'All things are an exchange for fire and fire for all things, as goods for gold and gold for goods' (B90). Fire, as Heraclitus' key element, can be exchanged for any stuff, as can gold at the marketplace. 'This world-order (*kosmos*], the same of all, no god nor man did create, but it ever was and is and will be: everliving fire, kindling in measures and being quenched in measures' (B30). The whole world is in some sense fire, but not at the same time. It is by kindling here and being quenched there that the world is constantly renewed. Here we begin to see the pattern: 'Changing it rests' (B84a). There is a unity in opposites (an important Heraclitean theme) which allows for changes within a constant framework.

The elements change into each other, but do so in proportion and order, so that a balance of elements is maintained (B31). 'A road up and down is one and the same' (B60). There is one road that offers a route uphill or downhill, depending on your direction. The balance of traffic up and down, out and back, maintains order. The road becomes emblematic of the change of elements from earth to water to fire to water to earth. The constant change maintains a constant unity. In a river the waters are constantly changing while (or: so that) the river stays the same (B12). Wisdom is knowing that all things are one (B50, B41).

For Heraclitus his predecessors have seen the basic patterns of the cosmos but missed the point: what is crucial is not the stuff the world may be made out of or the story of how the world arose, but the thesis that it functions as a unified whole, balancing opposites against each other (as Anaximander glimpsed in his story of cosmic justice). For Heraclitus knowledge consists of grasping the unity in the complexity. We need to be observant, but we also need to have insight, which comes by solving puzzles like the unity of the river and the unity of the road. In one sense, Heraclitus has restored a godlike power to the knower, to see in a sudden flash of understanding the connectedness of everything, and

38   *Knowledge in Ancient Philosophy*

to understand how the cosmos itself is a self-sustaining reality: 'War [cosmic process] is father of all and king of all; and some he manifested as gods, some as mean; some he made slaves, some free' (B53).

Heraclitus offers a powerful vision of the dynamic unity of the cosmos. Ultimately, he offers no epistemic justification for that vision. He does seem to recognize, perhaps for the first time, that information from observation cannot of itself explain anything; what is needed is some kind of synthetic perspective that connects the diverse processes into a unified system. There is, for Heraclitus as for his predecessors, a story of natural order, but natures are hidden (B123) and 'the invisible structure is greater than he visible' (B54). Yet his account of knowledge remains more intuitive than systematic.

4. Transcendent knowledge in Elea

Perhaps soon after the riddling critiques of Heraclitus, Parmenides of Elea in southern Italy offered an even more radical critique of Ionian thought. He composed a poem in the epic meter of Homer and Hesiod, depicting a youth who meets an unnamed goddess; the goddess reveals to him truths about being and knowledge. Parmenides uses the literary tools and religious imagery of traditional culture to call into question traditional wisdom and current philosophical theory.

At the outset of her address to the youth, the goddess states,

> It is right for you to learn all things,/ both the unshaken heart of persuasive Truth,
> and the opinions of mortals, in which there is no truth reliance.
> But nevertheless you shall this too, how beliefs
> should have been acceptable, all things just being completely. (B1.28–32)

Parmenides makes a strong distinction, which goes on to structure the argument of the poem, between Truth and Opinion, the former reliable and invariable, the latter unreliable and variable. The goddess then begins by offering a dichotomy, with a moral:

> Come now and I shall tell, and do you receive through hearing the tale,
> which are the only ways of inquiry for thinking:
> the one: that it is and it is not possible not to be,
> is the path of Persuasion (for she attends on Truth);
> the other: that it is not and that it is right it should not be,
> this I declare to you is an utterly inscrutable track,

Presocratic Epistemology

for neither could you know what is not (for it cannot be accomplished),
nor could you declare it [or: point it out]. (B2)

There are two ways, one that says it is, one that says it is not. What is the subject referred to by 'it', and what is the sense of 'is' being invoked here? There are a number of possibilities here, leading to a number of interpretations. (There is also the question of the modal terms, possibility, necessity, obligation, and the like, generating more interpretations.) But whatever the referents of the argument, Parmenides sees a simple choice between a positive and a negative way or route (*hodos*). There is a binary decision (*krisis*) to be made: is it or is it not? (B8.15–16). At the end of B2, the goddess points out that the negative route does not lead anywhere and must be ruled out, leaving only the positive route; for 'you cannot know what is not' (line 7). Evidently, then, the conclusion of the comparison reveals that the former route leads to what-is and allows knowledge of it, whereas the latter offers only what-is-not, an unattainable end.

The goddess goes on to reject a third way of inquiry (although whether it is really a third way is controversial), the one followed by 'mortals knowing nothing', for whom 'to be and not to be are thought to be the same/ and not the same' (B6.8–9). What, or who, Parmenides' target is here is not clear. But there are hints that it is Heraclitus (although that identification is controversial)[4]; in any case, Heraclitus at least seems to furnish fodder for such a refutation. For he says that '[c]old things warm up, hot things cool off, wet things become dry, dry things become moist' (Heraclitus B126) and that '[f]or souls it is death to become water, for water death to become earth, but from earth water is born, and from water soul' (B36). In Heraclitus and thinkers like him, one thing can perish as another thing comes to be; there is an interchangeability between being and not-being.

After arguing against this third way, the goddess admonishes the youth:

Never shall this prevail, that things that are-not are.
But you, withhold your thought from this way of inquiry,
nor let habit born of long experience force you along this way,
to wield an unseeing eye and echoing ear
and tongue. But *judge by reasoning* the very contentious examination
uttered by me. (B7; emphasis added)

This final exhortation embodies a rejection of empirical evidence and an appeal to reasoning. To be sure, the goddess does not reject the evidence of the senses in every context, but she does declare it irrelevant for the present discussion (thus Barnes [1982: 296–8]). And she appeals to rational argument to settle the dispute. Significantly, the goddess-preceptor does not play the divine-authority card: you should believe this, she tells the youth, on the basis of the argument itself, not because of who is telling it to you. Further, this is the first time in the history of Greek philosophy where we get something like an identification of pure reason as the proper basis for a theoretical understanding of the world. As for the theory of knowledge, Parmenides seems to offer for the first time an a priori basis for truth. The knowledge of what-is does not depend on the senses or owe anything to them. The goddess presents us with a kind of proto-rationalism.

The conclusion of the argument so far is drawn in fragment 8:

> Only one tale is left of the way:
> that it is; and on this are posted
> very many signs, that (1) what-is is (a) ungenerated and (b) imperishable,
> (2) a whole of one kind, (3) unperturbed, and (4) complete. (B8.1–4)

What we are seeking has to be something that is, and that thing has four properties, which Parmenides argues for in order. The longest and most detailed argument is that for (1) and in particular (1a). If something came-to-be, it would have to come-to-be from what-is-not; but we have already determined that what-is-not is not, so it cannot come-to-be (B8.6–9). Similarly, (2) if something is not all alike, there will be what-is-not, which is not allowed. Likewise anything that is must be (3) motionless and (4) complete in itself, lacking nothing. We still have not defined what the argument is all about, but the result seems to be that anything we can inquire about will have to be knowable; and to be knowable, it will have to have to be; and if it is, it will have the four properties he argues for in fragment 8. Let us call the properties Eleatic properties, and recognize them as properties essential to anything that is.

Here, it appears, we have the beginnings of a formal ontology. That ontology grows out of strong epistemic assumptions about what we can know. We can know what-is but not what-is-not. What-is, if it truly is, must be without coming-to-be and perishing, all alike, motionless, and complete. If there is only one thing that satisfies these conditions, Being itself, then Parmenides is espousing a strong form of monism. (This interpretation is dominant among Greek commentators.) But if the properties are only constraints on what can count as an object of knowledge, then we might have a pluralistic application of the theory.

Parmenides does not stop here. His goddess seems to recognize that the very abstract theory she has presented does not cover most of the practical questions people have about the world. She goes on to leave her 'faithful account and thought about truth' and consider 'mortal opinions' (B8.50–1). Mortals have distinguished 'two forms', Light and Night, the former rare, light (in weight), and bright, the latter dense, heavy, and dark (B8.54–9). These act like elements that mix together to make all things (B9). They seem to have Eleatic properties, at least as far as is possible for them. The goddess goes on to develop a cosmology like those of Parmenides' predecessors, pronouncing her words to be 'deceptive', but asserting that her account is 'completely likely' and superior to other theories (B8.53, 60–1). Parmenides' theory is indeed superior to any previous theory, particularly in empirical advances: he recognizes for the first time that the moon gets its light from the sun, that the morning star is the evening star, and that the earth is spherical in shape. These observations will bring about a revolution in astronomy.[5]

But what is the philosophical status of Parmenides' cosmological theory? He clearly views it as lacking the certainty of his ontological theory. Does he offer the cosmological theory to show its superiority to competing theories, and then to disavow it so as to say: cosmology is impossible? Or does he offer it as the best one can do with a domain of knowledge that is incorrigibly indeterminate? The latter option would remind us of Plato's view of the natural philosophy, which he develops tentatively in the *Timaeus*; Plato does not deny the existence of a phenomenal world, but he does view it as inferior in being and knowability to the world of ultimate Being (*Timaeus* 29b-d). We do not get any final answer to this question. But we can say that Parmenides goes to a great deal of trouble to develop his impressive cosmology, more than he needs to merely to refute the project. In general he manages, in the Truth part of the poem, to produce a transcendent account of what-is, one which seems to achieve absolute certainty; and in the Opinion part of the poem, he offers by far the best reconstruction of scientific knowledge available in his time, but presented under a cloud of epistemic suspicion. It is possible that he could endorse what Xenophanes says about the lack of certainty in this area, while allowing the possibility of epistemic progress. His own focus, however, is on attaining certainty about what-is in the realm of Truth.

5. Neo-Ionian models of knowledge

Parmenides clearly marks a turning point in early Greek thought. The standard view sees subsequent cosmologists as responding by desperately trying to rescue cosmology on the basis of pluralistic physics or metaphysics, but failing to refute Parmenides' theories. The so-called Pluralists or neo-Ionians do continue to provide cosmological theories, typically on the basis of positing a plurality of realities with Eleatic properties (Barnes 1982). But they do not seem to be as desperate as advertised, and they never seem to even try to argue against Parmenides. I think they can be better understood as interpreting Parmenides' Opinion as offering a genuine application of the Truth, that is, showing how a priori principles can be applied to explain empirical phenomena.

Parmenides' dualistic physics, with Light and Night as complementary components of the world, presents a model of how entities with Eleatic properties can explain a changeable world. Although the components, the elements, are everlasting and in important ways changeless, they can interact to create a changing world of appearances. The neo-Ionians often echo Parmenides in their statements of principles, but seem dissatisfied with the two elements of Parmenides. Anaxagoras posits an unlimited number of elements, corresponding to every kind of stuff we experience, for instance, water, earth, wood, bone, flesh, and perhaps even qualities such as wet and dry, hot and cold (B1, B4, B7). Empedocles posits four elements: earth, water, air, and fire, which will become the most popular theory for some 1,500 years. His elements roughly correspond to the major regions of the cosmos, with earth below, sea covering much of earth, air in the atmosphere, and fire in the heavenly bodies. But the most successful theory of all, in the long run, was that of the atomists Leucippus and Democritus, who posited infinitely many tiny particles moving in a void of empty space. The atomists seem to be the most anti-Eleatic of theorists, since their void is almost a perfect nothing or not-being. Yet from another point of view they are the most faithful to Parmenides' Opinion theory. Night and Light are opposed as dense and rare; what would happen if the dense became completely full and the rare completely empty? The former would become impenetrable matter, the latter insubstantial void. And that is just how the atomists present their 'elements' (Leucippus A6).

Yet how do we know what the elemental bodies are? We have several competing theories, but no clear criterion by which to choose between them. Anaxagoras can argue that his theory makes the fewest demands because every element is already present in the cosmic soup; certain actions like the vortex motion can separate the elements into their own regions so that they become manifest, for the stuff that is greatest in quantity in the mixture determines its phenomenal properties. But, he claims, the separation is never complete: everything is always mixed with everything – though in different proportions in different places. Yet there is a problem in perceiving Anaxagoras' elements. By hypothesis we never encounter anything that is purely water or earth or bone or flesh. How then do we know what the elements are?

Empedocles can claim that his four elements are the basic building blocks of the cosmos because we see the cosmos as articulated into four regions corresponding to the four elements. Everything else can be explained as a compound of the four. Thus blood, bone, flesh, are compounds of earth, water, air, and fire. Empedocles' ontology is much simpler than Anaxagoras'. But now we have something new emerging, coming-to-be in a strong sense, Anaxagoras might object, namely, the blood, bone, and flesh, and any other compound of elements. But these compounds, Empedocles replies, are not real. They are only temporary states of the real things, which are the four elements.

The atomists, meanwhile, maintain that everything we experience is mere appearance. In reality there are only atoms and the void. Properties such as hot and cold, wet and dry, light and dark exist only 'by convention' or perhaps by the projection of our sense organs. We can never in principle perceive the atoms themselves. How then can we know they exist?

The neo-Ionians have a good deal to say about perception. Anaxagoras says we perceive like things by unlike (A92); Empedocles that we perceive like by like (A86). Democritus has an elaborate theory of how different kinds of atoms affect the senses. Both Empedocles and Democritus believe that bodies give off 'effluences' or films that travel through space and produce images in the eye (Empedocles B89; Democritus A135). Empedocles and Democritus also talk about how accurate perception and clear thought occur when the elements of the soul are mixed in even proportions (Empedocles B105, B107, B108; Democritus from Theophrastus *On the Senses* 58 = A135; cf. Parmenides B16). Commenting on his predecessors, Aristotle points out that they tend to assimilate thought to perception (*On the Soul* III.3, 427a19–29). But he goes on to criticize them for failing to make appropriate distinctions between perception and thought. Can the neo-Ionians answer problems of knowledge, including those raised by their own theories?

Anaxagoras makes the strongest distinction between mind and matter. His material elements are always mixed with each other, whereas his mind is found in some things but not others. Mind is 'alone all by itself' and 'all alike', so that it can 'rule' (*kratein*) over matter (B12). While mind has spatial and structural properties, it is different enough from material things that we can see Anaxagoras as offering a kind of proto-dualism between mind and matter. Mind somehow 'comprehends' (*egnō*) all things and rules all things, and instigates the cosmic

44   *Knowledge in Ancient Philosophy*

vortex (B12). Some things, but not all, have mind (B11), so that apparently human beings can think by virtue of having a portion of mind. But how can we comprehend the world around us if everything is mixed with everything, so that we never experience any pure element? Anaxagoras' answer seems to be that we experience all of them directly. I perceive water (see it, smell it, taste it, touch it). Water of course has every other element in it in trace amounts. But what I perceive is really water. Anaxagoras has a what-you-see-is-what-you-get theory. He offers a principle of perception: 'Appearances are a vision of the invisible' (B21a). Appearances (*phainomena*) allow us to grasp the nature of things by analogy. As water is a mixture of things put into it, something can be manifestly water but contain other components.

Empedocles for his part has a materialistic theory of thought. We think with blood, which is an equal blend of all the four elements, centred in the heart (B98, B105, B107). By each element in us we perceive the corresponding element outside us (B109). He has to distinguish between the everlasting elements and ephemeral compounds of these. According to him, the four elements are the vehicles of perception. Yet all of this seems to be driven by theory rather than by empirical evidence. We can, to be sure, recognize the four elements in the cosmic masses, but we do not have any specific evidence for his theory of elements.

The atomists have to make a strong distinction between perception and knowledge, for the simple reason that we never do or can in principle perceive the atoms. Democritus in fact endorses Anaxagoras' dictum (B21a) that '[a]ppearances are a vision of the invisible' (Democritus A111). In some sense we must infer the structure of matter at the microscopic level from appearances at the macroscopic level. The atomists often, in fact, use analogies such as the gathering of birds or stones on a beach to understand the behaviour of atoms (B164). 'By convention', says Democritus, 'sweet, by convention bitter, by convention hot, by convention cold, by convention colour, but in reality atoms and the void' (B125). We experience the world only by convention (*nomōi*) or by the representation of our senses; but we do not experience the real components of the world and their properties, namely, shape, order, and orientation (Leucippus A6). Democritus goes on to observe,

Of cognition (*gnōmē*) there are two kinds, one legitimate, one bastard. Of the bastard kind are these: sight, hearing, smell, taste, touch. And there is the legitimate kind, which is distinct from the latter. Whenever the bastard kind is no longer able to see anything smaller or hear, smell, taste, or perceive by touch, but <must make> finer discriminations, <the legitimate kind takes over>. (B11)

Here the evidence of the senses is a kind of illegitimate offspring of thought. Only some genuine kind of cognition can account for how things are. Yet we must use evidence of the senses to infer the existence of atoms. Democritus seems conflicted about this predicament: 'In reality we know nothing; for truth is in the depths' (B117). In one place, he has the senses speak out against the mind in an imaginary dialogue: 'Wretched mind, after taking from us your evidence, do you overthrow us? Our fall will be your defeat!' (B125). Here, as in Parmenides, we get a contrast between a reliable realm of knowledge and an unreliable realm of opinion; but unlike Parmenides, the atomists have no a priori justification for their ontology, but must base their ontology on the shaky foundation of sense perception and inference.

In the Pluralists we begin to glimpse the outlines of a theory of knowledge as arising from sense experience. There is indeed evidence of an early theory of sense experience, in a passage of Plato. In the *Phaedo* he has Socrates recount his early experience studying natural philosophy. 'Do we think with our blood, or air, or fire, or none of these, and does the *brain* provide our *senses* of hearing and sight and smell, from which come *memory* and *opinion*, and from memory and opinion which has become stable, comes *knowledge*?' (96b, trans. Grube; emphasis added). This pre-Platonic theory seems to feature the brain as the centre of cognition, as a construction of knowledge from sense experiences, memory, and opinion or judgement. No author is named (could it be Alcmaeon of Croton, who championed the brain as the organ of thought?).[6] In any case, this theory seems to prefigure the epistemology of Aristotle in a text written around the time Aristotle was born (*Posterior Analytics* II.19; *Metaphysics* I.1). Alongside the proto-rationalism of Parmenides, we get a proto-empiricism growing up among the Pluralists.

One final thinker from the Pythagorean tradition offers some important insights into the question of knowledge. Philolaus of Croton says this:

> Concerning nature and harmony, this is how it is: the essence of things, being eternal, and nature itself admit of divine but not human knowledge; except that it is not possible that any of the things that exist and are known by us could have come to be unless the essences of things, from which the world-order is composed, existed – namely limiters and unlimiteds. And since the sources were not alike nor of the same kind, it was impossible for them to be organized unless a harmony came upon them, in whatever way it did. Now things that were unlike and of the same kind had no need of harmony, but things that were unlike and of a different kind and rank, these had to be combined by harmony, if they were to be held fast in an arrangement. (B6)

Here Philolaus, writing in the late fifth century, recognizes conditions on knowledge and being. The world itself must consist of two kinds of things, as he says: 'The nature in the world-order was constructed from unlimiteds and limiters, both <the> world-order [*kosmos*] and everything in it' (B1). The unlimiteds (*apeira*) presumably include the physical stuffs such as elements, while the limiters (*perainonta*) are structures. Without the latter principles, which tend to get overlooked by other Presocratics, there could be no order. And without order, there could be no human knowledge. By this argument we get something like a Kantian transcendental argument: knowledge presupposes order [*harmonia*], which presupposes limiters and unlimiteds. Philolaus seems to glimpse something like Aristotle's distinction between form and matter, and to see these two fundamental components as necessary to nature and the knowledge of nature.

6. Conclusion

This brief survey of early Greek philosophy has taken us from a mythological understanding of knowledge and its sources to the beginnings of philosophical theories about knowledge. Although much of the focus of early philosophy was on the workings of nature, reflection on how that was possible led to questions about the sources and possibility of knowledge. Roughly, the religious thinkers made a strong distinction between divine and human knowledge, based especially on access to an understanding of the future and the distant past, which only the gods had. Early Ionian thinkers focused on human knowledge, recognizing its limits but also trusting that some progress could be made. Heraclitus came to see that a godlike knowledge was implicit in the structure of the world, while Parmenides discovered an a priori understanding of being, which could provide tools for a human knowledge of the natural world. Pluralist thinkers pursued the latter project, drawing on a posteriori experience, gradually developing a kind of proto-empiricism to balance the proto-rationalism of Parmenides. Philolaus recognized the need to harmonize both material and formal elements to account for the orderly world we live in and our knowledge of that world, achieving a synthesis of the a priori and the a posteriori. As yet, however, the science of knowledge was in its infancy. Contemporary critics could complain that the Presocratics were using vain assumptions (*kenē hypothesis*) about unknowable phenomena, with no method for arriving at the truth (*to saphēs*).[7]

Notes

1 For studies of Presocratic epistemology, see Hussey (1990), Laks (1999), Lesher (1999, 2008), and Brunschwig (2000).

2 Translations my own, except as otherwise noted. Translations of Presocratics from Graham (2010).

3 The standard reference system for the Presocratics comes from Diels and Kranz *Die Fragmente der Vorsokratiker* (1951): 'testimonies' or ancient reports of the philosophers are designated by 'A' numbers (A1, A2, etc.), 'fragments' or quotations from the philosophers themselves by 'B' numbers.

4 I have argued for a connection (Graham 2002).

5 See Graham (2013).

6 Thus Barnes (1982: 149–50).

7 Hippocrates *Ancient Medicine* 1; cf. Xenophon *Memorabilia* 1.1.11, 13.

References

Barnes, J. (1982 [1979]), *The Presocratic Philosophers*, revised edn, London: Routledge & Kegan Paul.

Brunschwig, J. (2000), 'Epistemology', in J. Brunschwig and G. E. R. Lloyd (eds), *Greek Thought: A Guide to Classical Knowledge*, Cambridge, MA: Harvard University Press.

Graham, D. W. (2002), 'Heraclitus and Parmenides', in V. Caston and A. Mourelatos (eds), *Presocratic Philosophy: Essays in Honour of Alexander Mourelatos*, Aldershot: Ashgate.

Graham, D. W. (ed. and trans.) (2010), *The Texts of Early Greek Philosophy*, 2 vols, Cambridge: Cambridge University Press.

Graham, D. W. (2013), *Science before Socrates: Parmenides, Anaxagoras, and the New Astronomy*, Oxford: Oxford University Press.

Hussey, E. (1990), 'The Beginnings of Epistemology', in S. Everson (ed.), *Epistemology*, Cambridge: Cambridge University Press.

Laks, A. (1999), 'Soul, Sensation, and Thought', in A. A. Long (ed.), *The Cambridge Companion to Early Greek Philosophy*, Cambridge: Cambridge University Press.

Lesher, J. (1999), 'Early Interest in Knowledge', in A. A. Long (ed.), *The Cambridge Companion to Early Greek Philosophy*, Cambridge: Cambridge University Press.

Lesher, J. (2008), 'The Humanizing of Knowledge in Presocratic Thought', in P. Curd and D. W. Graham (eds), *The Oxford Handbook of Presocratic Philosophy*, Oxford: Oxford University Press.

Lloyd, G. E. R. (1966), *Polarity and Analogy: Two Types of Argumentation in Early Greek Thought*, Cambridge: Cambridge University Press.

3

Epistemology in the Sophists

Noburu Notomi

1. The Sophists and their activities

In the early history of philosophy, epistemology was not a particularly important subject of inquiry. Early Greek thinkers during the sixth and fifth centuries BCE sporadically discussed epistemology, but their main topics of concern were cosmology and natural philosophy. Philosophy began to focus on epistemology in the mid-fifth century BCE, when the Sophists engaged the topic wholeheartedly. This chapter will focus on two major Sophists, Protagoras and Gorgias, and examine their early contributions to the study of epistemology, contributions which focused not so much on purely theoretical concerns as on their intellectual activities within the larger society. To understand this distinction, we must first define what the Sophists were.

Professional intellectuals and teachers who called themselves Sophists (*sophistēs*/pl. *sophistai* in Greek) first appeared in the Greek world during the latter half of the fifth century BCE, and their influence grew throughout the fourth century BCE. These Greek Sophists are sometimes referred to as the Older Sophists (Diels and Kranz 1952; Sprague 1972) to distinguish them from the later Second Sophistic which would arise during the time of the Roman Empire. The Sophists were independent thinkers who competed with and often criticised one another. While many Sophists held divergent or even conflicting views, there are nevertheless certain features or tendencies common to them all which allow historians of philosophy to group them together under the rubric of 'the Sophistic Movement' (Kerferd 1981; Notomi 2014).

Protagoras of Abdera (c. 490–415/411 BCE) is traditionally regarded as the first Sophist (cf. *Suda* P.2958, Diogenes Laertius, *Lives of Eminent Philosophers* 9.51–4). One main source of this view comes from Plato's *Protagoras* in which he identified Protagoras as the first to use this title for his own profession. Protagoras purportedly added that 'disguised sophists' had preceded him, including poets (Homer, Hesiod, Simonides), mystics (Orpheus, Musaeus), medical doctors, and gymnastic and musical teachers (316d-317c). This list of predecessors suggests that Protagoras regarded himself not as a natural philosopher but as a successor of traditional poets and experts who had historically been respected as educators in ancient Greece. The great poets such as Homer and Hesiod formed the basis of the whole of Greek culture and education, and the Sophists interpreted works of these forerunners as part of their own teaching. Although the Sophists covered some aspects of natural science such as astronomy and mathematics, their main concerns were with other fields such as language, society, religion, and epistemology. Therefore, it is reasonable to distinguish the Sophists from the natural philosophers of Ionia and South Italy.

Besides Protagoras, the traditional list of major Sophists includes Gorgias of Leontini, Polus of Acragas, Hippias of Elis, Prodicus of Ceos, Thrasymachus of Chalcedon, Euthydemus and Dionysodorus of Thurii, and Antiphon. All of these thinkers were featured in Plato's dialogues except for Antiphon, whose identity remains controversial even today.[1] These figures are well known to us because Plato vividly depicted them as formidable opponents of Socrates in his dialogues.

After the Persian War, Athens became a centre of politics, economy, and culture in Greece. Intellectuals came to Athens to publish and exchange their views on philosophy, literature, politics, and other sciences, and among them were the natural philosophers Anaxagoras and Archelaus. Anaxagoras remained in Athens as an advisor of Pericles before eventually being expelled for impiety. Protagoras also became a confidante and advisor to Pericles and was asked to compose the laws of Thurii, a new city founded by Pericles in Southern Italy. Another great Sophist, Gorgias (c. 485–380 BCE), travelled to many cities after his hometown Leontini was conquered by Syracuse, and we know from Plato's *Gorgias* that he occasionally visited Athens to lecture. Regular visits to Athens by these individuals were enthusiastically welcomed by the local citizens, and in particular by rich and ambitious young men who wanted to study under these thinkers as preparation for their future roles in public life.

The subjects presented by the Sophists in their professional teaching ranged from various sciences and skills to virtue (*aretē*). The profession of 'teaching virtue' became fashionable because the Athenian democracy created the possibility of advancement for all of its citizens, advancement that was dependent on each citizen's own capabilities rather than on origin or social rank. However, the Sophist approach to teaching, which included charging fees for lectures, was novel enough to shock contemporary Greeks (de Romilly 1992). This may explain why the Sophists were passionately praised by young people but also severely condemned by conservative citizens who viewed them as corrupting the youth of Greece.

The availability of higher education for citizens in a democratic society necessarily led to theoretical reflections on knowledge and expertise. New questions were raised: Can virtues or excellence be taught? What can human beings know? What can they *not* know? Under what conditions can knowledge be obtained? The common desire for success within society invited the Sophists to inquire into political and social systems, laws, and moral values. They discussed the origin of human civilization and considered differences in norms and values between societies and cultures. These questions naturally led them to epistemology.

Since the Sophists (except for Antiphon) came from foreign cities and stayed in Athens for teaching, Plato criticised them as itinerant intellectuals who charged money for civil education. Following Plato's lead, Aristotle defined the Sophist as 'one who makes money from apparent but not real wisdom' (*Sophistical Refutations* 165a22–3). While each Sophist developed different thoughts, they were treated as a single group or a movement by the philosophers of their day who viewed them as counterparts and, perhaps, as opposition (Notomi 2014).

The Sophists' own writings have scarcely survived except three short pieces by Gorgias which will be discussed below.[2] To examine their contributions to epistemology, two points must be remembered. First, what we know about the Sophists comes mostly from Plato, who severely criticised them in order to defend Socrates and to dissociate him from the Sophists. Later sources are more or less influenced by the Platonic dialogues (as the traditional list of the Sophists itself shows) so that it is difficult to evaluate their original thoughts in an independent manner. Second, only a small number of works and fragments (quotations or paraphrases) of the Sophists remain, but we should not compare them with the dialogues of Plato (*Corpus Platonicum*) or the lectures of Aristotle (*Corpus Aristotelicum*). The philosophers' written works aimed at systematic inquiry into sciences and philosophy and at constructing theories. The Sophists, however, emphasized oral teaching and performances in front of either a large audience or a small group of pupils, and they did not make it a priority to write down theoretical treatises on their ideas in any systematic way. For example, two extant rhetorical pieces of Gorgias, the *Encomium of Helen* (DK 82 B11, LM GORG. D24) and the *Defense of Palamedes* (DK 82 B11a, LM GORG.

D25), are playful works probably intended as advertisement of his art of speech among prospective pupils (Buchheim1989). Rather than establishing systematic doctrines, the Sophists raised intellectual issues, often in radical or provocative manners, thus challenging both society and philosophy.

In the case of Protagoras, judging from the scarcity of both direct quotations and citations of his works by other writers of antiquity, his written works probably disappeared soon after his death. While Diogenes Laertius reports the titles of a handful of treatises (9.55),[3] we possess only two fragments of them. The famous 'Man-Measure thesis' (DK 80 B1) originally appeared at the beginning of his book *Truth* (also known as *The Throws*) and is quoted in Plato's *Theaetetus* and repeated by later traditions.[4] The other, a notorious agnostic statement on gods (B4) was originally located in the opening of his book *On Gods* (*Peri theōn*) and is also alluded to in the same dialogue by Plato, though later references to it differ much with respect to wording. This indicates that the ancient authors used secondary sources without the original book on hand. This lack of sources prevents us from reaching a comprehensive view of the Sophistic epistemology, but we should be content with a sketch of some important aspects.

2. Truth as the power of speech

While Protagoras and other Sophists professed to 'teach virtue', what they mainly taught was the art of speech (*technē logōn*). Athens was a notoriously litigious society in which anyone could become involved in a lawsuit and thus have to defend himself for survival. In addition to giving effective speeches for accusation and defence in court, Athenians needed effective skills for persuasive public speaking and for putting forth political proposals at the council or general assembly. The Sophists' teaching methods certainly fulfilled this social expectation.

The art of speech, later called 'rhetoric', is said to have been born in Sicily in the first half of the fifth century BCE. When the Sicilian city of Syracuse turned from tyranny to democracy, many lawsuits were brought to the court. This led Tisias and Corax to devise the skill set that would one day evolve into rhetoric. Gorgias, a pupil of Tisias, further developed this art and introduced it to democratic Athens in 427 BCE with a legendary speech at the Athenian Assembly. Antiphon of Rhamnus was also active in the development of rhetoric in Greece, and several other foreign Sophists such as Thrasymachus stayed in Athens to teach rhetoric.

Protagoras also taught rhetoric, but he seems to have been more interested in the theoretical aspects of the subject than in styles or figures of speech. He distinguished four basic forms of speech (wish, question, answer, and command), and discussed the 'division of time' (often interpreted as verb tenses) and the genders of nouns and adjectives (Diogenes Laertius 9.53–4). Prodicus of Ceos shared an interest in language with Protagoras, and both of them discussed the correct use of names (*orthoepeia*). In this manner, the Sophists established the study of language and grammar.

Concerning the art of speech, Protagoras supposedly claimed that 'there are two sides to every question, opposed to each other' (Diogenes Laertius 9.51; Schiappa 2003 [1993]). This method of antilogic (counterargument) is most useful in the forensic context where one must argue persuasively both for defence and attack. The eristic Sophist Dionysodorus, who was influenced by Protagoras' ideas, boldly claimed that 'whichever way the boy answers, he will be refuted', in Plato's *Euthydemus* (275e). One Sophistic treatise titled *Dissoi Logoi* (preserved in the manuscript of Sextus Empiricus: Robinson 1979) presents opposing arguments on such ideas as good and bad, beautiful and ugly, just and unjust, and true and false. The work clearly shows the strong influence of Protagoras.

Antilogic relates to another Protagorean claim that 'there is no contradiction', for if there is no contradiction between opposite claims, one can argue well on both sides. If this implies that the same statement is true for one side but false for another (but with no contradiction), it leads inevitably to the Man-Measure thesis.

Gorgias, in addition to giving lectures both in public (to appeal to the general public) and in private (for those who paid the requisite fees), published and circulated written works of speech performance. His two extant works, the *Encomium of Helen* and the *Defense of Palamedes*, used mythological figures and are full of playfulness. In the *Encomium of Helen*, the author sought to defend the notorious mythic beauty Helen of Sparta as innocent of triggering the Trojan War. He presented a series of arguments that considered the four alleged causes of her guilt, namely, gods or necessity, force, speech, and love, and dismissed three of them. Instead, the author focused on the impact of speech, proposing a mighty power of *logos* that persuaded Helen into flight to Troy. The attractive speech that demonstrated the power of the spoken word illustrated how rhetoric can seduce an audience. To argue that Helen is innocent is paradoxical (contrary to ordinary belief), but this *paradoxologia* reveals the essence of Gorgias' art.

First, Gorgias declared that the glory of a speech is truth (*alētheia*) and its contrary, falsehood, is a disgrace (1). He presented the goals for his own rhetoric as follows: 'by giving reasoning to my speech to put an end to the blame of her had reputation, and by exposing her detractors as liars, and by revealing the truth to put an end to their folly' (2). Gorgias' initially clear distinction between truth and falsehood becomes obscure when he later emphasized the divine power of speech. He insisted that '[s]peech is a great potentate, who by means of the tiniest and most invisible body achieves the most godlike results. For it is able to dispel fear, to assuage grief, to inculcate joy, and to evoke pity' (8). Speech can produce any desirable emotions and feelings within the audience and can thereby control them (9). By reference to religious songs, he claimed that its power 'charms, persuades, and transforms it by witchcraft'. Witchcraft and magic generate errors in the soul and deceptions of judgement (10). Persuasive speech is a drug-like power that compels the soul of the audience to agree (14). In this way, Gorgias deliberately blurred the distinction between opinion and knowledge.

A sharp contrast between truth and opinion is assumed in traditional epistemology, such as that of Xenophanes, Heraclitus, and Parmenides, but Gorgias fused the two concepts in the course of defending Helen. Deception turns out to be not a vice to condemn but a magical power to which one should aspire. Persuasion brings about a necessity just like a physical force. Truth is not what is judged in correspondence with independent facts, but rather whatever one is persuaded and convinced of. This drastic proposal challenges our ordinary view of truth and knowledge. Persuasion does not depend on knowledge and truth. On the contrary, it creates them. In other words, truth in rhetoric (which some might call 'rhetorical truth': Notomi 2007) is not an objective value, but the result of persuasion.

This concept of truth can be best understood in the context of courts of law. For example, if an ignorant audience must judge whether a person accused of violence is guilty or not within a limited time for accusation and defence speeches, the absolute truth can hardly be achieved, but they nevertheless must decide the issue depending solely on the persuasiveness of the speeches presented by the prosecution and the defence. Once a judicial decision is made, however, it becomes both truth and reality. It is in this context that Gorgias makes his bold announcement of the absolute power of speech.

Rhetorical truth aligns with the relativism of Protagoras because it entirely depends upon each person who makes judgements. Gorgias' emphasis is on the change or control of the others' opinions by means of speech. In Plato's *Gorgias*, he proclaimed that the use of rhetoric can enslave other people, in particular, experts in each subject. The art of speech bestows a political power. He also explained the ease of acquiring this omnipotent art without knowledge or expertise, thereby seducing young people into learning his art. Thus, the new teachings of the Sophists generated new ideas of knowledge and truth.

3. Human wisdom against divine authority

The original features of the Sophistic Movement can be observed more clearly in contrast to earlier philosophies. The main difference lies in attitudes towards tradition. The Ionian thinkers, from Anaximander to Herodotus, composed their writings in prose by declaring that the author stated the results of inquiry from his own voice. The poet Xenophanes, in contrast, cast sceptical doubt on human understanding (DK 21 B34, 35, 36, 38) while advancing a hope for development of human science over time (B18). Xenophanes shared an interest in natural inquiry with the other Ionian philosophers, but he took a pessimistic view on human knowledge from the poetic tradition. In hexameter, poets appeal to the goddesses (Muses) often at the beginning of composition in hopes of receiving inspiration because they required divine or superhuman power to speak the truth about the remote past or matters pertaining to the gods. It is in this divine perspective that poets expressed the limits and weaknesses of human cognition.[5] Just as Xenophanes uttered his epistemological pessimism in epic poetry, Parmenides and Empedocles, both putting their thought into verse, told the truth from the divine viewpoint. Heraclitus also presented his wisdom in a written book of aphorisms dedicated to the shrine of Artemis. His oracular sayings declared that people could not understand his *logos*, the truth of the universe.

The Sophists departed clearly from the traditional wisdom expressed in such verse as well as from the new scientific inquiry into nature. Not only did they avoid writing in verse, they also cast serious doubts on gods and religious authority. In fact, wisdom from divine authority was a main target of the Sophists. Instead, they put forward pessimistic views on human knowledge, not in the divine perspective (as the earlier thinkers and poets had) but within the human perspective. Self-reflection on human knowledge became possible through Sophistry, which challenged all authority and tradition, including that of philosophy.

Prodicus and Critias (who was not a professional Sophist but was still an intellectual strongly influenced by the Sophistic Movement) expressed the rationalistic view that gods are nothing but human creation, a result of the development of human civilization and society. Prodicus related Demeter to bread, Dionysus to wine, Poseidon to water, and Hephaestus to fire, and he insisted that religious ceremonies and the idea of gods had been generated in the human race from these things. We later see in Plato's *Phaedrus* that the rationalizing of myths was an emerging trend among the Sophists.

Similarly, the Sophist Antiphon resorted to the dichotomy of law or custom (*nomos*) and nature (*physis*) to cast serious doubt upon the idea of social justice (DK 87 B44). If law and justice are nothing but human conventions or parts of the social contract, one can gain profit by escaping or avoiding them. Thus, the separation of law from nature shakes the traditional view that the laws were given by the gods as an absolute standard of moral values. The application of rationalism to religion offered the people freedom from divine authorities. Truth was no longer a divine gift that came through inspiration or by religious authority. Instead, the Sophists challenged it to create a new epistemology.

In this context, we can properly understand the agnostic statement of Protagoras from *On Gods*. We have only the reconstruction of the first statement: 'As for gods, I cannot know either that they are or that they are not, or what they look like. For there are many obstacles that keep me from knowing these, both the obscurity and the shortness of human life.'[6]

The fragment contains a clear statement that it is impossible to know about the gods. First, the existence or non-existence of the gods is unknowable. Second, if they exist, their features or attributes are unknowable. The first part carefully escapes the charge of atheism (non-existence of gods), but the very challenge raised by the question suggests an atheistic viewpoint. Also, by limiting his statement with the first person 'I', Protagoras avoids committing to a general statement about human beings, but readers nevertheless understand that the idea is applicable to all of us.

Next, Protagoras presented two reasons based on human experience as to why the gods are unknowable. First, the object of the question, namely, the gods, is too obscure or unclear (*adēlotēs*) for one to grasp. This assumes a crucial distance between humans and gods, which is not entirely alien to traditional thought. Second, investigating such a huge question as the existence of gods would require enormous time and effort, but human life is very limited. Thus, it is impossible to reach any definitive view.

By these arguments, Protagoras twisted traditional and philosophical views into a new epistemological statement. His bold claim of agnosticism shocked ancient people, even if the anecdotes about the burning of his books, his impiety trial, his banishment, and his unfortunate death are later fictions or exaggerations. This demonstrates one aspect of why the Sophists were severely criticised as a dangerous movement. They shared a radical reconsideration of tradition, a clear departure from the divine authority, and a serious challenge to philosophy.

4. Gorgias' challenge to philosophy

Gorgias presented a similar agnostic claim – that human beings cannot know the truth – in the seemingly philosophical treatise *On What Is Not or On Nature* (*Peri tou mē ontos ē Peri physeōs*). This work has proven so difficult to interpret that commentators offer different views as to whether it is a serious attempt at constructing arguments on ontology and epistemology (in this case, nihilism and agnosticism) or a parody of earlier and contemporary philosophers such as the Eleatics. This chapter takes the second view and assumes that Gorgias aimed to subvert the arguments of Parmenides, Melissus, Zeno, and Leucippus by using their logical methods (e.g. argument *ad absurdum*) against them and putting their contradicting opinions together in opposition to one another. In this manner, he challenged the seriousness of those philosophers' paradoxical arguments by inducing incredible conclusions from them. This attitude accords with similar playfulness found in the *Encomium of Helen* (21).

In *On What Is Not or On Nature*, summarized in the pseudo-Aristotelian treatise *Melissus, Xenophanes, Gorgias* (*MXG*) and in Sextus Empiricus' *Against the Professors* (Laks and Most 2016), Gorgias sought to prove three claims. The first of the three proofs is as follows: If there is something, either *what is* or *what is not* (or both) is; however, it is denied that either of them is; therefore, nothing is. The second proof holds that, even if there is something, it is unknown. Then, the third proof concludes that, even if it is known, it cannot be transmitted to others.[7]

In the treatise, Gorgias employs a method to accumulate layers of negative arguments (a 'layering argument'). After proving not-P, he pursues a further argument in the hypothetical condition (or concession) of 'even if P', from which another absurdity results. After concluding that 'nothing is' in the first stage, Gorgias moves on to further argue (the second stage) that by assuming even if there is something, that something is unknown, and (the third stage) that even if something both exists and is known, its nature cannot be communicated. Such layering arguments look strange in philosophy, since if not-P is *proven*, it is unnecessary to further prove the case of 'even if P'. However, this type of argument is effective in rhetoric (and is, therefore, much used in the *Defense of Palamedes*), and one can see that Gorgias deliberately fused different ways of argumentation between philosophy and rhetoric.

The second and third stages, in particular, concern epistemology. Although the *MXG* and Sextus report different arguments and thus exact reconstruction is impossible here, it appears that Gorgias resorted to three devices: the correspondence between thought and the object, the difference of senses, and the relation between speech and the object. Each will be considered in turn.

First, Gorgias presented an argument *ad absurdum* by discussing thought and its object. The objects of thought are *what is*; but when one thinks of a man flying or a chariot racing in the sea, it *is not*; therefore, *what is* is not the object of thought and is unknown. One important assumption is that one cannot think of *what is not*. This epistemological claim, apparently shared by the Sophists under Eleatic influence, raises serious difficulties concerning falsehood which Plato tackled in the *Theaetetus* and eventually solved in the *Sophist*. Also, Gorgias discussed fictional creatures (such as Scylla and Chimera) and imaginary situations as counterexamples, both of which have no corresponding object in reality. The question of how to think meaningfully about non-existent things becomes a genuine problem to consider.

Second, Gorgias noted that the senses, such as sight, hearing, and even thinking (which Gorgias viewed as one of the senses), are different from one another and also independent of each other. Just as we can see something without hearing it, we can also imagine a chariot racing in the sea without seeing it. This point illustrates both the unknowability and the incommunicability of *what is*.

Third, speech and words correspond to things subsisting outside us. This raises two further questions: How does language represent or deliver what is outside, and since each person has different thoughts, how can people communicate with each other? Gorgias added that language does not reveal the multitude of subsisting things any more than sensing an object illuminates its true nature. With these points, Gorgias gave doubt to the utility of speech or language as a tool for communication and raised important questions about semantics and epistemology.

These arguments were meant to be paradoxes and were probably not intended to represent serious discussion, but they nevertheless raise several important issues to be solved. Gorgias' threefold argument as a whole shows his playful intentions. If the second argument is comprehended, then it must be admitted that it is incomprehensible, and if the third argument is admitted, it becomes necessary that what cannot be communicated is communicated. These positions are self-contradictory and absurd. Thus, the whole treatise should be regarded as a challenge to philosophy rather than a presentation of such philosophical positions as nihilism and agnosticism.

5. Protagoras' 'Man-Measure thesis'

The most important contribution of the Sophists to epistemology was the introduction of relativism. This concept was formulated for the first time by Protagoras in the form of 'Man is the measure of all things' (the 'Man-Measure thesis'). Although modern commentators rightly doubt that Protagorean relativism was widely shared by the other Sophists and became their standard position (Bett 1989), the thesis raised controversies among later philosophers. Relativism has been one of the most important positions in philosophy. We examine the thesis first, and then observe how it was treated in antiquity.

Protagoras first presented the Man-Measure thesis in his treatise *Truth* or according to Sextus Empiricus, *The Throws* (DK 80 B1): 'Of all things, the measure (*metron*) is man, of things that are, that they are, of things that are not, that they are not.'[8]

This opening statement allows several different interpretations (Guthrie 1971 [1969]). First, 'man' (*anthrōpos*) may refer to human beings as a genus (in contrast with other animals), or each human society or individual man. Also, 'things' (*chrēmata*) may be matters of fact, questions of moral values, or both. Accordingly, the thesis can be interpreted by different readers to encompass such positions as perceptual relativism, cultural relativism, linguistic relativism, conceptual relativism, and moral relativism. In addition to the theoretical difficulty in categorizing various types of relativism, it is almost impossible to identify Protagoras' Man-Measure thesis with one of them with confidence. A major difficulty comes from the lack of context or substantial information about the original thesis, but the indeterminacy may have been intended by the author, who might have supposed that if the thesis allows various interpretations, that very fact shows that relativism is valid.

Plato's *Theaetetus*, the most important testimony, explicates the thesis as indicating that each thing appears different for different persons. For instance, the same wind may feel cold to one person but warm to another. Some commentators simply follow this example and interpret it as an individual relativism of perceptual experience (e.g. Lee 2005). However, considering the general background of the thesis and some other passages in the *Theaetetus*, other options must be considered.

First, Plato clearly contrasted 'man' with other animals in the *Theaetetus* and also with 'god' in the *Laws* (4.716c). Socrates mockingly criticised Protagoras, saying that 'I was astonished that he did not state at the beginning of the *Truth* that "Pig is the measure of all things" or "Baboon" or some yet more out-of-the-way creature with the power of perception' (*Theaetetus* 161c). Socrates also mentioned 'god' and 'tadpole' in that passage, which seems to suggest that the thesis treats human beings as a genus.

Moreover, while individual relativism is a natural target in philosophy as practiced by Plato and Aristotle, Protagoras was an advisor to Pericles, and likely had an intention of defending democracy by suggesting that each society can posit its own norms and values. This view accords with the general contrast between *nomos* and *physis* as proposed by the Sophists.[9] If this is the case, social or cultural relativism may be a better fit for Protagoras' views. However, whether the thesis signifies individuals or societies, physical facts, or moral values or customs, Protagoras seems to have deliberately left the meaning open to interpretation, thus explaining why thinkers from Plato on have continued to discuss the meaning of the thesis.

The Man-Measure thesis, understood in the context of Athenian democracy and forensic rhetoric, definitely challenged traditional values and ways of seeing the world. It was no longer necessary to turn to the gods in considering law, custom, and moral judgement. Instead, human beings could deliberate and decide what to do by themselves. This marked a radical departure from traditional religion, which regarded the Olympian gods as the absolute source of morality and society. This new trust in human ability was widely criticised as impious by conservative citizens and as anti-philosophical by Plato.

Commentators differ on how successful Plato's criticisms were in the *Theaetetus*. His treatment was complex and multilayered. He first connected Protagoras' Man-Measure thesis (epistemology) with the Heraclitean flux theory (ontology) through 'secret doctrine', but we do not know how far that analysis represented the historical background of Protagoras' position. Above all, the so-called self-refutation argument (169d-171d) is a focus of assessment. To those who believe the Man-Measure thesis to be false, the thesis entails its own denial. Plato's *Theaetetus* was the first to appeal to this argument, and it is still controversial whether relativism is self-refuted or not.

However, Plato seems to have attached more importance to the pragmatic sides of the thesis. After all, if everyone can make judgements for themselves, why is Protagoras superior to others and his teaching worth paying for? To this objection, the imaginary Protagoras admits that there are better and worse judgements instead of true and false judgements, but the criticism casts serious doubt on the profession of Sophists as teachers of virtue.

In the history of philosophy, Protagoras is treated as the founder of relativism, but controversy lingers on his thesis and its connection to relativism in the modern sense (mainly in terms of conceptual frameworks: Zilioli 2007). It is unlikely that the other Sophists claimed any form of strong relativism (Bett 1989). Since Plato's *Theaetetus*, philosophers have discussed whether the Man-Measure thesis commits any kind of self-refutation (Burnyeat 1976a,b), and, accordingly, Protagoras has become a focus of epistemology (Lee 2005; Castagnoli 2010).

6. Later interpretations of the Man-Measure thesis

Interpretations and criticisms of the Man-Measure thesis were varied in antiquity. Protagoras' contemporaries and later philosophers of the era reacted to it critically, but generally only when presented in other forms. We have observed three simplified forms: 'no more this than that', 'all appearances are true', and 'all things are relative'. Each of these formulations represents some aspect of the original thesis but leads to different epistemological issues.

First, ancient philosophers occasionally took Protagoras as insisting on 'no more this than that' (*ou mallon*). As far as the Man-Measure thesis concerns measuring, it can naturally be interpreted in terms of 'more than': each man (A and B) being the measure, 'something is no more P (to A) than not-P (to B)'. Democritus, a younger compatriot of Protagoras during his time in Abdera, reportedly criticised the thesis as involving the 'reversal (*peritropē*)' (Sextus Empiricus, *Against the Professors* 7.389; DK 68 A114; cf. A8).[10] Plutarch noted this criticism clearly (*Against Colotes* 1108F-1109A; DK 68 B156): 'But indeed Democritus was so far from holding that *each thing is no more this than that*, that he attacked the sophist Protagoras for saying so, and wrote many convincing things against him.'

The Aristotelian commentator Asclepius of the sixth century questioned, '[W]hence is it obvious that I state truth no more than you?' (*On Aristotle's Metaphysics* 284.15–16 Hayduck). In applying 'no more P than not-P' to one person's truth (P) and another's (not-P), Asclepius suggested an objective way to express the Protagorean relativism. But this formula itself presented a non-relativistic truth, and therefore, the thesis involved 'reversal' (self-refutation). It is not certain whether Protagoras himself used this formulation, but certainly some of his opponents understood it in this way. This formula became a common device for later sceptics as Sextus discusses in the *Outlines of Pyrrhonism* (1.188–91).

The second formula, 'all appearances are true', is also assumed to be equivalent to the Man-Measure thesis. When Plato examined Protagoras' thesis in the *Theaetetus*, he occasionally dropped the qualification 'for someone' from the relativistic claim and criticised it in the simplified form. There is still controversy as to whether Plato's argument commits a fallacy of *secundum quid* or not, but after Aristotle, this simplified form became standard. While there are a few examples where the qualification 'for someone' is correctly kept in the relativist formula, ancient writers generally cared little about it (Aristotle, *Metaphysics* IV.5, 1009a6–9; DK 80 A19): 'From the same opinion also derives the thesis of Protagoras, and it is necessary that both either are or are not the case equally. For if all opinions and appearances are true, it is necessary that everything should be simultaneously true and false.'

Thus Aristotle criticised Protagoras (along with other thinkers) for violating the law of contradiction, and in doing so, he interpreted the thesis not as relativism (in the strict sense) but as subjectivism or infallibilism.[11] This simplified form allowed doxographers to classify Protagoras in the same group as Epicurus who insisted that 'all perceptions and appearances are true' while admitting to the possibility of falsehood in opinions. According to Epicurus, whereas sensory perception per se does not err, opinions added to it often lead to mistakes. In this type of infallibilism, the difference between truth and falsehood is meaningful and important. Protagoras' relativism, by contrast, denies the possibility of falsehood altogether. Doxographers contrasted both Protagoras and Epicurus with two groups of thinkers: Democritus and Xeniades, who claimed that all appearances are false; and Plato, the Stoics, and others, who insisted that some appearances are true while others are false (Sextus Empiricus, *Against the Professors* 7.369, 388).

The third formula, 'all things are relative', is again popular in discussion of Protagoras' thesis. Sextus treats relativity (*to pros ti*) as a consequence or implication of Protagoras' claim that 'all appearances are true' since every appearance is *relative to* a perceiver. It is notable that relativity is key to ancient scepticism as in Sextus' *Outlines of Pyrrhonism* (1.39, 135–40, 167).

If we combine the relative qualifier 'for someone' with the simplified form 'each appearance is true', this may come closer to Protagoras' original position of relativism, but these two claims are discussed separately in each doxographical context. If we attach 'for someone' to every appearance, the self-refutation argument, a common weapon of the ancient critics, no longer works against

Epistemology in the Sophists   63

the Protagorean position. Likewise, Protagoras cannot be criticised for violating the law of contradiction if each thing is relative to different perceivers. Aristotle discussed relativity in his examination of the Protagorean position (*Metaphysics* IV.6, 1011a17–20): 'If not all things are relative (*pros ti*), but some actually exist in their own right (*auta kath' hauta*), not every appearance will be true. For appearance is appearance for someone. Consequently, one who insists that all appearances are true makes relative all things that are.'

Later the anonymous commentator of the *Theaetetus* describes Protagoras' thesis as relativity (col. 62.39–44 Sedley and Bastianini) based on flux, since there is nothing in itself. This idea comes from Plato's *Theaetetus*, and it was Plato who first used the expression '*pros ti*' in relation to the Protagorean relativism (*Theaetetus* 160b): 'So if a man says anything "is", he must say it is to or of or in relation to something (*pros ti*) and similarly if he says it "becomes".' The relation between a percipient (one to whom something appears) and an object (what appears to him) is one way to explain Protagorean relativism, but there is a risk of reducing it to a specific kind of physical perception theory. Plato arguably paved the way for this explanation when he connected the Protagorean relativism with the Heraclitean flux theory. This commits Protagoras to a certain ontology which rejects absolute reality, that is, thing in itself (*kath' hauto*), but since the relation or interaction between the percipient and the object is objectively determinable, it becomes a dogmatic position of the objective truth about the external reality. Protagoras would probably deny such an interpretation if he had originally insisted on relativism.

This brief survey of the ancient interpretations of the Man-Measure thesis shows how the Sophists' arguments raised epistemological debates in later generations. They challenged the absolute philosophy of Parmenides, Plato, and Aristotle, and provided rich materials for rhetoric, social theories, and scepticism.

Notes

1 Antiphon of Rhamnus was the first rhetoric teacher in Athens and a contemporary of Socrates. He composed several works of rhetorical skills entitled *Tetralogies*. Later, he became known as an oligarchic politician before his execution as a leader of the Four Hundred Revolution in 411 BCE. Plato mentions his name only in passing as an inferior teacher of rhetoric in *Menexenus* 236a. Although he may be identical with the Sophist Antiphon, who wrote the philosophical treatise *On the Truth* (for which

64   *Knowledge in Ancient Philosophy*

only a few papyri fragments survive) and/or appears in Xenophon's *Memorabilia*, some ancient testimonies distinguished the two. Gagarin (2002) suggests a mutual identity, whereas Pendrick (2002) separates them.

2   Fragments and testimonies of the Sophists are included in Diels and Kranz (1952: original texts), Sprague (1972: English translations), and Graham (2010: both the original texts and English translations). Translations are from Graham (2010), unless otherwise noted.

3   The reported titles are *The Art of Contentious Arguments, On Wrestling, On Mathematics, On Government, On Ambition, On Virtues, On the Original State of Things, On Those in Hades, On Human Wrongdoing, Leadership, Trial for a Fee, Opposed Arguments I and II* (DL 9.55). In this list, we see no clear evidence that he wrote any treatise on epistemology, although the first and the last may contain some relevant arguments.

4   It is impossible to determine the original size and content of these books. Some theorize that this hopeless scarcity of testimonies may partly be due to the public burning of his books in the Athenian *agora* as a result of his impious claim in *On Gods* (Diogenes Laertius, 9.51–2).

5   For this poetic pessimism, see Snell (1953: chapter 7), Guthrie (1962: 398), Lesher (1999: 225–6), and Most (1999: 342–3). However, Hussey (1990) emphasizes the difference between Homer and Xenophanes.

6   While it is not cited in either Plato or Aristotle except for an allusion in *Theaetetus* 162d–e (DK 80 A23), the citations vary among other ancient writers (eighteen testimonies). The oldest reference is Timon, *Sylloi* II, fr. 5.3–6 *PGF* (Sextus Empiricus, *Against the Professors* 9.57; DK 80 A12). Diels and Kranz reconstruct fragment B4 slightly differently, and most editors follow this reconstruction. However, DK did not take all the extant citations into account, but used only Diogenes Laertius 9.51 and Eusebius, *Preparation for the Gospel* 14.3.7. As Capizzi (1955: 101-2n2) points out, DK missed a more important testimony of Aristocles, *On Philosophy*, recorded in Eusebius, *Preparation for the Gospel* 14.19.10. I present a new reconstruction considering all the testimonies; for the reconstruction, see Notomi (2008).

7   Since *MXG* and Sextus report different arguments in some places, commentators discuss which is more reliable. Sextus' version used to be regarded as more reliable, but recently *MXG* is treated more favourably.

8   The full form (with only a small variation of the negative particle) is quoted in five sources: Plato, *Theaetetus* 152A, Sextus Empiricus, *Outlines of Pyrrhonism* 1.21, *Against the Professors* 7.60, Diogenes Laertius 9.51, and Eusebius, *Preparation for the Gospel* 14.20.2. There are several partial quotations and rough references. See Notomi (2013).

9   Although there is no clear testimony of Protagoras' commitment to this contrast, Heinimann (1945/1980) ascribes its origin to Protagoras.

Epistemology in the Sophists

10 We see the same criticism against Protagoras in Plato's *Theaetetus* 170e-171a (DK 80 A15) and *Euthydemus* 286b-c (A19). In the *Cratylus*, Hermogenes, whose view of correct names is influenced by the Protagorean relativism, uses the same formula: 'the latter (sc. the new naming) is no more correct than the former (sc. the previous naming)' (Plato, *Cratylus* 384d). See also Aristotle, *Metaphysics* IV.5, 1009b10; Proclus, *On Plato's Parmenides* 631.6-10; Cousin, 17.3-6 Steel.

11 *Metaphysics* IV.4-6 (esp. 1007b18-24), 10.1 (1053a31-b3), and 11.5-6 (especially 1062b12-1063b35).

References

Bett, R. (1989), 'The Sophists and Relativism', *Phronesis*, 34: 139-69.

Buchheim, T. (1989), *Gorgias von Leontinoi, Reden, Fragmente und Testimonien*, Hamburg: Felix Meiner.

Burnyeat, M. F. (1976a), 'Protagoras and Self-Refutation in Later Greek Philosophy', *Philosophical Review*, 85: 44-69.

Burnyeat, M. F. (1976b), 'Protagoras and Self-Refutation in Plato's *Theaetetus*', *Philosophical Review*, 85: 172-95.

Capizzi, A. (1955), *Protagora, le testimonianze e i frammenti, edizione riveduta e ampliata con uno studio su la vita, le opere, il pensiero e la fortuna*, Firenze: G. C. Santoni.

Castagnoli, L. (2010), *Ancient Self-Refutation: The Logic and History of the Self-Refutation Argument from Democritus to Augustine*, Cambridge: Cambridge University Press.

Diels, H. and Kranz, W. (1952), *Die Fragmente der Vorsokratiker*, II, 6. Aufl., Dublin/Zürich: Weidmann (1. Aufl. 1903).

Gagarin, M. (2002), *Antiphon the Athenian, Oratory, Law, and Justice in the Age of the Sophists*, Austin: University of Texas Press.

Graham, D. W. (2010), *The Texts of Early Greek Philosophy: the Complete Fragments and Selected Testimonies of the Major Presocratics*, Part 2, Cambridge: Cambridge University Press.

Guthrie, W. K. C. (1962), *A History of Greek Philosophy, I. The Earlier Presocratics and the Pythagoreans*, Cambridge: Cambridge University Press.

Guthrie, W. K. C. (1971 [1969]), *A History of Greek Philosophy III, The Fifth-Century Enlightenment*, Cambridge: Cambridge University Press; repr. Part 1, *The Sophists*, Cambridge: Cambridge University Press.

Heinimann, F. (1945/1980), *Nomos und Physis, Herkunft und Bedeutung einer Antithese im griechischen Denken des 5. Jahrhunderts*, Basel/Darmstadt: Wissenschaftliche Buchgesellschaft.

Hussey, E. (1990), 'The Beginnings of Epistemology: From Homer to Philolaos', in S. Everson (ed.), *Companions to Ancient Thought 1: Epistemology*, Cambridge: Cambridge University Press.

Kerferd, G. B. (1981), *The Sophistic Movement*, Cambridge: Cambridge University Press.

Laks, A. and Most, G. W. (2016), *Early Greek Philosophy, Volume VIII, Sophists, Part 1; Volume IX, Sophists, Part 2*, Loeb Classical Library, Cambridge MA: Harvard University Press.

Lee, M.-K. (2005), *Epistemology after Protagoras: Responses to Relativism in Plato, Aristotle, and Democritus*, Oxford: Oxford University Press.

Lesher, J. H. (1992), *Xenophanes of Colophon, Fragments, a Text and Translation with a Commentary*, Toronto: University of Toronto Press.

Most, G. W. (1999), 'The Poetics of Early Greek Philosophy', in A. A. Long (ed.), *The Cambridge Companion to Early Greek Philosophy*, Cambridge: Cambridge University Press.

Notomi, N. (2007), 'Plato's Critique of Gorgias: Power, the Other, and Truth', in M. Erler and L. Brisson (eds), *Gorgias-Menon: Selected Papers from the Seventh Symposium Platonicum*, Sankt Augustin: Academia Verlag.

Notomi, N. (2008), 'Fragment and Tradition of Protagoras, *On Gods*', *Philologica*, 3 (in Japanese): 24–47.

Notomi, N. (2013), 'A Protagonist of the Sophistic Movement? Protagoras in Historiography', in J. M. van Ophuijsen, M. van Raalte, and P. Stork (eds), *Protagoras of Abdera: The Man, His Measure*, Leiden: Brill.

Notomi, N. (2014), 'The Sophists', in F. Sheffield and J. Warren (eds), *The Routledge Companion to Ancient Philosophy*, New York: Routledge.

Pendrick, G. J. (2002), *Antiphon the Sophist, The Fragments*, Cambridge: Cambridge University Press.

Robinson, T. M. (1979), *Contrasting Arguments: An Edition of the Dissoi Logoi*, New York: Arno Press.

Romilly, J. de (1992), *The Great Sophists in Periclean Athens*, trans. J. Lloyd, Oxford: Oxford University Press.

Schiappa, E. (2003 [1991]), *Protagoras and Logos: A Study in Greek Philosophy and Rhetoric*, 2nd edn, Columbia: South Carolina University Press.

Snell, B. (1953), *The Discovery of the Mind, in Greek Philosophy and Literature*, trans. T. G. Rosenmeyer, Oxford: Basil Blackwell.

Sprague, R. K. (ed.) (1972), *The Older Sophists, a complete translation by several hands of the fragments in Die Fragmente der Vorsokratiker edited by Diels-Kranz and published by Weidman Verlag, with a new edition of Antiphon and of Euthydemus*, Columbia: University of South Carolina Press.

Zilioli, U. (2007), *Protagoras and the Challenge of Relativism*, Aldershot: Ashgate.

4

Socratic Epistemology

José Lourenço and Nicholas D. Smith

1. Introduction

The main concern of Socrates'[1] thought concerned what type of life we should live. His inquiries into what can make life valuable for human beings led Socrates to pursue and in some cases endorse significant epistemological theses. In this chapter, we explore and document the epistemological positions attributable to Socrates. Certainly, the most famous among these commitments is his profession of ignorance or disavowal of knowledge. The profession of ignorance is itself a point of controversy among scholars, at least in part because Socrates also sometimes appears to maintain that both he and other people know some things. So one question we must explore is what Socrates does – and what he does not – intend to disclaim in his profession of ignorance. We will argue that studies of Socratic epistemology have generally not adequately recognized the different ways in which Socrates thinks that human beings can fall into ignorance, such that there can not only be different degrees of ignorance, but also different *kinds* of ignorance – some of which are much less readily remediated than others. So we also propose to consider more carefully what might be called a Socratic agnoiology – the Socratic views on the nature and causes of the forms of ignorance that impede our quest for happy lives. We find Socrates claiming that the improvement of our lives depends on a relentless search for the definitions of virtue, which he also characterizes as a kind of knowledge of essences. But if virtue is knowledge, and he and all other human beings lack that knowledge, does that indicate a very pessimistic assessment, not only of our epistemic condition, but even of our ultimate ethical condition? Related to this last question, we will argue, is Socrates' characterization of the wisdom by means of which one potentially would obtain the good life as at least analogous to craft or expertise.

2. The Socratic professions of ignorance and knowledge

It is worth stressing, as a preliminary observation, that the English words 'knowledge' and 'know' by which we customarily endeavour to translate different terms of the cognitive vocabulary of ancient Greek available to Socrates are likely from the outset to create significant distortion of our subject. In fact, to refer to the mental state that we usually call knowledge, Socrates used several Greek verbs (and their cognates) such as *gignoskō, oida, epistamai, sunoida, epaiō, phroneō,* and *phrontizō;* also nouns as *gnōsis, sophia, epistēmē, phronēsis,* and *technē.* These terms convey many different forms of cognition such as perception, recognition, intuition, acquaintance, thought, awareness, consideration, understanding, as well as the mastering of an art or skill, or having practical wisdom. If we begin our study of Socratic epistemology by stipulating that knowledge is, as Gail Fine (2008: 53) puts it, 'a truth-entailing cognitive condition that is appropriately cognitively superior to mere true belief', we may find that a number of important epistemological claims Socrates makes become either irrelevant or absurd. Certainly in the way in which he connects knowledge and wisdom to *technē* (craft, skill, or expertise) would seem to put more emphasis on what we now call 'know-how', rather than 'know-that', which is the focus of most contemporary theory of knowledge.

3. Socratic agnoiology, part I: risk and reward

Even so, Socrates does at least sometimes seem ready to recognize some cognitive states as instances of knowledge, even if he denigrates these as trivial. A good example of such a case appears in the *Euthydemus,* where Socrates makes an interesting claim:

> [Euthydemus speaking] Answer me, he said: Is there anything that you know?
> [Socrates] Certainly, I said, indeed many things, but small ones. (*Euthydemus* 293b; our translation)

We are inclined to think, given the context of this argument and also the focus of all of Socratic philosophical inquiry, that he regards the 'many things' he knows as 'small' because he does not find them particularly valuable when it comes to figuring out how to live the best human life and be happy. But this passage also gives us a good indication that when Socrates professes his own ignorance and also finds and exposes such ignorance in others, he should not be taken as some kind of global sceptic, or as entertaining the kinds of broad doubts about the human epistemic condition that Descartes, for example, seems to wrestle with in the first of his *Meditations*.

Another passage, we believe, is especially helpful in making clear what Socrates has in mind when he makes his profession of ignorance. In Plato's depiction of Socrates' defence at his trial, we find the philosopher considering a question he imagines his jurors would like answered: How is it that so many nasty rumours have arisen that characterize him in such negative terms (*Apology* 20c-d)? Socrates responds that the source of the prejudices against him turns out to be a peculiar sort of wisdom that Socrates actually has. This answer begins with the famous account of his friend's trip to Delphi, where Chaerephon asked the oracle if anyone was wiser than Socrates, and received a negative reply (20e-21a). Socrates reports that when he heard about this, he was extremely puzzled, for, as he says there, 'I'm aware that, in fact, I'm not wise at all' (*Apology* 21b).[2]

Socrates decides that he needs to figure out what the god might have meant to give such a strange answer to Chaerephon's question, and so he undertakes to interpret the meaning of the oracle by going and examining others who have reputations for wisdom. He begins with political leaders, and tells the jury about one such examination:

> I thought that this guy seems to be wise to many other people and, most of all, to himself, yet he isn't. And then I tried to show him that he thought he is wise, but he isn't. And so, as a result, I became hated by him and by many of those who were there. So, as I went away from him, I concluded to myself that I'm, indeed, wiser than this guy. I'm afraid that neither of us knows anything admirable and good, but this guy thinks he knows something when he doesn't, whereas I, just as I don't know), don't even think I know. At least, then, I seem to be wiser in this small way than this guy, because I don't even think I know what I don't know. (*Apology* 21c-d)

Here again, we find that Socrates is not professing a kind of global scepticism, so much as disclaiming any knowledge of what he would regard as 'admirable and good'. But as for those valuable subjects, he does have one 'small' advantage over the one he examined: unlike Socrates, the politician was ignorant of his own ignorance. Socrates' awareness of his own ignorance is the one advantage he has over others in terms of wisdom, which he calls his 'human wisdom' (20d), and it is this wisdom, he claims, that has led to all of the slanders and prejudices against him, which have resulted in his being brought to trial.

We should regard the Socratic profession of ignorance,[3] accordingly, as centrally concerned with what might be called ethical knowledge, which, again, would be the knowledge of how best to live. We may also reasonably assume that the sort of ignorance that Socrates finds in himself is what might be called 'privative ignorance' – a simple lack of whatever would count as its own relief. In this case, Socrates is aware of a lack in himself – a lack that is shared by the politician, but also not recognized by the politician in himself. Such ignorance would be relieved, plainly, but supplying what is lacking: the knowledge that both Socrates and the politician lack. However, precisely because Socrates is aware that he has such a lack whereas the politician remains unaware, there is a further error that the politician might make that Socrates does *not* make: The politician thinks he *knows*, because he mistakes what he merely *believes* as *knowledge*.

Curiously, among the dialogues normally counted as early only in Plato's *Meno* does Socrates make clear a distinction between true belief and knowledge (*Meno* 85c-d, 97a-98a).[4] But in many places, Socrates takes the acceptance of a *false* belief to be a clear indication of ignorance, and this sort of ignorance is not simply a privation, but a case in which one is actually in a condition that to some degree or other works against being relieved of one's ignorance: when we believe something, we are at risk of thinking we have knowledge. This is why we see Socrates targeting those who are regarded by others as wise, and especially those who regard themselves as wise, in his elenctic 'mission' in Athens. Only when one becomes aware – as Socrates is – that one does not have knowledge, can one have any hope of having the ignorance that is the privation of such knowledge at least to some degree remediated.

Here, however, is where Socrates' focus on know-how, skill, or expertise (*technē*) offers some hope where there might not otherwise seem to be any. Most contemporary epistemologists regard knowledge as what is called a 'threshold' achievement. If knowledge is a threshold achievement, in any given case, one either has knowledge, or not. But even in contemporary analyses, know-how does not work this way. Of course, one can be so deficient in some skill that it might be appropriate to say one really lacks the skill. For example, neither of the authors of this chapter would claim to be able, to know how, to perform an appendectomy. But in many cases, skills are what are called *gradable*. One can have a skill *to some degree*, and to that degree count *as skilled*.

Socrates also famously associates knowledge with happiness:

[Socrates speaking] [S]ince we all wish to be happy, and since we appear to become so by using things and using them rightly, and since knowledge was the source of rightness and good fortune, it seems to be necessary that every man should prepare himself by every means to become as wise as possible. (*Euthydemus* 282a)[5]

Scholars have debated whether Socrates' association of knowledge and happiness is one of necessity, sufficiency, or perhaps nomological in nature.[6] But in this passage, at least, the gradability of wisdom seems to be explicit, and we can thus associate that with a gradability in the happiness one might hope to achieve.[7] The gradability of each, accordingly, allows Socrates to think that we can, perhaps, achieve at least some measure of happiness – at least relative to those who are not merely ignorant, but also ignorant of their ignorance. Since, again, Socrates' interest is in the area of ethical practice, even if he is not especially optimistic about our ability as human beings to achieve complete ethical knowledge, the gradability of ethical skill might allow someone to obtain some (even if only marginal) measure of wisdom and thus happiness, if one will follow Socrates' advice and make every attempt to 'become as wise as possible'.

4. Socratic agnoiology, part II: aetiology and remediation

Given his ethical focus, we can now see why Socrates regards ignorance as not simply an epistemic fault, but also a profound threat to our quality of life. Accordingly, we might now wonder what he supposed were the sources of ignorance, and how they might be avoided. Here, too, we find an interesting novelty in Socratic philosophy. Socrates seems to have recognized the same kinds of epistemic processes that we now acknowledge, such as perception, various forms of reasoning, and the like. But in addition to these, he seems also to recognize a kind of cognitive process that is either overlooked or else denied in contemporary epistemology and cognitive psychology.

There has been a great deal of discussion recently of what has come to be known as 'Socratic motivational intellectualism'. While this is obviously not the place to undertake a detailed account of Socratic moral psychology, it is worth at least noting here that it is generally agreed that the moral psychology that Socrates did accept was an intellectualist one, and was therefore inextricably tied to his epistemology. According to Socrates, whatever any agent does in a given case will always reflect and depend upon what the agent thinks is best (for himself or herself), among the options the agent recognizes at the time of the action. This commitment is at the heart of Socrates' famous denial of (synchronic[8]) belief akrasia – that is, Socrates claims that no one ever acts in a way that is contrary to what they believe is best for them at the time of action. The consequence of this view, as Terry Penner (1990: 165) has famously put it, is that 'for Socrates, when people act badly or viciously or even just out of moral weakness, that will be merely a result of intellectual mistake'.

Until recently, scholars have tended to characterize the Socratic position as one that simply fails to recognize any motivational potency in psychological factors other than those we usually recognize as cognitive processes. But the attribution of such a view to Socrates not only seems to offend common sense, but also must confront many passages in the Socratic dialogues in which Socrates seems entirely aware that some other psychological processes (ones that are at least not obviously cognitive) can have effects on how people behave – processes such as those we associate with appetites and also those we regard as emotions or passions.[9] More recently, scholars have proposed that appetites and such actually constitute a different *kind* of cognitive process:

> A passage in the *Charmides* (167e) seems to indicate that human beings experience different kinds of desire, which target different sorts of goals. These include appetite (*epithumia*), which aims at pleasure, wish (*boulēsis*), which aims at what is good, and love (*erōs*), which aims at what is beautiful. Each of these seems to have an aversive alternative, as well: we avoid pains, what is bad, and what is ugly. Our natural attractions and aversions, we contend, are the grounds for a variety of non-rational beliefs: Insofar as something seems or promises to be pleasurable, beneficial, or beautiful, the agent will be naturally inclined to believe it to be something good; and insofar as something seems to be painful, detrimental, or ugly, the agent will be naturally inclined to believe it to be something bad. Unless the natural inclination to believe in such cases is mitigated or defeated by some other (for example, rational) belief-forming process, one will form beliefs about goods and evils accordingly. The beliefs created by these natural attractions and aversions, because they derive from non-rational processes, are veridically unreliable, but are also to some degree (by their nature as non-rational) resistant to rational persuasion and other belief-forming processes. (Brickhouse and Smith 2015: 14–15)

In this view, it follows that one important source of ignorance is that one allows a veridically unreliable cognitive process to produce one's beliefs – and this kind of process is not only unreliable; it also tends to lead the epistemic (and ethical) agent to resist other, more reliable cognitive processes. Recognizing this additional possibility, we contend, not only gives us better insight into Socratic agnoiology, but also into Socrates' famous philosophical practice, the *elenchos*.

5. The Socratic *elenchos*

In Plato's early dialogues, Socrates usually engages in refuting the opinions he elicits from interlocutors on ethical topics. The arguments vary greatly in complexity, form, and purpose, which has generated considerable controversy over Socratic methodology.[10] Generally, such questions of 'Socratic method' have focused on the logical and epistemological aspects of Socrates' arguments and so we should perhaps begin with these.

In his very important and controversial paper on the subject, Gregory Vlastos (1994) characterizes typical Socratic argumentation (called the '*elenchos*') as follows: (1) The interlocutor asserts a thesis which Socrates considers false and targets for refutation. (2) Socrates secures agreement to further premises, say q and r (each of which may stand for a conjunct of propositions). The agreement is ad hoc: Socrates argues from q and r, but not to them. (3) Socrates then argues, and the interlocutor agrees, that q and r entail *not-p*. (4) Thereupon Socrates claims that *not-p* has been proved true, p false (11). Other scholars have questioned whether Vlastos's reconstruction is entirely accurate to Socrates' practice, noting especially that (4) does not logically follow from (1), (2), and (3). (4) would only follow if we can secure the truths of q and r, but the way in which Socrates uses these secondary statements is left unsecured. All that logically follows, accordingly, is $\sim(p \,\&\, q \,\&\, r)$. Vlastos thus poses the question that has come to be known as 'the problem of the *elenchos*', namely, 'how can Socrates claim ... to have proved that the refutand is false when all he has established is its inconsistency with premises whose truth he has not tried to establish in that argument?' (3).

Vlastos's own account of 'the Socratic method' and also his attempt to solve 'the problem of the *elenchos*' has been target of many different criticisms and attempts of emendation.[11] Out of this more specific debate, however, a somewhat broader question has arisen: Was Vlastos even right to suppose that Socrates thought of himself as using a 'method' intended to establish falsehood or truth of positive moral doctrines; by contrast, might he not have intended all along only to display inconsistency in the belief-set of a person, and so revealing her ignorance? So called 'constructivist' accounts of Socratic argumentation have proposed versions of the first of these options; all such versions are rejected by so-called non-constructivist accounts, which defend the second alternative.[12]

It is not our place here to defend either side of this particular debate, so much as to make clear that they all agree on one point and also all make no attempt to engage the aspect of Socratic agnoiology that we brought out in the last section of this chapter. The point that both constructivist and non-constructivist interpreters all agree upon is that Socrates can and does use the *elenchos* to expose the kinds of confusion in his interlocutors that Socrates (plausibly) takes to show that they are not experts in the subject of how to live. Experts on a subject, he insists, will not all disagree with one another on the basic precepts of the subject in which they are experts. Even more importantly, they will not disagree with *themselves* about such precepts, but it is actually that condition that he reveals via the *elenchos*: his interlocutors accept and say things about how to live that are inconsistent.

In response to our propensity to have inconsistent beliefs, Socrates encourages everyone he meets to take up and engage as much as possible in what he calls 'the examined life' (*Apology* 38a), that is, a life of inquiring about how to live. In recommending 'the examined life' as a *way* of life, Socrates seems clearly to indicate that he thinks that living this kind of life is preferable to lives shaped by other sorts of pursuits – and he specifically contrasts the benefits of the sort of life he encourages with lives that focus more on the acquisition of wealth, political power, or social recognition (see *Apology* 29e).

Now, if we take his recommendation of 'the examined life' in a positive way, we are likely to lean in the direction of some 'constructivist' reading of 'the Socratic method'. But we might also take the recommendation in a negative way: Socrates might suppose that leading 'the examined life' might also make us less susceptible to the kind of culpable ignorance of people who are ignorant in the *privative* sense we identified above, but who are also ignorant of their own *privative* ignorance, and suppose, instead, that they have knowledge they do not actually have. A non-constructivist, thus, could regard Socrates' elenctic philosophical mission as one whose main goal is a kind of epistemic modesty.

6. *Elenchos* and the rational remediation of ignorance

At *Gorgias* 521d-e, Socrates makes a startling claim for someone famous for always professing his own ignorance[13]:

> I believe that I'm one of a few Athenians – so as not to say I'm the only one, but the only one among our contemporaries – to take up the true political craft and practice the true politics. This is because the speeches I make on each occasion do not aim at gratification but at what's best. They don't aim at what's most pleasant.[14]

Socrates' claim here is strange for a number of reasons, not the least of which is that he elsewhere says that he has had nothing to do with what is generally regarded as 'the political life' (see *Apology* 31c-32a). But for our purposes here, there is a different puzzle: as one who so consistently proclaims his own ignorance, but who also equates craft with knowledge, how can he, of all people, claim to have taken up the 'true craft of politics'?

In Section 2, above, we noted that the Socratic conception of knowledge was closer to our own conception of know-how, and not to be assimilated to our notion of 'propositional knowledge'. Because the Socratic conception of knowledge is gradable, it is entirely coherent for him to claim both that he has taken up a certain craft and also to disclaim being a master of that craft. He understands himself to have taken up the true political craft because he always aims at 'what's best' and not simply at gratifying those to whom he speaks – as he takes most 'politicians' to do. So we need not take Socrates' claim to conflict with his profession of ignorance, as long as we allow his conception of craft-knowledge to be gradable, and if we take the profession of ignorance to indicate that he regards his own achievement in the true political craft as being still very far from one of mastery.

Even granting this much, however, puts weight on a somewhat different question: precisely how does Socrates think he has come however far he thinks he has, so that he really has 'taken up' the true craft of politics.

We may reasonably assume that Socrates has assiduously followed his own advice that 'it seems to be necessary that every man should prepare himself by every means to become as wise as possible', as we earlier quoted him saying (in Section 2) at *Euthydemus* 282a. But how can he or anyone else undertake such a project? It seems the only answer Socrates ever gives to this question is that we should all endeavour to lead 'the examined life' (see *Apology* 38a), and it also seems that the only way we ever see Socrates accomplishing anything of this sort is in his elenctic examinations of others.

Now, we might suppose that examining others cannot possibly amount to leading an examined life, since it is almost never the case that Socrates is put in a position of answering elenctic questions, but mostly only plays the role of asking such questions. But this would be a mistake; Socrates makes clear that he takes his examinations of others to achieve a more general good for everyone involved, not only answerer and asker, but even others who witness such examinations:

[Socrates speaking] How could you possibly think that even if I were trying to refute everything you say, I would be doing it for any other reasons than the one I would give for a thorough investigation of my own statements – the fear of unconsciously thinking I know something when I do not. And that is what I claim to be doing now, examining the argument for my own sake primarily, but also for the sake of my friends. Or don't you believe it to be for the common good, or for that of most human beings, that the state of each existing thing should become clear? (*Charmides* 166c-d[15]; see also *Gorgias* 505e)

This means that the only way Socrates ever indicates, as to how we might lead 'examined lives', is for us to engage in elenctic argument about ethical matters. If so, we find at least some indication that Socrates regards his practice of elenctic argumentation as yielding constructive results. Of course, even this much of constructivism might be granted by so-called non-constructivists, who would no doubt happily count having one's ignorance exposed as a benefit – and this seems, at least, to be the benefit that Socrates explicitly indicates in the above passage. Non-constructivists might also grant that Socrates does accept that it would be 'for the common good ... that the state of each existing thing should become clear', but then maintain a non-constructive position about the ability of elenctic argument to deliver any such good.

Here again, however, we would do well to remind ourselves of the fact that Socrates regards the kind of knowledge that he pursues as *gradable*, and thus we might reasonably distinguish two very different questions: (1) Does Socrates think his elenctic arguments can produce the kind of precise knowledge he seeks? And (2) Does Socrates think his elenctic arguments can make some progress towards such knowledge – that is, does Socrates think that elenctic argument can produce some improvement in the *approximation* of such knowledge, some (gradable) improvement in our epistemic condition, relative to such knowledge? Non-constructivists have been focused entirely on the first of these questions, and find that the answer must be negative to this question. But notice that Socrates could actually be more interested in the second of these questions and be ready to give an affirmative answer to *this* question, even if he were inclined (as per non-constructivism) to answer the first of these two questions negatively.

It will help if we now remind ourselves that most Socratic examinations pursue what have come to be known as 'What-is-F-ness' questions: 'what is justice?' 'what is piety?' 'what is temperance?' and so on. In virtue of his search for answers to these, scholars have noted that Socrates seems to give some priority to *definitional* knowledge.[16] If we understand the first of our questions above, in application to this topic, we will be asking if Socrates thinks he can use elenctic argument to provide a complete and completely adequate answer to some definitional question. Here, we might advise caution, because on the one hand, we do find Socrates happily offering definitions that he seems to regard as fully adequate, though these are not definitions of *ethical* concepts (see *Laches* 192a-b on quickness; *Meno* 76a on shape). On the other hand, these definitions are never themselves exposed to elenctic examination in any of the dialogues, and in no dialogue do we ever get what is represented as a fully adequate definition of any ethical concept. So non-constructivists might rightly doubt that Socrates thinks he ever has – or perhaps ever could – obtain a fully satisfactory definition by using elenctic argumentation. But if we consider the second question we posed above, and ask now: Does Socrates think he (or his interlocutor, or both) can make progress towards better and better approximations of such definitions, then it seems to us the evidence of our texts tilts much more in the constructive direction.

Consider, for example, what happens in Plato's *Euthyphro*, which is obviously a 'dialogue of search' where the aim is to define what piety is. Socrates asks Euthyphro to provide such a definition (since Euthyphro regards himself as a very advanced expert in the field – see *Euthyphro* 4e-5a), and Euthyphro first responds simply by listing a number of examples of pious things (5d-6c). Socrates obviously thinks this is no way to give the sort of definition that he has asked for, and he clarifies that he wants a definition, not a list (6c-e). Euthyphro then claims that piety is what is loved by the gods (6e-7a). But Socrates points out that Euthyphro believes the gods quarrel and disagree, in which case what is loved by one god may be hated by another (7a-9d). Euthyphro then revises his attempt, and now says that piety is what is loved by all the gods (9e).

At this point in the argument, Socrates changes his approach a bit. In Euthyphro's first attempted definition, there were some things that would be pious (loved by some god) that would also be impious (hated by some other god). But in the remainder of the dialogue, Socrates never once suggests that there will be pious things that are not loved by all the gods, nor things loved by all the gods that are not pious. In other words, the revised definition Euthyphro has now given suffers from no 'scope inconsistency' between the definiens and definiendum.[17] At least in that sense, accordingly, Euthyphro has provided an improvement on his first attempt, though as the subsequent argument indicates, the definition he now provides is also still faulty, but now for a different reason.

Socrates points out that this revised definition has the problem that it seems to get the 'arrow of explanation' backwards: the gods all love what is pious *because it is pious*; it is not the case that what is pious is pious *because it is loved by all the gods* (9e-11b). So Euthyphro's revised definition also has failed. Euthyphro is now at a loss (called *aporia* in our texts), and seems not to know how to proceed (11b), and after an interlude, Socrates takes the lead in the discussion and begins to work towards yet another attempt to define piety – this time, as a part of justice (11e-12d). So now, Socrates indicates, all that is left for them to do is to say what part of justice piety is, and they will be done. Euthyphro, after struggling a bit to understand Socrates' proposal about parts and wholes, suggests that perhaps piety is that part of justice that is concerned with care of the gods, whereas the rest of justice concerns care of human beings (12e). Now Socrates responds, 'You seem to put that very well, but I still need a bit of information' (12e-13a).

The additional information has to do with how Euthyphro conceives of the 'care' we are supposed to provide for the gods. Euthyphro suggests that it is not the kind of care that produces some benefit that makes the gods better (13a-d), but rather a kind of service (13d). But as a service, it must be aimed at some goal or product (*ergon*; 13d). At this point, Euthyphro shows he is able to go no further. Challenged to indicate what the 'excellent aim' of our pious service to the god might be, Euthyphro falls back on the notion that our aim is to do whatever is loved by the gods (15b). When Socrates points out that this only returns them to the point of the earlier failed definition and so they must try again, Euthyphro hastily leaves the conversation and, as is usually the case, the search for a definition of piety has failed.

So, if we again try to apply our first question – does the *elenchos* succeed in providing a definition of piety? – we must surely agree that the answer is 'no' in this case. However, we have been given every indication along the way that the search for such a definition had made significant progress – only to founder on the question of distinguishing the unique *ergon* by which piety might be distinguished from the rest of justice. If we ask, accordingly, does the *elenchos* give us knowledge of the definition of piety – a question that seems to assume a threshold achievement – either we succeed in obtaining such a definition or we do not and we have to conclude that the *Euthyphro* gives us no indication of a positive answer. But if we – more aptly, in the view we have been trying to develop herein – ask instead, does the *Euthyphro* give us any indication that Socrates and/or Euthyphro might have become more skilled in knowing how to provide a definition of piety (even granting that their skills never reach the point of mastery), we have every reason to provide a very positive assessment. Each attempt that Euthyphro made to define piety was an improvement over the last attempt he made. And though Socrates always seemed to be in complete command of the discussion, we need not think that his command proves that his own skill in the project of defining piety was left wholly unimproved. If we take the question of improved skill in the quest for definitions as the right question to ask, given Socrates' 'crafty' conception of knowledge, we may conclude that the *elenchos* is shown to be a very valuable instrument for those who might wish to take up the 'true craft of piety' by becoming increasingly skilled in defining the subject matter of such a craft. As Socrates indicated early in his discussion with Euthyphro, the definitional goal has profoundly important practical consequences:

> Socrates: Instruct me then about what this very characteristic is in order that by looking at it and using it as a standard, I can say what either you or someone else might do is the sort of thing that is pious and that what is not of this sort I can say it is not pious. (*Euthyphro* 6e)

Socrates' search for definitions would, if completely successful, allow the one who knew the complete and adequate definition to be able to stand as an inerrant judge of whatever belongs to that subject. What about one who is in possession of no such definition or anything that even approximated such a definition? It seems that such a person – the complete ignoramus, we might suppose – would lack all judgement in that subject. But what about someone who takes up the true craft of that subject, but has not yet mastered it? What, in other words, about one who, like Socrates, might take up the true craft of politics and, though lacking in full mastery, may have made some progress in learning how to provide the essential definitions required? We would not expect such a person to make such 'rookie mistakes' as trying to explain justice or piety simply by giving some list of putative examples of each virtue. We would expect such a person to be able to give at least some approximation of an adequate definition of the subject-matter. And with such an approximation, such a person could then stand as a judge of whatever belongs to that subject who would be roughly as able a judge as his or her level of mastery over the field permitted. By leading an 'examined' life, accordingly, we would have every reason to think we could continue to improve our mastery of the ethical 'crafts'. It seems doubtful that Socrates would have supposed that mere human beings could ever become wise in the way of a god (so see *Apology* 23a-b), and thus it seems doubtful that any of us could ever really hope to become a master of any ethical craft. But even if it is our destiny always to fall short of such a lofty goal, that is no excuse for anyone not to try at least to take up ethical craft, and by leading an 'examined life' hope to create better and better understanding of our subjects, by creating better and better approximations of the definitions of their essential concepts,

80   *Knowledge in Ancient Philosophy*

and thus improving our judgements, becoming wiser, and thus also improving our life skills.

7. *Elenchos* and the irrational sources of ignorance

In Section 4, above, we noted that Socrates seemed to recognize a number of different belief-forming processes – much as we also recognize in contemporary epistemology. No doubt, Socrates accepts, as we do, such belief-forming processes as memory, sense perception, and ratiocination, and he refers to these in much the way we would expect. The significant novelty in Socratic epistemology on this point seems to be found in his motivational intellectualism, the best explanation of which indicates a belief-forming role for what he regards the operations of certain non-rational processes – or what we may regard as natural attractions and aversions, to pleasures and pains, respectively and thus from appetites, such as hunger, thirst, and lust, for example (which, Socrates claims, are experienced as pains, but whose satiations are experienced as pleasures). These he treats as unreliable cognitive processes, which – if not checked by some other more reliable cognitive process – can lead us into not just false beliefs about what is best for us, but also resisting attending to or even using the more reliable cognitive processes.

Several indications in our texts show that Socrates believes his elenctic refutations of others can also address faulty cognitive processing of this non-rational sort. So, for example, when he talks to his jurors in the *Apology* about what he does, we find him making liberal mention of *shaming* and *reproaching* those who suppose they are wise when they are not (see *Apology* 29e-30a, 30e), whose philosophical examinations make him like a gadfly who *stings* his victims (30e) and troubles them (41e), and who seeks to *discipline* those who seem to him to have allowed their appetites to play too large a role in how they function (*Gorgias* 505c). We believe that all of these kinds of passages – and the ways in which Socrates' interlocutors often show emotional responses – clearly indicate that Socrates does not think his way of talking with them is aimed only at *rational* remediation of their ignorance. Instead, we claim, Socrates understands that refutation – especially *public* refutation – can have effects on the non-rational cognitive processes that can not only lead to false beliefs, but also make one increasingly immune to reason. The way this works, presumably, is something he explains when he talks about how we need to keep our appetites in a disciplined condition (*Gorgias* 505a-b), by not allowing them to get too much of what they crave. Once they become too strong, however, damage is done to the soul, and once that damage is done, Socrates says, the only remediation possible is through a certain degree of pain and suffering (*Gorgias* 525b-c). While certain kinds of punishment must be left to the agency of the state, in its legal system (see *Apology* 26a), Socrates seems to think that it is an appropriate part of his philosophical mission to play the role of one who can 'discipline' his interlocutors in ways that go beyond simple logic and the rational presentation of epistemic evidence, and thus we see him attempting to remediate ignorance in non-rational as well as in rational ways, using his *elenchos*.

8. Summary and conclusion

In this chapter, we have tried to explain the various ways in which the primarily ethical focus in Socratic philosophy included several important epistemological commitments and insights. Central among these is Socrates' conception of the human epistemological condition and his characterization as an exemplar of epistemic modesty. The ethical aspect of his epistemology is to be found in his commitment to remediate his own and others' ignorance. We have paid special attention herein to belief-forming processes that Socrates seems to recognize as important problems for the human epistemic condition, and thus have also offered an account of how Socrates thinks that philosophizing can help us at least to moderate the effects of the processes most likely to lead us astray in our ethical and epistemic missions. We hope that making these aspects of Socratic philosophy clearer will allow others to assess more accurately than ever the significance of Socrates to Western philosophy.

Notes

José Lourenço is grateful to the CAPES/Ministério da Educação (Brazil) for funding that made his participation in this project possible.

1 When we talk about Socrates, we mean to refer only to the character of that name in Plato's early or Socratic dialogues. The relationship between this character in Plato's works and the historical Socrates is controversial, and we do not intend herein to take any position within that controversy, other than to go along with the general consensus among historians of philosophy that the 'Socrates' who is of the most interest to philosophers is the one who appears in the works of Plato.

2 All translations from *Euthyphro* and *Apology* included herein are those of Brickhouse and Smith (2002b).

3 There are many passages in Plato's works where such a profession appears, and each of these may reveal differences of emphasis or content, which we obviously cannot examine individually here. But for other examples of the Socratic profession of ignorance, see also: *Apology* 20c, 23b; *Charmides* 165b-c, 166c-d; *Euthyphro* 5a-c, 15c, 15e-16a; *Laches* 186b-c, 186d-e, 200e; *Lysis* 212a, 223b; *Hippias Major* 286c, 304d-e; *Gorgias* 509a; *Meno* 71a, 80d; *Republic* I.337e. In all of these passages, we contend, the focus is on knowledge or ignorance in ethical matters.

4 Most scholars regard the *Meno* as transitional, meaning that it is one of the first dialogues in which Plato begins to change the views he had Socrates express in the earlier dialogues. Among the novelties of this dialogue of interest here are not just the first clearly drawn distinction between knowledge and true belief, but also the doctrine that all knowledge is recollected from an earlier existence. Because we do not find such a doctrine in the (other) earlier dialogues of Plato, we will not discuss it further here. See Chapter 5 of this book for discussion.

5 Sprague translation, in Cooper (1997).

6 See Reshotko (2006: 135–55) for discussion of these options.

7 For a detailed defence of this claim, see Smith (2016).

8 Note that it does not rule out diachronic belief akrasia – Socrates can accept that people can do what they think is best at the time of action and later regret doing so, because they have changed their minds about what was best at the time of the action.

9 Examples of such texts include: anger, *Apology* 21b-23e, *Apology* 34b-d, *Protagoras* 352b-c; fear, *Apology* 29e-30a, *Apology* 32b-d, *Protagoras* 352b-c, *Gorgias* 525b-c; shame, *Apology* 29e-30a, see also especially Moss (2007), Sanderman (2004), Woodruff (2000); for *erōs*, *Charmides* 155d, *Charmides* 167e, *Lysis* 220e-221b; appetites, *Laches* 191e, *Charmides* 167e, *Lysis* 220e-221b, *Gorgias* 491d-e, *Gorgias* 493a, *Gorgias* 505a; pleasure and pain, *Protagoras* 352b-c, *Gorgias* 500d, *Gorgias* 507b, *Gorgias* 521d-e, *Gorgias* 525b-c.

10 On the question whether Socrates had a method or not, cf. Carpenter and Polansky (2002); Brickhouse and Smith (2002a); and Santana (2007: 254).

11 See Wolfsdorf (2013) for a comprehensive review of the reactions to Vlastos's treatment of elenchus.

12 A comprehensive review of all of the variations in such approaches in the recent literature is provided, again, in Wolfsdorf (2013).

13 Examples may be found at *Apology* 20c1-3, 21d2-7, 23b2-4; *Charmides* 165b4-c2, 166c7-d6; *Euthyphro* 5a7-c5, 15c12, 15e5-16a4; *Laches* 186b8-c5, 186d8-e3, 200e2-5; *Lysis* 212a4-7, 223b4-8; *Hippias Major* 286c8-e2, 304d4-e5; *Gorgias* 509a4-6; and *Republic* I.337e4-5.

14 Zeyl (trans.), in Cooper (1997).

15   Sprague (trans.), in Cooper (1997), slightly modified.
16   See Brickhouse and Smith (1994: 45–60) for discussion and analysis of the interpretive options.
17   We are here using the terminology given in May (1997), and much of our argument here is derived from the analysis she provides.

References

Brickhouse, T. C. and Smith, N. D. (1994), *Plato's Socrates*, Oxford: Oxford University Press.

Brickhouse, T. C. and Smith, N. D. (2002a), 'The Socratic Method?' in G. A. Scott (ed.), *Does Socrates Have a Method? Rethinking the Elenchus in Plato's Dialogues and Beyond*, University Park: The Pennsylvania State University Press.

Brickhouse, T. C. and Smith, N. D. (eds) (2002b), *The Trial and Execution of Socrates: Sources and Controversies*, Oxford: Oxford University Press.

Brickhouse, T. C. and Smith, N. D. (2015), 'Socrates on the Emotions', *Plato Journal*, 15: 9–28.

Carpenter, M. and Polansky, R. M. (2002), 'Variety of Socratic Elenchi', in G. A. Scott (ed.), *Does Socrates Have a Method? Rethinking the Elenchus in Plato's Dialogues and Beyond*, University Park: The Pennsylvania State University Press.

Cooper, J. M. (ed.) (1997), *Plato: Complete Works*, Indianapolis: Hackett.

Fine, G. (2008), 'Does Socrates Claim to Know That He Knows Nothing?', *Oxford Studies in Ancient Philosophy*, 35: 49–85.

May, H. E. (1997), 'Socratic Ignorance and the Therapeutic Aim of the *Elenchos*', in M. L. McPherran (ed.), *Wisdom, Ignorance and Virtue: New Essays in Socratic Studies*, *Apeiron*, 30 (Suppl.): 37–50.

Penner, T. (1990), 'Plato and Davidson: Parts of the Soul and Weakness of Will', *Canadian Journal of Philosophy*, 16 (Suppl.): 35–72.

Reshotko, N. (2006), *Socratic Virtue*, Cambridge: Cambridge University Press.

Santana, A. (2007), 'Constructivism and the Problem of the Socratic Elenchos', *Ancient Philosophy*, 27: 251–67.

Smith, N. (2016), 'Socrates on the Human Condition', *Ancient Philosophy*, 36: 81–95.

Vlastos, G. (1994), 'The Socratic Elenchus: Method Is All', in G. Vlastos, *Socratic Studies*, Cambridge: Cambridge University Press.

Wolfsdorf, D. (2013), 'Socratic Philosophizing', in J. Bussanich and N. D. Smith (eds), *The Bloomsbury Companion to Socrates*, London: Bloomsbury.

5

Epistemology in Plato's Middle Dialogues

Naomi Reshotko

1. Introduction

Plato's 'middle period' dialogues are multidimensional and among their riches one finds a large amount of epistemological content. Theories of inquiry and knowledge acquisition, like recollection and the method of hypothesis, are proposed. Plato paints striking epistemological images like the divided line and the cave. We encounter various candidates for subjects of knowledge: slaves, sophists, opiners, philosophers, and philosopher kings. It is difficult to organize these strands into one unified epistemological view and efforts to do so have resulted in much disagreement about the answers to some of the most fundamental and general questions about knowledge: What gets known: definitions, propositions, perceptibles, or Forms? Who, if anyone, can have knowledge: Gods, everyone, Socrates and his cohort, or Philosopher Kings? Also, with what resources does the knowledge seeker begin: nothing, true or false beliefs, some mysterious grasp of abstract ideas, or innate knowledge of the Forms?[1] As it is impossible to give all of the debates their due attention in this chapter, I will summarize only some of them and will discuss some of these in more detail than others. I will focus on the theory of recollection (TR) and the epistemological images of the *Republic* from which will emerge a brief description of hypothesis as a means for knowledge acquisition.

It is easy to get the impression that Plato's middle period epistemology is far more positive than what we find in the so-called Socratic dialogues. In those 'earlier' dialogues, Socrates frequently professes ignorance or, at best, knowledge that his own knowledge is worthless. If there is no hope for Socrates, there is even less hope for any of his interlocutors let alone those of us who cannot benefit from Socrates' tutelage. In contrast, it appears that, beginning with the

86 Knowledge in Ancient Philosophy

theory of recollection initiated in the *Meno*, Plato becomes far more optimistic and democratic about the possibility of human knowledge. Still despite his focus on knowledge acquisition, I will suggest that Plato tempers any optimism by theorizing about knowledge in such a way that its object, while approachable, is out of reach for at least the vast majority of human beings.

While *Republic* I is considered an early or Socratic dialogue, *Republic* II–X, which contain the passages I will be focusing upon in this chapter, are agreed to be from Plato's middle period. The *Meno*, upon which I also focus, is regarded as 'transitional'. The parts that show Plato's familiarity with Pythagoras, which include everything about recollection, are considered middle. The *Phaedo* is uncontroversially a middle dialogue.

2. Meno's paradox and recollection

At *Meno* 80e, Plato has his characters discuss a paradox (MP). It is introduced by Meno and then, perhaps, reframed by Socrates. In this dialogue, Plato introduces the theory of recollection (TR) for purely epistemic reasons; for the specific purpose of resolving this paradox.[2] Having led Meno into *aporia* concerning the nature of virtue (80b-d), and having confessed that he doesn't know at all what it is (71a), Socrates says that he is hoping that, now that Meno and he agree that neither of them knows what virtue is, they might search for it together. Meno responds by asking Socrates how he will recognize virtue when he does meet up with it if he doesn't know it to begin with: 'And how will you inquire, Socrates, into something when you don't know at all what it is? {B}Which of the things that you don't know will you propose as the object of your inquiry? {E}Or even if you really do stumble upon it, how will you know that this is thing you didn't know before?' (trans. in Scott [2006: 76]). Socrates responds: '{B} it's impossible for someone to inquire into what he knows or doesn't know: he wouldn't inquire into what he knows, since he already knows it and there is no need for such a person to inquire: nor into what he doesn't know, because he doesn't even know what he is going to inquire into' (80e1-5; trans. in Scott [2006: 77–8]).

I have inserted {B} and {E} into these curly braces in order to introduce a debate that has arisen concerning this paradox: Meno appears to raise a problem for both beginning an inquiry {B} and ending an inquiry {E}.[3] Socrates responds by repeating only the beginning problem. Many interpreters have found reason to resolve the two problems back into one. For example, Scott, noticing that resolution of {E} will also resolve {B}, says that recollection is introduced to

Epistemology in Plato's Middle Dialogues   87

resolve {E}. Benson (2015: 62–3) notes that the discussion concludes with the statement that we ought to proceed on the assumption that {E} can be resolved, even if Socrates only appears to mention {B} in his recounting of Meno's paradox, and so, agrees with Scott (1995: 30–1).

I will suggest, but not be able to follow up upon, a different way of thinking about this: the TR is addressed somewhat differently in each of the three dialogues in which it arises. The *Meno* and *Phaedo* give mysterious, but perhaps conclusive, evidence that TR resolves {B}. Despite concluding that we are better off if we do inquire, thus proceeding on the assumption that we can resolve {E}, Plato never really finds a solid resolution to {E}. Still, Plato suspects his understanding of metaphysics and epistemology will allow us to do the best we can with respect to {E}.

Plato's strategy in introducing the TR can be clarified by breaking what he has just said at 80e1–5 into four claims:

1. Everything is either something I know or something I don't know (implicit).
2. I can't inquire about what I already know.
3. I can't inquire about what I don't already know.
4. Therefore, I can't inquire.

The third claim might seem surprising. It could be explicated by pointing out that if I make an inquiry about something I don't already know, understood as something about which I am completely ignorant, then {E} I won't be able to judge whether or not I have found out about it. It's also the case that {B} I can't 'point' my inquiry at something about which I am completely ignorant. If I don't already know what x is, I won't know when I am learning about it or when I have learned about it.

Making sense of (3) by understanding 'don't know' as 'don't know at all' will lead to a specific interpretation of (1). For (1) must then be understood as 'everything is either something I know or something I don't know at all'. This reveals a problem with inquiring about something I don't already know since we have come to understand it as something about which I am completely ignorant. If that's the case, then it is not clear what allows my inquiry to be about x or what allows it to keep on being about x as I arrive at various hypotheses – some of which are likely to be false – about x. So, (1) treats a subject's knowledge of any x as an all or nothing affair. Thus, if one is to try to avoid the conclusion that we cannot inquire, the key might be to reject the first claim and to imagine that there is something in between knowing an object completely and not-knowing an object at all. It is roughly this strategy that interpreters take Plato to have in mind when

88   *Knowledge in Ancient Philosophy*

he introduces the TR to defeat MP.[4] Our having learned and then forgotten what we come to know in this life allows us to both know it (understood as having some unspecified – perhaps unwitting – antenatal relationship with it) and not-know it (understood as never having any postnatal relationship with it prior to or during sense experience) when we first begin to recollect it. If this is Plato's strategy, then the *Meno* discussion is at least *also* concerned with initializing our ability to think about and, therefore, inquire about an object {B}.[5]

Fine (2003: 64) finds the theory of recollection insufficient to resolve the paradox in the *Meno*:

> The theory of recollection (in contrast to the elenctic reply) does not by itself provide a sufficient answer to the paradox – for if one once knew, but now lacks the ability to inquire, the prior knowledge is idle. We should therefore be reluctant to place the whole weight of Plato's reply on the theory of recollection; and on my account of its role, we need not do so.

The 'elenctic reply' is Socrates' geometric demonstration with the slave. Fine (2003: 56) points out that, in contrast to other instances of Socratic questioning, this *elenchos* does not end in *aporia*. Rather, the slave is brought beyond *aporia* to true belief. Thus, the slave serves as a counterexample to our inability to inquire. He didn't have the answer and was able to come to discover it anyway. The claim that one cannot inquire into that concerning which one is ignorant has been shown to be false. Geometry is not relevantly different from virtue, so we can inquire into virtue as well.

In Fine's view, Plato does not disarm the paradox by reasoning against it, but by providing a brute counterexample. She speculates that all that recollection is supposed to explain is our tendency towards the truth as we inquire. But the truth of such speculations plays no role here, all that Plato needs is the brute fact that we obviously do succeed in inquiring into, and developing true beliefs and knowledge about, things concerning which we were once ignorant. This alone lays {B} to rest. It is safe to say that there is consensus that Plato thinks inquiry is possible. Whether and how recollection plays a role in this might be clearer if we take a look at the *Phaedo*.

3. Recollection in the *Phaedo*

The *Phaedo* prefaces its discussion of recollection with some principles: recollection is of that which our souls learned at a previous time when they were not in human form (72e-73a).[6] Recollection is when, perceiving one thing, a person comes to think of a further, distinct thing (73c). It can also be occasioned by things that are similar to one another and – in the case where there is similarity – one must necessarily bring to mind whether that similarity is complete or deficient (74a).

It is this final case – where that which is recollected is similar to that which is known, but the similarity is incomplete – that is dwelt upon in the particular argument Socrates gives in this dialogue. The argument is brief (74b-c):

> Don't equal sticks and stones, the same ones, sometimes appear to one [man][7] equal, to another not?
> Yes indeed.
> What then, have the equals themselves ever appeared unequal to you, or equality [ever appeared to be] inequality?
> Oh never, Socrates.
> Therefore they are not the same [thing], Socrates said, the equals and the equal itself.[8]

This argument can be understood as a nonidentity of discernibles; Socrates wants to show that equality-itself is not identical to equal physical perceptibles (equal sticks and stones), but exists in addition to them. He does this by demonstrating that equal sticks and stones have a feature that equality-itself does not have – the feature of appearing equal to one and not to another (one man will say of a pair of sticks that they are equal, while a second man will disagree, saying that they are unequal). But – to follow the parallel in a literal manner – it is not the case that one man will say of equality-itself that it is equal while another man will call it unequal.

As such, the key to understanding the argument will be to decide to which exact feature of equality Plato is trying to point in making this argument. A common interpretation assumes that it is perfection:

(P1) equal sticks and stones are imperfectly equal whereas
(P2) equality-itself is perfectly equal, hence
(C) equality-itself must be something other than equal sticks and stones.

This approach can be further divided into two interpretations based upon what this notion of perfection is assumed to imply. Some have interpreted it as implying something like mathematical perfection.[9] Another interpretation understands perfection as equal in all respects, always, everywhere.[10] A third approach does not take the feature to be perfection but, rather, finds Plato

90   *Knowledge in Ancient Philosophy*

comparing the corrigibility of our beliefs about sticks and stones with the incorrigibility of our beliefs about equality-itself.[11]

There is controversy over whether Plato intends to show that *everyone* has cognitive access to the Forms. Plato's use of the slave in the *Meno* easily leads us to conclude that whatever this intermediate state is, it is democratically distributed. This is coupled with further concerns about whether recollection, as presented in the *Phaedo*, would actually alleviate concerns over the paradox.

Bostock (1986: 110) (who suggests that Plato takes us to be recollecting something like the meanings of words) argues that Plato's solution simply leads to further telescoping paradoxes, and concludes that 'Plato, and the traditional account, are wrong about the only way of learning the meaning of a word'. In reference to the *Phaedo*, Scott (1995: 56–7) argues that recollection can't be used to explain ordinary concept formation as such an assumption would result in absurdity and paradox.[12]

> Plato is right to point out that if we are to be reminded of *x* by *y*, then we must have a recognition of *y* that does not involve knowledge of *x*, otherwise we have the absurd result that in recognizing *y* we are already thinking of *x*, and so recollection of *x* is impossible. But if we insist that Plato is using recollection to explain concept formation ... then we invite just that absurdity.

Scott elaborates an alternative understanding of recollection for Plato upon which it does not explain ordinary concept formation, but only the philosopher's knowledge of the Forms. Thus, Scott (1995: 53–73) takes TR to solve both {E} and {B}, but only for the philosopher.

4. Recollection as constitutive of recognition

There is, however, a further alternative to Scott's reconstruction. Plato might have intended the presence of equality in one's soul to provide a relationship with equality that is in between knowing and not-knowing but that is also unwitting. If I can inquire into what I don't know by asking questions about it and be assured that the answers that I find, in the form of hypotheses to be tested, are *about* that particular thing concerning which I asked, then I might be able to seek that which I do not know. I might be able to grope at the truth through a bunch of beliefs all of which are unstable and unreliable and maybe even false, if I already – even without realizing it – have some sort of inner connection to the object of inquiry.

It seems Scott supposes that when Socrates talks about comparing particulars to Forms, he talks about doing so consciously. Otherwise his concerns would not arise. But several scholars have responded that Plato may have thought that both the comparison and our contact with the Form take place unwittingly. Kelsey (2001: 94) agrees with Scott that *Phaedo* 75b shows Plato committed to the view that we 'cannot recognize equal sticks without having the Form of Equality "in mind".[13] However, since Plato must have assumed that everyday adults recognize equal sticks and stones, Kelsey counts this as 'strong evidence' that Socrates thinks that recollection of the Form is required in order to explain ordinary, everyday, cognitive achievements. In Kelsey's view, this suggests that Socrates did not think that recognition of the Form of Equality occurred *subsequent* to seeing equal sticks and stones, but rather that a grasp of the Form (whatever that amounts to) is constitutive of the recognition of the equality of perceptibles. The recognition of the equality of sticks and stones comes about by virtue of our having the equal itself 'in mind'. Thus, Kelsey takes it for granted that the TR is part of an analysis of everyday concept formations and does not require the kind of 'articulate understanding' of the Form of equality that Scott implies it does.

Franklin (2005: 295) agrees with Kelsey that recollection describes everyone's ordinary learning. However, he is sensitive to Scott's point as well: the exercise conducted at *Phaedo* 75b is designed to help philosophers *understand* the TR – not to help them *see* the equality of sticks and stones. Franklin agrees with Scott that, in order to *understand* the TR, one must already have an articulated understanding of the Forms.[14] But understanding the TR and being able to inquire are two different activities requiring different degrees of philosophical sophistication.

5. Recollection's purpose and results

Whatever the TR assumes about those who recollect, there is also controversy about whether it is ever presented as resulting in actual knowledge in those who do it. There are those who think that the text shows that even the slave boy has recollected and ends up with at least some knowledge by the end of Socrates' demonstration. Unsurprisingly, those who think that recollection is reserved for the likes of Socrates and Simmias think that it results in knowledge for those who are philosophically inclined (Scott 1995: 45).[15] Others, particularly those who think cognitive contact is unwitting, find the results more understated.

92   *Knowledge in Ancient Philosophy*

There are also those who believe that Recollection begins with unwitting contact and ends with full blown knowledge. I will here treat the results of the *Meno*'s slave demonstration as parallel to the recognition in the *Phaedo* that the sticks and stones are equal: That is, I will proceed to discuss whether recollection results in knowledge of the Forms or anything else for individuals like the slave, not whether the sticks and stones argument in the *Phaedo* allows philosophers to understand that learning is recollection.[16]

It might appear that at *Meno* 85c-d Socrates states incontrovertibly that recollection yields knowledge, but there Socrates says of the slave only that 'in the end his knowledge about these things [will] be *as accurate as anyone's*' (emphasis added). Given that Plato says in the *Phaedo* that no one knows the beautiful, the good, the just, or the pious and holds them parallel to the greater, the smaller and the equal (75c-76c), and, given that Plato says multiple times throughout the dialogues that knowledge must be infallible (*Theaetetus* 152c, *Euthydemus* 280a, *Meno* 97c, *Republic* 477e), this level of accuracy could easily fall short of what he holds out as knowledge.[17] While he does call the entire process from initial grasping to gaining knowledge 'recollection', Plato never indicates that recollection allows us to gain something knowledge-like any more quickly than we gain it through a slow process of empirical research and rational deliberation.[18] So, presumably, Plato would think the consequences with respect to acquiring knowledge (as opposed to a lot of interconnected, mostly true, mostly reliable, beliefs) would be about the same for recollection as it is for our empirical endeavours.

There is also debate about whether the position that people are in prior to recollection (the one that is in between knowing completely and not knowing at all) constitutes knowledge or even true belief. In the *Meno*, Socrates demonstrates that recollection is begun after an experience of *aporia* (79e-80b, 84a-b), which is at least a profound lack of confidence concerning one's beliefs.

When Irwin (1977: 138-9) and Fine (2003: 222n16) turn to interpreting the text's suggestions as to how we get to refer to that about which we are inquiring, they do it on the assumption that we have at least some true beliefs about it. But White (1976) and Nehamas (1999) both find textual evidence that supports the claim that Plato has the person who recollects begin from complete ignorance: Socrates pronounces that he does not know 'in any way at all (*to parapan*) what virtue itself is' (71a). Socrates, here, disclaims all knowledge of the nature of virtue and he does so again at 71b, using '*to parapan*'.[19] Furthermore, Socrates continues, saying that not knowing at all what something is means not knowing at all what qualities it possesses (71b). He is ignorant of virtue and cannot answer any questions whatsoever about it (71a). Socrates then questions Meno, who does profess to know something about virtue, leading him into *aporia*. Subsequently, Meno arrives at his own confession of ignorance also using *to parapan* and claiming that he is numb in both his tongue and his soul. When Meno is once again prodded by Socrates to say what virtue is, he asks how they can possibly go on with the inquiry and suggests the paradox, once again using *to parapan*: 'How can you search for something when you are completely ignorant of what it is?' (80d).

Much has been made of the fact that, in restating the paradox, Plato has Socrates eliminate *to parapan*, saying only, 'a man cannot search either for what he knows or for what he does not know' (80e) (Moravcsik 1971: 57; Scolnicov 1976: 52; Thomas 1980: 128–9). But others argue that if Plato were trying to have Socrates reduce the effect of complete ignorance in a philosophically significant way, one would expect him to be more overt about it. The real effect of Socrates' reformulation is to show that Meno has presented a dilemma, both sides of which are closed. If it really is a dilemma, then 'the function of *to parapan* is important and ineliminable' (Nehamas 1999: 9).

According to Irwin (1977: 138–9), the paradox is resolved because it relies upon the assertion that I cannot inquire into an object if I know nothing about it whatsoever. He thinks that Socrates rejects the assumption of complete ignorance. He points to 85c where it is agreed that the true beliefs which blossom in the slave after the inquiry must have already been in him prior to the inquiry (316n14). However, as Nehamas (1999: 14) argues, 'These true beliefs are recovered by the slave at the end of his examination by Socrates; they could not therefore play the identificatory role Irwin asks of them and that requires them to be there consciously at its very beginning.' Nehamas goes on to point out that the knowledge the slave is said to be able to eventually recover is also said to be in him. So there is no difference between the slave's access to his true beliefs and to his knowledge prior to recollection and, as a result, the true beliefs cannot serve as the hook for recollection of the knowledge.[20]

I would argue that, even setting aside any evidence concerning *to parapan*, there is a chicken and egg problem for the inquirer with any kind of belief, true or false. The true or false belief has to be *about* the object that makes it true or false *in order* to have a truth value and, so, unwitting cognitive contact must have been made with whatever makes one's belief true or false (I would argue that Plato takes this to be the Forms) *prior* to the belief's acquisition of that truth value. This makes me think that it is the constitutive view that offers the most promise for a unified notion of learning and knowledge in Plato's middle period and that Plato thinks that, in principle, we *can* inquire while having only false beliefs about our object of inquiry. Recollection, I would argue, is Plato's explanation for how that unwitting reference takes place and thus, mysteriously, resolves {B}.[21] Plato feels comfortable doing this, perhaps due to the brute evidence (as demonstrated with the slave) that we do inquire. He is not willing, however, to resolve {E} in a mystical manner, as there is no brute evidence that we can recognize our own knowledge. In fact, his anti-Protagorean and anti-Heraclitean metaphysics produces a quagmire for any sure solution to {E}.

6. Other methods

Some take it that Plato proposes recollection as a means for attaining actual knowledge of such things as virtue and equality, while others think that it only gives us the kind of connection to the Forms that will allow us to pursue knowledge of them. In any event, Plato had good reason to complement recollection with other methods. In the middle dialogues, he is thought to have displayed a predilection for hypothesis. If the TR only connects us to the Forms so we can begin to inquire about them, then one of these additional methods must be utilized in order to probe them further. We will look at a discussion of hypothesis when we decipher the image of the divided line at *Republic* 509c-511d. First, let us look briefly at the object of knowledge.

7. Knowledge, opinion, and ignorance

The tripartite distinction at *Republic* 476e-479d that places knowledge over what-is, ignorance over what-is-not, and opinion over what-is in between what-is and what-is-not has led to a wide range of interpretations. It has given rise to the 'two world' theory: Plato thought that the world of knowledge and the world of opinion were utterly separate from one another so that opinions and knowledge could not have the same object.[22] This theory further commits Plato to the view that the world accessed by knowledge has 'more being' than that accessed by opinion.[23]

Alternatively, the claim that knowledge is set over what-is as opposed to what-is and is-not has also been interpreted by supplying a predicate: reading what-is and is-not as 'what-is and is-not F'. This reading has Plato placing degrees of 'being-F' (being a good example of beauty, equality, etc.), on the table, rather than degrees of existence (Vlastos 1965, 1973; we can know that beauty itself is beautiful, but we cannot know that beautiful things are beautiful because they are all both beautiful and ugly at the same time (*Republic* 477e-479d). Or perhaps the world of opinion is composed of propositions that are and are-not F, where the supplied F is replaced by 'true' (Fine 2003: 87–95). The opiner's set of beliefs contains both true and false ones.

There are those who disagree with all three of these interpretations. Translating the Greek *epi* (lit. over) so that what knowledge, belief, and ignorance are *epi* is their *object* assumes that Plato sees the objects of knowledge and opinion as different. Alternatively, understanding the *objects* of knowledge and opinion as the *products* of the *interaction* between the powers of knowledge and opinion and that which they are, respectively, *epi*, leads to the conclusion that one way of looking at the world produces knowledge, another opinion, and yet a third, ignorance about the same objects – namely, the Forms.[24]

I believe there is significant textual evidence against the two world view: There are many places where knowledge and opinion appear to entertain the same object (*Meno* 98a-b; *Theaetetus* 201a-c).[25] Plato treats being something and being nothing at all as mutually exclusive and exhaustive ontological possibilities in the very same passage in which some think he makes the claim that knowledge and opinion have different objects (*Republic* 478b). This makes any notion of degrees of being an unappealing interpretive suggestion. Further, saying that, for example, the Form of Beauty is absolutely beautiful while beautiful perceptibles are both beautiful and ugly treats all Forms as literally self-predicating, which poses significant problems for Plato's metaphysics.[26] The view that the knower has only true beliefs while the opiner has some true and some false ones makes the controversial assumption that Plato regarded knowledge as propositional.[27] I would argue that we can understand Plato to be characterizing knowledge and belief as directed towards different kinds of objects (Forms and perceptibles, respectively), yet both are *about* the Forms. Knowers recognize that they aspire towards knowledge of the Forms, while opiners mistakenly take their opinions to be about perceptibles. As perceptibles are governed by the Forms, understanding perceptibles necessitates an understanding of the Forms and how they relate to one another (Reshotko 2014).

8. The divided line and the method of hypothesis

The claim that there are epistemological 'methods' in the dialogues is controversial and variously understood. On one end of the spectrum lies the notion that Plato

96　　　　　　　　　*Knowledge in Ancient Philosophy*

consciously developed some sort of *content neutral* method, which he deploys in many places on diverse subject matter.[28] On the other end, there is resistance to the notion that Plato understood his own metaphysics to allow for some kind of truth preserving, content neutral form that benefits all reasoning on any subject (Penner 1987: 287–91). While I can't discuss these metaphysical concerns here, it is worth noting that such reasoning might presuppose objects of knowledge that are facts, definitions, or propositions rather than Forms. As we have seen, there is ample textual evidence to suggest that Plato's objects of knowledge are Forms.

As discussed earlier, it is common to associate the term 'dialectic' with these methods, if indeed there are some. The method used in the middle dialogues would be the hypothetical method. While I have my own doubts about the benefits of isolating Plato's methods for understanding his epistemology, he certainly discusses hypothesis in the two intelligible parts of the divided line.[29] So let us examine those (brief) descriptions as a way of understanding the relationship for Plato between hypothesis and knowledge.

The image of the divided line closes book VI of the *Republic*. Warning that much will be omitted, but agreeing to give as full an explanation as possible (509c9), Socrates distinguishes the intelligible from the visible and proceeds to give an image of these two realms as a line divided first into two unequal parts with each part again unequally divided.[30] The four parts, working from the intelligible end, are labelled *noesis* (understanding), *dianoia* (thought), *pistis* (belief), and *eikasia* (imagination). The first two are intelligible, the second two are visible.[31]

Setting aside the proportions (their relative sizes represent clarity and obscurity), let's label the four sections **n**, **d**, **p**, and **e**, according to their Greek names. **n** is supposed to be clearer than **d**, and **p** is supposed to be clearer than **e**, just as **n+d** is supposed to be clearer than **p+e**. Working from least to most clear: the contents of **e**, *eikones*, are cashed out as shadows (*skias*) and also reflections (*phantasmata*) in water and on reflective surfaces. These seem to be images of sensible objects. **p** contains the things that create those images – living creatures, plants, and artefacts – the sensible objects themselves. This is the visible realm which has the same relationship to the intelligible realm as **p** and **e** have to each other. This is established when Socrates and Glaucon agree to a summary, which now introduces the terms *doxa* and *gnosis*. That section which contains *doxa* bears the same relationship to the section that contains *gnosis* (the known) as that which is similar (an image) does to its model (509e-510a).[32]

Epistemology in Plato's Middle Dialogues   97

While it is common to interpret the divided line as a metaphysical thesis and to see it reinforcing the two world theory, if one has diagnosed that theory elsewhere (Cornford 1945: 221), if one has not presupposed some sort of hierarchy of existence, the vocabulary itself points to epistemological concerns: **n+d** covers that to which the philosopher looks in order to gain knowledge. On such a view, **p+e** points to that which the person who employs the Forms unwittingly thinks she is trying to come to know and can't: perceptibles and their images.[33] The divided line represents an epistemic – not a metaphysical – conceptualization of what we encounter in trying to understand the world we inhabit. Philosophers explore the Forms by means of images. They stay on the **n+d** – the *gnosis* – segment of the line. This is why they are *philosophers*; lovers of knowledge. Ordinary people think of perceptibles as the ultimate substances, subordinate to nothing and superordinate to anything that might naturally or intentionally resemble or represent them; they stay on the **p+e** – the *doxastic* – part of the line. That is why they are *opiners* or lovers of opinion (*Republic* 475d-480a).

These realizations can help us to resolve some existing confusions about the contents of **d** and to see how Plato thinks hypotheses work with intelligibles. It seems straighforward to agree that **n** contains the Forms, **p** contains perceptible objects, and **e** contains images of perceptibles. But there has been much debate and consternation over the contents of **d**.[34] Since the two super-segments of the line are supposed to be analogous and proportional to one another, and it is clear that the subsections of the doxastic super-segment contain a subordinate subsegment that consists in the images of the contents of its superordinate subsegment, we are safest if we assume that the same relationship holds of the subordinate and superordinate subsegments of the gnostic super-segment: the contents of **d** must be the analogue for images of the contents of **n**.

n is the Forms, so **d** is 'images' of the Forms. Furthermore, in describing the epistemic super-segment of the line, Socrates says that, in the subordinate segment, 'the soul using as images what before were models is compelled to investigate from hypotheses, proceeding from these, not to a first principle, but to a conclusion' (Grube 1974: 510b). So what is in **d**? Philosophers and opiners both cast their senses upon perceptibles in trying to understand their world. While opiners just see them as perceptibles, those who understand that they are trying to come to know the Forms, understand the perceptibles (and the images that resemble them) by reference to the Forms. Thus, in the case of *dianoia*, they use perceptibles as means for looking beyond those perceptibles at hypothesized abstract objects. In other words, they use perceptible objects as a means to form hypothetical universals: to make hypotheses about which Forms exist.

98   *Knowledge in Ancient Philosophy*

Returning to our textual information, it says that in dealing with **d**, the soul is compelled to investigate from hypotheses and proceed to a conclusion rather than a first principle. When Glaucon asks for more explanation, Socrates points out that students of geometry agree upon a wide array of suppositions, which they take as given and for which they do not argue. Because they all posit the same such things as the odd, the even, three kinds of angles and many others, when they investigate the same things using these as their starting points, they reach the same conclusions. Socrates next associates the visible figures that geometers draw and use with these conclusions. But Socrates also makes it clear that this dianoetic process is limited: because all parties to the conversation agree on what seem to be obvious suppositions, they end up arriving at the thing that their search was designed to investigate: a hypothesized geometrical object. While it seems reasonable to assume that there are, in some cases, Forms that answer to their hypotheses, this practice does not allow them to know whether this is the case with any specific hypothesized Form. *Dianoia* might lead to some fruitful hypotheses about Forms, but it cannot tell us which hypotheses are vindicated by what-is. Socrates continues, saying that the geometers do not talk about the visible figures themselves, but use the visible figures to talk about their models – the square itself and the diameter itself. They use what used to be models as images in order to talk about what cannot be seen 'except in thought'. While the practitioners of the so-called sciences do not have *nous* of their subjects, they have something better than *doxa*; they are looking beyond perceptibles to the Forms. But they are not able to be sure to what degree the Forms answer to their hypotheses.

This is different from the way hypothesis works in **n**: 'In the second section, which leads to a first principle that is not hypothetical, the soul proceeds from a hypothesis without using the images of the first section, by means of the Forms themselves making its investigation through them' (Grube 1974; slightly revised: 510b). Socrates later (511c-d) clarifies that here one is not using hypotheses as first principles. One uses hypotheses as stepping stones in order to reach, 'what is beyond hypothesis, the first principle of all that exists'. He makes it clear that, in this kind of reasoning, nothing visible is used and it proceeds 'by means of Forms and through Forms to its conclusions, which are Forms'. Who conducts these inquiries? The earlier use of hypothesis was conducted by 'so-called scientists'. These inquiries are conducted – if at all – by those who can start with the Forms, not perceptibles, and use Forms to learn about some first principle, which is a Form. But who can start with the Forms?

I hope it is clear that our answer to this question will depend on how our interpretation has led us to answer the earlier questions: Is the object of

Epistemology in Plato's Middle Dialogues

knowledge the Forms themselves, or facts and propositions in which the Forms figure? If it is facts and propositions, then what does it mean to use Forms to discover Forms by means of Forms? Does recollection yield knowledge of the Forms or just an ability to think about them as one conducts one's inquiry? If the latter, it is not clear that anyone can populate this uppermost part of the divided line. If recollection yields knowledge of the Forms, does it do so for all or just for a select few? If for all, then maybe anyone can be groomed to *noesis*. If only a few, then maybe even geometers are left with *dianoia* alone. Plato's optimism about the possibility of human knowledge will vary with the answers to these questions. Is he explaining what it is for actual human beings to possess knowledge? Or is he speaking theoretically and *per impossible* about what human knowledge would have to be like and why, given that it is of Forms that cannot be accessed via the senses, we are left practicing the so-called sciences but without anything that rises to the level of knowledge?[35]

Easily the most popularly recognized image in Plato's dialogues is the allegory of the cave that opens *Republic* VII (514a-518d). It's not unreasonable to see the four divisions of the line translated into the chronologically ordered encounters of men who have been trapped in an underground cave from childhood, tied and fettered so that they cannot turn their heads.[36] The unfettering and subsequent movements of the prisoners in the cave can illustrate the same person encountering and becoming aware of progressively different kinds of things upon which to focus her epistemological gaze. The prisoner's appreciation of what creates these things and why they exist will be enhanced to the degree to which she realizes that each one brings understanding only by referring it to that first principle that allows it to be. In the allegory of the cave, the shadows, puppets, and reflections of actual men and other things in water, all must be referred to actual men and other actual things together with the sun. Is there some clue here about who, if anyone, can escape the cave?[37] Various passages indicate that prisoners vary in their abilities to make unwitting use of Forms for science-like activities.[38] Yet, while this would suggest that access to the Forms is democratically distributed, it might also suggest that even those with access to dianoetic objects and activities – even geometers – reside in the cave.

9. Conclusion

I began this chapter by noting that a superficial look at the middle period dialogues might give a reader the impression that Plato has a far more positive outlook on human knowledge at this stage of his writing than he had in the earlier 'Socratic' period, where many would take him at his word that he knows only that his knowledge amounts to nothing (*Apology* 23a-b). We have since observed that it is debatable that recollection results in knowledge. If it does, it might bring knowledge only to a select few. Even if recollection brings some kind of knowledge of the Forms to all, it is not clear that the methods Plato appears to recommend for human beings to further investigate the Forms or to figure out how to live well are bound to get us very far. The emphasis Plato places on the necessity of reaching beyond opinion and the perceptible world, towards a world that so-called science shows us only through hypotheses, also gives the impression that he worries that regular human beings – even those who are aware that it is worth striving to become philosophers and even those who are on the road to becoming philosophers – might never get far enough to be able to rely on their knowledge more than they must rely on their awareness of their own ignorance in order to lead the best lives that they can.

While I don't take a strong stand on the 'middle' dialogues being chronologically in the middle, I believe they do represent tension and compromise – being stuck in the middle – for Plato the epistemologist. He is confident that the Form is the best kind of object to use as an object of knowledge and that it is the best way to respond to the metaphysical puzzles laid out for him by his predecessors: Forms offer solutions to the difficulties of reconciling Heraclitus' world of flux with Parmenides' unchanging one, they resist the materialism and reductionism of the atomists, and they overcome the relativism that Protagoras creates when he collapses metaphysics and epistemology. But Plato recognizes that positing the Forms as the metaphysical foundation for the natural world raises very serious questions about how human beings – who, once embodied, must discover the world through sense experience – can come to know anything as they must start by knowing the Forms that regulate, but are not found in, the world of experience.

Notes

1 One glaring omission here is the question 'What is knowledge?', which is not discussed overtly in the dialogues that I am covering. The *Theaetetus*, which does take up this question, is treated by many (including the editor of this volume) as late.

2 This contrasts with other dialogues. At *Phaedo* 72a-77a, he uses it to bolster a theory of the immortality of the soul, in addition to using it as an explanation for how we come to know equality and inequality. At *Phaedrus* 249c, recollection is referred to as what allows humans to understand speech by bringing many appearances under reasoned unities.

3 This point was perhaps made most forcefully by Scott (1995, 2006), who distinguishes {B} as the paradox of inquiry and {E} as the paradox of discovery. My terminology of beginning and ending is taken from Benson (2015), whose treatment of this debate I have found particularly clear and helpful.

4 Scott (2006: 80) agrees that this is the logical way to solve the eristic dilemma, but does not think this is Plato's strategy in introducing recollection. Dancy (2004: 226) doesn't quite take it this far. He says that we can only learn what we (have) already know(n), but that Socrates emphasizes that it is not known at the moment of recollection. Benson (2015: 51) points out that one alternative is to have a teacher who already knows. Fine (2014) thinks that (1) should be interpreted differently, and argues that TR is designed to show that (3), and not (1), is false.

5 We will look at Scott's (2006: 77) suggestion that {E} could refer to a later part of the process in the context of the *Phaedo*.

6 If we had been in human form then we would have been stuck in the same situation – beholden to all of the same epistemological paradoxes that we are at the moments when we are forced to recollect.

7 Something needs to be supplied to the Greek text here. It's also possible to supply 'stick' or 'stone' here, with ramifications for interpreting the argument (Bostock 1986: 72–85). I won't address these issues here as I believe they force a choice that is more relevant to Plato's metaphysics than to his epistemology. See also note 12 below.

8 This translation follows Penner (1987: 57–8).

9 Here, the idea is that equality is only found in abstract mathematical objects and is not possessed by physical objects. Penner (1987: 44–55, 181–90) calls this the 'traditional approach'. Some examples are Geddes (1885), Bluck (1955), and Hackforth (1955). Gulley (1962) might be said to follow this approach as well, but he does so somewhat self-consciously.

10 Owen (1957) and Vlastos (1965) take this approach. Bostock (1986: 101) at least once refers to equality-itself as a 'perfect paradigm'.

11 Thus equality-itself is differentiated from equal sticks and stones by the fact that we have incorrigible beliefs about equality-itself (i.e. that equality ≠ inequality), but not about equal sticks and stones. In other words, equal sticks and stones are able to deceive our perceptions, equality-itself is not. This is Penner's approach.The choice among these three versions of the sticks and stones argument is critical to a proper understanding of Plato's Theory of Forms. It also might determine whether this

102   *Knowledge in Ancient Philosophy*

passage represents the theory of Forms as a plausible one. The view that Scott calls the 'traditional view' sees it as an argument for the existence of Forms.

12   Scott refers this insight back to Gulley (1954: 197–8) and Ackrill (1973: 183). Scott (1995: 31) also maintains that Plato is really talking about discovery, not inquiry, and should have used the Greek word '*heuriskein*' rather than '*zetein*'. That is, he takes Socrates' restatement of Meno's concerns at 80e1-5 to be evidence that Plato is at work on the 'ending problem' or the 'paradox of discovery'. Further Scott suggests that any solution to the paradox of discovery will also solve the paradox of inquiry. While that might be true, I take TR to resolve the paradox of inquiry and think that Plato might think that we never confirm that we have found that after which we inquired. Benson (2015: 88–91) appears to entertain this possibility.

13   This is Kelsey's way of tracking Plato's use of the Greek word '*ennoein*' and its equivalents.

14   Franklin (2005: 291). See also Williams (2002) and Harte (2006) for further support of the constitutive view. While I don't have space to rehearse it here, I find the unwitting awareness of the Forms to be a major contributor to Plato's middle and late epistemology. See Reshotko (2014) on its role in the *Republic*. I would argue that it also plays a major role in Plato's discussions of false belief and false statement in the *Theaetetus* and *Sophist*.

15   Again, one of the chief frustrations with Scott's view is that it offers no account of where the philosopher started in life (do philosophers begin as ordinary people?) and how he or she became a philosopher (Williams 2002: 150). Nor does it answer the question of whether or not ordinary people have immortal souls (Harte 2006: 38).

16   Thus, Scott's suggestions are put aside for the remainder of this discussion. There is much to debate about the continuity between the two arguments for recollection in any case. It's been pointed out that the *Meno* shows recollection of 'truths' and the *Phaedo* recollection of Forms – and certainly that is what a prima facie look at the text indicates.

17   I would argue that, particularly due to the infallibility requirement, Plato has, and believes in having, a very high bar for what counts as knowledge rather than particularly well 'tied-down' (*Meno* 97c-98b) true beliefs.

18   Hackforth (1955: 75) says that recollection is a long and gradual process. Gulley (1962: 13) has three explicit stages of knowledge acquisition, only the first of which is associated with recollection.

19   See Nehamas (1999: 5) for his agreement with Bluck (1964: 209) concerning reading *to parapan* at 71a closely with *oude*.

20   Scott (2006: 76) also states unequivocally that unless the inquirer described by Meno has a 'total blank' with respect to the object of inquiry, the absurdity of questions {B} and {E} will lose their force.

Epistemology in Plato's Middle Dialogues   103

21 I would compare what Plato thinks we get from Recollection to what Kripke and Donellan and their descendants think we get from 'direct reference'. I may be departing from Kelsey and Franklin here as they seem concerned with recognition (at least Kelsey [2001: 94] says that ordinary people recognize equal sticks). I think that this unwitting reference resolves {B}, but is not relevant to the resolution of {E}.

22 See Fine (2003: 68n1) for a comprehensive list of those who hold that knowledge is only of Forms and belief only of sensibles. As Fine notes, there are passages (like *Meno* 98a-b) where Socrates speaks as if knowledge and true belief can be of the same thing.

23 This has the further consequence that Plato seems to no longer follow Parmenides with respect to the notion that existence does not admit of degrees.

24 See Smith (2000), for a commentator who makes this move.

25 In these same dialogues, Plato also discriminates between true and false beliefs, something he does not do in the *Republic*'s discussion of *doxa*.

26 See Vlastos (1954) and Penner (1987: 205–31, 251–99).

27 In the *Republic*, if anywhere, Plato appears to present Forms, not propositions, as the objects of knowledge. In other places he represents bodies of skills like navigation and horse-training as such. Also see Gonzalez (1996, 1998).

28 See Benson (2015), whose project is to recover the forms of the *elenchos* and the hypothetical method and isolate their structure. Benson does not claim that Plato always deploys them fully and rigorously, or that Plato finds them foolproof.

29 I find it best to focus upon why Plato thought the Forms were the best candidates for objects of knowledge in trying to understand his epistemology.

30 The text specifies the proportions of the division so roughly that many translators who try to draw the line draw it differently. Compare, for example, the original Grube (1974) translation by Hackett with the one revised by Reeve (Grube 1992), which both differ from Smith (1996). It can be proven that the two middle sections will have to be the same size, but some say it is not at all clear that this was Plato's intention (Ferrari and Griffith 2000: 219n32). That these two sections are the same size lends support to Smith's interpretation as he thinks they contain the same things (perceptible objects) and to mine, as I think that they involve looking to the same things, but contain different things as the thoughts that come from looking to the same things are about different things in the two middle segments of the line.

31 Any effort to reconcile the divided line with the *Republic* 475d-480a passage must be tempered by the fact that these are not the same terms that Plato uses there: *epistēmē, gnōsis, doxa,* and *agnōsia* do not appear in the four subsegments of the line and only *gnōsis* and *doxa* are on the line at all.

32 In talking about **n+d** and **p+e**, we have returned to the terminology of *Republic* 475d-480a. **n+d** are *gnōsis* (knowledge). **p+e** are *doxa* (opinion). We should expect

the things in **p+e** to be the things over which opinion is set, and indeed they are. We should expect those in **n+d** to be that over which *epistēmē* was set, here it is *gnōsis* that governs them. *Gnōsis* is the opposite of the word used for 'ignorance' (*agnōsis*) in that same passage. Ferejohn (2006: 218) identifies *epistēmē* with **n+d** as well.

33 Ignorance is not found on the divided line, which is not surprising as it is represented as having no content at *Republic* 475d-480a. Ignorance is a non-starter. Indeed, I would argue that Plato only uses 'ignorance' at *Republic* 475d-480a in order to appease the Lovers of Sights and Sounds by saying that while they are not philosophers, they could be far worse epistemologists than they actually are. Yet, I would also argue that Plato thinks opinion can constitute ignorance.

34 One of the more unusual is Smith's (1996: 40–2) claim that both **d** and **p** contain the same thing: sensibles.

35 It is important to note that the method of hypothesis was introduced, back in the *Meno*, as the geometers method (86e-87b). The comments made about geometers and so-called scientists here seem *apropos* of my suggestion that Plato thinks recollection solves {B} albeit mysteriously, and that some other 'method' would be needed to resolve {E}, but that while the hypothetical method might be useful it does not result in foolproof recognition of what we were seeking, so it doesn't resolve {E}.

36 Although there is some controversy in this regard, see Annas (1981: 254–8) and Smith (1996: 34n23, 36–7).

37 There are at least suggestions that it will be a great struggle and that very few will succeed.

38 See Ferejohn (2006: 206–13) and Harte (2006: 26).

References

Ackrill, J. (1973), '*Anamnesis in the* Phaedo: Remarks on 73c–75c', in E. Lee, A. Mourelatos, and R. Rorty (eds), *Exegesis and Argument. Phronesis Suppl.* I, Assen: K. Van Gorcum.

Benson, H. (2015), *Cleitophon's Challenge*, Oxford: Oxford University Press.

Bluck, R. (1955), *Plato's Phaedo*, London: Routledge and Kegan Paul.

Bluck, R. (1964), *Plato's Meno*, Cambridge: Cambridge University Press.

Bostock, D. (1986), *Plato's Phaedo*, Oxford: Oxford University Press.

Cornford, F. (1945), *The Republic of Plato*, Oxford: Oxford University Press.

Dancy, R. (2004), *Plato's Introduction of the Forms*, Cambridge: Cambridge University Press.

Ferejohn, M. (2006), 'Knowledge and Recollection in the Middle Books of the *Republic*', in G. Santas (ed.), *The Blackwell Guide to Plato's Republic*, Malden, MA: Blackwell.

Ferrari, J. and Griffith, T. (trans.) (2000), *Plato: The Republic*, Cambridge: Cambridge University Press.

Fine, G. (2003), *Plato on Knowledge and the Forms*, Oxford: Oxford University Press.

Fine, G. (2014), *The Possibility of Inquiry: Meno's Paradox from Socrates to Sextus*, Oxford: Oxford University Press.

Franklin, L. (2005), 'Recollection and Philosophical Reflection in Plato's *Phaedo*', *Phronesis*, 50: 289–314.

Geddes, W. (1885), *The* Phaedo *of Plato*, London: Routledge.

Gonzalez, F. (1996), 'Propositions or Objects? A Critique of Gail Fine on Knowledge and Belief in *Republic* V', *Phronesis*, 941: 245–75.

Gonzalez, F. (1998), 'Nonpropositional Knowledge in Plato', *Apeiron*, 31: 235–84.

Grube, D. (trans.) (1974), *Plato's Republic*, Indianapolis: Hackett.

Grube, D. (trans.) (1992), *Plato's Republic*, rev. C. D. C. Reeve, Indianapolis: Hackett.

Gulley, N. (1954), 'Plato's Theory of Recollection', *Classical Quarterly*, N.S./4: 194–213.

Gulley, N. (1962), *Plato's Theory of Knowledge*, London: Routledge.

Hackforth, R. (1955), *Plato's* Phaedo, Cambridge: Cambridge University Press.

Harte, V. (2006), 'Beware of Imitations: Image Recognition in the *Phaedo*', in F. Hermann (ed.), *New Essays in Plato: Language and Thought in Fourth Century Greek Philosophy*, Swansea: The Classical Press of Wales.

Irwin, T. (1977), *Plato's Moral Theory*, Oxford: Oxford University Press.

Kelsey, S. (2001), 'Recollection in the *Phaedo*', in J. Cleary and G. Gurtler (eds), *Proceedings of the Boston Area Colloquium in Ancient Philosophy*, Leiden: Brill, 91–121.

Moravcsik, J. (1971), 'Learning as Recollection', in G. Vlastos (ed.), *Plato I*, Notre Dame: Notre Dame University Press.

Nehamas, A. (1999), *Authenticity of Virtue*, Cambridge: Cambridge University Press.

Owen, G. (1957), 'A Proof in the *Peri Ideon*', *Journal of Hellenic Studies*, 57: 103–11.

Penner, T. (1987), *Ascent from Nominalism*, Dordrecht: Reidel.

Reshotko, N. (2014), 'Plato on the Ordinary Person and the Forms', *Apeiron*, 47: 266–92.

Scolnicov, S. (1976), 'Three Aspects of Plato's Philosophy of Learning and Instruction', *Paideia*, 5: 50–62.

Scott, D. (1995), *Recollection and Experience*, Cambridge: Cambridge University Press.

Scott, D. (2006), *Plato's* Meno, Cambridge: Cambridge University Press.

Smith, N. (1996), 'Plato's Divided Line', *Ancient Philosophy*, 16: 25–46.

Smith, N. (2000), 'Plato on Knowledge as a Power', *Journal of the History of Philosophy*, 38: 145–68.

Thomas, J. (1980), *Musings on the* Meno, Boston: Springer.

Vlastos, G. (1954), 'The Third Man Argument in the *Parmenides*', *Philosophical Review*, 63: 319–49.

Vlastos, G. (1965), '*Anamnesis in the Meno*', *Dialogue*, 5/2: 143–67.
Vlastos, G. (1973), 'Degrees of Reality in Plato', in G. Vlastos (ed.), *Platonic Studies*, Princeton: Princeton University Press.
White, N. (1976), *Plato on Knowledge and Reality*, Indianapolis: Hackett.
Williams, T. (2002), 'Two Aspects of Platonic Recollection', *Apeiron*, 35: 131–52.

6

Plato's Later Epistemology

Hugh H. Benson

1. Introduction

Plato's later[1] dialogues are replete with epistemological explorations, many of which are familiar from his earlier works. They contain discussions devoted to the nature of memory (*Philebus* 33c-36c), perception (*Theaetetus* 155c-159d, 182a-b; *Timaeus* 42e-47e, 61c-69a; *Philebus* 32a-39c), appearance (*Sophist* 259d-264b), true and false belief (*Theaetetus* 187c-200d), true and false statement (*Sophist* 259d-264b), warrant or justification or explanation (*Theaetetus* 201c-210a), dialectic or philosophical method (*Parmenides* 137c-166c; *Theaetetus* 147c-151d; *Sophist* 251a-259e; *Philebus* 16e-19e; *Politicus* 262b-263b, 285a-286e), and even an entire dialogue evidently devoted to answering the most epistemological question of them all: 'What is knowledge (*epistēmē*)?' (*Theaetetus*). These discussions are philosophically sophisticated, provocative, and perplexing. They have been open to many careful scholarly investigations leading to a variety of interpretations – sometimes widely divergent. On the one hand, these dialogues have an empirical flavour, focusing on our cognitive contact with ordinary physical objects. On the other hand, they reiterate the other worldly epistemology of contemplation of eternally divine Forms, evident, for example, in the early pages of the *Phaedo*. Indeed, they are the locus classicus of the alleged Platonic ideal of assimilation to god.

A chapter of this sort has no hope of addressing all of these issues or even addressing one in any kind of complete way. Consequently I propose – rather dogmatically – to focus on some key passages in which Plato's focus on empirical knowledge comes to the fore. By 'empirical knowledge' I do not mean knowledge that can be acquired *only* on the basis of perception, as some understand a posteriori knowledge. I mean knowledge of empirical facts, for example, knowledge that Theaetetus is the son of Euphronius of Sunium (*Theaetetus*

108 *Knowledge in Ancient Philosophy*

144c), the wind is cold (*Theaetetus* 152b), the stone is white (*Theaetetus* 156e), Theaetetus is over there in the field (*Theaetetus* 193b-c), Alcibiades committed the robbery (*Theaetetus* 201a-c), 'SO' is composed of 'S' and 'O' (*Theaetetus* 203a), and the sun is the brightest of bodies that move around the Earth (*Theaetetus* 208d). In focusing on empirical knowledge I do not presume to maintain that this is Plato's only focus in these dialogues nor even that these are the only passages relevant to a full consideration of this focus. Indeed, I do not even propose to offer a very detailed discussion of these passages. Instead, I offer these passages as an indication of the rich and sophisticated flavour of Plato's epistemological interests in his later period.

2. Theaetetus

Let us begin with Plato's *Theaetetus*. Roughly, sixty-five of its sixty-eight pages are devoted to an investigation concerning the nature of knowledge (*epistēmē*). Plato's focus in the *Theaetetus* tends to be on *epistēmē* throughout, although he employs *gnōsis* and *sophia* and their cognates (including *eidenai*) in a way that belies a technical vocabulary. Nor is such a technical vocabulary indicated elsewhere, at least so I would argue, although Plato's use of *epistēmē*, *nous*, and *phronēsis* in the *Philebus* may suggest otherwise. I will generally follow Plato's lead in this regard, although I will try to indicate which word is being used when it may be thought to make a difference.

Theaetetus' first answer to the "What is knowledge?' question according to which knowledge is geometry, and the other things which he learns from Theodorus, namely, astronomy, music, and arithmetic (146c7-d3), is abandoned rather quickly for reasons familiar from earlier dialogues. Theaetetus, next, proposes that knowledge is perception (*aisthēsis*; 151e). It is a bit surprising that Theaetetus should propose such answer in light of his first response. But, Plato's immediate contention that Theaetetus' second answer is saying the same thing as Protagoras' famous man is the measure doctrine may indicate an explanation. As Plato explains, according to Protagoras everything is (*estin*) to a person as it appears to her (152a) and appearance is the same thing as perception (152b-c). Consequently, according to Protagoras, 'Perception, then, is always of what is (*to on*), and not false (*apseudes*), as though being knowledge' (*Theaetetus* 152c).

Plato here indicates that what motivates Theaetetus' second answer is perception's alleged satisfaction of two conditions for knowledge: (1) knowledge is always of what is, and (2) knowledge is true.

Plato's Later Epistemology 109

It is difficult to know what to make of these criteria. Readers of Plato have met with them before. In the famous argument at the end of *Republic* 5 (477a, 477b, 478c), Plato maintains that knowledge is always set over (*epi*) what is (*toi onti*), while ignorance is set over what is not, and belief is set over what is and is not. Plato also maintains that knowledge makes no mistakes (*anamartēton*), while belief does (5.477e-478a). But understanding of this *Republic* argument is no less difficult than understanding the passage in the *Theaetetus*, so we would do well to focus on the latter. The *Theaetetus* passage is open to two quite opposed interpretations. According to the first – strong – interpretation the first criterion is aimed at restricting knowledge to a special set of objects – realities, intelligibles, or perhaps Forms.[2] The other criterion should be read as indicating that knowledge is infallible.[3] According to the second – weak – interpretation, the apparently distinct criteria are meant simply to indicate that knowledge entails truth.[4] According to this reading, the being (*to on*) of the first criterion should be read veridically.[5]

The context of the passage tells against the strong reading. The strong reading begs the question against Theaetetus' proposal that knowledge is perception, rather than supporting it. If we begin our investigation into the nature of knowledge with an understanding of knowledge indicated by the strong reading of these criteria, the thought that knowledge is perception looks like a nonstarter. But, the examination of the viability of Theaetetus' second answer that knowledge is perception occupies almost half of the dialogue – considerably more attention than either of Theaetetus' third or fourth answers. Moreover, the appeal to the Protagorean thesis that as each thing appears to a person, so it is to that person, together with the identity of appearance and perception, appears intended to support Theaetetus' second answer. It has the result that perception entails truth. The appeal to Protagoreanism cannot explain how Theaetetus' answer would satisfy the criteria on the strong reading, but it can explain how it would satisfy the criteria on the weak reading. Thus, Plato maintains that in defining knowledge as perception Theaetetus is saying the same thing as Protagoras.

Having maintained that Theaetetus' second answer meets at least a minimal necessary condition for knowledge on the assumption of Protagoreanism, Plato next supports Protagoreanism by appealing to a doctrine which he playfully suggests was taught by Protagoras in secret and which has the authority of the wisest of the Greeks, among whom are mentioned by name Homer and Heraclitus. In the course of presenting this so-called Secret Doctrine Plato presents a theory of perception which accounts for perception's always being true. The general idea of the theory is the following. According to the Secret

110 *Knowledge in Ancient Philosophy*

Doctrine everything moves (Heraclitean flux), but some things are slow movers and some are swift movers. Among the slow movers, some are active and some are passive. The intercourse of the active and passive slow movers gives birth to twin swift movers. The swift moving offspring are divided into two groups, the first consisting of perceptions (*aisthēseis*) – things like sight, hearing, smelling, feeling cold, feeling warm, feeling pleasure, and feeling pain, and the second consisting of perceptibles (*aisthēta*) – things like colours, sounds, and warmth. The former are associated with the passive slower movers – things like eyes, and ears, and the latter with the active slow movers – things like rocks, sticks, winds, dogs, and cats. Thus, the intercourse of an eye and a rock, for example, gives birth to sight and whiteness. The eye is filled with sight and so sees and the rock is filled with whiteness and so is white. The seeing of the eye is always in conjunction with (because a twin of) a colour of an active slow mover. As a result the eye never sees something white without there being something white that the eye sees. So, perception is always true.

Plato goes on to provide a number of objections to the Protagoreanism, perhaps the most famous of which is referred to as the *peritrope*, according to which Protagoreanism cannot be consistently maintained. Roughly, either those who deny Protagoreanism (and so believe that there are false beliefs) are mistaken and so there are false beliefs, or they are not mistaken and so there are false beliefs.[6] Either way, at least some appearances or beliefs are false, contrary to Protagoreanism. Next, Plato offers a similar objection to the Heraclitean flux doctrine, according to which if it were true it would be impossible to say anything, including the doctrine itself.

Neither of these arguments are aimed at or successful against the theory of perception just adumbrated. The *peritrope* argument may succeed in refuting the thesis that whatever one believes is true (e.g. that Protagoreanism is true or that it is false), but it appears to leave untouched a weaker thesis to the effect that whatever one perceptually believes is true – where a perceptual belief is one involving perceptible things or properties (e.g. that the rock is white or the wind is cold) understood along the lines of the theory of perception. The argument against Heracliteanism may succeed in refuting radical flux – that is, the view that everything is changing in every way, but the radical view is only necessary for the stronger epistemological view that whatever one believes is true. A weaker version of flux according to which only perceptibles and perceptions are changing would survive this argument, and allow the theory of perception so restricted to survive as well. Refuting that whatever one believes is true suffices to refute the second answer that knowledge is perception, on the assumption that there is non-perceptual knowledge. (Note the wax tablet model of false belief – at *Theaetetus* 191a-196d – is abandoned on the grounds that it cannot account for false non-perceptual belief.) Nevertheless, the theory of perception and the possibility of empirical knowledge have not been refuted. This has led some to suppose that Plato remains committed to the theory of perception found in the *Theaetetus*.[7]

Plato's concluding argument against Theaetetus' answer that knowledge is perception indicates Plato's awareness of this possibility. The structure of the argument is simple, but its interpretation controversial. Structurally, the argument goes as follows.

1. Perception cannot grasp being (184b-186c)
2. Grasping truth requires grasping being (186c)
3. Knowledge requires grasping truth (186c-d)
4. So, perception cannot grasp truth (186e) – from (1) and (2)
5. So, knowledge is not perception (186e) – from (3) and (4)

We meet again the criteria of knowledge with which we opened the discussion of Theaetetus' second answer – being and truth. Here the relationship between the first and the second is explicit. Grasping truth requires grasping being, and so knowledge, in requiring the grasping of truth, requires grasping being. But grasping being no longer looks equivalent to grasping truth, but rather a necessary condition for the latter.

Some scholars take grasping being to amount to grasping Forms.[8] Thus, perception in being unable to grasp Forms cannot grasp being, and so cannot grasp truth. Again, this is familiar from dialogues like the *Phaedo* and the *Republic* where knowledge is in some way associated with Forms, as opposed to sensibles.[9] One difficulty for this approach is that no argument has been offered in the *Theaetetus* for the substantive and hence controversial premises that perception cannot grasp Forms or that grasping truth requires grasping Forms, as the proponents of this view would concede.[10]

Others take grasping being as having nothing to do with Forms but rather only indicating something like grasping a proposition or having a propositional structure.[11] Thus in maintaining that grasping truth requires grasping being Plato is indicating that grasping truth requires grasping a true proposition, like that the wind is cold, and grasping the true proposition that the wind is cold requires grasping the *is* or *being* in the proposition that the wind *is* cold. Perception however fails to grasp being because it is not propositional. To feel is simply to feel coldness, not to feel that the wind is cold. The difficulty with this interpretation is that at least since as far back as the introduction of the Protagorean man is the measure doctrine Socrates has been treating perception as propositional in character. If the current argument is aimed at denying the possibility of perceiving that the wind is cold, then the previous arguments seem to provide immediate counterexamples.

As a result of these difficulties a variety of interpretations have been proposed allowing for the propositional nature of perception without appealing to the apparently absent Forms. Thus, grasping being may indicate being able to judge how a thing is objectively as distinct from how it appears (Cooper 1970), or how a thing is related to other things (Modrak 1981), or to actively or rationally judge something to be the case (Lorenz 2006: chapter 6).

Notice that none of these interpretations – neither the moderate ones just mentioned nor the more extreme interpretations they are aimed to avoid – refute the possibility of empirical knowledge, like the knowledge that the wind is cold. They do show that such knowledge, if it is possible, cannot simply rely on perception or the theory of perception proposed earlier. Such knowledge requires, since it entails that it is true that the wind is cold, some grasp of a propositional structure, objectivity as opposed to subjectivity, how the wind is related to coldness, a rational activity, or even the Forms themselves, which perception alone (at least understood along the lines of the theory of perception proposed earlier) cannot provide – for distinct reasons relative to the individual interpretation. Of course, unless Plato denies the possibility of true belief or that true belief grasps truth, true belief must grasp being as well. Thus, the arguments in this portion of the *Theaetetus* succeed in showing that perception is insufficient for knowledge. Nevertheless, they leave open the possibility of empirical knowledge, appropriately supplemented. Indeed, the arguments of this portion of the *Theaetetus* indicate what it would take – what a theory of perception needs to look like and what else in addition to perception is required – for such empirical knowledge to be possible.

Following the refutation of Theaetetus' answer that knowledge is perception, Theaetetus proposes his third answer that knowledge is true belief (*alēthēs doxa*). Plato quickly dispatches this answer by means of a counterexample (201a-c). According to the counterexample, a jury when persuaded correctly about some robbery that only an eyewitness could know has true belief, but not knowledge, concerning the robbery. This leads Theaetetus to propose his final answer that knowledge is true belief plus a *logos*. The indication that only the eyewitness can know who the robber is may suggest that the jury lacks direct acquaintance with the robbery and that this direct acquaintance is required for

Plato's Later Epistemology 113

knowledge. A similar point applies to the road to Larisa example in the *Meno*. But Theaetetus' response to this counterexample, namely, that knowledge requires a *logos* in addition to true belief, suggests instead that it is justification or explanation that is required for knowledge. When the jury decides the guilt of an individual robber whom they did not witness committing the crime, what they lack is something like justification or explanation (*logos*) for their verdict, not direct acquaintance. Perhaps this is because the length of time permitted to the presentation of argument and evidence by the water-clock is insufficient for a justified or explained verdict. Nevertheless, Plato quickly dispatches Theaetetus' final answer as well, by proposing three accounts of *logos* and showing that the answer that knowledge is true belief plus a *logos* fails on all three accounts (206c-210a). This quick refutation is surprising in light of a similar passage at the end of the *Meno* where Socrates appears to maintain that knowledge is true belief that has been tied down by working out the reason (*aitias logismōi*; *Meno* 98a).

This account of knowledge in the *Meno* is motivated by an example similar to the jury counterexample. Plato distinguishes between an individual with true belief about the way to Larisa and an individual with knowledge (because he has been there) about the way to Larisa. Both these examples suggest the possibility of empirical knowledge – both the knowledge of who the robber is and how to get to Larisa. Of course, these examples do not require the possibility of empirical knowledge. Plato may simply be indicating that the distinction between knowledge and true belief *is like* the distinction between an individual who guides correctly but has not been to Larisa and an individual who guides correctly but has been there, and like someone who gets the right verdict as a result of a jury trial and someone who gets the right verdict because he was an eyewitness to the crime.

Before turning to the refutation of Theaetetus' final answer, Plato has Socrates recount a dream he has had which Theaetetus' answer has caused him to recollect. In this dream Socrates heard people saying that everything was either a primary element or a complex composed of those elements. The primary elements can only be named and so do not have a *logos*; the complexes have names that are woven together, and so do have a *logos*. Thus, the primary elements are without a *logos*, unknowable, and perceptible, while the complexes are knowable, have a *logos*, and can be truly believed (202b). The dream concludes that when one has a true belief without a *logos* of such complexes, one does not know the complex, but when one also gets hold of the *logos* of the complex, one knows it completely (202b-c). The Dream theory, then, presents an asymmetrical foundational account of *logos* and knowledge according to which perceptible, unknowable,

114 *Knowledge in Ancient Philosophy*

and *alogos* elements serve in some way as the epistemological foundation for the things that are knowable through having a *logos*.

Unfortunately, Plato is dissatisfied with this Dream theory. Plato employs an example which he uses frequently in the late dialogues – the example of our knowledge of letters and syllables (*Politicus* 278c-d, *Sophist* 253a-e, *Philebus* 16c ff.). He explains the source of his dissatisfaction by means of two arguments. The first, the dilemma argument (203c-205e), argues against the knowledge asymmetry thesis (AK) – the unknowability of the letters (elements) and the knowability of the syllables (complexes) (203c). The second, the argument from experience (206a-b), argues against the specific version of the asymmetry thesis assumed in the Dream theory.

The dilemma argument goes roughly as follows:

1. Either the syllable 'SO' is the same as its letters 'S' and 'O' or it is not (203c)
2. If the syllable 'SO' is the same as its letters 'S' and 'O', then if A knows 'SO', then A knows 'S' and 'O' (203c-d)
3. If A knows 'S' and 'O', then A knows 'S' and A knows 'O' (203d)
4. So, if the syllable 'SO' is the same as its letters 'S' and 'O', then if A knows the syllable 'SO', then A knows the letter 'S' and A knows the letter 'O' (203d)
5. So, if the syllable is the same as its letters, then both the letters and the syllables are knowable, i.e. not AK (205d-e)
6. If the syllable 'SO' is not the same as its letters 'S' and 'O', then the syllable 'SO' is some one thing coming to be from the letters 'S' and 'O' (203e, 204a)
7. If 'SO' is some one thing coming to be from 'S' and 'O', then 'SO' has no parts (204a)
8. If 'SO' has no parts, then 'SO' is an element and has no *logos*, and cannot be known (205c-d)
9. So, if the syllable 'SO' is not the same as its letters 'S' and 'O', then both the syllable 'SO' and the letters 'S' and 'O' are unknowable, i.e. not AK (205e)
10. So, it is not the case that the elements are unknowable and the complexes knowable, i.e. not AK (205e)

The Dream theory and the dilemma argument presented against it raise a variety of important textual and philosophical issues, too numerous to attempt.[12] Moreover, a number of objections have been raised against the dilemma argument itself, not the least of which is that it commits fallacies of referential opacity and division.[13] Some of these objections are more easily met than others.

Nevertheless, I focus on the tension between this argument and the argument from experience which follows.

The argument from experience considers how we learn how to read and write. According to this argument, we do so by first learning the letters and later the syllables. As a result the letters are in some way more knowable or epistemically tractable than the syllables. Thus, it is the letters (elements) that are epistemologically prior to the syllables (complexes), not the other way around as the Dream theory's AK would have it. According to the argument from experience, then, there is an epistemological asymmetry between the letters and the syllables, contrary to the dilemma argument. It is just that the asymmetry goes the other way round.

Some scholars focus on the dilemma argument and take Plato to be arguing against the thesis that some things have a *logos* and some things do not – the *logos* asymmetry thesis (AL). The idea is that the thesis that knowledge requires an account (KL), which receives Platonic endorsement elsewhere,[14] together with the *logos* asymmetry thesis (AL) entails the knowledge asymmetry thesis (AK). But since Plato rejects the asymmetry of knowledge (AK) via the dilemma argument, Plato must be rejecting the asymmetry of *logos* (AL). In rejecting the asymmetry of *logos* Plato is rejecting a foundational account of justification or explanation[15] and endorsing a coherence account. That is, what it is for a true belief to have a *logos* is for that belief to be part of an interrelated system of beliefs, each serving as a *logos* for the others.[16]

Other scholars focus on the tension between the dilemma argument and the argument from experience. According to this line, the tension indicates that something must be wrong with one or the other of the arguments. Plato cannot both think that the syllables and their letters are equally knowable or unknowable, as the dilemma argument suggests, and that the letters are more knowable than the syllables, as the argument from experience suggests. Thus, he expects the reader to see the flaw in one or the other argument. Once we look for the flaw, the dilemma argument looks problematic, in particular its reliance on a specific understanding of the premise that the syllable is the same as its letters, an understanding which Plato appears to question, for example, at *Parmenides* 146b, 157b-158d, *Sophist* 251a-259e, *Philebus* 28d-29a, 64d-e, and *Timaeus* 29d-33b.[17]

On either interpretation, the Dream passage is struggling with issues associated with the nature of justification or explanation. If we think Plato endorses the dilemma argument, then he appears to endorse a holistic model of knowledge based on an interrelated system of true beliefs. But we are given

116 *Knowledge in Ancient Philosophy*

no reason here to exclude true empirical beliefs. Indeed, such beliefs should be included in a fully holistic system, and so the possibility of empirical knowledge remains. If we think Plato endorses the argument from experience, then he appears to endorse a foundational account of knowledge which takes seriously the possibility that these foundations are composed at least in part by perceptibles. That Plato views at least some of these foundations as perceptible is indicated by his use of *aisthēta* (perceptibles) at 202b and the general empirical nature of the examples considered in the knowledge is true belief plus a *logos* section of the dialogue: letters and syllables, a wagon and its parts, the sun, Socrates and Theaetetus. A Platonic endorsement of such a foundational account is indicative of an Aristotelian solution to a similar regress problem which distinguishes between kinds of knowledge – knowledge of elements which does not require a *logos* and knowledge of complexes which does.[18] In either case, even here near the conclusion of the *Theaetetus* the focus on the role that perception has in knowledge and the possibility of empirical knowledge remains.

3. Timaeus

Plato's *Timaeus* also displays an interest in the role of perception and the possibility of empirical knowledge. Of course, this should come as no surprise. The *Timaeus* has a claim to being Plato's *peri phuseōs* (natural science or physics) and cosmology.[19] How we are to understand the likely story (*eikōs muthos*) by which he pursues this physics and cosmology is a matter of debate.[20] But that Plato is offering some kind of account (*logos*) of the nature and cause of the world of becoming, as opposed to the world of being (29b-e) is clear.[21]

I only have space to highlight two aspects of Plato's account: first, Timaeus' theory of perception and, second, a well-known argument for the existence of Forms.

The *Timaeus* contains a second fairly detailed account of the nature of perception at 42e-47e (esp. 45b-47e) and 61c-69a.[22] The *Timaeus* discussion tends to focus more on the nature of perceptibles (especially the second of the two passages) than the process by which those perceptibles are cognized. Nevertheless, according to the discussion of sight at 45b-46a the body emits an internal ray of fire which is impacted by external rays of fire emanating from external objects and the resulting motions are transmitted back along the internal ray first to the body and then to the soul. When one turns to Timaeus' account of the other perceptual powers (taste, smell, hearing, and touch), emanations from the

Plato's Later Epistemology 117

perceiver are no longer needed, and the focus is on the impact of the perceptible objects on the body as a whole or the individual perceptual organs. Both here and in the theory in the *Theaetetus* perceptions are understood as motions, the perceiver is primarily taken to be passive, and a corresponding object for every perception is assumed. When perception goes wrong it looks to be in virtue of a failure of calculation or reason. The irrational mortal soul – located between the midriff and the navel – passively receives the impressions on the body or individual perceptual organs, but it cannot reflect upon them and so lacks belief, calculation, and understanding (*doxēs men logismou to kai nou*; 77b-c). It is only through the interaction of the rational immortal soul – located in the head – with the irrational soul that judgements concerning the things which created these impressions through their impact on the body and individual perceptual organs get made and so can go wrong.[23] Moreover, while portions of these *Timaeus* passages find fault with perception (see, e.g., 46d-e), the overwhelming sentiment of the passages is the benefit, perhaps necessity, perception provides for acquiring knowledge. Indeed, sight is explicitly credited with all of Timaeus' statements about the universe (*tou pantos*), the invention of number, the thought of time (*chronou ennoian*), and the inquiry concerning the nature of the universe (*peri te tēs tou pantos phuseōs zētēsin*) (see, e.g., 46e-47e and 68e-69a).

Despite the credit and attention devoted to perception in the *Timaeus*, it contains perhaps one of the most straightforward arguments for the existence of Forms – based on the distinction between knowledge and true belief. The argument goes as follows.

1. If knowledge (*nous*) and true belief (*doxa alēthēs*) are distinct, then there are Forms (51d)
2. If knowledge and true belief are not distinct, then there are no Forms (51d)
3. Knowledge and true belief come to be independently (51e)
4. Knowledge and true belief are unlike each other (51e)
5. Knowledge comes to be through teaching; true belief comes to be through persuasion (51e)
6. Knowledge is always with a *logos*; true belief is without a *logos* (51e)
7. Knowledge is unmoved by persuasion; true belief is moved by persuasion (51e)
8. Knowledge is possessed by a few; true belief is possessed by all (51e)
9. So, knowledge and true belief are distinct (51e) – from (3) through (8)
10. So, Forms exist (51e-52a) – from (1) and (9)

118   *Knowledge in Ancient Philosophy*

The precise understanding of the individual premises of this argument require more attention, but the general structure of the argument is clear. Indeed, we have an elegantly brief argument against Theaetetus' third answer that knowledge is true belief. Perhaps this explains why Plato can so quickly dismiss Theaetetus' third answer that knowledge is true belief with a counterexample in the *Theaetetus*. Plato's commitment to premise (6) is not at odds with his rejection of Theaetetus' fourth answer that knowledge is true belief plus a *logos*. If knowledge has a *logos*, it does not follow that knowledge is true belief plus a *logos*. The *Timaeus* argument does, however, reinforce the familiar Platonic idea that accounting for the nature of knowledge without appealing to Forms (or Form-like entities) will be difficult, if not impossible. The arguments found in the *Parmenides* (130a-135c) have suggested to some that Plato has abandoned his commitment to Forms (and yet 135b-c appears to indicate a continued commitment to the necessity of Forms for thought [*dianoia*] and dialogue [*dialegesthai*]). This may explain why Forms appear to be missing in the *Theaetetus*. The explicit appearance of Forms in the *Timaeus* can be explained by taking the *Timaeus* to predate the *Parmenides*, denying that the *Parmenides* indicates Plato's abandonment of Forms, or taking Plato to be committed to entities like Forms which are not subject to the objections in the *Parmenides*.[24] In any case, the argument in the *Timaeus* does not deny the possibility of empirical knowledge. It does require that such knowledge is not possible simply on the basis of grasping perceptibles. One must also grasp Forms (or Form-like entities).[25] But having grasped such Forms, one might then be able to know that the wind is cold, at least if something like the theories of perception as found in the *Theaetetus* or the *Timaeus* is true, although *Timaeus* 27d-28a may suggest otherwise.

4. Philebus

I want to conclude with a fascinating passage from Plato's *Philebus*. The *Philebus*, often considered Plato's examination of pleasure,[26] might look like an odd place to conclude a chapter devoted to Plato's late epistemology. But we should remember that the question that introduces the *Philebus* is whether the good is pleasure, as Philebus maintains, or knowledge, as Socrates maintains. While much of the *Philebus* is devoted to an examination the nature of pleasure (31b-55b), Plato turns to an examination of the kinds of knowledge at 55b before attempting to settle the main question of the dialogue at 59e-66c. (A different account of the kinds of knowledge can be found at *Politicus* 258b-261e.)

Plato begins his examination of the kinds of knowledge by distinguishing between craft-like (*dēmiourgikon*) knowledge and knowledge concerned with education and nurture. Plato here appears to be employing his method of division introduced at *Philebus* 16c-17a, and employed extensively in the *Politicus* and *Sophist* (see also *Phaedrus* 265c-266c, 273d-e, and 277b). The use of the method here in the *Philebus* is awkward. Plato's first division between craft-like knowledge and knowledge concerned with education and nurture, for example, goes unexplained and Plato offers no examples of the latter. Nevertheless, Plato immediately distinguishes two kinds of craft-like knowledge. One kind – the stochastic expertise (*technē*) – lacks arithmetic, measurement, and weighing and proceeds by guessing or estimating achieved through training the senses (*aisthēseis*) by experience and routine (*empeiriai* and *tribēi*). As a result it contains unclarity, imprecision, and little stability. Examples of this kind of knowledge include music, medicine, farming, sailing, and generalship. The other kind of craft-like knowledge – technical expertise – employs measurement and tools like straight-edges and compasses. As a result they are more precise and include building expertises (like house-building and ship-building), commerce, arithmetic, measurement, and weighing. Next, Plato distinguishes two kinds of arithmetic, measurement, and weighing: the popular kind and the philosophical kind. The former makes use of unequal units (e.g. different sizes of oxen or armies), while the latter employs only identical units. Here again the division is awkward. First, the philosophical mathematical expertises (as well as dialectic) do not look like they should fall under craft-like knowledge. And second, the popular-philosophical division does not look like a division of the technical expertises. It is hard to imagine that Plato is committed to philosophical house-building, for example. Perhaps Plato is distinguishing between two types of the technical expertise: the building expertises and mathematical expertises, and then dividing the latter type into popular and philosophical. Alternatively, a bit later at 56e-57a Plato suggests that the technical building crafts make use of the mathematical crafts and the popular-philosophical distinction applies to the mathematical crafts used by the building crafts.[27] In any case, Plato sums up these divisions by indicating that philosophical mathematics is purer because it is clearer, more accurate, and truer[28] than the other kinds of knowledge distinguished. Finally, Plato distinguishes all of these from dialectic, and here we find the more familiar Platonic point that the most genuine (*alēthestatē*) knowledge concerns being and that which does not change (58a). Due to the stability, purity, truth, and clarity of that which is and does not change, knowledge of this gets the noblest of names 'thought' (*nous*) and 'intelligence' (*phronēsis*).

120 *Knowledge in Ancient Philosophy*

Plato here offers a rather inclusive account of the nature of knowledge. It is true that the discussion of dialectic comes close to restricting knowledge properly so-called to knowledge of some unchangeable reality (59b). But even in this case the idea does not go unqualified. At 59b Plato writes, 'Then there can be no reason or knowledge *that attains the highest truth* about these subjects [viz. those that are subject to change]' (Frede (1993) trans.; emphasis added); and again at 59c, 'Either we will find stability, purity, truth, and what we may call clarity among the things that are forever in the same state, without anything mixed in it, *or we will find it in what comes as close as possible to it'* (adapted from Frede (1993) trans.; emphasis added). Nevertheless the tone of the passage is overwhelmingly inclusive. Music, medicine, farming, sailing, generalship, house-building, ship-building, building in general, commerce, arithmetic, measuring, weighing – in both the popular and philosophical varieties, and dialectic are all explicitly described as kinds of knowledge (*epistēmai*).[29] The criteria for knowledge – stability, clarity, precision, purity, truth, and being – we have met with before. Stability is suggested in distinguishing knowledge from true belief near the end of the *Meno* (97d-98b) and used of the objects of knowledge at *Timaeus* 51d. Clarity is familiar from the Plato's Divided Line image at the end of *Republic* 6 (509c-511e) and clarity, precision,[30] truth, and being from *Phaedo* (65a-66a). And, we have met with truth and being in the *Theaetetus*. In the *Philebus*, however, the emphasis is on their admitting of degree or their convergence.[31] But perhaps most remarkable, when Plato turns to answering the primary question of the dialogue – whether pleasure or knowledge is the good – following his account of the kinds of knowledge, he explicitly includes all the kinds of knowledge just adumbrated in the best life (62a-d). Of course how this is all to be understood and whether it is consistent with other things Plato maintains about knowledge in this dialogue and throughout his corpus requires further investigation. But, in one of Plato's latest dialogues he displays an openness, if not explicit commitment, to the possibility and value of empirical knowledge.

5. Conclusion

We have seen then that in the *Theaetetus* and other late dialogues much of Plato's interest is focused on issues related to the nature and possibility of empirical knowledge. This interest tends to raise more puzzles and difficulties than answers and solutions. And other interests capture his attention as well.

Plato's Later Epistemology 121

Nevertheless, Plato's focus on the nature and possibility of empirical knowledge is in keeping with his openness to its possibility. I do not propose that Plato's later epistemology explicitly maintains the possibility of empirical knowledge. But I do hope to have displayed his interest in its possibility and value.[32] In Plato's final thoughts about the nature of knowledge, the possibility and value of empirical knowledge occupies much of his attention.

Notes

1 I here stipulate that, by the late dialogues, I mean (in alphabetical order) *Critias, Laws, Parmenides, Philebus, Politicus, Sophist, Theaetetus*, and *Timaeus*. That the *Parmenides* and *Theaetetus* post-date the *Phaedo, Phaedrus, Republic*, and *Symposium* is relatively uncontroversial. The *Timaeus'* position vis-à-vis the *Parmenides* is debated. See note 24 below.

2 The debate about whether and, if so, why Forms are absent from the *Theaetetus* is long-standing and cannot be addressed in this chapter.

3 Gerson (2003: 198) refers to the first criterion as the 'reality criterion' and the second the 'inerrancy criterion'. Gerson offers a reading of the *Theaetetus* as a whole based in part on the strong reading of these criteria (194–238). See also, for example, Cornford (1950: 32) and Giannopoulou (2013: 58).

4 The clearest statement of the weak reading is Bostock (1988: 43). See also McDowell (1973: 120) and Dancy (1987: 99 n18).

5 For the various readings of being (*to on*) – existential ('exists'), predicative ('is F'), identity ('is identical to') and veridical ('is true') – see, for example, Brown (1986).

6 Notice the move from perceptions and appearances to beliefs. This goes unremarked in the text.

7 Those who take Plato to be committed to the theory of perception, though not the knowledge is perception answer, maintain Burnyeat's (1990: 8–9ff.) interpretation A, while those who take Plato to dispose of the theory of perception along with the answer it is associated with maintain Burnyeat's interpretation B.

8 See, for example, Cornford (1950: 108–109), Ross (1951: 103), and Chappell (2004: 146–8).

9 See, for example, *Republic* 5.475e-480a, 6.507a-511e, and *Phaedo* 65d-66a. I use the vague 'in some way associated with Forms' to leave open the variety of interpretations concerning how this required 'association' is to be understood.

10 The closest one comes to such an argument is 184b-186c, where Plato argues that perception cannot grasp the so-called commons – things like sameness, difference, likeness, unlikeness, and being. But whether these 'commons' are the Forms of the *Republic, Phaedo*, or even *Sophist* is a matter of considerable controversy.

11 See, for example, Kahn (1981: 119–20; 2013: 67).

12 Many of these issues concern this section's focus on knowing and believing (grasping) objects rather than knowing and believing propositions. See also 187c-200d. For now, I simply point out that Plato also repeatedly focuses on knowing and believing propositions (see the knowledge is perception section at 151e-183c, the argument at 184–6, and the jury counterexample). How these two features of Plato's discussion can be accommodated goes to the core of the *Theaetetus*.

13 See, for example, Harte (2002b: 12) and Sedley (2004: 166).

14 See *Meno* 97d-b, *Phaedo* 76b, 97d-99d, *Symposium* 202a, *Republic* 534b, *Timaeus* 27d-28a, 51d-52a.

15 I here leave open whether the *logos* attached to true belief is meant to be a justification or an explanation. See Burnyeat (1990: 133) for a good brief introduction to this issue. My general point remains in either case.

16 See, for example, Fine (1979). She also cites *Philebus* 18c.

17 See, for example, Harte (2002a: chapters 3–4).

18 See, for example, *Posterior Analytics* 1.3 and 2.19.

19 See, for example, the title of Johansen's (2004) monograph on the *Timaeus* – namely, *Plato's Natural Philosophy: A Study of the* Timaeus-Critias.

20 Perhaps the best place to begin coming to terms with this controversy is Burnyeat (2005). See also Johansen (2004: 48–68).

21 For the substitution of *eikōs logos* for *eikōs muthos*, see 29b-c, 29c, 29d, 30b, 48d, 53d, 55d, 56a, 57d, 59c, 68b, 68d, 90e.

22 In what follows, I assume that Timaeus represents the views of Plato (as most scholars do) and that the *Timaeus* post-dates the *Theaetetus* (as many scholars do). See note 24 below.

23 For a defence of an indirect theory of perception found in the *Timaeus*, see Ganson (2005). At 64b, Plato appears to distinguish between motions created by the impact of external objects which are perceptions and those which are not by indicating that the former continue until the movements arrive at *to phronimon* (intelligence?). The role of *to phronimon* in perception is explicit. Either *to phronimon* must be located in the irrational soul or the movements in the irrational part of the soul cannot count as perceptions until they reach the rational soul where *to phronimon* is located. In either case, the irrational soul contains perceptions and yet lacks belief, calculation, and understanding. Perhaps the phrase 'and reports the property that produced the reaction' at 64b6 indicates that while there can be perception in the irrational soul, there cannot be judgement, calculation, or understanding until a report is made to the rational soul from the irrational soul and some further cognitive action is undertaken concerning the object which caused the movement culminating in the rational soul. See, for example, *Philebus* 38c-d. For a very helpful discussion of these issues, see Carpenter (2010).

24 On the relative date of the *Timaeus* to the *Parmenides* in light of Plato's apparent continued commitment to Forms, see the classic debate between Owen (1953) and Cherniss (1957).

25 This does raise the question of what it is to grasp Forms (or Form-like entities). To some extent, this is a concern of *Theaetetus* 187a-210a. But addressing this question appears at the service of examining the nature and possibility of empirical knowledge.

26 See, for example, the title of Hackforth's (1945) translation and commentary of the *Philebus* – namely, *Plato's Examination of Pleasure*.

27 The awkwardness of these divisions leads Hackforth (1945: 114–15) to maintain that Plato here forces the method of division on a subject matter for which it is inappropriate. See also Cooper (1977: 719) who finds only three kinds of knowledge distinguished here: applied empirical knowledge, pure mathematical knowledge, and dialectic. Carpenter (2015: 183-4n10) is more generous.

28 Only truth is not explicitly put in the comparative form, although later see 61e. But 57d maintains that philosophical mathematics surpasses the others with respect to accuracy and truth. For the superlative of truth, see, for example, 58c, 58d, 59b.

29 Hackforth (1945: 117n3) points out that Plato refers to the stochastic expertises as 'so-called expertises' at 56c, perhaps suggesting that Plato does not endorse their expert status. But, Plato describes them as expertises or knowledges without any such qualification at 55d, 55e, 56b, 57a-b, 57b, 57c.

30 Gosling (1975: 128) doubts a substantive distinction between clarity and precision. Carpenter (2015: 191) suggests otherwise.

31 For an attractive interpretation of this *Philebus* passage which nicely accommodates this feature of the criteria, see Carpenter (2015).

32 For a very different reading of the *Theaetetus*, for example, see Sedley (2004: esp. 179) who thinks that Plato takes knowledge and belief (or judgement) to be two different cognitive states or capacities, and that the former is restricted to Forms and the latter to the sensible world.

References

Bostock, D. (1988), *Plato's* Theaetetus, New York: Oxford University Press.

Brown, L. (1986), 'Being in the *Sophist*: A Syntactical Inquiry', *Oxford Studies in Ancient Philosophy*, 4: 49–70.

Burnyeat, M. F. (1990), *The* Theaetetus *of Plato* (trans. M. J. Levitt), Indianapolis: Hackett.

Burnyeat, M. F. (2005), 'Εἰκὼς μῦθος', *Rhizai*, 2: 143–65.

Carpenter, A. (2010), 'Embodied Intelligent (?) Souls: Plants in Plato's *Timaeus*', *Phronesis*, 55: 281–303.

Carpenter, A. D. (2015), 'Ranking Knowledge in the *Philebus*', *Phronesis*, 60: 180–205.

Chappell, T. (2004), *Reading Plato's* Theaetetus, Indianapolis: Hackett.

Cherniss, H. (1957), 'The Relation of the *Timaeus* to Plato's Later Dialogues', *Journal of Philology*, 7: 225–66.

Cooper, J. M. (1970), 'Plato on Sense Perception and Knowledge: *Theaetetus* 184 to 186', *Phronesis*, 15: 123–46.

Cooper, J. M. (1977), 'Plato's Theory of Human Good in the *Philebus*', *Journal of Philosophy*, 74: 714–30.

Cornford, F. M. (1950), *Plato's Theory of Knowledge*, London: Routledge & Kegan Paul.

Dancy, R. M. (1987), 'Theaetetus' First Baby: *Theaetetus* 151e–160e', *Philosophical Topics*, 15: 61–108.

Fine, G. (1979), 'Knowledge and *Logos* in the *Theaetetus*', *Philosophical Review*, 88: 367–97.

Frede, D. (1993), *Plato: Philebus*, Indianapolis: Hackett Publishing.

Ganson, T. S. (2005), 'The Platonic Approach to Sense-Perception', *History of Philosophy Quarterly*, 22: 1–11.

Gerson, L. P. (2003), *Knowing Persons: A Study in Plato*, Oxford: Oxford University Press.

Giannopoulou, Z. (2013), *Plato's* Theaetetus *as a Second* Apology, Oxford: Oxford University Press.

Gosling, J. C. B. (1975), *Plato:* Philebus, Oxford: Oxford University Press.

Hackforth, R. (1945), *Plato's Examination of Pleasure*, Cambridge: Cambridge University Press.

Harte, V. (2002a), *Plato on Parts and Wholes*, Oxford: Oxford University Press.

Harte, V. (2002b), 'Plato's Problem of Composition', in J. J. Cleary and G. M. Gurtler (eds), *Proceedings of the Boston Area Colloquium in Ancient Philosophy*, Leiden: Brill.

Johansen, T. K. (2004), *Plato's Natural Philosophy: A Study of the* Timaeus-Critias, Cambridge: Cambridge University Press.

Kahn, C. H. (1981), 'Some Philosophical Uses of "To Be" in Plato', *Phronesis*, 26: 119–27.

Kahn, C. H. (2013), *Plato and the Post-Socratic Dialogue: The Return to the Philosophy of Nature*, Cambridge: Cambridge University Press.

Lorenz, H. (2006), *The Brute Within: Appetitive Desire in Plato and Aristotle*, New York: Oxford University Press.

McDowell, J. (1973), *Plato:* Theaetetus, Oxford: Clarendon Press.

Modrak, D. K. (1981), 'Perception and Judgment in Plato's *Theaetetus*', *Phronesis*, 26: 35–54.

Owen, G. E. L. (1953), 'The Place of the *Timaeus* in Plato's Dialogues', *Classical Quarterly*, NS2: 79–95.

Ross, W. D. (1951), *Plato's Theory of Ideas*, Oxford: Clarendon Press.

Sedley, D. (2004), *The Midwife of Platonism*, Oxford: Oxford University Press.

7

Aristotle on Understanding and
Practical Wisdom

Corinne Gartner

1. Introduction and background

Aristotle divides sciences or systematic fields of understanding (*epistēmē*) into three branches, based on their ends: theoretical fields of knowledge have no end other than understanding itself, while both practical and productive fields have ends outside themselves.[1] The end of practical understanding is action (*praxis*) (*Nicomachean Ethics* [*NE*] I.3.1095a5–6),[2] and Aristotle considers political science (*politikē epistēmē*) the topic of investigation in his ethical treatises (*NE* I.2.1094b10–11), a field of practical study. Aristotle uses the term *epistēmē* to refer both to the cognitive state of an individual and to the systematic field of knowledge in relation to which the individual exercises this cognitive state, as he does in dividing the sciences. Throughout, I translate *epistēmē* as 'understanding' when it is used in relation to the cognitive state in the soul of an individual who possesses it, following Burnyeat (1981).

Aristotle denies, *contra* the Socratic view, that the virtues are themselves types of knowledge or understanding: that is, Aristotle rejects the view that understanding, for example, justice makes an individual just the way that understanding geometry makes an individual a geometer (*Eudemian Ethics* [*EE*] I.5.1216b2–15). And he notoriously downplays the role of understanding, as opposed to experience, in matters of action. Perhaps this is in part because, when it comes to action, the subject matter does not lend itself to the precision of a field like geometry, for its premises, and therefore its conclusions, hold only for the most part (*NE* I.3.109419–22); in order to become adept in acting well, interpreters of Aristotle have often thought, one needs practice and not theoretical understanding. It is thus easy to read Aristotle's division in branches of study or sciences as a sharp one. Although he terms all of them 'sciences' (*epistēmai*), there seems to be a substantial break between, for instance, understanding that all triangles have interior angles equal to two right angles and understanding that it is good not to flee one's post on the battlefield: the former is universal and necessary in a straightforward way, while the latter may be a decent heuristic but its truth remains conditional on facts about the particular agent and his current circumstances.

In both the *Posterior Analytics* and the *Nicomachean Ethics*, Aristotle explains that understanding in the strictest sense must be of what cannot be otherwise. He provides an account of unqualified understanding (*epistēmē haplōs*) at *Posterior Analytics* I.2.71b9–16:

> We think we understand a thing in an unqualified way (and not in the sophistical way, incidentally) when we think we know of the explanation because of which the object holds that it is its explanation, and also that it is not possible for it to be otherwise. It is plain, then, that to understand is something of this sort. And indeed, people who do not understand think they are in such a condition, and those who do understand actually are. Hence if there is unqualified understanding of something, it is impossible for it to be otherwise.[3]

Similarly, at *NE* VI.3.1139b19–24, after asserting that there are five states in the soul that grasp truth – craft knowledge (*technē*), understanding (*epistēmē*), practical wisdom (*phronēsis*), theoretical wisdom (*sophia*), and intelligence (*nous*) – Aristotle tells us that what is understood does not admit of being otherwise: 'Hence what is understood is by necessity. Hence it is everlasting; for the things that are by unqualified necessity are all everlasting, and everlasting things are ingenerable and indestructible.'[4] It would seem, then, that the proper objects of understanding for Aristotle are those that the astronomer or geometer studies, and not the politician or student of ethics.

Now, this might seem to us like a strange way for Aristotle to elucidate the state of soul that is understanding. Surely we can have different epistemic states in relation to the same objects of cognition, or the same propositions.[5] And, if so, why not think that one agent may have a weaker grasp of some ethical fact, while another agent's grasp of that same fact could rise to the level of unqualified understanding?[6] I return to this possibility again, but one difficulty is that, for Aristotle, there is a tight correspondence between objects in the world and our capacities or states: certain objects are suited to actualize specific capacities, or, to put it the other way, subjects of awareness are constituted such that they possess different faculties for apprehending different things in the world.

Aristotle opens his discussion of the virtues of thought in *NE* VI (= *EE* V)[7] by reminding us of his earlier division in the soul between the reasoning part of the soul and the part that can obey or listen to reason (*NE* VI.1.1139a3–5).[8] He then divides the reasoning part of the soul into two further subparts, the understanding part (*epistēmonikon*), with which we study things whose principles do not admit of being otherwise, and the calculating part (*logistikon*), which deliberates and deals with things that can be otherwise. 'For when the beings are of different kinds, the parts of the soul naturally suited to each of them are also of different kinds, since the parts possess knowledge (*gnōsis*) by being somehow similar and appropriate [to their objects]' (1139a8–11). In order for an object to be understood without qualification it must be understandable without qualification, and those objects with which the calculating part is concerned are not understandable without qualification.

Aristotle argues that the virtue of practical wisdom can be neither understanding nor craft knowledge, as the practically wise person is the one who deliberates finely about what contributes to living well (*NE* VI.5.1140a25–28, 7.1141b8–12). We deliberate about what is up to us in action (*NE* VI.5.1140a31–33; III.3.1112a30–31). Since we do not deliberate about what is by necessity and cannot be otherwise, practical wisdom cannot be understanding. Practical wisdom, then, is the virtue of the calculating part. The nature of an object of study licenses division in the soul, and the central distinction when it comes to differentiating unqualified understanding and practical wisdom is the distinction between things that cannot be otherwise and those that can be otherwise. So, again, it may seem that unqualified understanding in the domain of ethics, or unqualified understanding of political science, is impossible, and that practical wisdom, being deliberative, set over prospective particular actions, does not include understanding. Recent scholarship has, however, challenged these claims and sought to unify the theoretical and practical branches of knowledge within Aristotle's system.[9] In what follows, I explore, in the following section, whether there may be unqualified understanding of ethical facts, or at least some kinds of ethical facts – namely, ethical universals. And, in the third and final section, I consider how understanding might relate to practical wisdom: does the practically wise person need to have theoretical understanding of political or ethical science, if there is such theoretical understanding?

2. Could there be unqualified understanding of politics?

It is clear from the text of *NE* VI that practical wisdom cannot itself be a kind of unqualified understanding, but that leaves open the possibility that there could be unqualified understanding in the domain of ethics.

We should return to Aristotle's characterizations of unqualified understanding from both the *Posterior Analytics* and *NE* VI, where Aristotle made clear that unqualified understanding must be set over what cannot be otherwise. On a standard reading of Aristotle's account of unqualified understanding, there can be no unqualified understanding of anything in the domain of practical knowledge (*epistēmē*) because actions admit of being otherwise, and practical understanding is essentially concerned with actions. Drawing upon current approaches that aim to bring together the branches of investigation within Aristotle's system, I offer three compatible strategies for challenging the standard interpretation, all of which take seriously the claim that unqualified understanding must be of what cannot be otherwise. In so doing, I explore the strengths and weaknesses of each. Because Aristotle has a technical notion of understanding (*epistēmē*) and yet does not always employ the term *epistēmē* and its cognates in his strictest technical sense, determining whether political science (*politikē epistēmē*) may satisfy this technical notion, or whether there is some distinct theoretical ethical understanding is challenging. As will emerge, though promising, none of these strategies is an obvious success.

First, one might argue that, though particular actions must fall within the realm of things that can be otherwise, there are nonetheless necessary and unchanging principles of ethics or politics.[10] Indeed, the *Nicomachean Ethics* and the *Eudemian Ethics* both investigate these principles, insofar as they offer accounts of the human good or happiness (*eudaimonia*), the virtues that contribute to happiness, and explanations of various ethical or practical phenomena that run quite deep, relying on facts from other domains of understanding, such as psychology and metaphysics. In *NE* I.2 Aristotle indicates that there is a kind of science or capacity (*dunamis*) that aims at the human good, and this is political science, which makes use of all of the subordinate fields of study that concern the human good, such as household management as well as productive branches of study like rhetoric (1094a24-b3). And although the end of this type of understanding is action – action that constitutes the human good – Aristotle nonetheless analogizes understanding of the human good, for the student of political science, to an archer's possession of a target at which to aim (1094a22–4).

But there are some worries for the view that there are universals in ethics that can be understood in an unqualified way. Aristotle is often read as claiming that the subject matter of actions does not admit of such universals. In a commonly mentioned passage (*NE* V.10.1137b11–24), he explains that there is a disconnect between what the legislator sets down as law and what is in fact just and decent in practice. Law is universal, but 'the source of error is not the law or legislator, but the nature of the object itself, since that is what the subject matter of actions is bound to be like' (1137b17–19). However, what Aristotle here criticizes is the application of a universal prescription. The legislator does not err with respect to generating universal prescriptions – indeed, this is precisely what he should do, so it is no failure of his when a given prescriptive universal does not recommend the correct action, or simply fails to cover a specific case. And, at any rate, the universal laws at issue in the passage are the ones the legislator is creating, and not whatever universals might exist in the domain of action as objects of understanding: perhaps there are universals that cannot be implemented on a *polis*-wide scale because they require too much qualification, but nonetheless could apply on a smaller scale within subcommunities.

Moreover, there is a distinction between universal prescriptions and universal descriptive facts about the nature of happiness, so that even if the former cannot be necessary in the strict sense, the latter might well be. That happiness consists in virtuous rational activity can be used to recommend prescriptions which obtain only for the most part, even as the fact itself remains a changeless universal, grounded in further facts about human nature. But given that Aristotle repeatedly specifies that political science concerns actions – that actions are its subject matter – we might wonder whether the understanding of these necessary universals regarding the nature of the human good fall within a different sphere of study if they do not prescribe or directly concern action. Perhaps they are instead within the purview of what Aristotle calls 'theoretical moral philosophy' (*ta ēthikēs theōrias*) in the *Posterior Analytics* (I.33 89b9).

A second strategy to extend unqualified understanding to the ethical sphere lies in drawing an analogy between natural science and political science.[11] Aristotle seems to hold that we can possess unqualified understanding of natural phenomena, even though the relevant phenomena hold only for the most part – for example, human beings have two legs, adult male humans have hair on their chins. The fact that ethical phenomena, too, hold only for the most part would, similarly, constitute no barrier to having unqualified understanding of them.[12] That is, there must be some sense in which things that obtain for the most part nonetheless can obtain necessarily, and so feature in demonstrations. As Devin

130   *Knowledge in Ancient Philosophy*

Henry (2015) rightly explains, success of this strategy is contingent on Aristotle using 'for the most part' (*hōs epi to polu*) consistently across contexts. Yet close analysis of this phrase suggests different meanings (171–7). Nevertheless, Henry argues, there is one usage that applies in both natural and ethical realms: the causes (*aitia*) in question are necessary in the sense that they necessitate their effects if nothing impedes them. They have the status of ceteris paribus laws. Thus, the ethical universal that courage is good may be defeasible but still necessary; there may be particular instances where courage is not good, but this does not alter the necessity of the universal, for it holds for the most part in the relevant causal sense. While this observation effectively rebuts a common objection to thinking that there cannot be a proper science of ethics, thus going some way towards establishing a connection between unqualified understanding and understanding in the ethical sphere, it does not on its own go far enough, as will be clear shortly.[13]

Third, there seems to be some textual evidence to support the notion that Aristotle treats ethical facts as understandable, since he invokes some of them as examples within the context of the *Posterior Analytics*. For instance, in a passage at *Posterior Analytics* II.13.97b15–25, he gives as an example of establishing a definition through division the case of magnanimity: 'if we were seeking what magnanimity is, we should inquire, in the case of some magnanimous men we know, what one feature they have in common as such' (97b15–17). And *Posterior Analytics* II.11 features a number of practical or political examples to illustrate the four causes or explanations (*aitiai*), including a syllogistic case where the middle term exemplifies the efficient cause: 'Why did the Persian war come upon the Athenians? What is the explanation of the Athenians being warred upon? Because they attacked Sardis with the Eretrians – this initiated the change' (94a36-b2). The former case is seeking a definition, which is always universal and cannot be otherwise, and the latter case concerns something which happened in the past. We do not deliberate and decide about the past, for it does not admit of not having happened (*NE* VI.2.1139b7–9). These things, then, cannot be otherwise, yet seem to be both within the realm of political science and clearly important for the legislator or politician to understand.

The difficulty is that while the past does not admit of being otherwise now, past actions are still such as to once have been capable of being otherwise: the Athenians could have acted differently. Indeed, this fact, too, would also seem to be a crucial aspect of the legislator's knowledge. So although the practically wise person will not deliberate about the past, for deliberation and decision only concern currently available actions, the necessity at play in past actions is not that of the heavens or mathematics. Furthermore, Aristotle never uses *epistēmē* or its cognates in the second book of the *Posterior Analytics* after the first sentence; he uses weaker terms for knowing (*eidenai, gignōskein, gnōsis*) to describe what one gleans in these cases.[14] So the knowledge involved in these two ethical examples seems to be something weaker than understanding, and surely weaker than unqualified understanding.

There are further worries for these ways of reconciling the requirements on unqualified understanding with ethical understanding. For one thing, even if there are ethical universals, it is unclear whether and how they might feature in demonstrations.[15] But unqualified understanding is, Aristotle stipulates, a demonstrative state (*NE* VI.3.1139b31–2; *Posterior Analytics* I.2.71b17). In *Posterior Analytics* I.30 Aristotle introduces the distinction between demonstrations of necessary things and those that hold for the most part, making room for ethical demonstrations, but at *NE* VI.3.1139b23–4 demonstration is distinctive of things that are necessary without qualification, and in *NE* VI.5 he seems expressly to rule out ethical demonstration in separating understanding from practical wisdom (1140a33–5).[16] For another, it is not clear whether the reconciliation would even be amenable to Aristotle. If there were ethical or political unqualified understanding, it would seem to be quite removed from ethical practice: the more universal and necessary the object of understanding, the more removed from our experience, and the less immediately applicable to human decision-making and action. And yet, as Aristotle emphasizes, we study ethics with the aim of being good and not merely understanding what is good. Of course, he does think, as we have seen, that there are necessary facts about the nature of the human good, But the issues are whether there can be unqualified understanding of these abstract universals, whether there can be unqualified understanding of any ethical facts that are subordinate to them, and, if there can be, whether, in either case, that understanding is of political science. If the universals of political or ethical understanding are descriptive facts about the nature of the human good, a sharp divide remains between ethical understanding, on the one hand, and the practical side of ethics, on the other: descriptive universals do not prescribe.

Part of the trouble with attempting to get clarity on these issues is that Aristotle's use of the term *epistēmē* and its cognates is technical yet at the same time admits of laxity. In the two places where he is strictest with the term – *Nicomachean Ethics* VI and *Posterior Analytics* I.2 – he also expressly builds in room for a looser usage. At *NE* VI.3.1139b18–19 he indicates that he is speaking exactly about *epistēmē*, allowing that one might speak less exactly, as he does in other contexts, and at *Posterior Analytics* I.2.71b16 he refers to another kind of understanding, in contrast with unqualified understanding.[17] To limn the rest of the terrain in brief, the strictest variety of unqualified understanding is active demonstrative understanding of the objects that are most understandable without qualification – that is, the heavenly substances that are most eternal, and incapable of being otherwise in any sense because they are pure activity. But unqualified understanding in the fullest sense is characterized not only by the superiority of its objects, but also by both the breadth and depth of explanatory familiarity and preparedness. As Burnyeat (1981) point outs, achieving complete understanding, or expert mastery of a systematic field of inquiry, requires not merely grasping and being capable of connecting the propositions within a field of knowledge, but thoroughly internalizing them. Burnyeat likens this process to moral habituation; the end result is achievement of comprehensive understanding in the strictest or fullest sense.

Although such understanding is the pinnacle of human cognitive achievement, one may also plausibly understand without qualification objects admitting of other, looser forms of necessity. And one may understand a host of things with qualification, including those that can be otherwise, as well as individual propositions, the understanding of which may or may not presuppose understanding the entire systematic field of study to which those truths belong. For example, at *Posterior Analytics* I.1.71a27–9 Aristotle uses the verb cognate with the term for understanding (*epistatai*): it is possible to understand the proposition that the sum of the interior angles of a triangle equals two right angles, though he specifies that this fact is not understood without qualification, for he is describing the learner's, as opposed to the expert's, grasp of the fact. And in his analysis of akratic action in *NE* VII.3, Aristotle uses a verb form for 'understand' (*epistasthai*) in clarifying the ways that we can apprehend a proposition in order to explain what the akratic agent lacks with respect to a given proposition – for example, that this particular food in front of me is dry.[18] At *NE* VII.3.1147b18 Aristotle even modifies 'understanding' (*epistēmē*) with 'perceptual' (*tēs aisthētikēs*): there is a kind of perceptual understanding of the particular, which, Aristotle says, is responsible for controlling action.[19] In all of these cases, however, understanding has a core sense. The central notion of understanding that unifies the various instances is that of possessing an explanatory grasp of something. The individual who understands some phenomenon X is capable of providing an explanation of the cause(s) of X. In the strictest cases, this explanation is demonstrative, and the demonstration contains things which are necessary without qualification, but some of Aristotle's uses suggest that there may be instances of non-demonstrative understanding, depending on the phenomenon understood.

3. Aristotle's identification of practical wisdom and political science

As we just saw, there are various kinds of qualified understanding, various looser or extended senses of the term that cover given instances of understanding both a particular fact and of understanding objects which admit of fluctuation. If this is right, and political science is not understood without qualification but is instead understood in an incidental way (*kata sumbebēkos*), as C. D. C. Reeve (2012) has argued, then we might wonder whether practical wisdom just is political understanding. Throughout *NE* VI Aristotle repeatedly and explicitly distinguishes practical wisdom from understanding, but it is clear that what he means to differentiate from practical wisdom is unqualified understanding in the strictest sense. However, in differentiating theoretical wisdom from practical wisdom and political science, he seems initially to associate political science and practical wisdom (*NE* VI.7.1141a20–1). Likewise, in his account of practical wisdom in *NE* VI.5, Aristotle brings together practical wisdom and political science by remarking that we consider people like Pericles practically wise because 'they are able to study (*theorein*) what is good for themselves and for human beings; we think that household managers and politicians are such people' (1140b9–11). And, at the opening of *NE* VI.8, Aristotle claims, 'Political science and practical wisdom are *the same state*, but their being is not the same' (1141b23–4).

Whether or not practical wisdom is any sort of understanding, recent work has emphasized the close connections between these two states of soul in the intellectually and practically virtuous agent. Reeve (2012: 148–50, 157), for example, argues that practical wisdom involves both grasping ethical universals, which an understanding of political science supplies, and character virtue. And Karen M. Nielsen (2015: 32) similarly maintains that practical wisdom requires an understanding of the nature of the human good: 'Only someone who knows what the human good is can use deliberation and perception of particulars to make the right decision.' According to both views, then, the practically wise agent's deliberation is informed in some way by his theoretical ethical understanding. In what follows, I consider further whether practical wisdom could itself *be* a kind of understanding, and whether, or to what extent, the practically wise agent must possess understanding of political science.

134 *Knowledge in Ancient Philosophy*

Recall that, in *NE* VI.1, Aristotle divides the rational part of the soul into the scientific part (*epistemonikon*), which understands things that cannot be otherwise and the calculating part (*logistikon*), which reasons or deliberates about what admits of being otherwise. Each of these parts has its own function and corresponding virtue; theoretical wisdom (*sophia*), which is understanding (*epistēmē*) plus intelligence (*nous*), is the virtue of the scientific part, while practical wisdom is the virtue of the calculating part (*NE* VI.13.1144b14–17, 1145a3–4; cf. *NE* VI.12.1144a1–3). Aristotle thinks, 'A thing's virtue is relative to its own proper function' (*NE* VI.1.1139a16–17), and so in *NE* VI.2 he sketches the functions of each of these two parts of the soul in order to introduce the virtue of each part. Although the two parts of the rational soul are in part individuated by their objects, they are also in part individuated by their functions in relation to their proper objects.

The function of each of the parts of reason is apprehending truth, but Aristotle indicates that the type of truth that the calculating part grasps differs from that of the scientific part. He claims at *NE* VI.2.1139a26–7 that practical truth is a distinctive kind of truth, contrasting it with theoretical truth: the good functioning of a faculty of practical thought is truth in agreement with correct desire (1139a29–31). Although there is much interpretive controversy over how to make sense of Aristotle's notion of practical truth,[20] and what distinguishes it from theoretical truth, Aristotle commits himself to a clear separation between the two. But the separation between these two classes of truth also makes it hard to see how practical wisdom could itself be any type of understanding; understanding, even understanding within the ethical sphere, concerns universals. Universals cannot be otherwise, so they are within the purview of the scientific part. C. M. M. Olfert (2014) has recently argued that practical truth is the truth about what is good for a person when all of the features of his current circumstances and condition are taken into consideration.[21] According to her view, then, practical truth is crucially context-dependent, providing further reason for thinking that there are two non-overlapping sets of objects – those which cannot be otherwise, and those which can – with respect to which there are two different ways of apprehending two distinct kinds of truth.

Yet, in order for an agent to determine what is good for him, given his current condition and circumstances, he might plausibly need to know something about what is good for human beings more generally. That is, he may apply various ethical universals in order to arrive at a conception of what action would currently be good for him. At *NE* VI.7.1141b14–22 Aristotle states that practical wisdom is not only knowledge[22] of universals, indicating that it does concern universals, even though the particulars are more important, since, he explains, action is about particulars. Therefore, even if practical wisdom is not itself a kind of understanding, it may nonetheless necessarily involve or incorporate understanding.

A separate reason for thinking that practical wisdom cannot simply be a sort of understanding is that, in *Eudemian Ethics* VIII.1, Aristotle addresses a puzzle inspired by the Socratic identification of practical wisdom and understanding.[23] His response to the puzzle expressly rules out the possibility that practical wisdom is understanding on the grounds that, if it were, one could misuse it, just as one can use, for example, his understanding of medical knowledge to promote health or illness. But, Aristotle insists, practical wisdom does not admit of misuse; it is a virtue, and another type of knowing (*gnōsis*) (*EE* VIII.1.1146b35–6). It must be controlling or ruling (*EE* VIII.1.1146b9–11), making use of other branches of knowledge to achieve its aims. Thus, according to one possible account of the relationship between theoretical understanding of ethics and practical wisdom, although they are not to be identified, the latter makes use of the former.

However, Aristotle also explains, 'Moreover, practical wisdom does not control theoretical wisdom or the better part of the soul, just as medical science does not control health. For medical science does not use health, but only aims to bring health into being; hence it prescribes for the sake of health, but does not prescribe to health' (*NE* VI.13.1145a6–9). One might think, on the basis of the analogy with medicine, that practical wisdom cannot use the better part of the soul – the scientific part. But then how might understanding of theoretical ethical truths inform or relate to the operation of the calculating part? Even though practical wisdom acts for the sake of theoretical wisdom, according to this passage, it neither prescribes to nor receives prescriptions from theoretical wisdom. Theoretical wisdom is not prescriptive; rather, just as medical understanding requires grasping truths about health, even though it does not use health, so too practical wisdom requires grasping truths about value. As we have seen, however, the truths that actually constitute practical wisdom are distinct from theoretical truth, including theoretical ethical truth. There thus remains a gap in accounting for the relationship between the rational activity of the scientific part of the soul and that of the calculating part of the soul.

We might wonder in what way the practically wise agent must grasp theoretical ethical truths. Practical wisdom is the virtue of the calculating part of the soul, and, in addition to being the part of the soul that deliberates, this is also the part of the soul that houses beliefs, for both deliberation and belief concern what can be otherwise (*NE* VI.5.1140b25–8, VI.13.1144b14–15). In

EE VII.2, in the context of his *Eudemian* account of friendship, Aristotle raises a puzzle about the object of love, and resolves the puzzle by equating what is loved with what is desired: we desire both what we believe to be good and what appears to us to be good, but belief and appearance are in different parts of the soul (1235b25–9). Appearances belong to the part of the soul that can listen to reason, but does not itself possess reason, while beliefs belong to reason. But the fact that belief seems to be the epistemic state responsible for rational desire (*boulēsis*), as opposed to something stronger, in combination with the fact that belief is housed in the part of the soul the virtue of which is practical wisdom, may suggest that the practically wise agent's grasp of theoretical ethical truths need not rise to the level of understanding. Perhaps the practically wise agent can deliberate finely with true beliefs about ethical universals.[24]

That the calculating part possesses beliefs does not entail that the practically wise person need not also possess theoretical understanding of the same ethical universals about which he has beliefs, and indeed, there are some difficulties for thinking that one could have beliefs about universals at all, the most serious being that belief concerns what can be otherwise and, as we have seen, universals do not admit of being otherwise. Moreover, practical wisdom is a state that grasps truth (*NE* VI.5.1140b4–6, 20–1), and beliefs need not be true, so it would be strange if the practically wise person's calculating part were virtuous, in part, insofar as it possessed mere true beliefs. Last, at *NE* VII.2.1145b36–1146a7, Aristotle implicitly contrasts belief and practical wisdom when he considers and rejects two candidate explanations of akratic action.

We might think that the practically wise agent's true beliefs are explained and justified at the level of the scientific part of the soul. Perhaps, in reasoning about how to act, he need not employ his theoretical ethical understanding in the sense that he need not attend to, for example, the explanation of the nature of the human good, even as he does employ his true belief that the human good consists in virtuous rational activity. But this also opens up room for the practically wise agent who can account for a practical truth with an explanation that appeals to a theoretical ethical truth, and yet does not understand – that is, cannot himself explain – that theoretical ethical truth: why think the practically wise agent must be able to offer an adequate theoretical explanation of *why*, for example, it is, ceteris paribus, good to be courageous? In fact, Aristotle indicates that an explanation at the level of the theoretical truth may be inappropriate to the task of the ethics:

> We must also remember our previous remarks, so that we do not look for the same degree of exactness in all areas, but the degree that accords with a given

subject matter and is proper to a given line of inquiry. For the carpenter's and the geometer's inquiries about the right angle are different also; the carpenter restricts himself to what helps his work, but the geometer inquires into what, or what sort of thing, the right angle is, since he studies the truth. (*NE* I.7.1098a26–32)

Though one could inquire about the right angle qua carpenter or qua geometer, these inquires will look very different, for the carpenter's is shaped by his productive ends. So, one might conclude, the practicing practically wise politician need not possess proper theoretical understanding of the human good, just as the carpenter need not possess the geometer's account of the right angle in order to use the results of geometry well. Each actor needs only the results from the corresponding branch of understanding that are relevant for his purposes.

At the very end of the *Nicomachean Ethics*, however, Aristotle explains why understanding legislative science is essential for the practically wise legislator, suggesting that, on the contrary, practical wisdom and understanding are quite closely connected:

> Nonetheless, a doctor, a gymnastics trainer, and everyone else will give the best individual attention if they also know universally what is good for all, or for these sorts. For sciences are said to be, and are, of what is common. Admittedly someone without scientific understanding may well attend properly to a single person, if his experience has allowed him to take exact note of what happens in a given case, just as some people seem to be their own best doctors, though unable to help anyone else at all. Nonetheless, presumably, it seems that someone who wants to be an expert in a craft and a branch of study should progress to the universal, and come to know that, as far as possible; for that, as we have said, is what the sciences (*hai epistēmai*) are about. Then perhaps also someone who wishes to make people better by his attention, many people or few, should try to acquire legislative science, if laws are a means to make us good. For not just anyone can improve the condition of just anyone, or the person presented to him; but if someone can, it is the person with knowledge, just as in medical science and the rest of which there is some attention and practical wisdom. (*NE* X.9.1180b13–28)

Although Aristotle has argued, directly preceding this passage, that individual education and attention is better than a common education, he makes clear that the person in the best position to offer this care to all sorts of different people is the expert who also grasps the relevant universals. And not only must the expert grasp the universals within his branch of expertise, but he must grasp them *as far as possible*; his understanding should, it seems, be as thorough as the given branch of study allows. Just as an individual needs medical understanding to be a doctor, so too one needs understanding of legislative science in order to be a practically wise legislator. But in this passage Aristotle also mentions the person who is able to prescribe well in his own case with respect to health, the person who is his own best doctor, even though he could not cure anyone else because he lacks understanding of the relevant medical science. Why not suppose, then, that there might be a practically wise individual who does not possess a deep enough understanding of the human good to make anyone else good – certainly not enough to legislate well – and yet manages to care effectively for the health of his own soul?

Aristotle concedes that the type of practical wisdom concerned with the individual himself is most of all considered practical wisdom (*NE* VI.8.1141b29–30), but quickly offers a qualification explaining the origin of this widespread view and signalling that the individual's own welfare cannot be divorced from that of the communities of which he is a part. And, after equating practical wisdom and political science at 1141b23–4, Aristotle treats legislative science and household management as species of practical wisdom, which might be taken to suggest that the practically wise agent must possess understanding of all of these subordinate branches of political science.

Recall, though, that practical wisdom concerns those things about which the agent deliberates, and an agent deliberates about what is up to him, what he can achieve in action. Aristotle's target audience in the ethics is primarily composed of future politicians, and so it will be important for political leaders, in particular, to understand how to make other people good and thereby happy, just as it is important for a doctor to understand how to make other people healthy. Legislators and politicians are the people whose individual spheres of action immediately includes the good of the polis: they enact decrees which may promote the common good, and they will be in a position to gain experience with respect to making decisions on behalf of the city as a whole. There are thus actions and experiences open to the politician that are not open to the private, reclusive citizen, and so potential for deliberation about a wider range of actions which must plausibly be informed by an understanding of legislative science in order for the legislator to be a practically wise. But it does not follow that any given practically wise agent must possess understanding of, say, legislative science. Perhaps the particular systematic fields of understanding and depth of understanding required in the case of a given practically wise agent will depend on that agent's sphere of action.

I mentioned earlier that when he differentiates theoretical wisdom from practical wisdom, Aristotle initially pairs practical wisdom with political science at *NE* VI.7.1141a20–2, contrasting them both with theoretical wisdom. As the argument continues, however, he separates practical wisdom from political science, distinguishing them in turn from theoretical wisdom. The practically wise agent is the one who effectively studies questions about his own good, which is why, Aristotle claims, even some of the beasts are considered practically wise, for some of them, 'are evidently capable of forethought about their own life' (1141a27–8).[25] But political science concerns the good of human beings, in particular, as distinct from other species. As we saw earlier, states and capacities are individuated for Aristotle on the basis of their objects, so we might expect that the state of soul concerning the human good would be singular. When Aristotle claims that practical wisdom and political science are the same state, then, but not the same in being, he means that, in human beings, both are, in some way, concerned with the same object: the human good.

But what does Aristotle mean when he says that practical wisdom and political science are not the same in being? I have already alluded to one possibility. Aristotle treats political science, along with legislative science and household management, as different kinds of practical wisdom, just as knowledge of what is good for oneself is also one kind (*eidos*) of practical wisdom (*NE* VI.8.1141b33–4). In NE X.9 we saw that understanding the universals of legislative science facilitates a politician's ability to make other people good on the broadest scale. The practically wise person who is in a position to govern a city must possess this type of practical wisdom, since he must understand the universals that are relevant to making decisions about the good of the city as a whole. And, more generally, political science is concerned with the good of others, the common good, while practical wisdom includes the common good to varying extents, based on the place that an agent occupies within a community and so the actions available to him. That is, practical wisdom is always concerned with the agent's own good, but, because one's own good depends on the good of others in his communities, he may also, to be practically wise, need to possess an understanding of the good of these communities insofar as he is in a position to promote their good directly in his actions.

One might worry that the distinction between an agent's own good, with which practical wisdom is concerned, and the good of his community, with which political science is concerned, collapses once we recognize the mutual interdependence between these two domains of value, for, as Aristotle repeatedly tells us, human beings are political animals (see, e.g., *Politics* I.2.1253a7–8). Even

140   *Knowledge in Ancient Philosophy*

though the good of all members of the *polis* is intertwined, there are still decisions that an individual must make which centrally concern her own well-being – for example, whether to eat some bird meat (*NE* VI.7.1141b18–21). When an agent decides to eat *this* piece of bird meat, his action is centrally concerned with his own good. Of course, his decision may impact others, and where the well-being of others is immediately salient, since he is virtuous and practically wise, he will include their good in his decision-making. He would not, for instance, selfishly hog all the bird meat at the dinner table. He need not, however, possess an understanding of legislative science in order to make a decision about eating bird meat, and so his understanding of political science may be quite limited, shaped by what is up to him to achieve in action.

By contrast, in deliberating about whether, for instance, to implement a given change to the city's current educational system, a politician must invoke a thorough and sophisticated understanding of legislative science, political science in the highest degree. Yet this is nonetheless an exercise of his practical wisdom as well, for in this case his good is both indirectly influenced by the impact of his decision on the polis and directly influenced because *he* is the one acting. So even if practical wisdom and comprehensive understanding of political science are fully aligned in the case of the politician, who legislates both on a city-wide scale and governs at home, it does not follow that everyone must have the understanding of a politician, nor does it follow that all of the politician's own exercises of his practical wisdom will require his understanding of legislative science, for he, too, decides whether to eat this bird meat.

There is another potential difficulty for Aristotle's explicit claim that practical wisdom and political science are the same state. If they are the same state, then this state must be in one part of the rational soul. Aristotle makes clear that practical wisdom is the virtue of the calculating part, so we have strong reason for thinking that the singular state at issue is a state of the calculating part of the soul. However, if political science is understanding of the theoretical truths of ethics – universals, such as the claim that the human good is virtuous rational activity – and these are truths about things that cannot be otherwise, then it would seem that political science belongs to the scientific part of the soul. We could grant that political science is thoroughly deliberative, preserving the same state claim, but at the expense of the possibility that understanding of political science could be quite close in kind to unqualified understanding, both housed in the scientific part of the soul. We thus confront a tension. According to the first option, practical wisdom and political science are the same state, a state of the calculating part of the soul, in which case this state may be informed by but does not consist in theoretical ethical understanding, for such understanding is a product of the scientific part of the soul. According to the second option, we would have either to reinterpret Aristotle's claim that practical wisdom and political science are the same state, or renege on his commitment to the claim that practical wisdom is the virtue of the calculating part. The first option is preferable, for it avoids obvious inconsistency with the text: we should attribute an understanding of political science, along with the virtue of practical wisdom, to the calculating part, but questions about the way in which theoretical understanding of ethics may contribute to the reasoning of the practically wise agent remain.

Notes

I have benefited from Ravi Sharma's and Nicholas D. Smith's helpful comments on this chapter.

1 See, for example, *Topics* VI.6.145a15-16, though he later treats the main division as that between practical and theoretical (*Topics* VII.1.152b4), and *Eudemian Ethics* I.5.1216b11-18, where Aristotle instead lumps political science in with medicine as productive, in opposition to astronomy and natural sciences, which are theoretical. Analysis of the relationship between practical and productive sciences is outside the scope of this project, though Aristotle often relies on analogical arguments that assimilate these two branches of study, contrasting them with the theoretical.

2 See also, for example, *Eudemian Ethics* 1216b12-20; *Metaphysics* 993b20.

3 Translations from the *Posterior Analytics* are those of Barnes (1993), with minor modifications.

4 I follow the translation of Irwin (1999) for the *Nicomachean Ethics*, with minor modifications.

5 To be sure, Aristotle does consider the way in which there could be both belief (*doxa*) and understanding in relation to the same thing in *Posterior Analytics* I 33, but he still denies that there can be belief and understanding in relation to the same thing *in every way* (*pantōs*) (89a23-4). For one account of this puzzling chapter, see Fine (2010).

6 I refer variously to an agent understanding facts, objects, and phenomena. These facts are linguistically represented in propositions and claims, but, for Aristotle, mind-independent things (*pragmata*) in the world are what we understand.

7 I cite *Nicomachean Ethics* VI in discussing the intellectual virtues, but it is worth keeping in mind that *NE* VI is a common book; it is also *Eudemian Ethics* V. Aristotle's ethical accounts of understanding and practical wisdom occupy both treatises.

142   *Knowledge in Ancient Philosophy*

8   See *NE* I.13.1102b13-1103a3 for the initial argument dividing the part of the soul that is reason strictly speaking and the part capable of listening to reason.

9   For example, Reeve (1992, 2012, 2013), Charles (1999, 2015), and Lear (2004) analogize practical and theoretical reason, albeit in different ways. And a recent volume edited by Henry and Nielsen (2015) is dedicated to establishing connections between the Aristotelian branches of study. I cannot hope to address the myriad ways of relating theoretical and practical wisdom. I set aside ethical connections to natural science, potential methodological similarities, including how we come to acquire a grasp of principles in each domain, as well as comparison of the theoretical demonstrative syllogism and the practical syllogism.

10   Reeve (2012, 2013) and Nielsen (2015) adopt this strategy.

11   My account of this strategy is heavily influenced by Henry's (2015) discussion. He argues persuasively that, 'even if it turns out that Aristotle does not think we can acquire genuine scientific understanding (*epistēmē*) about matters of conduct, it is not because they hold only for the most part' (188). Others who adopt the strategy of analogizing natural and ethical fields of study include Reeve (1992, 2012), Anagnostopoulos (1994), and Irwin (2000).

12   Henry (2015: 171) helpfully reconstructs the standard version of this argument.

13   Henry (2015: 170, 189) himself never indicates that this strategy is sufficient to establish ethical understanding; indeed, he makes clear that he hopes only to militate against one common objection.

14   For a convincing account of the way that Aristotle uses these various terms for knowledge, see Bronstein (2016: 16–21, 77–8).

15   If Henry (2015) is right, however, and ethical facts can be necessary, they would then be capable of demonstration.

16   Henry (2015: 179n18) also addresses this tension.

17   Though it seems most natural to take the contrast at *Posterior Analytics* I.2.71b16-17 to be between unqualified understanding, which Aristotle has just finished characterizing, and a different sort – a qualified sort – of understanding, Bronstein (2016: 53–6) instead reads the contrast here as forward-looking, distinguishing demonstrative and non-demonstrative unqualified understanding, including intelligence (*nous*) under unqualified understanding.

18   Aristotle also uses understanding (*epistēmē* and cognates) throughout *NE* VII.2–3 in an extended sense. One worry with Aristotle's use of the term in the *akrasia* discussion is that he is replying to the Socratic view about the impossibility of acting against knowledge, and so may be using *epistēmē* more in accordance with the Socratic usage. For a helpful discussion of distinctions among modes of understanding in the context of Aristotle's *NE* VII.3 discussion, see Lorenz (2014).

19   Various commentators have sought to emend the text to avoid this outcome, but Lorenz (2014) offers a compelling way to make sense of the notion of perceptual

understanding. For a succinct but accurate take on this portion of the text, see 259n22.

20 For differing recent accounts of practical truth, see, for example, Broadie and Rowe (2002), Lear (2004), and Olfert (2014).

21 Competing accounts of practical truth, such as those of Broadie and Rowe (2002), as well as Lear (2004), make practical truth even more distinctive and removed from truth in the theoretical sphere. Olfert's reading preserves Aristotle's standard notion of truth.

22 Aristotle uses other terms for knowing (*eidenai, gignōskein*), not *epistēmē* or cognates, when referring to the practically wise agent's knowledge of universals and particulars.

23 One may worry that, as with his usage of *epistēmē* in the *akrasia* discussion of *NE* VII.2–3, Aristotle is not employing his own conception because he is replying to the Socratic dissenter on the dissenter's own terms (see also note 20).

24 Nielsen (2015: 34) seems to suppose this when she explains, 'For prudence it suffices that we understand the results of the enquiry conducted by the science of ethics. Here we should recall that Aristotle envisions a division of labour between theoretical ethics and statesmanship. The latter art uses the results of the former ... The statesman employs the findings of political science to create a well-ordered polity.' The practically wise person need not conduct his own enquiry into theoretical ethics, according to her view.

25 For a sustained defence of the view that, according to Aristotle, certain animals are capable of practical wisdom, see Henry (forthcoming).

References

Anagnostopoulos, G. (1994), *Aristotle on the Goals and Exactness of Ethics*, Berkeley: University of California Press.

Barnes, J. (ed.) (1993), *Aristotle:* Posterior Analytics, with trans. and commentary, 2nd edn, Oxford: Oxford University Press.

Broadie, S. and Rowe, C. (trans.) (2002), *Aristotle:* Nicomachean Ethics, with commentary, Oxford: Oxford University Press.

Bronstein, D. (2016), *Aristotle on Knowledge and Learning:* The Posterior Analytics, Oxford: Oxford University Press.

Burnyeat, M. F. (1981), 'Aristotle on Understanding Knowledge', in E. Berti (ed.), *Aristotle on the Posterior Analytics*, Padua: Editrice Antenore.

Charles, D. (1999), 'Aristotle on Well-Being and Intellectual Contemplation', *Proceedings of the Aristotelian Society Supplementary Volume*, 73: 205–23.

Charles, D. (2015), 'Aristotle on Practical and Theoretical Knowledge', in Henry and Nielsen (2015).

Fine, G. (2010), 'Aristotle's Two Worlds: Knowledge and Belief in *Posterior Analytics* I.33', *Proceedings of the Aristotelian Society*, 110: 323–46.

Henry, D. (2015), 'Holding for the Most Part: The Demonstrability of Moral Facts', in Henry and Nielsen (2015).

Henry, D. (forthcoming), 'Aristotle on Animals', in P. Adamson and F. Edwards (eds), *Oxford Philosophical Concepts: Animals*, Oxford: Oxford University Press.

Henry, D. and Nielsen K. M. (eds) (2015), *Bridging the Gap between Aristotle's Science and Ethics*, Cambridge: Cambridge University Press.

Irwin, T. (trans.) (1999), *Aristotle:* Nicomachean Ethics, with commentary, 2nd edn, Indianapolis: Hackett.

Irwin, T. (2000), 'Ethics as an Inexact Science: Aristotle's Ambitions for Moral Theory', in B. Hooker and M. Little (eds), *Moral Particularism*, Oxford: Oxford University Press.

Lear, G. R. (2004), *Happy Lives and the Highest Good*, Princeton: Princeton University Press.

Lorenz, H. (2014), 'Aristotle's Analysis of Akratic Action', in R. Polansky (ed.), *The Cambridge Companion to Aristotle's Nicomachean Ethics*, Cambridge: Cambridge University Press.

Nielsen, K. M. (2015), 'Aristotle on Principles in Ethics: Political Science as the Science of the Human Good', in Henry and Nielsen (2015).

Olfert, C. (2014), 'Aristotle's Conception of Practical Truth', *Journal of the History of Philosophy*, 52: 205–31.

Reeve, C. D. C. (1992), *Practices of Reason: Aristotle's* Nicomachean Ethics, Oxford: Oxford University Press.

Reeve, C. D. C. (2012), *Action, Contemplation, and Happiness: An Essay on Aristotle*, Cambridge, MA: Harvard University Press.

Reeve, C. D. C. (2013), *Aristotle on Practical Wisdom:* Nicomachean Ethics VI, with trans. and commentary, Cambridge, MA: Harvard University Press.

8

Aristotle: From Perception to Understanding

Keith McPartland

1. Introduction

In his *Posterior Analytics* Aristotle has an extended discussion of a cognitive achievement that he calls '*epistēmē haplōs*'. In using the word '*haplōs*', Aristotle indicates that he is talking about unqualified *epistēmē*, or *epistēmē* in the strictest sense, which, following Myles Burnyeat, I propose to treat as *understanding* or *scientific understanding* in my discussion.[1] '*Epistēmē*' is a noun related to the verb '*epistasthai*' which along with a number of other verbs (e.g. '*gignoskein*', '*eidenai*', and '*gnorizein*') is justifiably translated as 'to know' in many contexts.[2] It might seem completely natural for an interpreter trying to understand Aristotle's epistemology to focus her attention on Aristotle's discussion of *epistēmē* in the *Posterior Analytics*.

However, it soon becomes clear that Aristotle sets the bar for understanding extremely high. He writes thus: '(T1) We think we understand each thing in an unqualified way (*epistasthai haplōs*), and not in the accidental and sophistical way, when we know (*gignōskein*) that the cause because of which the thing is the case is the cause of that thing, and that it is not possible that it be otherwise' (*Posterior Analytics* 71b9–12).[3] In this passage and the surrounding discussion, Aristotle constrains the objects of *understanding* to universal facts that cannot be otherwise (71b15). In order to possess *it*, a person must grasp that things cannot be otherwise and must be incapable of being persuaded to change her mind (72b3–4). Understanding, therefore, involves both objective necessity and subjective certainty. Aristotle, however, demands even more. A person has understanding of a fact only when she knows the proper ultimate explanation of that fact, knows that it is the proper ultimate explanation of that fact, and has the ability to give a deductive demonstration of the fact from ultimate

146   *Knowledge in Ancient Philosophy*

explanatory principles. The requirements for understanding thus seem to go far beyond those we normally take to govern mere knowledge. Rather, the person who has understanding is an expert with a deep, systematic, and explanatory understanding of a field of enquiry.[4]

In order to understand something, a person must be able to demonstrate it from first principles. In *Posterior Analytics* I.3, Aristotle disallows both circular demonstration and infinite chains of demonstration. He concludes that first principles cannot be demonstrated and that they, therefore, cannot be objects of understanding. Since Aristotle denies that we can have understanding as a result of demonstration without knowing the principles of demonstration, he claims that there must be another form of knowledge that we have of the principles. In *Posterior Analytics* II.19, Aristotle identifies our knowledge of the principles as *comprehension* (*nous*), which he claims is a cognitive state superior even to understanding. He claims that the principles that we comprehend must be true, primitive, and indemonstrable. They must also be explanatory of, prior to, and more knowable by nature than the conclusions of scientific demonstrations of which we possess *understanding* (*Posterior Analytics* 71b25–32). As he does in the case of understanding, Aristotle places conditions on comprehension that go far beyond those that we ordinarily place on knowledge.

Aristotle takes a person to know whatever she comprehends or understands, but thinks that knowledge extends further than understanding and comprehension. In (T1) we see Aristotle characterize *understanding* by using a different Greek knowledge verb, '*gignōskein*'. In other passages, we can see that Aristotle takes '*gignōskein*' and other knowledge words to be properly applicable in cases where a person lacks understanding and comprehension.

At the outset of the *Posterior Analytics*, Aristotle writes:

> (T2) All intellectual (*dianoêtikê*) teaching and learning arises from pre-existent knowledge (*gnōsis*). This becomes clear by attending to all the cases. For the mathematical sciences and each of the other arts come to be present in this way. And it is similar in the case of deductive and inductive arguments, since both of these produce their teaching through what is already known (*progignōskein*). Deductive arguments begin from premises we are assumed to grasp, and inductive arguments prove something universal through the particular case's being clear. (71a1–9)

By restricting himself to intellectual learning, Aristotle means learning that results from some sort of reasoning or argument. Whenever someone learns something by a deductive or inductive argument, she needs to begin from something that she already knows. In deductive arguments, she needs to grasp the premises to learn the conclusion. In inductive arguments, the individual cases must be plain for her to derive anything more universal. In each of these cases, Aristotle credits the learner with some kind of pre-existent knowledge. What is important for present purposes is that this knowledge need not and, in many cases, cannot meet the stringent standards that Aristotle imposes on understanding and comprehension.

Second, Aristotle thinks that we begin our quest for understanding already in the possession of knowledge: '(T3) It is when we know (*eidenai*) the fact (*to hoti*) that we seek the reason why (*to dioti*). For example, when we know that it is eclipsed or that the earth moves, we seek the reason it is eclipsed or the reason it moves' (*Posterior Analytics* 89b29–31). The knowledge of the fact with which we begin is neither comprehension nor understanding. Instead, we possess knowledge of a different sort before we possess a scientific demonstration.

Finally, Aristotle allows that there is knowledge involved in practical matters that falls short of the standards that he imposes on understanding and comprehension. He identifies practical wisdom (*phronēsis*) and craft (*technē*) as intellectual virtues concerned with things that can be otherwise. Neither practical wisdom nor craft can be straightforwardly identified with knowledge of contingent matters of fact, but each crucially involves such knowledge.[5]

In contrast with craft and practical wisdom, understanding and comprehension are intellectual virtues concerned with what cannot be otherwise. Aristotle takes wisdom (*sophia*) to consist in understanding and comprehension. The wise person in any scientific field comprehends the first principles of that field and, through her possession of scientific demonstrations that proceed from these first principles, understands the theorems of that field. Aristotle takes the exercise of wisdom to consist in the activity of contemplation (*theoria*), which he identifies both as the activity that is proper to god and as the highest activity of which human beings are capable. The exercise of comprehension and understanding is, therefore, a fundamental component of the realization of the human end, that is, living well or being happy.

Since understanding and comprehension play such vital roles in his thought, Aristotle takes the time to discuss them in a careful way. However, he spends less time giving a precise characterization of knowledge in general. It is difficult, therefore, to find a simple statement of Aristotle's general epistemology. Furthermore, some of the central concerns that drive modern or contemporary epistemologists receive little treatment by Aristotle. He never, to my knowledge, undertakes a general discussion of justification or warrant. His treatment of scepticism is brief and can

148 *Knowledge in Ancient Philosophy*

look like it simply misses the point. Furthermore, as we will see in the next section, Aristotle's way of carving up the cognitive landscape can look somewhat peculiar to a person used to contemporary discussions in epistemology and the philosophy of mind.

Nevertheless, I think that it is possible to reconstruct Aristotle's general epistemology from the claims that he makes in a number of different works. My goal in what follows is to offer only the outline of such a reconstruction. I will suggest that Aristotle has a broadly naturalist and externalist theory of epistemology. To understand his brand of epistemic naturalism, it is crucial to understand the central role that teleology plays in Aristotle's theory of nature. We have knowledge because we truly represent the world as a result of exercising capacities that have accurate representation of the world as their constitutive natural end.

2. Aristotle's cognitive landscape: *epistēmē, gnōsis, doxa,* and *hupolēpsis*

I have already claimed that Aristotle generally reserves '*epistēmē*' for a particularly high-level and specialized kind of knowledge. If we want to look for more general account of epistemology in Aristotle, we need to turn our attention elsewhere. Aristotle uses the verbs '*gignōskein*' and '*eidenai*' and the noun '*gnōsis*' in talking about knowledge more generally. He uses '*gnōsis*' in a particularly broad way, and he is willing to credit even non-human animals with *gnōsis* as a result of their having perception. In the *Generation of Animals*, Aristotle distinguishes animals from plants by the fact that the former have the power of perception:

> (T4) [T]he function (*ergon*) of the animal is not only to reproduce (for this is common to all living things), but all share in some sort of knowledge (*gnōsis*), some more and some less, and some very little altogether. For they have perception, and perception is a sort of knowledge (*gnōsis*). And the worth of this differs greatly depending on whether you examine it in relation to intelligence (*phronēsis*) or in relation to the kind of things without a soul. In relation to intelligence it seems like nothing to share in only touch and taste, but in relation to the absence of sensation it seems like a really great thing. For it is would be desirable to have even this sort of knowledge and not to lie around as a dead and non-existent thing. (731a30-b4)[6]

Animals, including human beings, have some sort of knowledge simply as a result of perception. This type of knowledge is significantly less valuable than the sort of knowledge that we find in the case of human beings with a capacity for intelligence. However, even the most basic perceptual capacities of touch and taste are good for the animals that possess them, since even taste and touch allow an animal to live a life that is better than that of a plant or an inanimate object.

In contemporary epistemology, the claim that knowledge requires belief is extremely widespread. However, Aristotle denies that non-human animals have the ability to form what he calls '*doxai*' generally translated as 'opinions' or 'beliefs'.[7] In *De Anima* III.3, Aristotle argues that opinion requires conviction (*pistis*) and that conviction requires reason (*logos*) (428a18–23). Since non-human animals do not possess reason, they are incapable of opinion or thought.[8] Animals do possess perception and perceptual imagination (*aisthētikē phantasia*), which is a capacity for the formation of sensory appearances even in the absence of an external object currently affecting the perceptual organ. Imagination differs from opinion because the former does not involve the kind of conviction that arises from being rationally persuaded. It is easiest to understand what Aristotle means by conviction and persuasion here, by looking at a case in which someone has an opinion that conflicts with how things appear. Aristotle notes that the sun appears to be quite small. However, most people presented with this appearance still have the true belief (*hupolēpsis*) that the sun is very large. Human beings have the capacity to reflect on the representational purport of an appearance and to deny (or to affirm) that the appearance accurately represents world. Furthermore, they can be convinced that the world is other than it appears to be. Non-human animals do not have this capacity.

In addition to the fact that belief requires conviction, I suspect that Aristotle takes belief to have a different sort of content than perception. One of the most striking differences between human and non-human animals is that only human beings possess a capacity for language, and this capacity for language is closely related to the capacity for reason and thought. In his *De Interpretatione*, Aristotle claims that spoken words are signs of affections in the soul which, in turn, are likenesses of things in the world. Aristotle also refers to these affections in the soul as 'thoughts' (*noēmata*), and he distinguishes simple thoughts from complex thoughts in which these simples are combined.

Simple thoughts are akin to names and verbs taken in isolation and are not truth-evaluable. Some complex thoughts are akin to truth-evaluable assertions in natural language in which names and verbs are combined. The proper combination of simple thoughts thus yields truth-evaluable propositional content. This content can be the object of conviction which yields opinion, and these opinions can be expressed in spoken and written language. Non-human animals are incapable not only of language, but of the sorts of thoughts that language is used to express.

The difference between human and non-human animals seems especially clear in the case of thoughts that signify universals. Consider the case of the opinion that a particular stone is white and the assertion that expresses this opinion. Both the term 'white' and the simple thought of which it is a sign indicate something universal, that is, something of a sort to be predicated of many things. Aristotle, however, denies that animals possess such universal thoughts. Furthermore, as we will see below, Aristotle thinks that even human animals need to do a good deal of work in order to come to possess universal concepts. Even before she comes to have a universal concept, however, Aristotle is willing to credit a person with perceptual and experiential knowledge.

While perceptual knowledge does not involve opinion, we can locate a structural similarity between perceptual knowledge and the sort of knowledge that is unavailable to non-human animals. Furthermore, this structural similarity justifies the claim that perceptual knowledge is a sort of knowledge that epistemologists do and should take seriously. For the structural similarity to work, we need to take cases of perception as well as cases of imagination to be cases in which a subject is presented with an appearance. Appearances are sometimes accurate and sometimes inaccurate. When Aristotle talks about perception as a form of knowledge, however, he is talking about the activity of perceiving which is always veridical. Perceptions are accurate appearances. Furthermore, perceptions are not coincidentally or accidentally accurate. Rather, they are accurate because they are the result of the proper exercise of our perceptual capacities. I discuss Aristotle's notion of proper exercise of a capacity in more detail below.

I have already argued that Aristotle takes non-human animals to be capable of knowledge that does not involve opinion. We might think, however, that opinion is necessary for the forms of knowledge proper to human beings. In *Posterior Analytics* I.33, however, Aristotle tells us that opinion and understanding are set over different sorts of objects:

(T5) The understandable and understanding are different from the opinable and opinion *(doxa)*, because understanding is universal and arises through what is necessary, and the necessary is what cannot be otherwise. But there are things that are true and are the case, but which can be otherwise. It is clear that there is not understanding of these things, since then what cannot be otherwise would be capable of being otherwise. Nor is there comprehension of them (by comprehension I mean the principle of understanding), i.e. there is not indemonstrable understanding of them which is belief in an immediate proposition. But comprehension, understanding and opinion (as well as the things called after these) are the things that are true. The remaining possibility, therefore, is that opinion concerns what is true or false but which could be otherwise. And this (opinion) is belief (*hupolēpsis*) in an immediate proposition that is not necessary. (88b30–89a4)[9]

Aristotle here characterizes both opinion and comprehension in terms of *hupolēpsis*. There is good reason to take Aristotle's use of '*hupolēpsis*' to correspond fairly closely to our notion of belief. In *De Anima* III.3, he claims that understanding, opinion, and practical wisdom (*phronēsis*), as well as their opposites, are all kinds of *hupolēpsis* (427b24–6). What exactly Aristotle means by the opposites of belief, understanding, and practical wisdom is a bit unclear. A bit earlier (427b8–11), he tells us that thinking (*noein*) can be correct or incorrect. Understanding, practical wisdom, and true belief are forms of correct thinking, and the opposites of these are forms of incorrect thinking. I suggest that 427b24–6 is trying to make the same point about *hupolēpsis*. The correct or true forms of *hupolēpsis* will include understanding, practical wisdom, and true opinion. The incorrect of false forms of *hupolēpsis* will include false opinions concerning contingent matters as well as false beliefs that a person takes to be necessary. Each of the varieties of belief that Aristotle talks about will be unavailable to non-human animals, and will involve thoughts of the kind Aristotle discusses in the *De Interpretatione*. These beliefs admit of truth and falsity, and are expressed by assertions in natural language. Opinion (*doxa*) is a subkind of belief (*hupolēpsis*), in which the content is not taken to be necessary. Understanding and comprehension (and their opposites), however, belong to a different subkind of belief in which a subject takes the content of her belief to be necessary.

I noted above that Aristotle takes practical wisdom and craft knowledge to involve knowledge concerning things that could be otherwise. In *Nicomachean Ethics* VI.1, Aristotle claims that there are two parts of the soul that possess reason. We contemplate things that cannot be otherwise with one of these parts, which Aristotle calls 'the understanding part' (*to epistēmonikon*). We consider things that can be otherwise with a part that he refers to as 'the calculating part' (*to logistikon*) or 'the opining part' (*to doxastikon*). The function of both these parts of the soul is to grasp the truth concerning their objects, and Aristotle claims that each part comes to possess knowledge (*gnōsis*) by becoming like its proper objects. Knowledge of contingent truths plays a vital role in both practical wisdom and craft expertise, and Aristotle identifies practical wisdom

152 *Knowledge in Ancient Philosophy*

as an excellence of the opining part of the soul. This contingent knowledge also plays a vital role in the development of understanding and comprehension.

We are now in a position to give a rough taxonomy of the various sorts of knowledge that Aristotle accepts, and we can identify some of the conditions that are necessary for each type. We can begin with the perceptual knowledge that is available to non-human animals.

(Perceptual Knowledge) A creature has perceptual knowledge of some fact only if (i) it has an appearance that represents that fact as obtaining and (ii) the appearance is accurate.

Perceptual knowledge involves appearance rather than belief. The content of an appearance in non-conceptual and does not involve thoughts. Each of the other kinds of knowledge that we will consider requires belief, where belief requires both conviction and the sort of content that we find in complex thoughts. I will use 'that Φ' clauses in my subsequent discussion of beliefs and the cognitive states that involve beliefs. We can begin with opinion.

(Opinion) A person has an opinion that Φ only if (i) she believes that Φ and (ii) does not take it to be necessary that Φ.
(Contingent Knowledge) A person has contingent knowledge that Φ only if (i) she believes that Φ, (ii) it is true that Φ, and (iii) she does not take it to be necessary that Φ.

Contingent knowledge seems to encompass a pretty broad range of cases. In some cases, contingent knowledge will simply involve a conceptually articulated belief that represents what a person perceives. When my dog sees a black ball, he has an accurate appearance of the black ball and thus has perceptual knowledge. Having this accurate appearance, however, does not require that he have any concept of blackness. When I see a black ball I have perceptual knowledge involving the same sort of non-conceptual content. However, I can go on to form the belief or opinion that the ball is black. This opinion does require that I have a thought that represents the universal blackness. In a typical case, I will also come to have contingent knowledge that the ball is black. The conditions above do not give us the resources to distinguish true opinion from contingent knowledge. I suggest below that the story will be similar to that suggested in the case of perceptual knowledge. A person will have contingent knowledge because her true opinions are warranted by being the result of the exercise of capacities that aim constitutively at true beliefs about contingent matters. Before turning to a discussion of warrant, however,

Aristotle: From Perception to Understanding 153

it will be useful to give a preliminary characterization of understanding and comprehension.

(Understanding) A person understands that Φ only if (i) she believes that Φ, (ii) it is true that Φ, (iii) she takes it to be necessary that Φ, (iv) it is necessary that Φ, and (v) she has a demonstration that Φ is the case proceeding from first principles that she comprehends.

(Comprehension) A person comprehends that Φ only if (i) she believes that Φ, (ii) it is true that Φ, (iii) she takes it to be necessary that Φ, (iv) it is necessary that Φ, and (v) she properly takes the fact that Φ to be an indemonstrable first principle.

In the case of understanding we do have some account of the sort of warrant involved – the sort of warrant that a demonstrative argument produces. In the other cases, we have said very little. I turn to this task in the next section.

3. Externalism and teleological naturalism

Aristotle is best understood as having broadly externalist and reliabilist views about warrant. His view is externalist in the sense that a person need not have access to all of the features that play a role in warranting her belief.[10] Furthermore, our being warranted in at least some of our beliefs will not be a result of our having an articulable reason for that belief. Rather, our being warranted is a result of the fact that these beliefs come to be in a way that reliably tracks the truth. Very roughly, a person knows that Φ because she has a true belief that Φ which comes to be, at least in part, as a result of its being the case that Φ, and she would not have believed that Φ had it not been the case that Φ. Furthermore, on Aristotle's view, these beliefs come to be as a result of the proper exercise of faculties that naturally and constitutively aim at the accurate representation of the world. A person will have knowledge that Φ only if she has a true belief that Φ which results from the proper exercise of her various truth-aimed cognitive faculties.

Aristotle's epistemology is also naturalistic. He assumes that knowledge is the natural result of our interaction with the world, and he does not seem much concerned with sceptical challenges to our knowledge claims. Rather, he aims to give a careful discussion of the various biological and psychological processes by which we typically come to have knowledge. In thinking through Aristotle's brand of epistemological naturalism, it is essential to remember that

154   *Knowledge in Ancient Philosophy*

his understanding of biology is thoroughly teleological. A proper understanding of any organism crucially involves grasping that organism's end (*telos*). This end is the successful achievement of the various activities that are characteristic of that organism's form of life. We understand the nature of a dog, for example, when we understand the activities involved in living a successful canine life. Furthermore, we fully understand various features of dogs, say their physiology or social behaviour, only in relation to the role these features play in living the successful canine life. In Aristotle's view, organisms are naturally endowed with the capacities necessary for their characteristic activities, and organisms will, for the most part and in the right circumstances, naturally exercise these capacities in the course of living their lives.

The notion of a successful life is important here. While survival and reproduction are certainly important, we saw in (T4) that Aristotle does not take survival and reproduction to exhaust the animal's natural function. Rather, for an animal to realize its function is for it to come to have perceptual knowledge through the natural exercise of its perceptual capacities. For the animal to exercise its perceptual capacities, however, is for it to get certain things right about the world.

Aristotle's account of seeing serves as an excellent example of his teleological naturalism. Aristotle claims that the proper object of sight is colour and that sight is either infallible with respect to colour or not very prone to error when it comes to colour.[11] Aristotle takes colours to be real intrinsic properties of objects in the world.[12] By virtue of having the colours that they do, objects have an active capacity to affect the souls of sighted creatures. By virtue of having the sorts of souls that they do, creatures have a correlative passive capacity to be affected by the colours of objects. When a thing with the active capacity comes into contact with a thing with the correlative passive capacity, in the proper circumstances and in the absence of interfering conditions, both these capacities are exercised.[13] The organism sees – that is, it takes on the visible form of the object without its matter – and the visible properties of the object are seen.[14]

The natural exercise of the capacity to see is the accurate representation of certain features of the world. In Aristotle's view we fully and properly understand a capacity only in relation to the activity that counts as the capacity's proper exercise. Furthermore, capacity and activity come in layers. The activation of a lower-level capacity can itself be a capacity in relation to a further activity. For example, the eye, taken as a material organ, grounds a first-level activity consisting in an organism's possessing a psychological power, the power of sight.

The power of sight is itself a capacity that is further exercised when we actually see something.[15] On Aristotle's view activity or actuality is metaphysically and epistemologically prior to capacity or potentiality.[16] What it is to be a given capacity just is to be the capacity for a given activity, while the converse is not the case. Furthermore, we understand a capacity only in terms of the corresponding activity while the converse is not the case. So, we understand what the eye is only in terms of its role in giving an animal the capacity to see, and we understand the capacity to see only in terms of actual seeing. But seeing involves accurately taking on the visible form of an object without its matter. The accuracy of the vision is thus worked into Aristotle's full and proper biological account of sighted animals.

What distinguishes animals from plants, according to Aristotle, is the fact that they have the capacity to perceive. Animals, however, are not simply plants that happen to have perception. Instead, the ability to perceive goes along with a type of life that is distinctive of animals. For an animal to live its life is for the animal to take in information about the world and to deploy this information in directing its behaviour. In most cases this information will be used to shape the way in which the animal moves through the world. For an animal to be successful in living its life is for it both to take on accurate information about the world through its perceptual faculties and to respond to this information in an appropriate way.

It is instructive to contrast Aristotle's account with an attempt to ground the reliability of our perceptual faculties in natural selection. While accurate perceptual representations might increase the evolutionary fitness of an organism, so might certain kinds of systematically inaccurate representations. For example, an animal might be better at avoiding predators if it incorrectly represents them as being closer than they are. Whether or not a perceptual faculty is reliably accurate thus comes apart from whether it conduces to survival, and selection favours increased survival rather than accuracy. On Aristotle's view, however, the fact that an animal's perceptual capacities are reliably accurate is internal to his account of the animal's natural function.

The fact that our perceptual faculties aim at truth does not mean that they are infallible. While Aristotle claims that the senses are authoritative with respect to their proper objects, he does not take this to show that we are never mistaken about the perceptual qualities of objects. In *Metaphysics* Γ.5, he denies that all appearances are equally true. The fact that some wine appears bitter to a sick person and sweet to a healthy person does not show that there is no truth about the sweetness of the wine or that the wine in both sweet and

156 *Knowledge in Ancient Philosophy*

bitter. Nor does it show that sweetness and bitterness are simply properties relative to perceivers. Rather, in response to this sort of problem of conflicting appearances, Aristotle writes:

> (T6) Again, it is fair to express surprise at our opponents for raising the question whether magnitudes are as great, and colours are of such a nature, as they appear to people at a distance, or as they appear to those close at hand, and whether they are such as they appear to the sick or to the healthy … and whether truth is what appears to the sleeping or to the waking. (*Metaphysics* Γ.5 1010b1–9)

In response to what looks like the beginnings of a sceptical problem, Aristotle simply takes it to be obvious that the waking, healthy, and nearby person gets things right. The sick person gets things wrong because her sickness interferes with the proper function of her faculty of taste. We need to distinguish the failure of a capacity to be exercised with the exercise of a different capacity. The wine does not exercise a capacity to taste bitter to sick people when a sick person drinks it. Nor does the sick person exercise a correlative capacity when she drinks the wine. There simply are no such capacities. The exercise of a perceptual capacity involves getting things right about the world. Cases of misperception are cases in which some chance element interferes with the natural exercise of a capacity.[17] Furthermore, Aristotle does not talk about cases such as veridical hallucinations in which an accurate appearance arises from some process other that the natural exercise of the perceptual capacities.[18]

We are now in a position to see the sort of story that Aristotle can tell about warrant in the case of perceptual knowledge. An animal has perceptual knowledge by having an accurate appearance that arises as a result of the natural exercise of its perceptual capacities. When an appearance does not arise from the natural exercise of its perceptual capacities, an animal fails to have perceptual knowledge. Usually these appearances will fail to be accurate and the animal will be misperceiving the situation. Furthermore, cases of misperception might not even be particularly rare. Aristotle suggests that the soul spends a good deal of its time in error that involves false appearance (*De Anima* 427a31ff). However, these errors get corrected as a healthy animal continues to exercise its perceptual capacities. An animal gets the colour of an object wrong when it is far away from the object but comes to perceive the colour correctly when it gets closer. Perceptual errors are corrected by further perception, and what seems to have the most legitimate claim on reliability is not the process by which each individual momentary appearance is produced, but the continual functioning of the perceptual system over time. Animals are warranted in acting on perceptual appearances that remain stable over time because they are naturally constituted in a way that makes it very likely that these appearances will be accurate.

Animals navigate the world by responding to their appearances. While appearances can play a similar role in shaping human behaviour, they can also lead to the formation of beliefs. These beliefs can then play a role in various types of reasoning, for example, in deliberation about how to act, or in inductive or deductive arguments about what else one should believe. In human beings, therefore, part of the function of perception is to lead us to form true beliefs.

In *Topics* I.11, Aristotle points out that only certain cases of puzzlement are properly resolved by argument. In other cases, he claims that the person who is puzzled needs perception or punishment rather than argument. For example, the person who is puzzled about whether to honor the gods or to care for his parents needs punishment and the person who is puzzled about whether snow is white needs perception (105a2–7). In denying that such people need an argument, Aristotle indicates that perception should be able to settle certain questions directly. In human beings, the exercise of the perceptual capacities will immediately result in beliefs about the objects in the world. We have a strong prima facie warrant for these beliefs because of the accuracy of the perceptual capacities and the reliability of the process by which perception leads to such beliefs in a human subject.

In cases where my perceptions are not accurate or where reliance on my senses leads to false beliefs, Aristotle will hold that something has interfered with the proper exercise of my capacities. As noted above, Aristotle also seems to think that cases of misperception, false appearance, and the resultant false belief will generally be corrected. In some cases, this correction will occur because I come to have accurate perceptions. For example, I believe that a thing has one shape when I am far away but change my belief when I get closer. In other cases, I will have come to have further beliefs that will break the causal link between appearance and belief. For example, a stick looks bent but I notice that it is in water and refuse to form the belief that it is bent. Even in cases where there is error, Aristotle takes the proper function of our capacities to include mechanisms of correction. We are likely to end up with true singular beliefs by using our senses in the proper circumstances. We are even more likely, however, to weed out false beliefs over time. Furthermore, these true singular beliefs play a vital role in our realization of the human end. First, these beliefs are crucially involved in deliberation about how to act and are vital to our exercise of practical wisdom. Second, these beliefs form the foundation of our theoretical pursuits. In

158   *Knowledge in Ancient Philosophy*

the next section, I will examine Aristotle's discussion of how understanding and comprehension come to be for human beings.

4. Understanding and comprehension

Aristotle takes the search for understanding to begin with what is more familiar to us and to proceed to what is more familiar by nature. Particular objects of perception are most familiar to us. Universals, however, are initially less familiar to us but are most familiar by nature (*Posterior Analytics* II.2). We have already seen that Aristotle takes understanding and comprehension to concern necessary relations between universals. Furthermore, we have seen that understanding any of the theorems of a science presupposes comprehension of the first principles of that science.

In *Posterior Analytics* II.19 and *Metaphysics* I.1, Aristotle outlines a process that begins with perception and ends with comprehension and understanding. His discussions of this process are quite compressed. Furthermore, there are at least three different things that Aristotle needs to explain. First, he needs to explain the way in which we come to have general concepts. I argued above that such concepts will be necessary even for the beliefs about particulars that we base directly on perception. Second, Aristotle needs to explain the way in which we come to have the knowledge of the fact that we then seek to explain by finding the correct principle. Third, Aristotle needs to explain how we come to have comprehension of the principles by virtue of which we know the reason why. These three tasks are closely linked in Aristotle's discussion and can be difficult to tease apart.

It will be useful to start with an extensive quotation of the texts from *Posterior Analytics* II.19 and *Metaphysics* I.1 in which Aristotle summarizes the process by which perception leads to further cognitive achievements.

(T7) For all animals have an inborn discriminatory capacity which is called perception. Given that perception is present, for some animals there comes to be a retention of the percept, while for others this does not come to be. For those in which there is no retention, there is no knowledge outside of perception ... But in the case of some of those perceiving, it is possible are able to hold what is perceived in the soul. When such thing has happened many times, there is a difference: an account (*logos*) comes to be for some of them from the retention of such things, but not for others. So, from perception memory comes to be, as we say, and from repeated memory of the same thing

Aristotle: From Perception to Understanding 159

experience comes to be. For a single experience comes from memories that are many in number. And from experience, or from the whole universal having become fixed in the soul, from the one beside the many which is one and the same in those things, comes to be the principle of art and understanding: of art if it is about what comes to be, of understanding if it is about what is. (*Posterior Analytics* 99b35–100a9)

(T8) By nature animals are born having perception. Memory does not arise out of perception for some of them, but it does arise for others. And because of this, the latter are more intelligent and capable of learning than the ones that are not capable of remembering ... The other animals live by appearances and memory, but have only a small share of experience, but human kind lives also by art and reasoning. In human beings experience arises out of memory. For many memories of the same thing produce in the end a capacity for a single experience. And experience seems to closely resemble art and science, but art and science come to men through experience ... And art comes to be, when from attending to experience many times there comes to be a single universal judgment concerning similar objects. For to have a belief that when Callias was ill with this disease this did him good, and similarly in the case of Socrates and many individual cases, belongs to experience; but to judge that it has done good to all such people, distinguished as being of a single kind, when they were ill with this disease – for example, to the phlegmatic or the bilious ones who were ill with a fever – belongs to art (*technê*). (*Metaphysics* I.1.980a27–981a12)

While perception relates us to particulars, Aristotle holds that universals are already present in a nascent form in perception. Say, for example, that we look at Callias and come to have a visual representation. This representation is of the individual Callias or his visible features, but the character of the visual appearance is not the way it is because this individual is being represented. What properly matters to vision is the distribution of colour and the various visible features of Callias, not that Callias is this particular individual.[19] Our visual appearance would have been exactly the same were it caused by something other than Callias as long as that thing had the same distribution of visible features. The particular distribution of visible features, call it being Callias-looking, is something that could, at least in principle, be present in a variety of things. Various colour universals and universals corresponding to sensible properties characterize the particular perception of Callias.

While the proper object of sight is a particular distribution of colour, Aristotle thinks that Callias, the particular human being, is an incidental object of sight. This is not simply because this colourful object happens to be a human being,

160   *Knowledge in Ancient Philosophy*

but because sight allows us to detect the presence of instances of humanity rather than simply instances of colour. Colour is the proper object of sight because we see an incidental object such as Callias or this human being *by* seeing colour. In addition to colour universals and universals ranging over his properly visible features, the universal *human being* is already present in Callias, and is already, if only in a nascent and indeterminate way, represented in our first visual impression of Callias. Everything that is going on thus far seems to be something that we share with other sighted animals. The additional steps in the process that Aristotle outlines above involve the universal coming to be present in the soul in an increasingly determinate way, until a fully explicit general concept arises. This is the simple thought that will be deployed in belief, opinion, and propositionally articulated knowledge.

In some animals, perceptual affections are retained in the soul even when the animal has stopped perceiving. These animals have the power of memory in addition to the power of perception. In an animal that only has access to present perceptions, there can be no shaping of the animal's future behaviour by past events. In an animal with memory, however, such shaping of the animal's behaviour by the environment is possible. The first time a puppy sees a cat he runs over to investigate and gets scratched. The older dog will then have a getting-scratched memory appearance going along with a cat-looking memory appearance. When he perceives a cat, the similarity of the present cat appearance to the memory appearance will result in his being more wary. On Aristotle's account all of this is possible without the dog's having any *noemata* which are the kinds of thought corresponding to language.

What differentiates human animals from non-human animals is the way in which repeated memories can lead to thought. In both the passages quoted above, Aristotle claims that repeated memories of the same thing first lead to a single experience. Experience then leads to the presence of the universal in the soul, at which point the person possesses the universal thoughts necessary for belief.

This process seems to involve a shift in kinds of content. Aristotle conceives of memories as imagistic likenesses of the perceptions in which they have their origin. In the animal without experience, memories can be similar to one another either because they have the same perceptual origin or because they originate in similar perceptions. However, each memory will be tied back to the particular object that was involved in the original perception and will represent that particular object.

There is a transition when a person goes from having a multitude of similar memories to having a single experience. The single experience still concerns particulars. But it bears a different kind of representational relation to the particulars than the multitude of memories do. The content of the single experience does not seem to be tied to any one of the objects that we perceived in opposition to any other. Furthermore, the single experience seems to involve a degree of abstraction from the particular memories. Imagine the single experience as something like a scale model of a prefabricated house. We construct the model after having perceived many examples of this sort of house. The model functions as a representation of each qualitatively indistinguishable house without being a model of any one of them in particular. It represents the various particular houses indifferently. Furthermore, looking at the model will turn out to be useful when we run into any new house of the same kind. We'll be able to navigate the new house by attending to the model.

The doctor who has experience but lacks craft is in a similar position. He has various memories of people who had a disease with these perceptible symptoms and who were cured by a certain treatment. Each individual memory will be a copy of the perceptions that the doctor had with an individual patient, and will represent what happened to that patient. Because of the perceptible similarities between the cases, the doctor also comes to have a single experience in which the situation with each patient is represented indifferently. When a new case of the disease comes up in which the perceptible features are like those in the experiential model, the doctor will be able to act correctly. Up to this point, the doctor need not have any representation that involves a universal thought of the specific disease that ailed Callias and Socrates.

The representation of the universal arises when the person is able to mark off all of the particular cases represented in perception, memory, and experience as belonging to a single kind. In this marking off of the cases, the universal comes to be present in the soul as one thing apart from the many instances that is the same in all of them. The shift here involves going from a single experience that indifferently represents the many particular instances to having a thought that represents the single universal that is present in each of those instances.

What we have so far is an account of how a human being comes to have universal thoughts that correspond to the universal features that are present in the world. Aristotle is a realist about which universal features are present in the world. He also thinks that the human end involves the accurate discernment and representation of these features. The process by which we go from perception to a grasp of the universal involves the successive activation of various cognitive capacities that naturally aim at an accurate representation of the structure of world.[20]

A person that has the ability to have universal thought also gains the ability to form the complex thoughts that are the contents of belief. When a human being sees a black ball, she will also come to have the belief that the ball is black. Coming to have accurate beliefs of this sort is a crucial step in the realization of the human end, and these beliefs will constitute knowledge. A person with these beliefs also has the ability to deploy these beliefs in inductive and deductive reasoning. In many cases, knowing the universal fact that needs to be explained comes about as a result of induction.[21] Just as repeated perceptual exposure to a kind of thing leads to the ability to have simple universal thoughts, inductive reasoning from many beliefs about particulars of a certain kind will lead to universal beliefs. These universal beliefs will count as knowledge of the facts that we seek to understand because they have come to be by the proper exercise of our various cognitive capacities.

However, more is needed for us to have comprehension and understanding. It is not enough for our thoughts correctly to represent the universal features in the world as a result of a process that begins with perception and proceeds through induction. Rather, we need to demonstrate various necessary connections between universals from first principles that we comprehend. To comprehend a first principle is to grasp the essence of a kind or to grasp an indemonstrable necessary relationship between kinds. The sort of grasp that a person has of a universal when she knows that a fact obtains need not be a full grasp of the essence.[22] For example, a person can have the ability to recognize an eclipse and the ability to classify all and only eclipses as belonging to a single kind without yet knowing the essential nature of the eclipse. She might even know that eclipses happen with a certain sort of regularity and be able to predict when the next eclipse will be. Coming to comprehend the essential nature of the eclipse is an explanatory project.

Imagine that a person has already come to have thoughts that track certain astronomical features of the world correctly. She can recognize lunar eclipses and properly identifies them as being of a single kind. She also has had plenty of experience with light and shadows. She already has a good deal of knowledge as a result of perception and induction. First, she knows that the moon periodically suffers eclipses in which it loses its light. Second, she knows that opaque objects cast shadows when they are interposed between a light source and another object. She wants an explanation of the fact that the moon periodically undergoes eclipse. As she searches for the explanation she comes to believe that the sort of loss of light involved in the eclipse is a case of a thing falling into shadow, rather than, say, an extinguishing of a fire. She knows that the eclipse is not just any

Aristotle: From Perception to Understanding 163

sort of loss of light, but is loss of light of the enshadowing variety. She knows that shadows come about when something opaque comes between a light source and an object. She tries to figure out what the light source and the interposing opaque object could be. Eventually, she figures out that the light source is the sun and that the interposing object is the earth. She also comes to know that this interposition is the cause of the loss of light that we observe in cases of eclipse. Our astronomer has now found the proper explanatory middle term for her scientific demonstration, that is, interposition of the earth between the sun and moon. Furthermore, she knows that the middle term explains the moon's loss of light. As a result, she is in the position to produce a demonstration.[23]

1. The enshadowing sort of loss of light belongs to all things that suffer interposition.
2. Suffering interposition of the earth between it and the sun belongs to all cases of the eclipsed moon.
3. Therefore, the enshadowing sort of loss of light belongs to all cases of the eclipsed moon.

Assume that (1) and (2) cannot be demonstrated from more basic premises, and that our astronomer grasps that they cannot be. At this point, Aristotle takes her to understand the conclusion expressed in (3) and to comprehend (1) and (2). Remember that Aristotle takes understanding and comprehension to be about things that cannot be otherwise. It is interesting to consider what sort of necessity he takes to be involved in cases of scientific demonstration. In comprehending (2) Aristotle takes us to grasp the essential nature of the eclipse. For the moon to be eclipsed just is for the moon to suffer interposition. The necessity in (1) might similarly involve understanding the essential nature of shadows. In the case of (2), we came to grasp the essence as a result of our search for an explanation of (3). In the case of (1), however, it seems that we come to grasp a certain kind of natural necessity as a result of perception and induction. Repeated exposure to opaque objects, light sources, and shadows leads us to know not only that all objects of a certain sort do cast shadows, but also that it couldn't be otherwise.

What we have here is only a sketch of how perception and a host of other human cognitive capacities can be exercised to provide a way that leads eventually to comprehension and understanding. What is essential for an understanding of Aristotle's epistemology is that comprehension and understanding do result from the proper exercise of these capacities. Furthermore, we have these capacities because our natural end essentially involves their exercise. We have

164   *Knowledge in Ancient Philosophy*

these capacities because of the role they serve in allowing us to obtain wisdom and to exercise this wisdom in the contemplation of eternal truths.

Notes

1   Burnyeat (1981) is the *locus classicus* of the view that *epistēmē haplōs* is understanding rather than simple knowledge.
2   For an illuminating discussion of Aristotle's epistemic vocabulary, see Burnyeat (1981, 2011) and the works cited therein. The discussion in Barnes (1993) is also very helpful on this topic and many others arising from a study of the *Posterior Analytics*.
3   The translations in this chapter come from Barnes (1984), although they have been modified in several instances. The translation of passages from the *Posterior Analytics* also relies heavily on Barnes (1993) and Ross (1949).
4   It is worth noting in that the word '*epistēmē*' can also be used, like the English word 'science', as a count-noun like the English word 'science' for an explanatorily unified branch of knowledge; for example, 'Biology is a science.'
5   Aristotle claims that craft (*technē*) is 'a state accompanying true reason concerned with production (1140a9-10)', and that practical wisdom (*phronēsis*) is 'a true state accompanying reason concerned with action regarding human goods' (1140b20-1). Both practical wisdom and craft are states that are essentially related to truth. Both of them involve epistemic success. However, neither should be straightforwardly identified with propositional knowledge. For one thing both involve the ability to reason properly to a conclusion regarding what should be made or done in a given circumstance. What is important for present purposes, however, is simply that Aristotle takes the practically wise person and the master craftsman to know various things about contingent matters. This knowledge cannot be understanding or comprehension.
6   I am following the text of Peck (1953) and my translation relies on his.
7   A few notes are in order here. First, I will use 'opinion' rather than 'belief' as a translation for Aristotle's use of '*doxa*'. Part of the reason for this choice is that Aristotle takes *doxai* to concern only matters that can be otherwise. However, he uses the word '*hupolēpsis*' to include both opinions and beliefs about necessary matters. Part of my contention in this chapter is that we should identify *hupolēpsis* with belief and take opinions (*doxai*) to belong to a subcategory of belief. This does not change Aristotle's point about animals, however, because Aristotle denies that animals have *hupolēpsis*. My thinking about these matters owes a lot to discussions with Jessica Moss.
8   I am using 'thought' to capture Aristotle's use of '*phronein*', '*noein*', and '*dianoein*'. I do not think that Aristotle is marking a distinction in his usage of these three terms in *De Anima* III.3. In particular, I do not think that '*phronein*' is here reserved for practical thought.

Aristotle: From Perception to Understanding 165

9 It can be useful to compare Aristotle's treatment of opinion and understanding with Plato's. In the *Meno*, Socrates claims that true opinion becomes knowledge (*epistēmē*) when tied down by an explanatory account. Similarly in the *Theaetetus* Socrates considers the position according to which knowledge (*epistēmē*) is true belief with an account. In the *Republic*, however, Socrates suggests that opinion and knowledge (*epistēmē*) are distinct capacities set over different objects.

10 I put things in terms of belief, but an analogous story can be told for the warrant that we have to rely on appearances in cases of perceptual knowledge. For an animal to have perceptual knowledge of the apple's being red, the apple has to be red, the animal has to have a red apple appearance, and the red apple appearance has to be the result of the proper exercise of the animal's perceptual capacities.

11 See *De Anima* 418a12-18, 427b11-13 428b18ff. In addition to proper sensible objects, Aristotle recognizes common and coincidental sensibles. Common sensibles are grasped by more than one sense. For example, shape can be detected by both sight and touch. Coincidental sensibles are entities that are objects of the senses by being coincident with proper sensibles. For example, the son of Diares is a coincidental object of sight by being coincident with an instance of colour that is a proper sensible. Aristotle claims that we are more liable to error in the case of common and coincidental sensibles.

12 We can contrast Aristotle's view about colour with a secondary quality view according to which colours essentially involve relations between the primary qualities of an object and a perceiver. For a careful discussion of Aristotle's views on the nature of colour and of Aristotle's theory of perception, see Everson (1997). With Everson, I think that colour is best seen as an intrinsic property of an external object rather than as the capacity to affect the visual capacity of an organism. This intrinsic property of the external object and the intrinsic properties of the perceptive organism ground the existence of a correlative pair of capacities: a capacity to affect (in the external object) and capacity to be affected (in the organism). When the external object and the organism are placed in suitable circumstances, these capacities are simultaneously activated. For an alternative view, according to which colours are identified with the power to affect the visual capacity, see Marmodoro (2014). For extremely helpful discussions of active and passive capacities, see Beere (2012) and Marmodoro (2014).

13 See *Metaphysics* IX, especially 1047b31-1048a24, for a discussion of capacity and activity.

14 See *De Anima* 424a17ff. What exactly is involved in the sense's taking on the perceptible form without the matter has been a source of great controversy. For an illuminating discussion, see Cohen (1995) and the papers cited therein. The discussions in Everson (1997) and Shields (2016) are also helpful.

15 Aristotle distinguishes first and second actuality in his discussion of the soul in *De Anima* II.1, and claims that the soul is the first actuality of a natural body having

life potentially. Having perceptual capacities is part of what it is to have an animal soul and to live an animal life.

16 See *Metaphysics* IX.8 for a discussion of the priority of activity/actuality to capacity/potentiality.

17 In an important way, misperception is not going to count as an occurrence that happens *by nature*. What happens by nature is what happens always or for the most part. When Aristotle talks about what happens 'for the most part', he means something that involves the realization of a thing's end rather than a mere statistical regularity. Misperception is something that is contrary to nature and which has no teleological explanation. In *Physics* II.5, Aristotle contrasts what happens always or for the most part with what happens by chance.

18 I suspect that Aristotle would take this to be a case of luck. What occurs by luck is what does not occur for the sake of an end but is of the same sort as what does occur for the sake of an end. See Aristotle's discussion in *Physics* II.4–6.

19 Shape is a common rather than a proper sensible, because it is detectable by more than one sense. See Everson (1997) and Marmodoro (2014) for further discussion.

20 The story that Aristotle tells about the acquisition of universal thoughts is extremely individualistic. However, in Book I of his *Politics*, Aristotle emphasizes the social nature of human beings. Furthermore, he claims that the ability to use language is part of what makes human beings political rather than merely social. Aristotle continually emphasizes the role that education plays in the acquisition of ethical virtue and practical wisdom. It is somewhat surprising that he does not allow for a similar role in our coming to track the right universal kinds. We rarely come to represent a kind without relying heavily on instruction by other people who already grasp the kind. I suspect that there is room in Aristotle's account for the role of sociality in the acquisition of theoretical knowledge, but I leave it aside here.

21 'Induction' is the translation of Aristotle's '*epagōgē*'. For a discussion of *epagōgē*, see Hamlyn (1976), Engberg-Pedersen (1979), and Bronstein (2016).

22 For a fuller account of the difference between the sort of knowledge of the universal that we have before and after coming to possess a scientific demonstration, see Bolton (1976) and Charles (2000).

23 For a fuller discussion of Aristotle's scientific method, see Bolton (1987; 1991), Gotthelf (1987), Goldin (1996), Ferejohn (2013), and Bronstein (2016).

References

Barnes, J. (1984), *The Complete Works of Aristotle*, 2 vols, Princeton: Princeton University Press.

Barnes, J. (1993), *Aristotle: Posterior Analytics*, trans. with commentary, 2nd edn, Oxford: Clarendon Press.

Beere, J. (2012), *Doing and Being*, Oxford: Oxford University Press.

Bolton, R. (1976), 'Essentialism and Semantic Theory in Aristotle: *Posterior Analytics*, II.7–10', *Philosophical Review*, 85: 514–44.

Bolton, R. (1987), 'Definition and Scientific Method in Aristotle's *Posterior Analytics* and *Generation of Animals*', in A. Gotthelf and J. Lennox (eds), *Philosophical Issues in Aristotle's Biology*, Cambridge: Cambridge University Press.

Bolton, R. (1991), 'Aristotle's Method in Natural Science: *Physics* I', in L. Judson (ed.), *Aristotle's* Physics: *A Collection of Essays*, Oxford: Clarendon Press.

Bronstein, D. (2016), *Aristotle on Knowledge and Learning*, Oxford: Oxford University Press.

Burnyeat, M. (1981), 'Aristotle on Understanding Knowledge', in E. Berti (ed.), *Aristotle on Science:* The Posterior Analytics, *Proceedings of the Eighth Symposium Aristotelicum*, Padova: Editrice Antenore.

Burnyeat, M. (2011), 'Episteme', in B. Morison and K. Ierodiakonou (eds), *Episteme Etc.: Essays in Honour of Jonathan Barnes*, Oxford: Oxford University Press.

Charles, D. (2000), *Aristotle on Meaning and Essence*, Oxford: Oxford University Press.

Cohen, S. M. (1995), 'Hylomorphism and Functionalism', in M. C. Nussbaum and A. O. Rorty (eds), *Essays on Aristotle's* De Anima, 2nd edn, Oxford: Clarendon Press.

Engberg-Pedersen, T. (1979), 'More on Aristotelian *Epagoge*', *Phronesis*, 24: 301–19.

Everson, S. (1997), *Aristotle on Perception*, Oxford: Oxford University Press.

Ferejohn, M. (2013), *Formal Causes: Definition, Explanation and Primacy in Socratic and Aristotelian Thought*, Oxford: Oxford University Press.

Goldin, O. (1996), *Explaining an Eclipse: Aristotle's* Posterior Analytics 2.1–10, Ann Arbor: University of Michigan Press.

Gotthelf, A. (1987), 'First Principles in Aristotle's *Parts of Animals*', in A. Gotthelf and J. Lennox (eds), *Philosophical Issues in Aristotle's Biology*, Cambridge: Cambridge University Press. Reprinted in A. Gotthelf, *Teleology, First Principles and Scientific Method in Aristotle's Biology*, Oxford: Oxford University Press.

Hamlyn, D. W. (1976), 'Aristotelian *Epagoge*', *Phronesis*, 21: 167–84.

Marmodoro, A. (2014), *Aristotle on Perceiving Objects*, Oxford: Oxford University Press.

Peck, A. L. (1953), *Aristotle: Generation of Animals*, Cambridge, MA: Harvard University Press.

Ross, W. D. (1949), *Aristotle's* Prior *and* Posterior Analytics: *A Revised Text with Introduction and Commentary*, Oxford: Clarendon Press.

Shields, C. (2016), *Aristotle:* De Anima, trans. with commentary, Oxford: Clarendon Press.

9

Epicurean Epistemology

Pierre-Marie Morel

1. Introduction

The Epicureans' foremost claim about knowledge and science is that sensation is the first criterion of truth. In their mind, it means not only that each belief, judgement, or opinion should be assessed from sensation and evaluated in light of common experience, but also that sensation itself is always true. Similarly, affections (*pathē*) of pleasure and pain are criteria in the practical sphere, because they indicate immediately what is pleasant or painful in a given time and, consequently, what is to be pursued or avoided. Falsity and illusions are brought about by our judgements and opinions regarding what is perceived or conceived, and not by sensation itself. An uncontrolled use of reasoning, or the false assumption that reason can govern itself apart from the senses, would necessarily jeopardize one's ability to reach true knowledge. At first sight, then, Epicurean epistemology appears as a mere empiricism. In fact, one of its main features is a deep mistrust of reason as such.

Nevertheless, Epicureans do not give up the idea of elaborating a real and consistent epistemology, based on a complex methodology of judgement. They do not even reject 'ideas', taken as general and common notions or simple thoughts. Such 'ideas' are neither intelligible entities existing in an intelligible realm, like Platonic ideas, nor pure constructions of our mind apart from experience. After all, even an empiricist philosopher may admit, without inconsistency, the validity of this kind of 'idea', since each of us, in everyday life, resorts to general representations, like time, being, human being, and so on. Indeed one may consider that the word 'ideas' can be applied to a wide range of cognitive states, as does John Locke at the beginning of the *Essay Concerning Human Understanding* (1.1, Intro. sec. 8). Moreover, the Epicureans think that some notions, 'preconceptions' (*prolēpseis*) according to them, have a status, which is similar to that of sensations and affections (pleasure and pain), insofar as they reveal, immediately and without ambiguity, what they are related to: the preconception of 'human being' is a reliable representation or idea of what this or that particular human being is. Last, they develop a global world view, beyond ordinary experience, a comprehensive explanation of the physical world, which necessarily involves judgements about *adēla*, that is: non-perceptible things and principles, like atoms and void. Now, this is not a secondary task for the Epicureans. This project coincides with the ultimate goal of their philosophy as a whole: the ethical perspective of psychic *ataraxia*, absence of disturbance.

Taken that way, the question is not whether Epicureans are empiricist philosophers – they definitely are empiricists – but which kind of empiricists they are. If they are not radical empiricists, who would not admit any true knowledge but sensation, are they 'ashamed' empiricists, who are in contradiction with their own principles because they are led to admit non-empirical beliefs and representations? Ancient critics of Epicureanism, especially Cicero and Plutarch, could lead us down one of these roads, because they point out what they denounce as inconsistencies in Epicureanism and because they aim at its alleged incompetence in logic and epistemology. Actually, Epicureanism is rather a sort of rational empiricism, which fully legitimates the use of reason, in accordance with experience. This reading is probably the most fruitful, if one aims to understand the twofold goal of the Epicurean epistemology: to give a strong basis (at the same time empirical and logical) to our scientific hypothesis and claims, on the one hand, and to reach a reassuring world view which contributes to the pursuit of happiness, on the other.

2. The Epicurean tradition and our sources on Epicurean epistemology

The philosophical tradition founded by Epicurus (341–270 BCE) is one of the most homogeneous of antiquity, although a certain evolution may be observed after the first period of the Garden (Epicurus' school, founded around 306–305 in the immediate environs of Athens). This evolution is due to successive polemics (especially against sceptics and Stoics), historical conditions, and the literary and philosophical temperament of authors, particularly Lucretius in his Poem *On the Nature of Things* (*De Rerum Natura*; quoted below: *DRN*). Nonetheless, the doctrine remains basically the same until Diogenes of Oenoanda, the last Epicurean in Antiquity (second century CE). The Epicureans refer constantly and with great respect to their first teacher. Epicurus wrote a considerable body of work, now largely lost. Fortunately, Book 10 of Diogenes Laertius' *Lives and Opinions* contains a 'life of Epicurus' which gives important information on Epicurus himself and the organization of the Garden. It also presents a valuable overview of Epicurean philosophy, which pays particular attention to epistemology (paragraphs 29–34). As we will see later, this passage contains important indications on the criteria of truth and the epistemic function of sensations and preconceptions. Diogenes adds (paragraphs 35–135) the three philosophical texts that constitute the basis of our documentary evidence: the *Letters* to Herodotus (below: *Hdt.*), Pythocles (below: *Pyth.*), and Menoeceus (below: *Men.*). These are followed by forty Principal Maxims, or Key Doctrines (below: *KD*). They focus mainly on ethics, but contain important information about epistemological issues as well, like *KD* 37–38 on the preconception of what is just, or *KD* 24 on the preeminent role of sensation. All the same, let us keep in mind that Diogenes Laertius cites forty-one titles of works by Epicurus and specifies that he is mentioning only his best works (10.27–28). Among these, *On Nature* (*Peri phuseos*), in thirty-seven books, must have been the most important, not only with respect to its volume, but also because it contained a detailed development of thesis, which are only summarized in the *Letters*. We have a few fragments of it, thanks to the excavations at Herculaneum and the papyrological studies based on them.

Despite the strong personality of the founder of the Garden and the traditional orthodoxy of his pupils and heirs, Epicureanism cannot be reduced to Epicurus' own thought. His first-generation disciples – Hermarchus, who succeeded to the headship of the Garden, and after him Colotes, Polystratus, and Metrodorus – contributed to deepening the doctrine. Colotes' criticisms against scepticism, in particular, which are known thanks to Plutarch's treatise *Against Colotes*, reveals that the Epicurean theory of knowledge, after Epicurus, is built up, to some extent at least, against the philosophical tradition as a whole, including Presocratic philosophers (like Parmenides and Democritus), Plato, Socrates, and the sceptics. Colotes, indeed, reduces all these doctrines to scepticism itself, because they cast doubt on our most evident knowledge, like everyday experience. How could anyone be certain, if perception is never reliable, that he is a human being, that fire is dangerous for him, and so on? So doing, they spread confusion in our lives and contribute to psychic disturbance.

The influence of the Athenian Garden gradually extended to such an extent that in the first century BCE, Italy became the site of an important Epicurean revival, thanks to the diffusion of Epicurean ideas in the cultivated circles and to the debates between the great philosophical schools, as depicted in several of Cicero's works like *De finibus bonorum et malorum*, *Tusculana*, *De natura deorum*, or *De fato*. Our main Epicurean witnesses to this phenomenon are Philodemus of Gadara and above all Lucretius (first century BCE). Both of them take part in the epistemological debate and tackle the issues of their time, regarding scientific methodology and the criterion of truth.

Philodemus, a Greek philosopher from Syria, is the author of several treatises dealing with ethics, economics, aesthetics, politics, logic, theology, and the positions of the various philosophical schools. The fragments of his books are preserved in the papyri of Herculaneum and constitute a source that is damaged but very valuable for the historical development of Epicureanism and for its new areas of interest, such as poetry and the history of philosophical movements. He is the author of a treatise 'on signs and inference' (usually mentioned under the title of *De signis*), where he echoes the epistemological debates in which Epicureans face the other schools, especially the Stoics, and he is probably the author, as well, of a treatise on sensation. Moreover, with Philodemus, not only in his epistemological writings but also in other treatises, the preconception seems to acquire a greater importance (Tsouna 2016): in the practical sphere (like economics) it indicates what is good in a given activity (for instance, what is the 'idea' of the good manager, i.e. the sage himself); from the epistemological point of view, it seems to be more closely connected to definition.

Regarding Lucretius, the situation is quite different: we know almost nothing about his life, but we have a continuous text of his poem *On the Nature of Things*, which offers a good idea of his philosophical project. Lucretius himself claims to be a mere translator or imitator of Epicurus (*DRN* 3.6). Actually, his fidelity should not conceal a great formal originality and a genuine intention to elaborate the doctrine on several fundamental points. Lucretius has also to face the philosophers of his time who are declared opponents to the first-period Epicureanism, like Stoics and sceptics. The latter are permanently in the background when epistemological issues are dealt with, as can be seen from Lucretius' anti-sceptical arguments in favour of perception, in Book 4 of his poem. Finally, the fragments of Diogenes of Oenanda's mural inscription, in Lycia, attest to the persistence of the Epicurean tradition until the second century CE, even if they are contemporary with the decrease of its influence in the ancient world. Diogenes of Oenoanda seems to be more concerned, at least in the small

Epicurean Epistemology 173

part of his inscription we know (which amounts to perhaps a fifth of the total), with ethics and physics than with epistemology, but several clear attestations of faithfulness to the Epicurean empiricism and scientific methodology are still to be found there.

3. Sensation as primary evidence

Sensation is always true, according to Epicurus and his followers. As Lucretius puts it, '[W]hatever impression the senses get at any time is true' (*DRN* 4.499). Nonetheless we are often victims of sensory illusions. To say the least, the imprecision of information coming from the senses is commonly noticed. It is even a sort of topos in the history of philosophy. How could it be that sensation is our first criterion of truth?

Epicurean texts offer several arguments to escape this difficulty. Some are based on positive statements, whereas others are inferred from negative arguments. Let us start with the positive arguments in favour of sensation. One of the most elaborated arguments is physical or physiological. The physiological explanation of sensations runs as follows: vision, for example, results from the reception of replicas (*tupoi*) or images (*eidōla*) coming spontaneously from the seen object. Because these transmitted emanations preserve the structure and properties of the object, they produce, in the sensory organs of the perceiver, a representation or appearance (*phantasia*), which remains in 'sympathy' (*sumpatheia*) with the object, that is, with the 'substrate' or 'underlying reality' (*hupokeimenon*), as Epicurus says (*Hdt.* 49–53; see also Lucretius, *DRN* 4.46–268).

One should not believe, however, that sensation is nothing but a physical reception of corpuscular bodies. The sensory impression does not actually become an appearance (*phantasia*) unless we 'grasp [it] by applying ourselves to it through thought or else through the sense organs' (*Hdt.* 50). Sensation, like the mind's perception, entails an *epibolē*, that is, an 'application', or 'focusing' or 'projection' towards the object. The latter is thus not merely received, but also 'aimed at'. Its image is at the same time a projection-of-an-image (*phantastikē epibolē*: *Hdt.* 50-1). Consequently, sensation involves both the physical receptivity that makes it true, and the mental act of attention without which it could not inform us about what we perceive.

Conversely, the appearance is not purely subjective, and even less strictly mental: what we perceive in ourselves, through our sense-organs, is the very result of a physical process. Now, a physical process is something real (i.e.

something true); hence, what happens in sensation is the immediate and reliable attestation of a physical reality. In other words, we perceive something that the object itself brings about, and the process through which we perceive this thing can be described in the same way as any other natural process. Because our sensations are physically similar to their objects, they can be called 'true' prior to any judgement about their truth or falsity. The explanation of the origin of sensations thus leads to an assimilation of truth to reality. In this sense, one may talk about a 'physicalist' and realist conception of truth.

This is not only important for the everyday knowledge and life and for natural experience: the immediate reliability of sensation is also a justification for the appeal to empirical evidence on the epistemological level, for it applies derivatively to representations that are not immediately sensory. Paragraphs 37–8 of Epicurus' *Letter to Herodotus* (Long and Sedley 1987) clearly show that sensations play the role of criteria for scientific investigation, and not only for everyday knowledge:

> First, then, Herodotus, we must grasp the things which underlie words, so that we may have them as a reference point against which to judge matters of opinion, inquiry and puzzlement, and not have everything undiscriminated for ourselves as we attempt infinite chains of proofs, or have words which are empty. For the primary concept corresponding to each word must be seen and need no additional proof, if we are going to have a reference point for matters of inquiry, puzzlement and opinion. Second, we should observe everything in the light of our sensations, and in general in the light of our present focusings whether of thought or of any of our discriminatory faculties, and likewise also in the light of the feelings which exist in us, in order to have a basis for sign-inferences about evidence yet awaited and about the non-evident.

I will come back later to the methodological aspects of this passage. For the moment, let us just notice that sensation is said to be true and reliable, not only within the sphere of practical life and common experience, but also in the epistemological and scientific areas, and this for two reasons. First, sensation corresponds to the necessary limit of the demonstration and demonstrative knowledge, since what is evident, by definition, does not need any further demonstration; so sensation prevents from the *regressus ad infinitum*, the infinite research for a primary cause. Second, as a basis for the method of inference, it constitutes a guarantee for inferences on non-evident (i.e. non-empirical) realities; thus, it is a compulsory step for anyone who wants to grasp the principles (atoms and void), which are below the objects of experience.

Epicurean Epistemology   175

Still, an objection may be raised: If sensation is true right from the start, how are we to account for perceptual errors, hallucinations, or optical illusions? In fact, under non-standard conditions, the abovementioned sympathy of images will only be partial. Let us take the famous example of the square tower: the air that wears down the simulacra is responsible for the effect that, seen from a distance, a tower that is in fact square seems round to us (*DRN* 4.353–63; Sextus Empiricus, *Against the Mathematicians* 7.208–9). This is objectively an illusion: if we assess this image throughout a methodical comparison with better conditions of observation (if the observer is closer, moves around the tower, etc.), it cannot be taken as a reliable information about what is seen. Nevertheless it remains the case that the impression itself is constituted via an immediate sympathy with the flow of simulacra or images, and thus that it is constituted in sympathy with the objective conditions of their production: it is true that the tower appears to be round.

In addition, the Epicureans use negative and defensive arguments in support to sensation as a criterion. Indeed, to say the least, the point is a matter of controversy in Antiquity. Before Epicurus, Democritus had set out many arguments against sensation, particularly regarding our knowledge of the physical reality (see especially: Sextus Empiricus, *Against the Mathematicians* 7.135–9; *Outlines of Pyrrhonism* 1.213–14; Galen, *Elements According to Hippocrates* 1.2; Diog. Laert. 9.72). Now, Epicurus endorses the main thesis of the Democritean physics, according to which atoms and void make up all things. One may reasonably guess that Epicurus' theory of 'sympathy' in *Letter to Herodotus* is a response to this criticism against empirical knowledge. Then the followers of Epicurus had to give responses to new opponents, especially the Academic Sceptics and the Stoics. Lucretius's Fourth Book of *De Rerum Natura* offers a good example of this polemical context. Against the sceptics' classical arguments, Lucretius defends the infallibility of sensations by showing that no sense, such as sight or smell, can be corrected by a different sense: sight cannot be corrected by hearing, or hearing by touch, or touch by taste, since each sense has a particular and distinct power (*DRN* 4.486–90). As for reason, it comes from sensation and so cannot refute it, since it would refute itself in claiming to refute its own origin (*DRN* 4.483–5; see also Diog. Laert. 10.32). We must therefore admit that error comes from some other mental movement distinct from sensation. If I see a square tower in the distance as round, it is not sensation itself that deceives me, but rather my judgement or opinion – that is, the belief I form when I have the sensation (*DRN* 4.353–63). The distortion of the images (*eidōla*) is an epistemologically neutral physical process. The error really comes

176 *Knowledge in Ancient Philosophy*

from that which is 'added by opinion' (*prodoxazomenon*) and is not subsequently subjected to an attestation capable of confirming it (*Hdt.* 50). This judgement, it is true, depends on sensations, but it is distinct from them.

In fact, beside the physical explanation, sensation itself is defined in a negative way: it does not require *logos* – reason or discourse – or even memory to establish the truth of what it expresses. According to Diogenes Laertius (10.31), '[A]ll sensation, he [Epicurus] says, is irrational (*alogos*) and does not involve memory.' Being deprived from any kind of rational activity, it cannot judge; hence it cannot fail. Indeed error and illusion ever presuppose a propositional content *plus* a belief (or what Stoic philosophers of the same period call an 'assent') related to this propositional content. Now, this twofold operation requires the use of a rational faculty.

However sensation is not the only criterion of truth. Diogenes Laertius (10.31) reports that, according to Epicurus' *Canon*, the criteria of truth are sensations, preconceptions (*prolēpseis*), and feelings or affections (*pathē*): 'Thus Epicurus, in the *Canōn* ("Yardstick"), says that the sensations, preconceptions, and the feelings are the criteria of truth. The Epicureans add the "focusings of thought into an impression"' (cf. also Sextus Empiricus, *Against the Mathematicians* 7.203–16). It does not mean that these criteria are opposed to one another. On the contrary, each one plays its part, according to the particular situation. Affections reveals in an evident manner pleasure and pain to the agent (Diog. Laert. 10.34), and for this reason play a central role in ethics and in the Epicurean explanation of conduct. We do not have, in the Epicurean texts, any account expressly dedicated to preconceptions, but Diogenes Laertius' summary indicates that they have two correlative functions: the retention in memory and generalization of repeated sensations – the notion of man derives from the sensory experience we have had of individual human beings – and the anticipatory apprehension, through general notions, of objects that may correspond to later sensations – what appears to me in the distance may be a horse, an ox, or a man (10.33). Preconceptions intervene, not only in sciences and theoretical knowledge, but also in practical (ethical, political, ordinary) situations. Let us now focus on this very important feature of the Epicurean epistemology.

4. Preconceptions: genesis and methodology

What allows Epicurus to count preconception as a criterion is its immediate evidence. Although it comes from sensation, preconception is, like sensation, a self-evident knowledge: when I have in my mind the preconception of a horse, a cow, or a human being, I have a clear, unambiguous idea of it. A preconception, indeed, has two features, which can explain this evidence: on the one hand, its proper immediacy and clarity; on the other hand, the continuity that links preconception to sensation.

Let us begin with immediacy. One could object to the Epicureans that the evidence of preconceptions is secondary or derived, since it comes from another act of knowledge: sensation, which precedes preconception, by definition. Now, if preconception is derived, it constitutes a sort of second-rank knowledge, distinct from what is originally evident; hence, one may guess that there is some intermediate stage, between sensation and preconception, which makes room for false judgements. Nonetheless, the Epicureans seem to respond to this objection that there is no intermediate phase, because preconception (once formed in our mind) is immediately given with the corresponding external stimulus: the sensation of the object or the corresponding linguistic signifier. Consequently, because preconception is a spontaneous manifestation of the main properties of the object, there is no room for judgement. This response appears in the following text, the most complete extant account of Epicurean preconception:

> Preconception, they [the Epicureans] say, is as it were a perception, or correct opinion, or conception, or universal 'stored notion' (i.e. memory), of that which has frequently become evident externally: e.g. 'Such and such a kind of thing is a man.' For as soon as the word 'man' is uttered, immediately its delineation also comes to mind by means of preconception, since the senses give the lead. Thus what primarily underlies each name is something self-evident. And what we inquire about we would not have inquired about if we had not had prior knowledge of it. For example: 'Is what's standing over there a horse or a cow?' For one must at some time have come to know the form of a horse and that of a cow by means of preconception. Nor would we have named something if we had not previously learnt its delineation by means of preconception. Thus preconceptions are self-evident. And what we inquire about we would not have inquired about if we had not had prior knowledge of it. For example: 'Is what's standing over there a horse or a cow?' For one must at some time have come to know the form of a horse and that of a cow by means of preconception. Nor would we have named something if we had not previously learnt its delineation by means of preconception. Thus preconceptions are self-evident. And opinion depends on something prior and self-evident, which is our point of reference when we say, e.g., 'How do we know if this is a man?' (Diog. Laert. 10.33; Long and Sedley 1987)

The formula 'as soon as' is to be emphasized. 'As soon as' I hear the word 'man', I have in mind, through the preconception, like a déjà vu, the corresponding delineation (or 'schema' or 'impression': *tupos*). In other words, I do not ask for any additional data, because the link between the preconception and the word is immediate, as is the link between the preconception and the object of my first sensible experience. So, when I think of 'man' generally speaking, I reach the same level of evidence as I do while perceiving a particular man through the senses. Consequently, one may say that 'preconceptions are self-evident', as it is claimed in the text.

Moreover, there is a natural continuity between sensation and preconception, which is well expressed by the psychological and physical account (Goldschmidt 1978). Diogenes of Oinoanda (fr. 9.III.6–14: see Smith 1993) describes quite clearly what occurs when a preconception is being formed: 'and after the impingements of the first images, our nature is rendered porous in such a manner that, even if the objects which it first saw are no longer present, images similar to the first ones are received by the mind'.

The repetition of sensations of the same kind (say: of an indefinite number of human beings) produces continuous modifications in the sense organ, and this phenomenon is the physical basis of the similarity which characterizes the preconception (the common idea of human being). As we have seen, sensation is deprived of reason and memory: it is an instantaneous grasp. Preconception is a sort of memory insofar as it retains the common features of successive and similar experiences. It is also an active remembering of what has been experienced previously (Glidden 1985; *contra* Hammerstaedt 1993). Hence, preconception is truly self-evident because it consists in a sort of immediate, and therefore reliable, actualization, by thought, of the state – the mental image – produced by the preceding sensible experience (Tsouna 2016).

However, one may wonder if preconception is in itself rational or not, and, if it is, how it can be saved from the possibility of false predication (Striker 1996: 41). It is not clear if the Epicureans think that preconception has a propositional content, for example, 'human being is such and such' as alleged propositional content of the preconception 'human being'. At any rate, they seem to think that preconception is already rational insofar as it is a sort of notion or 'idea', in the broad sense already mentioned. Diogenes Laertius (10.32) attributes to the Epicureans a typology of general representations according to which each kind of notion is a rational construction: 'Also, all notions *(epinoiai)* arise from the senses by means of confrontation, analogy, similarity and combination, with some contribution from reasoning too.' Taken that way, preconception, which is a kind of *epinoia* – perhaps the sort of notion which arises from the senses by means of 'similarity' – is something more elaborated than a mere sensory apprehension of the object. Consequently, it probably depends on the rational part of the soul. Nevertheless, the Epicureans obviously think that there is at least one kind of notion that comes right after the sensation, without intermediary, because it is obtained in the most natural way: preconception.

Besides, preconceptions are not just spontaneous productions of the mind, or natural generalizations: they are also very important tools for scientific inquiry (see, especially, Long 1971; Asmis 1984; Morel 2008; Tsouna 2016). Preconception, in the Epicurean methodology, has at least three functions: it serves (a) as a primary concept for scientific inquiry, (b) as an invariant or a critical point of comparison for other representations or judgements, and (c) as a sort of definition.

(a) An interesting testimony by Clement of Alexandria (*Stromates* 2.4) echoes Epicurus' inferential methodology as it is developed in *Letter to Herodotus* (37–8). Clement's text defines Epicurean preconception as 'a focusing on something evident and on the evident notion of the thing' and adds that 'it is impossible to look for anything, to have doubts or opinions about anything or even to refute anything without preconception'. Taken that way, preconception is not only a particular kind of representation among others: it gets a very important epistemological and logical function insofar as it is necessary for any subsequent investigation. Without preconception, indeed, there would be neither issues, nor opinions, nor research. One may suppose that this theory of preconception is the Epicurean response to the famous issue of Plato's *Meno*. As a self-evident notion and as a criterion, preconception must be referred to, in order to assert any proposition on a given subject.

(b) Besides, the *Letter to Menoeceus*, in paragraph 123, invites us not to add to the 'common notion' (*koinē noēsis*) of God (a notion of which we have the outline in ourselves) an opinion that contradicts it, that is to say, an opinion that is contrary to the idea that the gods are happy and incorruptible. Now, we learn next that this common notion is a preconception,[1] as opposed to the false assumptions that the majority of men make:

> For there are gods – the knowledge of them is self-evident. But they are not such as the many believe them to be. For by their beliefs as to their nature the many do not preserve them. The impious man is not he who denies the gods of the many, but he who attaches to gods the beliefs of the many about them. For they are not preconceptions but false suppositions, the assertions of the many about gods. (Epicurus, *Letter to Menoeceus* 123–4)

180   *Knowledge in Ancient Philosophy*

It is clear from this text that we have in ourselves a stable representation of the gods, as happy and incorruptible beings. All passages insisting on the presence of preconceptions *in us* tend to show the same thing. This is particularly true, in Cicero's *On the Nature of Gods* (*De natura deorum*), of the exposition by the Epicurean Velleius, who insists repeatedly on the inherence of a notion of the gods, as nature itself has inscribed them in every mind (1.43: *in omnium animis eorum notionem impressisset ipsa natura*), whence the proposition: 'we have ingrained, or rather innate, knowledge of them' (1.44: *insitas eorum vel potius innatas cognitiones habemus*). However, we may also have acquired false ideas about them: the gods of Olympus are often jealous, envious, and cruel, and many people are terrified at the thought of divine punishments in the Hades. These opinions are not only incompatible with divine happiness; they also bring about psychic disturbance. To save ourselves and other people from psychic troubles arising from these false beliefs, we must use the right preconception of gods as an invariant to which we can refer in order to compare with it the various opinions that we may have concerning the gods.

In that very particular case of the preconception of gods, preconception serves first of all as a negative criterion for characterizing its content: it defines what the gods are not. Conversely, it has, by virtue of its very imprecision, a positive function: a prolepsis is the condition for the validity and legitimacy of our statements concerning its object. Thanks to it, one can accept various representations of the gods, and concede some points to the traditional, imagistic theology, for instance, that the gods have this or that shape and in particular a human shape (Cicero, *De natura deorum* 1.46), or that they live in a community and speak Greek (Philodemus, *On Gods* 3.14; Diels), or even that some things in nature may be called by the names of gods. Lucretius makes this quite clear in Book II of his *Poem*:

> If anyone is resolved to call the sea Neptune and corn Ceres, and likes rather to misuse the title of Bacchus than to utter the true name of the vine-juice, let us grant that he may proclaim that the world is the Mother of the gods, if only in very truth he forbear to stain his mind with shameful religious awe. (*DRN* 2.655–60)

The situation is analogous to the case of the prolepsis of justice (Goldschmidt 1977). We have two maxims of Epicurus on the topic, which make explicit reference to the preconception of justice:

> What is legally deemed to be just has its existence in the domain of justice whenever it is attested to be useful in the requirements of social relationships,

whether or not it turns out to be the same for all. But if someone makes a law and it does not happen to accord with the utility of social relationships, it no longer has the nature of justice. And even if what is useful in the sphere of justice changes but fits the preconception for some time, it was no less just throughout that time for those who do not confuse themselves with empty utterances but simply look at the facts. (Epicurus, *KD* 37)

Where, without any change in circumstances, the conventional laws – when judged by their consequences – were seen not to correspond with the preconception of justice, such laws were not really just; but wherever the laws have ceased to be useful in consequence of a change in circumstances, in that case the laws were, for the time being, just when they were useful for the social relationships of the citizens, and subsequently ceased to be just when they ceased to be useful. (Epicurus, *KD* 38)

The idea we have of political utility (i.e. of what is useful to a given political community in a given place and time, so that people do not do each other harm) must adapt itself to the preconception of justice. This must be, then, sufficiently stable to serve as an invariant and as a point of comparison. The conception of what is useful can change according to the circumstances, even as it remains consistent with the prolepsis of justice. This does not suffice, in and of itself, to *define* justice in a way that applies, without variations, to all times and all places; but it constitutes a framework for its variation or a rule of evaluation for particular situations in which the question of legal justice may arise.

(c) What characterizes prolepsis, apart from its function as a criterion which it shares with other modes of knowledge, is that its content is always something general – a god is always incorruptible and happy; body is not conceivable without a determinate number of constant properties, such as shape or size – and that this content consists in the essential determinate idea that corresponds to the word, thanks to which the prolepsis is apprehended (Manuwald 1972: 103–105). This point is confirmed by Philodemus (*De signis* 52; xxxiv–xxxv De Lacy's trans.), who specifies that preconception takes the place of definition: 'There is also the meaning that this is the particular definition of that, and this is the preconception, as when we say that body as body has bulk and resistance, and man as man is a rational animal.'

Epicurus and his followers are deemed to have vigorously criticized the definition as such (*Anonymous Commentary to Plato's Theaetetus*, 22, 39–47). Actually their target is a sort of abstract and purely logical definition, independent of any empirical attestation of its content. They know that we do need definitions, for the everyday life and, above all, in philosophy and sciences. Preconception,

182   *Knowledge in Ancient Philosophy*

insofar as it is closely connected to empirical data, is well equipped to play this role. To understand this third function of preconception, let us consider now the Epicurean attitude towards demonstration.

5. Criticism and use of demonstrations

The Epicureans not only reject abstract definitions: they also criticize dialectic (Cicero, *Academics II (Lucullus)* 30.97; Diog. Laert. 10.31) and have strong reservations on demonstration (*apodeixis*) (Asmis 1984: 35–9; 2009). Actually, Epicurus and his followers, in criticizing demonstrations, have three kinds of targets: purely formal demonstrations (when one does not take empirical data into account); non-relevant demonstrations (when one uses demonstrations, although this should not be done, e.g., about the meaning of words); *regressus ad infinitum* (when one intends to demonstrate the indemonstrable principles). A good example of this is the methodological introduction of Epicurus' *Letter to Herodotus* (37–8), already quoted.

In this passage, Epicurus does not argue against demonstration as such, but against certain uses of *apodeixis*. He criticizes, on the one hand, *ad infinitum* demonstrations and, on the other hand, additions of demonstrative arguments ('additional proof') when one should keep to the evidence of verbal expressions ('the things which underlie words'), of sensations, of affections, and of first notions ('primary concepts') of things (i.e. probably: preconceptions).[2] It is noteworthy that Epicurus does not confine himself to mentioning the criteria of truth (sensations, affections, and preconceptions) for their proper value, but sets out the necessary conditions for sign-inference (*semeiōsis*). If one takes all these conditions into account, one can rely on stable and manifest data in order to lead the inquiry about non-evident matters (like atoms and void). In other words, one has to start from indemonstrable data.

Now, this requires a clear distinction between what can be demonstrated and what is not demonstrable – that is, between what can be an object of demonstration and what is self-evident. It is the case of sensations, as well as of preconceptions: the latter are primary concepts, beyond which we must not go (since it is self-evident) at the risk of finding ourselves in an infinite regress towards some supposed prior self-evident thing. The Epicureans have an implicit doctrine of the 'indemonstrable' principles, taken as necessary conditions for scientific reasoning. Indeed, they do not reject all demonstration, and they think that some mental states – sensations, preconceptions, and affections – are by

Epicurean Epistemology 183

themselves evident, so that they play the role of indemonstrable principles of reasoning.

Consequently, one may reasonably suppose that the Epicurean criticism against demonstrations does not aim at logic as such (as attested also by Sextus Empiricus: *Against the Mathematicians* 7.15), but rather at misuses and false conceptions of deductive reasoning.

6. Judgement and science

Moreover, the Epicurean theory of criteria of truth, the 'canonic', does not content itself with a mere typology of self-evident knowledge or mental states: it is also the framework for a complex methodology of judgement and attestation, in connection with empirical data. From Epicurus himself (*KD* 24; first sentence), we have a short but enlightening text, which calls for the use of this methodology: 'If you are going to reject any sensation absolutely, and not distinguish opinions reliant on evidence yet awaited from what is already present through sensation, through feelings, and through every focusing of thought into an impression, you will confound all your other sensations with empty opinion and consequently reject the criterion in its entirety.'

This theory of the criteria of knowledge may seem at first sight to amount to a naive form of empiricism. Its application, however, shows that it does not, for the Epicureans in no way claim to reduce knowledge of hidden entities to a direct extension of the perception of phenomena. The very subtlety of Epicurean methodology lies in the different modes of transition from notions (*epinoia*) and opinions to sensations and conversely. These modes, and analogy in particular, relate propositions about hidden things to sensory evidence through a complex method for verifying beliefs. It might be the case that this theory of inference was fixed after Epicurus. Yet the testimonies of Diogenes Laertius and Sextus Empiricus (Diog. Laert. 10.34; Sextus Empiricus, *Against the Mathematicians* 7.211–16), Philodemus' treatise *On Signs*, as well as the argumentative procedures used by Epicurus himself and Lucretius, allow us to see in this theory the continuation of the doctrine of the criteria.

When beliefs relate to what can be the object of a direct sensory experience, their truth is established by attestation (*epimarturēsis*) and their falsity by non-attestation (*ouk epimarturēsis*). Thus, when I believe that Plato is coming towards me, I still need attestation or confirmation or its opposite, non-attestation, which sensory experience will provide when the man I see has come near. This is the same kind of situation Epicurus is alluding to, when he distinguishes, in the *KD* 24, between what is already evident and opinions which are still to be confirmed. When beliefs relate to hidden things, they can be the subject of a non-infirmation (*ouk antimarturēsis*) or an infirmation (*antimarturēsis*). In this case I must establish a relation of consequence (*akolouthia*) between the invisible and sensory evidence. The latter cannot be directly confirmed, but it can be established by non-infirmation. Take, for example, the existence of the void. We assume the existence of motion. Now this implies the existence of the void (*Hdt.* 40). Hence, we posit the existence of the void. Thus the contrary hypothesis is infirmed and the conclusion is warranted.

In the case of remote phenomena, like celestial or underground events and bodies, if the inference does not infirm the contrary hypothesis, it justifies a resort to multiple explanations. Epicurus' *Letter to Pythocles* is devoted to this kind of phenomena (see *Pyth.* 86–7, 93–6; *Hdt.* 79). Eclipses of the sun and moon, for example, can be explained either by their being extinguished, or by their being hidden by other bodies. Furthermore, the different explanations of a single phenomenon may not only be logically compatible – insofar as they are equally acceptable – but may even be conjoined (*Pyth.* 96). The most important, actually, is the very fact that a rational explanation can be given: it preserves our *ataraxia* by showing that it is pointless to invoke gods and, for example, their alleged anger, in order to explain natural events, such as thunders or earthquakes.

In sum, the Epicurean conception of knowledge is complex and subtle: it is not a radical empiricism, but rather a rational empiricism, equipped with efficient and clearly defined methodological tools (Morel 2009). Reason is not to be ruled out: it gets its own function and, in certain circumstances, produces its own results. This is the case with hidden properties and realities, which escape sensation. Our eyes see shade and light, Lucretius says, but they do not teach about the difference between them: 'reason (*ratio animi*) alone must discern them, and the eyes are unable to know the nature of things (*natura rerum*)' (*DRN* 4.384–5).

7. Conclusion: epistemology and ethics

Epicurean science does not aim at encyclopaedic knowledge and it is perfectly aware of its own limits. We can possess some certainties, since sensation, preconceptions, and affections are evident, and what is evident requires no proof. Nevertheless, the infinity of the All (or the Universe, which contains an infinite number of worlds) and the complexity and remoteness of some particular physical processes entail that a comprehensive (and not extensive) conception of the science of nature should be favoured. For instance, after comparing atomic combinations to those of the letters that make up the verses he is writing, Lucretius says that atoms, which create the diversity of things, have power to work much more combinations (*DRN* 1.827–9). In other words, human discourse is unable to cover the totality of that for which it nonetheless gives a comprehensive explanation. Knowledge of nature is sufficient, however, to free us from terror in the face of death or psychic and bodily sufferings, and to provide a secure base for happiness (Morel 2006).[3]

Notes

1 See the use of the vocabulary of preconception about the notion of gods in Philodemus, *On Piety*, 1. 441–3; 1300; 1887 (Obbink 1996).
2 Several arguments can be invoked in favour of the identification of these primary concepts to preconceptions. For more details, see Morel (2008). On the positive use of the vocabulary and the procedure of demonstration in Epicurean methodology, see Morel (2016).
3 I wish to thank Dimitri El Murr for his valuable reading of this text.

References

Asmis, E. (1984), *Epicurus' Scientific Method*, Ithaca: Cornell University Press.
Asmis, E. (2009), 'Epicurean Empiricism', in J. Warren (ed.), *The Cambridge Companion to Epicureanism*, Cambridge: Cambridge University Press.
Giannantoni, G. and Gigante, M. (eds) (1993), *Epicureismo Greco e romano. Atti del congresso internazionale*, Naples: Bibliopolis.
Glidden, D. K. (1985), 'Epicurean Prolepsis', *Oxford Studies in Ancient Philosophy*, 3: 175–217.
Goldschmidt, V. (1977), *La Doctrine d'Épicure et le droit*, Paris: Vrin.
Goldschmidt, V. (1978/2006), 'Remarques sur l'origine épicurienne de la "prénotion"', in J. Brunschwig (ed.), *Les Stoïciens et leur logique*, Paris: Vrin.
Hammerstaedt, J. (1993), 'Il ruolo della *Prolêpsis* epicurea nell' interpretazione di Epicuro, *Epistula ad Herodotum* 37 SG', in Giannantoni and Gigante (1993).
Long, A. A. (1971), '*Aisthesis, Prolepsis* and Linguistic Theory in Epicurus', *Bulletin of the Institute of Classical Studies*, 18: 114–33.

Long, A. A. and Sedley, D. N. (1987), *The Hellenistic Philosophers*, Cambridge: Cambridge University Press.

Manuwald, A. (1972), *Die Prolepsislehre Epikurs*, Bonn: Habelt.

Morel, P.-M. (2006), 'Epicureanism', in M. L. Gill and P. Pellegrin (eds), *A Companion to Ancient Philosophy*, Malden, MA: Blackwell.

Morel, P.-M. (2008), 'Methods and Evidence. On the Epicurean Preconception', *Proceedings of the Boston Area Colloquium in Ancient Philosophy*, 23: 25–48.

Morel, P.-M. (2009), *Épicure. La nature et la raison*, Paris: Vrin.

Morel, P.-M. (2016), 'Esperienza e dimostrazione in Epicuro', in D. De Sanctis, E. Spinelli, M. Tulli, and F. Verde (eds), *Questioni epicuree*, Sankt Augustin: Academia Verlag.

Obbink, D. (1996), *Philodemus: On Piety, Part 1*, critical text with commentary, Oxford: Clarendon Press.

Smith, M. F. (1993), *Diogenes of Oinoanda: The Epicurean Inscription*, Naples: Bibliopolis.

Striker, G. (1996), *Essays on Hellenistic Epistemology and Ethics*, Cambridge: Cambridge University Press.

Tsouna, V. (2016), 'Epicurean Preconceptions', *Phronesis*, 61: 160–221.

10

Stoic Epistemology

Marcelo Boeri

1. Stoic epistemology and its platonic background

Cicero reports that the Stoics were especially concerned with highlighting the coherence of their philosophical system. In *On Ends* 3.74, Torcuatus admits that he was attracted to the wonderful structure of the Stoic system and the extraordinary sequence of the topics they deal with. He also states that there is no conclusion inconsistent with its premise or any discrepancy between an earlier and a later statement. As such, the interconnection of the parts of philosophy is so well structured that if a single letter were altered, the whole building of philosophy would tumble. However, 'there is nothing which it would be possible to alter'.

The Stoics maintain that logic is our engagement with discourse (*logos*), which is the same as dialectics (Aëtius 1.2). Stoic logic includes not only formal logic and semantics, but also epistemology. Stoic epistemology makes emphasis upon two points that have a Platonic flavour: first, knowledge (*epistēmē*) and belief/opinion (*doxa*) are two radically contrasting powers (Plato, *Republic* 5); second, if one has knowledge, his knowledge exhibits stability. Similarly, a Stoic knower cannot be a psychologically weak person who changes his mind all the time. Cicero's passionate defence of the coherence depicted by Stoic philosophy stresses a logical consistency. But such coherence can also be understood as an inner consistency both of the system as a whole and of the individual.

Now, the Stoics were keen to argue that opinion should be identified with baseness, and knowledge with wisdom. This explains why if you are a Stoic knower, you are a wise person, both in an epistemic and in a moral sense. So, it appears that the Stoics were interested in emphasizing a practical mark which underlined both the theoretical and practical character of Stoic wisdom and its ideal instantiation of such coherence in the virtuous person, the one who possesses both the theory and the practice of what should be done (Epictetus, *Dissertations* [*Diss.*] 3.2 ff.; Diogenes Laertius [DL] 7.126; LS 61I; Stobaeus, *Excerpts* (*Ex.*) 2.63, 11–12; *SVF* III 280; LS 61D; Musonius Rufus, *Dissertations* 5). This detail is important in order to understand what the Stoics take to be knowledge (or so I shall argue).[1]

This chapter proceeds as follows: in the next section, I shall discuss some crucial topics that can be regarded as a sort of starting point in Stoic epistemology – perception, concept formation, impression (*phantasia*), and assent. There has been a great deal of discussion regarding the way in which the Greek *phantasia* should be rendered (for discussion, see LS 1987: 239; Annas 1990: 187n11; Frede 1999: 201; Long 1999: 575; Hankinson 2003: 60n1). In this chapter I will use 'impression', following the Stoic view that a *phantasia* is a 'printing' – *tupōsis* – in the mind which is produced when an external object, a *phantaston*, the 'impressor' (LS' translation), strikes the mind through sensation (DL 7.45, 50; *SVF* 2.55; LS 39A. Cicero, *Academica* [*Acad.*] 1.40). Some aspects of Stoic psychology will be briefly discussed: unlike Plato and Aristotle, the Stoics argue for a materialistic soul. In their view, such a materialistic approach, while avoiding the 'complicated way' in which Plato and Aristotle explain the relation between soul and body (two entities supposedly distinct in nature), would contribute to a clearer account of our psychological functions and explain more accurately the state of mind we call 'knowledge'. Indeed, perception, impression, and assent are all psychological items: that is why, in the Stoic view, it is more reasonable to account for the way in which, for example, an extra-mental object (what they technically call 'impressor') is able to produce an impression in one's mind: both the impressor and the impression are bodies. Thus, the unbridgeable gap between body and soul can be overcome. The Stoics hold that if the soul is in the body (as it is), and if the soul is able to move the body, the soul should be a body as well. Later on, after dealing with these matters, we shall be in a position to discuss briefly the three states of mind which are closely linked to each other and which play a crucial role in Stoic epistemology: knowledge, opinion, and cognition. In this section, both the Stoic criterion of truth and the Stoic theory of impressions will be dealt with. The way in which the Stoics discuss impressions is particularly relevant, since they distinguished several kinds of impressions and one of them was declared to be 'the criterion of truth' (the 'cognitive impression'; *phantasia katalēptikē*).

Among Hellenistic philosophers the expression 'criterion of truth' became a trademark phrase when discussing the issue of knowledge.[2] The Skeptical

Stoic Epistemology 189

Academy's attack on the Stoic cognitive impression is a very interesting chapter of this story, but for the sake of brevity I will omit it (for a full discussion of this issue, see Allen 1994, Schofield 1999: 338–45, and Gerson 2006: 115–24) and will briefly refer to some critiques addressed by the Sceptic philosopher Sextus Empiricus. Finally, I shall summarize the achievements of this chapter and provide some concluding remarks.

2. Perception, impression, assent, and concept formation in the background of a material soul

Both the Older and Middle Stoics took the soul to be a body. However, the soul is not the same kind of body as one's skull. It actually is, as reported by several Stoic sources,[3] a 'subtle body', 'breath', or rather, 'psychic breath'.[4] In line with some contemporary physicalist assumptions, the Stoic world is causally closed (Kim 2005: 21–2). The Stoics are committed to arguing that perceptive phenomena (such as the nerve impulses produced in the retina in a visual perception) can be physically explained as 'streams of breath': sight, for instance, is just breath (a bodily item in the Stoic ontological map) extending from the 'commanding-faculty' (another bodily item) to the eyes (another body; Aëtius 4.21, 1–4; *SVF* 2.836; LS 53H; the same thing applies to the other senses). Even though the Stoics did not know that the movement of one's arm is caused by a nerve impulse which sends orders to one's muscles, and that impulses are caused by other nerve impulses in the brain cortex, they, based on their ontological physicalism, had an entirely coherent manner to account for the physical connection among a psychological state (one's belief or desire), an extra-mental object (the cake), and the intentional movement of one's arm approaching the object of desire. The chain of events starting in one's desire to eat and ending in one's eating the cake can be explained, in the Stoic view, only because *all* the items involved are corporeal.

This quick description of how the Stoics explain the way in which perceivers interact with their environments is helpful to start discussing perception, impression, and assent. Perception and impression are the primary cognitive faculties. Within the Stoic empiricist framework, they are what trigger all the other psychological events that take part in a cognitive process, including thought, which is taken to be a kind of concept, which stems from perception 'or not without perception' (Plutarch, *On common notions* 1085a-b; *SVF* 2.847; LS 39F; Sextus Empiricus, *AP* 8.56–61; *SVF* 2.88; see also Hankinson

190 *Knowledge in Ancient Philosophy*

2003: 64). A Stoic concept sometimes is characterized as a 'stored thought', and a thought is said to be a 'rational impression' (Ps. Galen, *Medical Definitions* 19.381, 12–13).

The Stoic Zeno asserts that the soul is divided into eight parts: the five sense organs (*aisthēteria*; sometimes 'the five senses', *aisthēseis*, which should be the meaning of *aisthēteria* in Nemesius, *On the nature of man* 72, 7–13), the phonetic (i.e. the speech: *to phōnētikon*), the generative (*to spermatikon*), and the thinking part (i.e. the 'commanding part' in Nemesius and other sources: *to hegemonikon*; DL 7.110). The 'phonetic' part of the – *to phōnētikon* – is characterized as breath extending from the commanding part to the throat, tongue, and the related organs (Aëtius 4. 21, 4). It allows us to speak; it can be a little intriguing why the Stoics took this to be 'a *part* of the soul', but they probably were pointing out that speaking (in its most physiological sense) should depend on a 'part' of the soul, suggesting this way that the 'vocal or phonetic part of the soul' is one specific *function* of one's psyche. In other sources the thinking part is identified with 'the commanding part' of the soul, which is 'the highest part' and is responsible for producing impressions, assents, perceptions, and impulses (**T1**: Aëtius 4.21, 1–4; *SVF* 2.836; LS 53H). Although this passage is relevant (in fact, it describes almost all the abilities belonging to rational and irrational animals), it is a little misleading, too. From the commanding part, it is said, seven parts of the soul arise and stretch out into the body ('as the tentacles of an octopus'). That is, there are eight parts of the soul but all of them depend on and derive from the commanding part. Five of these seven 'parts' are the senses (or the senses organs identified with the senses), which are explained in physicalist terms. In the Stoic world everything is breath in different degrees of tension – breath that, by virtue of its subtleness, is able to pervade every bit of matter. If this is so, it is not surprising that perception is explained in terms of contact between breath and the commanding part. Furthermore, sight, smell, hearing, and so on are physical events that take place when the sense organ and the soul meet at a point, so to speak. One might think that this just describes an inner experience within the perceiver; but how about the extra-mental object?

The Stoic corporeal soul allows the subject 'to be in touch' with the external world; otherwise it would not be possible to have a sensory experience. Perception is the starting point of the whole process that ends in knowledge; such a process starts when the subject is affected in his or her perceptive capacities by perceptible objects. Stoics and Epicureans, albeit rivals in some important respects,[5] shared a common background: (i) they were empiricists, and (ii) materialists. According to (i), the possession of knowledge presupposes that the knower has had a perceptual experience before being able to know. Sometimes it seems as if the Stoics had in mind the Platonic doctrine of innateness: very roughly, Plato's view states that knowledge is nothing but the recollection of certain things we have come to know when our soul was in a state preceding our current human life (*Meno* 81d5; 82a; *Phaedo* 72e-77e). By contrast, the Stoics heavily rely on an empiricist account, according to which there is nothing in our souls before our perceptual experience has taken place. In a crucial passage attributed to the Stoics, the soul is said to be like a 'blank slate ready to be written upon' (**T2**: Aëtius 4.11.1–5; LS 39E).[6] What is inscribed in the 'sheet of paper' (one's mind) is each of our concepts, and the first manner of inscription or writing, the Stoics claim, is through the senses. What starts filling our soul are the senses or, rather, our perceptual experiences; in fact, when one perceives something endowed with a certain quality (such as white), one retains a memory after the object goes away. Memory is taken to be the upshot of the very sensory state one is experiencing. The Stoic strategy to explain memory seems to concentrate on the fact that, due to the sensory state produced by a certain quality, and given that such a quality is dependent on a bodily object, one is able to remember such a sensory state in the future because such an object leaves an imprint in one's soul. If one retains a memory of the sensory experience, given that both the imprinting object and the mind are bodies, what one retains should be something bodily. Any sensory experience, in being a certain activity of one's soul, is a bodily event in one's mental life.

Now, according to **T2**, what one retains is the concept of the experienced object; the Stoics contend that the person inscribes on the sheet of paper 'each and every one of his concepts'. This is produced through the senses: if by perceiving something white the subject has a memory of it when it has departed, one might assume that, under similar sensory experiences (when one sees snow the day after a snow storm), the person would be able to recognize that a quality like white is present in different objects of the world and thereby the subject will be able to say 'this *x* is white'. This must be so because such a person has already acquired the concept 'white', and such acquisition occurs because the person has already had the perceptual experience 'white'.

According to the Stoics, the perceptible objects are conceived (or thought: *enoēthē*) (i) by 'confrontation' ('contact' or 'direct experience' – *periptōsis* – as suggested by Sandbach [1971: 35 n15]), (ii) by 'similarity' (like conceiving of Socrates on the basis of a picture of him), (iii) by 'analogy' (sometimes by magnification, as in the case of Tityos and Cyclopes, and sometimes by diminution, as in the case of the Pigmy),[7] (iv) by 'transposition' (like eyes on the chest), (v) by 'combination' (like the Hippocentaur), (vi) by opposition (like death). (vii) Some things, such as 'sayables' (meanings, predicates, arguments, etc.) and place (incorporeal items in Stoic ontology), are thought by 'transition' (DL 7.52–3; *SVF* 2.87; LS 39D). (viii) What is just and good is thought 'naturally', (ix) what lacks hands is thought by privation. As is clear, without a sensory experience, there is no way to acquire concepts and thereby, insofar as things are grasped by means of concepts (DL 7.42), there is no knowledge.

Now, as stated by **T2**, one has experience when many memories of a similar kind have occurred. Experience is defined as a 'plurality of similar impressions'. Thus, insofar as one inscribes in one's mind each of one's concepts, and the first method of inscription is through the senses, the result of one's perceptual experience must be a concept. According to the Stoics, some concepts come into being naturally 'without technical elaboration' (such as the case of what is just and good), but others come into being through teaching and care. The latter are called 'concepts' (*ennoiai*), whereas the former are also called 'preconceptions' (*prolēpseis*; for this view, cf. Epictetus, *Diss.* 2.17, 1–13). This introduces the issue of innatism which can turn out to be rather complicated within an empiricist epistemology like that of the Stoics. In some Stoic passages (Epictetus, *Diss.* 1.2, 5–82; Plutarch, *On Stoic self-contradictions* 1041e-1042a; *SVF* 3.69; 545, citing the Stoic Chrysippus) the idea of 'inborn (*emphutoi*) preconceptions' is introduced. If one would like to avoid the problem, one could probably say 'implanted preconceptions', that is, implanted by sensation. **T2** is clear: without sensation, there are no concepts, and as suggested by the text, concepts stem from a certain accumulation of perceptual experience.

Cicero (*Acad.* 2.21; LS 39C), developing a Stoic view, argues that there are some things that we grasp with our mind, that is, they are said to be perceived by the senses, but by them 'in a certain respect' (such as 'that is white', 'this is sweet', 'that is a horse', etc.).[8] What we strictly perceive with our senses is the sweetness of the honey. But we also *perceive* 'this is sweet', even though we do not perceive this with the senses, but with the mind. Actually, this perceiving must be the understanding we have of the proposition at stake, or the way in which we can articulate in language our perceptual experience. Again, if one states that preconceptions are implanted by sensation, they arise naturally in us (not because of a conscious pursuit) and derive from some primary impressions. What **T2** clearly contends is that without an accumulation of perceptual experience which allows memories to take place, there are no concepts, and memories become 'similar in kind' after a repeated experience (the same argument is recorded by Sextus Empiricus, *AP* 7.373; Cicero, *Acad.* 2.30).[9]

Stoic Epistemology 193

Now, if conceptions of things are not imprinted on us, there can be no understanding of anything. What the Stoics presumably thought is that one can have the concept of horse because one has previously seen a horse. And thanks to the acquisition of language, one is able to associate both the name and the sound 'horse' with a four-legged animal, one of whose characteristics is neighing, having a more or less long neck, being able to gallop, to carry a rider, and so on. So whenever I see such a four-legged animal again I will say, 'That is a horse.' One can do that because one's soul was somehow imprinted by the impression of an item of the world that in English is called 'horse', and further because such an impression has become a concept, insofar as one can recognize some characteristics that determine the object at stake as being the kind of object that it is. So, the first time that one saw that animal and then remarked, 'That is a horse', thenceforth one began to connect the word 'horse' with a particular object. This involves associating the sound with some specific features belonging to a certain kind of object, even though one does not yet know that the name 'horse' (and the uttered word 'horse') refers to a certain kind of animal with such and such characteristics.[10] The acquisition of language presupposes that the individual is able to understand meanings. But before a perceptual experience has taken place, the notion or concept of what a horse is did not exist in one's mind. As is clear, the role of memory in the whole process is decisive: without memory one would not be able to recognize the object in one's next perceptual experience where the object at stake is involved (in my example, 'horse'). But, of course, without the initial sense-perceptual experience, one could not retain a memory after it goes away.

Now we can turn to the issues of impression and assent. As already said, without a perceptual experience of a horse, there is no concept of 'horse'. An actual horse is an extra-mental perceptible object that impresses upon one's soul, this object technically being an 'impressor', which is able to form an impression in one's soul, when leaving a mark on it. This is what **T1** explicitly asserts: the cause of an impression is an impressor, for example, the actual horse one is perceiving. So the concept 'horse' is the mark left by the actual horse on one's mind, that is, an impression (after all, as indicated above, a concept is a kind of impression, a 'rational' impression).

Now, it must be clear why knowledge is so strongly rooted in perceptual experience; perception is basic because it is the factor that imprints on the soul the first marks. But in the process of apprehension of things, senses are not passive receptors of the data impressed on them from without. As we have seen above, when the soul is affected by the perceptible object, a stream of breath goes from the commanding part of the soul to the sense organ. After that, it returns to the percipient subject through the sense organ and deposits a sensory impression in her mind. The breath forms a sort of material bridge through which the sensory data travel in the mind. Once the impression has been deposited in the mind, such an impression can be evaluated by the perceiver. If she judges the impression to be true, she gives her assent to it.

This leads us to consider briefly the Stoic theory of assent; this is relevant for understanding the Stoic view on knowledge because it is said that the sage person, the one who really qualifies as a knower, does not give assent to what is 'non-cognitive', while the ignorant is the one giving assent to the non-cognitive. So, both knowledge and ignorance seem to be two different sorts of assent. Assent is usually taken to be a mental act that is given to a proposition; in fact, it is the mental act through which one somehow refers to a determined propositional content, taking it to be true.[11] If I give my assent to the proposition 'it is day', it is because I believe that it is day; if I assent to the proposition 'I ought to do F', this F being a certain kind of action, I act according to F since I take it to be true to do F. Every impulse stems from assent but not every assent yields an impulse: when you give your assent to a descriptive proposition (such as 'the sky is starry'), no impulse is necessarily followed. What activates impulse is the 'impulsive' (*hormetikē*) impression, whose propositional content can be 'it is appropriate to do F' (Stobaeus, *Ex.* 2.88, 2–6; *SVF* 3.171; LS 33I; for the relevance of this kind of 'motivating' impressions in Stoic action theory, see Inwood [1985: 56–86] and Sorabji [2000: 32–3, 42–4]). Thus, strictly speaking, assent is given to a propositional formula, not to an impression.[12] According to the regular sequence described in our sources, impression is first; then thought (which is 'expressive') communicates through reason what it experiences because of impression (DL 7.49). When the Stoics argue that an impression is an affective state, they are actually emphasizing the physiological aspect of it (Stobaeus, *Ex.* 2.88, 2–6; *SVF* 3.171; LS 33I).

But assent also can be understood as a mental act enabling sensory perception; as Cicero says (maybe having a Zeno's view in mind), without assent there is no sensory perception of things (*Acad.* 2.37–8; LS 40O). This somehow explains how it can be said that 'the mind itself is even identical with the senses' (*Acad.* 2.30; LS 40N) and how the Stoics assert that *every* sense-perception *is* an assent and a cognition (Aëtius 4.8.12; *SVF* 2.72). These kinds of remarks can be a little misleading, but the basic idea is that even though they are different psychological events, when they occur together, they are presented as being a unity: it is the person's soul as a whole that has sense-perceptions, that assents, and that knows.

The Stoics distinguished several kinds of impressions (persuasive, unpersuasive, persuasive and unpersuasive, neither persuasive nor unpersuasive; Sextus, *AP* 7.242-60; *SVF* 2.65; LS 39G, 40E, 40K). Persuasive (i) and unpersuasive (ii) impressions are particularly relevant in this context because they are said to be the kind of impressions that respectively induce and deter their being assented to. Examples of (i) are 'it is day', 'I am conversing', that is, impressions which exhibit an obviousness that cannot be rejected. By contrast, (ii) are the kind of impression whose falsehood is so obvious that one is not willing to assent to it (such as, 'if it is day, the sun is not above the earth', 'if it is dark, it is day'). According to Sextus, persuasive impressions can be divided into (i.1) true, (i.2) false, (i.3) true and false, and (i.4) neither true nor false. Impressions labelled under (i.3) describe the kind of impression that the madman Orestes had of his sister Electra: in his madness he had the impression of an existing thing (Electra, an 'impressor'), and hence Orestes's impression was true. But inasmuch as Orestes had an impression of a Fury (in fact, when he saw his sister, he confused her with a Fury), it was false. Orestes and anyone else undergoing a false and vacuous attraction to what is 'phantastic' (i.e. what the Stoics technically call *phantasma*, 'figment'; Aëtius 4.12.1-5; *SVF* 2.54; LS 39B) do not represent what exists, which means that it does not properly represent the object that produced the impression. This is a typical case of what the Stoics name '*non*-cognitive impression', that is, 'either that which does not arise from an existing thing, or from an existing thing but not exactly in accordance with an existing thing: one which is not clear or distinct' (DL 7.46).

As already indicated, the 'cognitive impression' is taken to be the criterion of truth. An impression is cognitive if it meets the following conditions: (i) it arises from an 'existent thing' (or from 'what is'; *hyparchon*); (ii) it comes from an existing thing and is exactly in accordance with said existing thing, that is, it is 'stamped and moulded in accordance with the existing thing itself', which clearly means that it accurately represents the object; (iii) it is 'of such a kind as could not arise from what is not existing', a remark added by some Stoics in response to some Academic sceptical objections (DL 7.46; *SVF* 2.53; LS 40C; DL 7.49-51; *SVF* 2.52, 55, 61; LS 39A. Sextus, *AP* 7.247-52; *SVF* 2.65; LS 40E). A cognitive impression is said to provide the subject who receives it a guarantee that it accurately and clearly represents the thing at stake. By contrast, a non-cognitive impression is that which is either not from an existing thing, or else is from an existing object but not (exactly) in accordance with it (it is neither clear nor distinct; cf. DL 7.46). There has been some deal of discussion over the meaning of *hyparchon*, which can mean either (a) 'existent' or (b) 'what is (the case)'. Reading (a) has its appeal since, in a very conservative Stoic account, one can say that the existent bodily thing is what causes the impression in one's mind. Reading (b) suggests that the impression that A is F is a cognitive one that must be rooted in the fact that A is F (Frede 1999: 302–304). However, according to Sextus (*AP* 11.182–3; *SVF* 1.73; 2.97; *AP* 7.247–60; *SVF* 2.65; 40E, 40K; FDS 273), a *hyparchon* is an existing thing rather than what is the case, since it is 'what sets the impression in motion' (i.e. it is what produces an impression in one's mind), so it must be the same as an impressor. If an impression comes from an existent thing but it does not represent the thing as it really is, it is non-cognitive. That is the case of Orestes, whose impression has an existing thing as its cause (Electra), but it does not represent the existing thing accurately and clearly (Electra is not a Fury).

The Stoics held that a cognitive impression 'induces' one to assent to it (it is 'so evident that it seizes us by the hair and pulls us to assent'; Sextus, *AP* 7.257, 402–10). This view involves some problems: it is a fact that base people do not assent to cognitive impressions. Furthermore, the Stoics sometimes say that non-cognitive impressions are those experienced by people in abnormal states (Sextus, *AP* 7.247). But, as pointed out by the Academic Sceptic Carneades in his effort to prove that cognitive impressions are indiscernible from the non-cognitive ones, there are impressions that depict all the features of the cognitive impressions and yet are false. And this can happen whether an individual is in a normal or abnormal state; so, there can be situations in which both the perceptual conditions and the individual are perfectly normal but it is hard to make a clear distinction between what is true and what is false. As Sextus puts it (*AP* 7.402–10; LS 40H), there can be objects so similar (such as two eggs or two twins) that they turn out to be indiscernible in virtue of the way they imprint our impressions. If this is so, they fail to meet the condition according to which a cognitive impression is stamped and moulded in accordance with the existing object itself (see condition [iii] above; this objection was designed to show both that there is no an impression which is able to provide an accurate grasp of its object and that such a perceptual impression is not self-evident; cf. Cicero, *Acad.* 2.68; 78). Another device used by the Sceptics against the Stoic criterion of truth was the sorites paradox (recorded and endorsed by Sextus, *AP* 7.415–42; LS 37F; for discussion, see Mignucci 1993; Williamson 1994: 22–31).

3. Opinion, cognition, knowledge, and the power of experience in knowledge

The distinction among opinion, cognition, and knowledge was particularly relevant for the Stoics (Cicero, *Acad.* 1.40–2; *SVF* 1.55, 60–1; LS 40B; 41B; Sextus, *AP* 7.151–7; *SVF* 1.67–9; 2.90; LS 41C).[13] Knowledge is usually characterized as 'a secure and stable cognition unalterable by argument' and as 'a condition (*hexis*) in the reception of impressions which is irreversible by argument' (DL 7.47; LS 31B; DL 7.165). Opinion is weak and false assent. Cognition is assent to a cognitive impression. As is clear, the kind of epistemic state one possesses depends upon the kind of assent one has given: if one's assent is weak and false, one's epistemic state is 'opinion' (so for the Stoics there is no true opinion); if assent is to a 'cognitive impression', one's epistemic state is cognition. One can intuitively grasp the sense in which it can be said that assent is weak. But what is a 'false' assent? The Stoics recognized two sorts of assent: (i) a wise person never makes a false supposition nor does he assent to anything which is 'incognitive'. By contrast, the base person, due to his cognitive state (opinion), moves swiftly, and his assent, which is the same as ignorance, is changeable and weak. A base person, in giving his assent to what is non-cognitive, gives his assent before having a real understanding (Stobaeus, *Ex.* 2.111, 17–112, 8). So, an assent is regarded to be false insofar as it is directed at false propositions that are taken to be true. Knowledge and opinion can be understood as two psychological states depending upon the kind of impressions people assent to. But there are other requirements that a state of mind must meet in order to be 'knowledge'.

There was a debate regarding the difference between cognition and knowledge, the clear separation of which was urged by the Stoics. As the Academic Sceptic Arcesilaus contends, (i) if the Stoics say that knowledge is present only in the sage, and opinion is only present in the base, and (ii) if both the sage and the base can have cognition (which is said to be the criterion of truth by some Stoics), then (iii) cognition cannot be a criterion and cannot stand in between knowledge and opinion. In fact, if (iv) cognition is assent to a cognitive impression, and cognition occurs both in the sage and the base, it cannot be true that it is knowledge when it is present in the sage, but opinion when it is in the base. Besides, (v) if cognition is assent to a cognitive impression, then cognition does not exist, since (v.1) assent is given not to impressions, but to propositions. And (v.2) there is no cognition because there are no true impressions such that there could not be false ones, and, given that there is no cognitive impression, cognition will not exist either (for cognition is assent to a cognitive impression).

Now if someone who is not wise is able to assent to a cognitive impression, and if cognition is defined as an assent to a cognitive impression (Sextus, *AP* 11.182–183) and the base person can have a cognition, it follows, Arcesilaus infers, that such person has knowledge. However, the matter is not that simple and, as we shall see, the Stoic distinction between cognition and knowledge might be suggesting that the passage from opinion to knowledge is not instantaneous, but it supposes cognition, a previous stage that, as Cicero reports, has been given to us by nature as the standard of knowledge and as its starting-point from which conceptions of things are printed upon the mind (Cicero, *Acad.* 2.42; LS 41B). Indeed, Arcesilaus makes a good point: if it is true that there is no cognitive impression (see v.2 above), there will be no cognition since this is defined as 'assent to a cognitive impression'. But if this is so, everything will be non-cognitive, and the wise person will opine since he will assent to the non-cognitive (which is tantamount to opining). A Stoic might reply that assenting to a cognitive impression is a necessary but insufficient condition of knowledge (LS, 1987: 257): one can give assent to a cognitive impression, but if one has not acquired a disposition in which one unfailingly gives assent *only* to cognitive impressions, one has no knowledge (Frede 1999: 313–14). So, even though both the sage and the base people can have cognition, such cognition can become knowledge if it is able to be unaltered by argument. Thus, it seems that the difference between cognition and knowledge is just a matter of 'degree of stability and firmness' (Stobaeus, *Ex.* 2.73, 19–74, 3; *SVF* 2.112; LS 41H. Sextus, *AP* 7.151. Cicero, *Acad.* 1.41; LS 41B). Finally, Arcesilaus' complaint that assent must be to a proposition, not to an impression, did not produce a problem for the Stoics either, since they assume that an impression *is* a proposition (Sextus *AP* 7.242–3). Although they assert that an impression is a physical change (an affection in one's soul, and so a physical item), its intentional content is propositional.

Now, even if cognition and knowledge are not the same thing, they share a common terrain. The 'intermediate position' of cognition is sometimes explained by saying that it is neither right nor wrong. However, it is reliable because 'it deserves to be believed' (Cicero, *Acad.* 1.42). The reliability belonging to cognition derives from the trust we give to the senses, since a cognition made by the senses is, as long as one is experiencing it, true and reliable. Indeed, the Stoics state that 'it is by sense-perception that we get cognition of white and black, rough and smooth' (DL 7.52; *SVF* 2.71; LS 40P), that is, the source of cognition is sense-perception. That cognition is true does not mean that it captures *all* the relevant features of the object, but rather all such features which concern it. If my sense organs are in good condition and in front of me there is a four-legged animal

Stoic Epistemology 199

that is barking and moving its tail, I'm experiencing a perceptual cognition of a dog. This is not a mere groundless opinion: when I see a dog and say that there is a dog there, I have the warrant of my senses concerning the truth of what I think. Cognition is especially (even though not exclusively) concerned with what is perceptual (DL 7.52; *SVF* 2.71; LS 40P; Cicero, *Acad.* 1.40–2; *SVF* 1.55, 60–1; LS 40B; 41B). Moreover, it can be understood in two ways: (i) as cognition of sense and (ii) as cognition of knowledge. Although cognition is generated by sensation of objects endowed with perceptible qualities, it is by reason that we get cognition of conclusions reached through demonstration (such as the gods' existence and their providence). If this is so, not all the cases of cognition are cases of sense-perception (cf. Frede 1999: 298–9; Gourinat 2000: 62–3).

It might be worthwhile to conclude this section by referring to the gesture used by Zeno the Stoic in order to explain the difference between impression, assent, cognition, and knowledge: when holding out his hand with open fingers he represented impression. Then when he closed his fingers a bit he said, 'Assent is like this', and then when he made a fist he said that this was cognition. Knowledge, finally, was explained by putting his left hand over his fist, a firm and secure state 'that no one except the sage person possessed' (Cicero, *Acad.* 2.145; *SVF* 1.66; LS 41A). This image illustrates quite well why knowledge is unaltered by argument: the Stoic knower's soul is so stable and firm, and his convictions for arguing what he argues are so well justified that his argument cannot be modified by another argument and it turns out to be irrefutable.

4. Concluding remarks

As I mentioned in passing above, based on their radical division of mankind into virtuous and base people, the Stoics think that opinion and knowledge should be identified with baseness and wisdom respectively (Stobaeus 2.99, 3–8; LS 59N). The word 'virtue' (*aretē*) almost immediately evokes moral perfection (such as temperance), and in the above cited passage from Stobaeus this is certainly the way in which *aretē* should be understood. But the Stoics surely were making reference to 'epistemic virtues', too. Dialectics (within which epistemology is included) is said to be a virtue, which incorporates 'specific virtues' (DL 7.41; LS 31A). The list of such virtues includes different types of cognitive abilities a person should be endowed with if he or she is going to be wise: (i) non-precipitancy, (ii) unhastiness, (iii) irrefutability (this dialectical virtue is reminiscent of Plato's claim that 'truth is never refuted'; *Gorgias* 473b) and (iv) non-randomness (DL

7.47; LS 31B). The Stoic sage person has non-precipitancy in his assent (as we have already seen, the role of assent is crucial for determining the epistemic state of the person); in having strength in argument ('so as not to be carried away by argument into the contradictory', presumably of his own thesis, as suggested by LS in their translation of the passage), he is irrefutable.

The possession of all these qualities will guarantee the wise person to be free of error in argument. But, of course, possessing these extraordinary cognitive qualities just belongs to wise people, since they are the only ones whose judgement is *always* correct rather than just sometimes, or even at random. All of this can seem like both appealing and impossible achievements: appealing because everyone would like to be a person who knows when he or she should assent and should not assent (this is non-precipitancy). Furthermore, to have 'a strong reason' is something epistemically desirable insofar as it allows one to be legitimately prepared with regard to what is likely, and what is thus 'dangerously seductive' in terms of assent. Finally, being irrefutable clearly has its epistemic appeal, insofar as it ensures one a strong reason for maintaining the view one is defending. However, this project seems to be impossible since, from the standpoint of healthy common sense, one can assume (or even be sure!) that, even though one can reduce the frequency of one's mistakes (at least in a specific field of expertise), it is in fact impossible not to be mistaken sometimes (both at the theoretical and practical level).

If the rather radical division of mankind the Stoics propose is accepted, one has to face the problem of moral and 'epistemic' progress. Indeed for the Stoics moral progress is a sort of epistemic progress: you cannot be a virtuous person if your cognitive state is not knowledge. But that knowledge is not limited to the theoretical domain. After all, a Stoic wise person is the one who possesses both the theory and the practice of what should be done.[14]

Notes

1 The most interesting epistemological insights stem from Ancient and Middle Stoicism. The fragmentary evidence is collected by von Arnim (1903–1905; abbreviated *SVF*, followed by the volume and text number) and is translated into English and commented on by Long and Sedley (1987; abbreviated LS, followed by the section and the text letter, e.g. LS 63B). In addition to LS, the reader can find accurate English translations in Inwood and Gerson (2008). We also keep 'complete works' both by Epictetus and Marcus Aurelius, where some relevant remarks can be found, too.

2 For the Stoics, see Sextus Empiricus, *Against the Professors* [*AP*] 7.152, 227; DL 7.54. For Epicurus, *Epistle to Herodotus* 52, 1 (=DL 10, 52).

3 Ps. Galen, *Medical Definitions* 29, vol. 19, p. 355, 11–17, (ed. Kühn) (*SVF* 2.780); Galen, *Commentary on Hippocrates' Epidemics*, vol. 17b, p. 246, 14–247, 5 (*SVF* 2.782; LS 53E); Nemesius, *On the Nature of Man* 16, 12–16 (*SVF* 2.773).

4 Galen, *Book on the Utility of Respiration*, vol. 4, p. 501, 12–502, 8 (ed. Kühn). See also Cicero, *Tusculan Disputations* 1.42 (reporting the view of the Stoic Panaetius).

5 The Stoics argue for a teleological structure of the cosmos; the Epicureans deny the existence of teleology.

6 Interestingly, Plato (in a 'non-innatist' passage) points out that when we are children our soul, understood as a sort of 'receptacle', is empty (*Theaetetus* 197e).

7 In a similar vein, David Hume argues that the 'creative power of the mind' amounts to the faculty of compounding, transposing, augmenting, or diminishing the materials provided by the senses and experience. He explains fictions (e.g. 'a golden mountain') as the combination of the ideas of gold and mountain. Hume (2007: sec. II, 5–6) also applies this argument to account for what he calls a 'sublime thought or idea', such as the idea of God.

8 There is a similar passage in Sextus Empiricus, *AP* 7.344–5, which is close to what Cicero ascribes to the Stoics here. See, however, Cicero, *Acad.* 2.30, where 'mind' is identified with 'sense'.

9 In his pioneering book on Epictetus and the Stoa, Bonhöffer (1890: 193–5, 200–203) attempted to show that the Stoic preconceptions do not depend on perceptual experience, since they are limited to practical concepts. Sandbach (1971: 22–3, 35n12) challenges Bonhöffer's reading by providing some textual evidence that shows that any concept or notion depends on experience. For a fresh discussion of the topic, see Scott (1995: 202–4), who defends a 'dispositional approach' to Stoic innatism. A new discussion of the Stoic innatism is provided by Løkke (2015: 51–6).

10 The Stoics distinguished between sound (*phōnē*) and speech (*lexis*). But language (*logos*) is even different from mere 'speech': language is *always* significant (*sēmantikos*), whereas speech can be meaningless (such as 'blituri', an articulated sound, but lacking significance). For evidence, see DL 7.57 (*SVF* 1.74; 2.136; 140; 147; LS 33A; 33H; 33M).

11 For assent as the act of approval of a propositional content and as a faculty depending on the agent, cf. Cicero, *On Fate* 39–44 (*SVF* 2.974) and *Acad.* 2.37–8 (LS 40O).

12 See Sextus Empiricus, *AP* 7.242–3 (*SVF* 2.65; LS 39G), where examples of impressions are 'it is day', 'I am conversing.' Even Marcus Aurelius continues to think that an impression is a proposition (*Meditations* 5.16).

13 We owe to Cicero the effort for trying to translate into Latin some Greek technicalities. The case of the Greek *katalēpsis* ('cognition') is particularly

interesting: he proposes three terms for it (*cognitio, comprehensio*, and *perceptio*, although, as is clear, *perceptio* does not solely mean 'sensory perception': Cicero, *On Ends* 3.17). When rendering *katalēptike phantasia* by 'représentation perceptive', Gourinat (2000: 63) seems to be following Cicero. All of these terms capture the idea that the subject apprehends what the object is.

14 I am very grateful to Nicholas D. Smith for his suggestions and editing work. This piece was written with the financial support of the Fondecyt project 1120127 (Chile).

References

Allen, J. (1994), 'Academic Probabilism and Stoic Epistemology', *Classical Quarterly*, 44: 85–113.

Annas, J. (1990), 'Stoic Epistemology', in S. Everson (ed.), *Companions to Ancient Thought 1. Epistemology*, Cambridge: Cambridge University Press.

Bonhöffer, A. (1890), *Epictet und die Stoa. Untersuchungen zur stoischen Philosophie*, Stuttgart: Ferdinand Enke.

Frede, M. (1999), 'Stoic Epistemology', in K. Algra, J. Barnes, J. Mansfeld, and M. Schofield (eds), *The Cambridge History of Hellenistic Philosophy*, Cambridge: Cambridge University Press.

Gerson, L. (2006), *Ancient Epistemology*, Cambridge: Cambridge University Press.

Gourinat, J.-B. (2000), *La dialectique des stoïciens*, Paris: Vrin.

Hankinson, R. J. (2003), 'Stoic Epistemology', in B. Inwood (ed.), *The Cambridge Companion to The Stoics*, Cambridge: Cambridge University Press.

Hume, D. (2007 [1748]), *An Enquiry concerning Human Understanding*, ed. Stephen Buckle, Cambridge: Cambridge University Press.

Inwood, B. (1985), *Ethics and Human Action in Early Stoicism*, Oxford: Oxford University Press.

Inwood, B. and Gerson, L. (2008), *The Stoics Reader: Selected Writings and Testimonia*, Indianapolis: Hackett.

Kim, J. (2005), *Physicalism, or Something Near Enough*, Princeton: Princeton University Press.

Løkke, H. (2015), *Knowledge and Virtue in Early Stoicism*, Dordrecht: Springer.

Long, A. A. (1999), 'Stoic Psychology', in Algra et al. (eds), *The Cambridge History of Hellenistic Philosophy*.

Long, A. A. and Sedley, D. N. (1987), *The Hellenistic Philosophers*, 2 vols, Cambridge: Cambridge University Press.

Mignucci, M. (1993), 'The Stoic Analysis of the Sorites', *Proceedings of the Aristotelian Society*, NS 93: 231–45.

Sandbach, F. H. (1971), 'Ennoia and Prolepsis in Stoic Theory of Knowledge', in A. A. Long (ed.), *Problems in Stoicism*, London: The Athlone Press.

Schofield, M. (1999), 'Academic Epistemology', in Algra et al. (eds), *The Cambridge History of Hellenistic Philosophy*.

Scott, D. (1995), *Recollection and Experience: Plato's Theory of Learning and Its Successors*, Cambridge: Cambridge University Press.

Sorabji, R. (2000), *Emotion and Peace of Mind: From Stoic Agitation to Christian Temptation*, Oxford: Oxford University Press.

Williamson, T. (1994), *Vagueness*, London: Routledge.

11

Ancient Scepticism

Paul Woodruff

1. Introduction

Ancient scepticism aimed at a suspension of belief (*epochē*) using argument schemata known as modes. By contrast, most modern scepticism is dogmatic, albeit in a negative way. Sceptics of the ancient schools avoided dogmatism both positive and negative. Modern sceptics who deny the possibility of knowledge commit themselves to the belief that knowledge is impossible – which is dogmatic. The essence of scepticism in ancient philosophy is not a doctrine or even an argument but a set of practices for maintaining a mind free of commitments and untrammelled by belief.[1]

Ancient sceptics in the Hellenistic period were embroiled in philosophically productive arguments with dogmatists, primarily Stoics who were committed to there being a criterion for truth. Sceptical challenges to Stoicism led that school to develop stronger epistemological theories. At the same time, dogmatic challenges to sceptics forced them to consider how it could be possible to live a safe and successful human life while abstaining from belief on all subjects. From this grew distinctions among attitudes that might seem to count as belief, along with (at one stage) a distinction between two levels of assent.

Ancient sceptics developed arguments that continue to be active in epistemology. They made a strong case that there could not possibly be a criterion for truth, and they developed strategies for living without commitment to the truth of any proposition or impression. In addition, they invented sceptical argument schemata that could be deployed against a wide variety of dogmatic claims.

Pyrrho of Elis (c. 360–270 BCE) was said to have been the founder of sceptical practices, but, having left no writings, he remains a mysterious figure. The ancestors of scepticism also include a number of non-sceptics who challenged common assumptions about knowledge – Socrates and some pre-Socratics in the fifth century, Plato and Aristotle in the fourth.

Two main types of scepticism flourished in the Hellenistic and Roman Periods: Academic Scepticism in the Hellenistic and early Roman periods and Pyrrhonism as revived in the Roman period. We do not know when the word 'sceptic' was first used, but it was not used by the early Academics, who thought of themselves as the successors of Plato in the Academy. The Pyrrhonian revival was not a formal school but a powerful intellectual movement. The differences between the two are a subject of controversy, but all scholars agree that the Academic sceptics were no more moderate than the Pyrrhonians, as both schools held back strenuously from commitments of belief. David Hume (in his *Dialogues Concerning Natural Religion*, published posthumously in 1779) represents the Academic school as milder, but this is wrong. The main differences lie in their argument strategies and in their goals. Argument strategies will be treated below. As for goals, Pyrrhonians explicitly aimed at *ataraxia*, tranquility; Academics did not do so explicitly.

This chapter will outline the history of scepticism from its antecedents to its demise and discuss the operation of sceptical practice and argument. Sceptics held no theories and so left nothing but their practices to discuss. Nevertheless, they levied serious challenges against dogmatic philosophers, and these will be covered in this chapter.

2. Precursors

Several early philosophers questioned the accuracy of perception. The sources and natures of things, they taught, are not exactly as they are perceived. 'Nature loves to hide', said Heraclitus, meaning, apparently, not that perception is useless, but that the truth is not obvious to perception (22 B 123). Atomism, as developed by Democritus, allows the existence of only imperceptible atoms and the void in which they move. Since this reality is not open to perception, Democritus labelled the senses 'illegitimate' sources of knowledge (68 B 11) – illegitimate, because they do not reveal the hidden natures of things, but sources of knowledge nevertheless, because no acceptable theory could come in conflict with the evidence of the senses. Generally, the early philosophers who posited unseen elements in the nature of things had strategies for throwing perception into doubt, and these would be adopted by sceptics.

Ancient Scepticism 207

In the later fifth century, Gorgias wrote: 'The nature of true things is not evident [meaning, not evident to the senses]; so that even if they are the case these things would not be knowable, at least not to us.'[2] Gorgias taught mainly rhetoric, and we do not know how seriously he meant this; he did not have an epistemology to offer. He was probably drawing on earlier thinkers who were in the service of dogmatic theories that explained change or the cosmos in terms of things unseen, such as atoms.

On the other side, Protagoras trusted nothing but perception, and may have taught that only what is perceivable exists. He was famous for maintaining silence about the gods because they had not been clearly perceived, and he insisted that a tangent touches a circle along a line, and not at a point.[3] Not being perceivable, points do not exist on his theory. We can be fairly sure that he was sceptical in the ancient sense about any claims made on behalf of imperceptibles: he held back from commitments on such matters.

At the same time, Protagoras was evidently a relativist of some kind. He taught something along these lines: Plato reports him teaching that what a person perceives to be true is true for that person – and therefore known by that person. We shall see that some later sceptics declared that everything is relative and therefore unknowable. Protagoras, however, was different in this respect: his relativism, he thought, entails that knowledge is possible for all of us, whereas sceptical relativism was supposed to undermine the possibility of knowledge.

Some ancient sceptics – the Academics – looked to Socrates and Plato as the origin of their school. They observed that Plato's use of the dialogue form insulates him from direct commitments to the doctrines entertained in his writings, and that Socrates' reliance on refutation, along with his disclaimers of wisdom, also make him appear to be a kind of sceptic.

Few modern scholars read Socrates or Plato as sceptics, however. Plato represents Socrates as making dogmatic claims on a number of points while disclaiming knowledge on others. In the *Apology*,[4] Socrates says he knows that he is worthless with respect to wisdom, but that is evidently consistent with his knowing many other things as well – for example, that no harm can come to a good man. In a nearby context, he disclaims knowledge of life after death, but is committed in the *Phaedo* (70d ff.) to the belief that the soul lives on, supporting this with argument, and provides a powerful case for this dogmatic conclusion in the *Phaedrus* (245c-e). In the *Crito* he affirms his belief that one must never commit injustice; his commitment to this belief is strong enough that he would rather die than compromise it. In the *Gorgias* he admits that he does not know the truth of his view about justice, but he is confident in holding it nonetheless, because all those who deny it can be refuted.

Socrates' method of argument has much in common with sceptical modes, as we shall see, but he does not use it in a sceptical way. Sceptics aim at a suspension of belief, Socrates at a continuation of the inquiry. At the end of a failed search for the definition of a virtue, Socrates and his companions agree on the need for more work; most sceptics, at such an impasse, would breathe a sigh of relief – they have succeeded in escaping the temptation to hold a belief on one side or the other. At the end of argument, by contrast, Socrates asserts dogmatically that certain answers to his question have been shown to be false. That, to a sceptic, is negative dogmatism.

In a rare case, Socrates uses his questioning to purify his partner of all beliefs on a matter, preparatory to leading the partner to discover for himself the right answer. That case is described in the *Meno*. The purifying (or kathartic) phase of argument would satisfy a sceptic. Plato has the Stranger describe purely kathartic argument in the *Sophist* (230bc), but never has Socrates used such argument except in the *Meno* (84a), where he goes beyond katharsis to ask questions that yield positive conclusions.

As for Plato, Aristotle and most modern scholars agree that he was committed to an ontology of transcendent forms – a commitment quite incompatible with scepticism. But for the sensible world, Plato appears to have been a sceptic. Knowledge of the world of appearances is impossible in his view, as only the transcendent Forms are knowable. Perceptible objects are not knowable because they are in an unceasing process of change, and because even at a given time they appear to have conflicting qualities.[5]

Aristotle introduced some sceptical arguments in his work on epistemology and was credited by later sceptics with starting the philosophical practice of arguing on both sides of every question (Cicero, *On Ends* 5.10). Aristotle introduced the practice of arguing pro and contra on particular subjects, not, like the Academic Arcesilaus, with the object of always arguing against everything, but in order that he might nonetheless set out all possible arguments on either side of a subject (Cicero, *On Ends* 5.10).

3. Origins: Pyrrho

Pyrrho of Elis is said to have been the first sceptic. In the late fourth century and early third century BCE he taught informally. He did not produce any written work, but is known to us through later sources. The most authoritative of these is Timon of Phlius, whose work survives in fragments. Timon is probably the source also for the reports on Pyrrho to be found in later sceptics. Tradition has it that Pyrrho followed his teacher Anaxarchus with Alexander's army to India, where he encountered naked philosophers, *gymnosophists*. If the story is true, his naked philosophers were probably Buddhists, but we can only guess at what he might have learned from them. We also have a report that he was influenced by the ethical teachings of Democritus.

Pyrrho taught his students to seek *ataraxia* (freedom from mental disturbance) and promised that this would lead to pleasure. In this he may well have influenced Epicurus in an early stage of the development of his theories. To achieve this goal, he taught that one should live without opinions or beliefs, and to help his students preserve the minds from opinion, he taught that all things are indeterminable. The contrast with Socrates is striking. Socrates' proto-scepticism is based on his beliefs about the difference between gods and humans: gods may well know the truth of things, but we do not. Pyrrho's view appears to have been that there is no truth for anyone – divine or human – to know.

What we can truly say about each thing, then, is only that it no more is than it is not – for whatever predicate we wish to supply. We do not know how Pyrrho and his immediate followers came to this conclusion, or exactly what they meant by it. But we can readily see that his conclusion runs into the danger of being dogmatic. Later sceptics will hold back from declaring a priori that things are indeterminable, and especially from declaring that it is the nature of things to be indeterminable, because such claims would be dogmatic to the taste of later sceptics, as we shall see.

Why should one seek a life without belief? Surely not on the basis of the belief that this will make one tranquil and therefore happy. That would be to compromise scepticism. Judging from later sceptic texts, we can sketch Pyrrho's thinking as roughly this: When we have come to accept indeterminability and suspended judgement about questions of value, our desires and passions will fall away, and we will find ourselves free of the disturbance that comes from thinking our condition should be better than it is. If nothing can be determined to be bad for us, then we have nothing to worry about.

Pyrrho's opponents apparently mocked his teaching on the assumption that any action entails belief. For example, if you act to avoid a danger, you must believe that the danger is real. So they promulgated stories in which Pyrrho was so indifferent to danger that his students had to protect him. But Timon insisted that Pyrrho lived a normal life, basing his actions on appearances.

4. Principal sceptics

Arcesilaus (316/5–241/0 BCE) became head of the Academy that Plato had started in 284 BCE. He was the first sceptic to lead the school. He may have been influenced by Pyrrho and his followers, but he believed that the foundation of his work was Plato's. His rise to influence came soon after Zeno of Citium founded the Stoic school of philosophy.

Carneades (214–129/8 BCE) shaped the arguments of Academic scepticism in response to defensive moves made by the Stoics. His brand of scepticism was found to be too close to the Stoics for the comfort of the early Pyrrhonians.

Philo of Larissa (159/8–84/3 BCE) was the last head of the Academy in residence, and is considered the last sceptical head of the Academy, although his was a weaker form of scepticism. An influence on Cicero.

Antiochus of Ascalon (125–68 BCE) was an Academic who broke with his teacher Philo over scepticism. An eclectic philosopher, he blended Stoicism and Platonism, but was an important thinker in his own right. His influence marks the end of the sceptical Academy. He was a teacher of Cicero.

None of the works of these Academics has survived; we know of them through ancient secondary sources and short quotations in ancient works. Our main source is Cicero.

Cicero (106–43 BCE) was a Roman lawyer, politician, and philosopher. He was drawn toward the Academy when Philo visited Rome, and he studied philosophy in an eclectic manner in Athens. He is an important philosopher in his own right, and he is also one of our main sources for Academic scepticism, primarily through his *Academica*.

Aenesidemus (first century BCE) appears to have been the founder of the Pyrrhonian revival, a school of scepticism that, for the first time, claimed the legacy of Pyrrho. He is said to have been the author of the Ten Modes, the principal argument schemata designed to be deployed against any sort of dogmatism, not just Stoicism. Like the Academics, Aenesidemus left no texts for us. We have summaries and paraphrases from other ancient writers as well as from an important Byzantine scholar.[6]

Agrippa, who followed Aenesidemus, is known only as the author of the Five Modes.

Sextus Empiricus (second century CE) was an empirical doctor – that is, one who preferred to use treatments that had been seen to work, rather than treatments recommended by abstract theory. He is the author of *Outlines of*

Pyrrhonism and other works collected as *Sceptical Treatises*. He is our main source for the various strains of Pyrrhonian philosophy.

5. Academic Scepticism

The two principal architects of the Academic philosophy were Arcesilaus and Carneades. So far as we know, they did not call themselves sceptics or followers of Pyrrho. Only with hindsight do we list them as sceptics.

Arcesilaus evidently used techniques of refutation learned from Plato's representation of Socrates. Socrates said that he knew he was worthless in wisdom, but Arcesilaus would not go so far. He did not know even that he did not know. Socrates refuted his partners in such a way that they suspected he was hiding his own beliefs on the matter, and in some dialogues he is shown arguing in favour of certain positions. But Arcesilaus' arguments were evidently designed not to commit him to any beliefs – or even to the soundness of any logical system of inference: 'By arguing against everyone's opinions [Arcesilaus] drew most people away from their own, so that when reasons of equal weight were found on opposite sides on the same subject, the easier course was to withhold assent from either side' (Cicero, *Academica* 1.43).

The Academic goal, then, was equipollence (*isosthenia*) between opposing positions. Once students feel the equal power of arguments on both sides of an issue, they will be unable to commit to either, with the result that they will remain in suspension of belief. But Arcesilaus is reported to have concluded from equipollence that one *should* suspend judgement on the issue. That, of course, would be a dogmatic normative claim. If Arcesilaus were consistent, he would have held back from such inferences. As we shall see, sceptics find it hard to preserve sceptical hygiene – total *epochē* – while deploying formal arguments against dogmatists.

In such case as this, sceptics have two safe alternatives. They can draw the dogmatists to conclude that they should suspend judgement, in view of their own criteria for judgement. For this, the argument will be a standard deductive one using dogmatist premises. Alternatively, they may be reporting their own experiences: faced with equipollence, they simply find that they feel like suspending judgement. Their arguments then need not be water-tight, so long as they make their audience feel like relaxing into *epochē*.

Carneades, the fourth head of the Academy after Arcesilaus, used similar strategies. As ambassador from Athens to Rome, he is said to have brought together all the arguments in favour of justice so that he could overturn them. He would defend justice on one day and attack it on the next. This excited young students in Rome, but it scandalized Cato the Elder and other conservatives, giving philosophy and Greek culture a bad door in Rome.

Thus far, Carneades followed the path set by Arcesilaus. But in two areas he expanded Academic philosophy. He introduced from Stoicism a distinction between two levels of assent, in order to explain how it could be possible for a sceptic to live an active life while suspending belief (see below). In addition, he took on a fundamental doctrine of the Stoics – determinism. His arguments were significantly original.

Stoics taught that every event is determined by antecedent causes, governed by a well-meaning providence. The only freedom we have is over our thoughts and emotions, which we can bring into line with the governance of the world. Acquiescence in the governance of the world is an essential part of wisdom. Take away the comfort of benign determinism, and the appeal of Stoicism to ordinary followers would fade away.

So, Carneades argued against causal determinism making crucial new distinctions. Carneades allows that time-indexed truths about contingent events in the future have always been true (this as a matter of what we would call tense logic), and so Carneades accepts logical determinism, but he denies that this entails causal determinism. The Stoics agreed that if every event had an antecedent cause (causal determinism), then every event would be causally determined, and a god who knew all would know what is coming to be (epistemic determinism). But if there are events that could not be known in advance, even by a god, then causal determinism is false.

Carneades argues that the failure of epistemic determinism entails the failure of causal determinism. He calls attention to contingent events with no antecedent causes which anyone could know about – such as the death at sea of a Roman consul. And there are events that spring from human choices simultaneous with the resulting action, such as Oedipus' killing of a man met by chance. These events have causes that are not antecedent. Even the god of oracles, Apollo, could not predict events that have no antecedent causes, and so myths about oracles foretelling contingent events or human choices must be false (Cicero, *De Fato* 26–33).[7] Therefore, causal determinism is false.

After Carneades, the Academy seems to have shifted back towards Plato and his texts. This is the period in which Thrasyllus produced the edition of

Plato's works that has come down to us. This is also the period of the Academic commentary on Plato's *Theaetetus*, a work that makes good use of that dialogue for sceptical ends. Philo of Larissa rejected the Stoic criterion; in his view there could be objective truths, but no one could be as certain of them as Stoics sought to be. We are therefore left with plausible opinions. So Philo did not rigorously suspend judgement. His pupil, Antiochus of Ascalon, rejected scepticism as incompatible with Plato's philosophy. He set out to show that Stoic theory was implicit in Plato from the start (as some Stoics claimed) and broke away to form what he called the Old Academy.

6. The Stoic-sceptic debate

For about 200 years sceptics and Stoics argued against one another, each school providing fodder for the other. As sceptics, the Academics had no doctrines they could deploy against the Stoics, but they could take Stoic doctrines and turn them against their own makers. Stoics took over and developed formal-style logic from the Megarian School, so that Academics were free to use such logic against Stoics without committing themselves to its validity.

Academics poked holes in Stoic epistemology, and Stoics moved quickly to plug them. The relationship between the schools rapidly became symbiotic – neither school would have had much life in it without the other. Having no doctrines, Academics would have had little to say if they had had no recourse to the generous structure of Stoic thought. And without the challenges of the Academics, Stoic thinkers would have had little to do besides repeating old teachings. The two centuries of this debate were the most dynamic period in ancient philosophy.

Early modern epistemological debate revived the ancient issues. The expression 'clear and distinct ideas' is a translation of the main idea behind the *phantasia kataleptikē*: a sense impression that carries in itself features that guarantee its truth. As Descartes showed, this is not as easy a target as it may appear. Although the Academics launched many attacks on the possibility of knowledge on Stoic grounds, none of their arguments had the devastating power that Descartes deployed in his thought experiment of the Evil Demon.

Before examining Academic arguments against Stoic epistemology, we must be clear that these arguments are not supposed to commit their makers to any beliefs – not even in the validity of the logic that they use. All the commitments are supposed to come from the Stoics. The Academic strategy is to ensnare Stoics in their own teachings while preserving their own sceptical hygiene. That was a difficult strategy to sustain as generations of dialecticians built on a standard repertoire of doctrines which, in the end, the two schools seemed to share. The Pyrrhonian revivals, as we shall see, made scepticism independent of Stoicism for the first time since Pyrrho himself. I will focus this section on two issues that divided sceptics and Stoics – the criterion and the possibility of action without belief.

7. Against the criterion

Academic argument was tailored to rein in the dogmatism of the rival Stoic school. Stoics claimed that there was a criterion of truth, and that it was empirical – the self-verifying sense impression, called *phantasia kataleptikē*. Such impressions, in Stoic theory, would ground knowledge of the world. The expression is also translated as 'cognitive impression', but 'self-verifying' conveys the meaning of the claim more clearly. To have a *katalēpsis* is to have a grasp of the truth. A sense impression is *kataleptic* (graspable) when it is such that the subject knows, from the impression alone, that this impression reveals the truth of its object. Such impressions are clear and distinct, like an impression made in soft wax by a signet ring. In what follows, I shall use 'graspable' as a technical term entailing 'self-verifying'.

This is a gift to scepticism. All the sceptic needs to do is to provide a thought experiment in which a false impression has all the perceivable features of a true one that was taken to be graspable. If that is possible – if we can be deceived by an impression that looks graspable but is not – then we cannot rely on any impression as being self-verifying in this way.

A well-known myth served their purpose. Zeus is said to have created a false simulacrum of Helen, using all his divine power to make her such that anyone who saw her would think she was the real Helen. She is designed to have all the perceivable features of the sort of impression the Stoics called graspable. Meanwhile, according to myth, the real Helen sat out the war in Egypt. A clear and distinct impression of the true Helen would have been self-verifying if the Stoic theory held up (the sceptics said), but it would not have differed in any perceivable way from an impression under good conditions of the false Helen. If we can be deceived by an impression that has all the earmarks of one that is perceived as self-verifying, then there can be no self-verifying impressions.

As a result of such arguments, Arcesilaus is said to have claimed that all things are incognitive – that is, that nothing is accessible by means of self-verifying

Ancient Scepticism

impressions. In claiming this he seems to be taking a negatively dogmatic stance – denying something about the world in his own persona. Sceptics always run this risk, that by refuting dogmatists they fall into commitments to negative conclusions. In this case, the report must be incomplete. What Arcesilaus should have said is that, given the Stoic theory of the criterion, *Stoics* must believe that all things are incognitive. He himself would suspend belief on the matter.

Such arguments stimulated the Stoics to refine their theory of the criterion. But a thought experiment in which a god uses his power to deceive us is hard to beat. Descartes would improve upon it later with his methodological doubt and the experiment of the Evil Demon.

8. Action without belief

Stoics were on the defensive in the debate over the criterion, but sceptics were on the defensive over action theory. Opponents of scepticism continued to press the argument first recorded as used against Pyrrho: how can anyone live a human life with no beliefs whatever? If action entails belief (as it appears to do), then sceptics will have to suspend action to the extent that they suspend belief. How could they not? This was the main question that sceptics in all periods were pressed to answer – the so-called inactivity or *apraxia* argument. It has a precedent in Aristotle's argument that a person who is equally drawn to contrary beliefs – such as a relativist like Protagoras – will be unable to act (*Metaphysics* 4.4).

On Stoic action theory, action entails belief: If you run from danger, that is because you have assented to your impression that you are in the presence of danger. To assent to an impression (they thought) is to believe the associated proposition: this object is dangerous. Take away assent, on this theory, and no action will follow. Therefore, if Stoic action theory is right, then sceptics who do take action are only pretending to live without belief. If, on the other hand, they truly live without belief, they will take no actions.

In response to this argument, sceptics mainly used one of these four strategies to explain how one could act while suspending belief.

1. *The sceptic assents to nothing.* Human beings act without belief when they act as animals do on Aristotle's theory, responding automatically to the stimuli of sense impressions – without deliberation about what is good or right or fitting in the circumstances. When they perceive danger, they flee, and so do we humans. This was the line Arcesilaus took.

2. *The sceptic assents weakly to some impressions, but without committing to a belief.* There is a high level of assent that does entail belief. Sceptics would hold back from this level of assent, and so would not take any impression to be true. But they would allow themselves to then act upon an impression they found to be persuasive (*pithanon*), while suspending judgement as to its truth, on the basis of weak assent.

   This concept of weak assent was taken by Carneades from the Stoics, who held that only the sage could know, and assent to, the truth of things. Non-sages would have to depend on a weaker mode of assent as the criterion for action. Carneades apparently adopted the criterion of action that the Stoics had proposed for non-sages – persuasiveness – taking this to be a criterion for action but not for truth. Some of his followers and some modern scholars have concluded that Carneades adopted this criterion as his own, but he may have used it merely as a dialectical step in a purely sceptical argument against the Stoics. By this he could show the Stoics that they themselves allowed for action without full-blown assent, thus blowing away their claim that action entails assent in the full sense. Still, Carneades left the impression on later sceptics that Carneades and his followers had been infected with Stoic theory – that they were Stoics fighting Stoics.

3. *The sceptic may assent to appearances, but not to dogmatic beliefs.* In this view assenting to appearances would entail beliefs about appearances, such as 'I am seeing red here now' or 'I feel that danger is near'. This strategy is hinted at in Sextus Empiricus but not developed. What would count as a dogmatic belief? The simplest interpretation ties dogmatism to claims about what cannot be perceived or what is known only through indicative signs. For example, smoke is a sign of an unseen fire.

   In dogmatic medicine, theorists held that certain symptoms indicate underlying conditions of health, but sceptical doctors like Sextus would not allow such inferences from the seen to the unseen. They would adopt treatments not on the basis of theory, but on the basis of appearances: 'This treatment appears to work.' A belief is dogmatic, in this view, if it presupposes the existence of anything that cannot be perceived and a theory is dogmatic if it is based on assuming a reality that is imperceptible.

   Stoic theory made much of indicative signs, against which sceptics developed modes of argument. These I will treat below.

4. *The sceptic complies with the lookouts that guide human life.* This does not entail assent. Later Pyrrhonians such as Sextus Empiricus adopted this

strategy explicitly. The four lookouts are[8]: nature, feeling, custom, and *technē* (technical knowledge).

Complying is obeying or going along with a guide, and it entails no more than passive acquiescence. By nature, we cannot help thinking certain things. A feeling such as like hunger drives one to find food and eat it; one does not have to assent to the proposition that eating is good. Custom commands us to live by values on which we have no need to reflect; we must live that way to live in society. Fourth, *technē* presses actions on us which we must take in order to carry out our tasks; if a gale blows up, the sailor takes in sail without asking whether that is a good thing to do. The sceptic complies with these four passively, without any form of assent, like small children being led around by servants. The children do not make choices and so do not assent; they go where they are taken.

9. The Pyrrhonian revival

The principal differences between Academic and Pyrrhonian scepticism are two: First, Academics sought relief from belief apparently as an end in itself, whereas Pyrrhonians practiced sceptical argument in order to find tranquility of mind. Second, Academics made detailed use of Stoic epistemology for dialectical purposes – to confront Stoics with contradictions in their own theories. In doing this they went so far that they have common ground with the Stoics. That made them seem like Stoics fighting Stoics to the Pyrrhonian reformers, who steered clear of Stoicism and developed general strategies – the modes – for helping any dogmatic philosopher hold back from belief.

The first Pyrrhonian revival was led by Aenesidemus, who was disgusted with what he saw as Carneades' tilt towards Stoicism, and he refused to follow Philo into the moderate scepticism of the Academy's twilight years. Instead, he broke away entirely from the Academy and started the Pyrrhonian revival. In this he was evidently followed by Agrippa, the reported author of the Five Modes. Together, they constitute the first phase of the Pyrrhonian revival.[9]

Aenesidemus returned to Pyrrho's goal of tranquility (*ataraxia*) and attacked negative dogmatism, to which he thought the Academy had succumbed. He wrote an attack on the Academy and developed modes of argument to use against all dogmatists, not Stoics alone. So it appears from the evidence we have that we are not sure of the man's dates, nor can we be certain of the authorship of the modes. Much of what we know of his philosophy comes from the summary in the ninth-century *Library* of Photius. The Ten Modes attributed to him survive in different versions given by ancient authors, primarily Sextus Empiricus, Diogenes Laertius, and Philo of Alexandria. The Eight Modes against the causes are found only in Sextus.

Aenesidemus taught that finding disparity in appearances and theories would lead to suspension of judgement. A good way to become aware of disparity is to recollect conflicting appearances or ideas. Then, once you are in a state of *epochē*, you will find that tranquility follows that condition 'like a shadow'. Tranquility simply happens to us after we suspend judgement; it is a psychological consequence that we each find true in our own case. Aenesidemus would not make a general claim on such a matter.

Such Pyrrhonians say they are happy in knowing that they have no firm cognition of anything. This raises a difficult issue. At the same time, Aenesidemus accuses the Academics of negative dogmatism, while seeming to draw strong negative conclusions himself. Most of the arguments attributed to him are refutations – *aporiai*. The word *aporia* in the sceptics, as in Plato, means an impasse or refutation. Later Pyrrhonians such as Sextus will balance every refutation with a positive argument, and then suspend judgement between the positive and the negative case. Aenesidemus appears to have been content to end with a refutation. I have argued that he is therefore our best example of an aporetic Pyrrhonist.[10]

For example, he argues that indicative signs (causes) do not exist at all, and that non-evident objects like gods are not subject to being grasped. But we shall see that his conclusions are negative in a different way from those of the Academics he rejects. When a Stoic would say, 'This is graspable' and an Academic, 'This is not graspable', Aenesidemus seems to have used the 'no more' formula (*ouden mallon*), and said: '[T]his is no more graspable than non-graspable.' This he understands in relativistic terms: '[T]his is graspable at one time but not at another, or by one person but not by another.' Evidently he thought that the Academics went wrong by not relativizing their claims under temporal or personal qualifications. In fact, Aenesidemus is said to have argued that all things are relative – meaning, I think, that he can find an argument with an *ou mallon* conclusion for anything. The *Ten Modes* are designed to do just such a task. His arguments rest on what I call the Platonic Principle. Plato assumes that Forms and other causes have essential natures such that they always affect whatever they affect in the same way. If the essential nature of fire is hot, then fire will bring heat to anything it affects. But if we find a case in which fire makes someone shiver, then fire is no more hot than cold:

PP. If an object is no more F than G, then it could not be the essential nature of that object to be either F or G.

If honey tastes sweet to one person and bitter to another, it is no more sweet than bitter; therefore it is not the case that it is the nature of honey to affect people in a sweet way. Thus, from a relativized conclusion – the sweetness of honey to an observer depends on the observer – we can draw a negative conclusion about honey – that it does not have the essential nature to affect people sweetly. This leaves open the question of whether honey has an essential nature. On that, the sceptic holds back.

Aenesidemus probably distinguished in practice between two kinds of negative conclusion, only one of which he found to be dogmatic. The difference is one of scope:

C1. It is the underlying nature of an object not to be F.
C2. It is not the underlying nature of an object to be F.

Now apply this to the question of what is graspable. Aenesidemus believes that he can show for any object that it is no more graspable than not. From this he can conclude by PP in each case that the object does not have an essential nature to be graspable. By contrast, the Academics seem to have argued that it was in the natures of things to be not graspable. That is the kind of dogmatism that Aenesidemus avoids.

The Ten modes and the Eight apparently delivered negative conclusions in their original formulations. But Sextus Empiricus tried to use them differently.

10. Sceptical argument

The modes are argument schemata for general use against dogmatism. We have records of two main lists of modes, the Ten and the Five, which were used at various times in the history of ancient scepticism, either independently or in some sort of systematic connection, mainly as tools of the Pyrrhonian revival.

The modes were compiled long after Pyrrho – the Ten probably by Aenesidemus,[11] and the Five by a shadowy figure named Agrippa. In addition, we have a list of *Eight Causal Modes* attributed to Aenesidemus.

The Five Modes are dissonance (disagreement), regress, relativity, hypothesis, and reciprocity. They seem to form a system. If theories seem to *disagree*, the sceptic should ask the dogmatist on one side for the grounds of that theory. Then ask after the grounds for that, and so on, with the result that the dogmatist will

220 *Knowledge in Ancient Philosophy*

fall into a *regress*, or else stake everything on an unsupported *hypothesis*, or else appeal to something that is in question (*reciprocity*). If all else fails, ensnare the dogmatist in the *relativity* of perception.

The Eight Causal Modes are designed to show that appearances cannot be explained with reference to what is unseen. The Fifth brings out the main problem: various dogmatic theories explain phenomena in different ways, by reference to different unseen elements. But we find no way to settle the disputes among dogmatists, since the elements to which they appeal are unseen. At this point we could turn to the Five Modes.

The most distinctively Pyrrhonian strategies are the Ten. The first seven modes show the relativity of perceptual appearances in various ways; these are summed up in the Eighth Mode, 'Relativity'. The Ninth and Tenth Modes deal with issues of value. The First Mode, from differences among animals, is typical (Sextus, *Outlines* 1.40, cf. 2.26).[12] Different animals have different sensory receptors; the same object will probably have different effects on different receptors; so different animals will probably receive different sensory impressions. As party to the issue, we humans cannot judge between our impressions and those of other animals, so the matter is undecidable or inarbitrable.

At this point, we must choose between two strategies. Following the *aporetic* Pyrrhonism of Aenesidemus, we would assume the premise that one ought not to take a position on an undecidable issue, and conclude that therefore one ought to suspend judgement in such matters. All reports of the first mode end this way, drawing a deontic conclusion. This is the strategy of demonstration.

To *ephectic* Pyrrhonians such as Sextus, however, the aporetic (refutative) strategy is dogmatic. The aporetics assume the validity of inference as well as the truth of the premises, and they assert its conclusion as if it were a belief. *Ephectic* Pyrrhonians prefer a rhetorical strategy: once you have been led by the argument to feel that both sides are equally powerful, you simply feel like suspending judgement. On this strategy, the goal of the modes is therapeutic. If you feel a bout of dogmatism coming on, go to your local Pyrrhonian practitioner and listen to modal arguments until your inclination to form beliefs goes away. Once you are free of that inclination, you will find that tranquility follows – a blessed relief from the anxiety of belief.

Notes

1　In preparing this chapter, I have drawn on the essays in Bett (2010). Translations of sceptical texts, unless otherwise indicated, are from Long and Sedley (1987).

Ancient Scepticism 221

2 Gorgias on knowledge, from *On Not Being* (DK 82B3, 77 ff. = Sextus Empiricus M7.77, ff.).

3 Protagoras on the gods, DK 80B4; on the tangent, Aristotle, *Metaphysics* 998A1-4.

4 For Plato's works, I recommend Cooper's (1997) edition.

5 Sceptics attributed to Plato himself the relativistic account of perception at *Theaetetus* 156c-157b. For the thesis that things are in constant change in the phenomenal world, see *Republic* 479a.

6 Photius, in a book called *Library*, wrote an extended account of Aenesidemus' work for colleagues of his who did not have access to the book itself, in the ninth century CE. For a translation, see Long and Sedley (1987: 71C, 468–9).

7 For a more detailed account, on which mine is based, see Long and Sedley (1987: 465–7).

8 The fourfold lookout or guide to life (*tērēsis*) is given at Sextus Empiricus, *Outlines of Pyrrhonism* 1, 23–4.

9 Woodruff (1988) and Bett (2000) have argued that there were two distinct phases of the Pyrrhonian revival, with Aenesidemus being the primary representative of the first, while Sextus (most of the time) speaks for the second. Hankinson (1995: 178) holds that Diogenes Laertius in his presentation of the mode of relativity 'looks back to an earlier, less developed Pyrrhonism'. Schofield (2007) has marshalled arguments to show that Aenesidemus was a Pyrrhonist in precisely Sextus' sense. Although my view of the matter is not changed, my interpretation of particular modes does not depend on the two-phase hypothesis.

10 The account that follows is defended in Woodruff (1988: 139–68; 2010: 208–31).

11 The Ten Modes are associated with Aenesidemus or his followers in Sextus Empiricus M 7.345 and by context in Diogenes Laertius 9.78 and Aristocles. As Aenesidemus is the founder of the Pyrrhonian revival, he is most likely in any case to have been the author of the Ten Modes.

12 Philo's version is at 171, in Diogenes' at 9.79–80. The First Mode is also found in Aristocles.

References

Bett, R. (2000), *Pyrrho, His Antecedents, and His Legacy*, Oxford: Oxford University Press.

Bett, R. (2010), *The Cambridge Companion to Ancient Scepticism*, Cambridge: Cambridge University Press.

Cooper, J. (1997), *Plato: Complete* Works, Indianapolis: Hackett Publishing Company.

Hankinson, R. (1995), *The Sceptics*, London: Routledge.

Hume, D. (2007 [1779]), *Dialogues Concerning Natural Religion*, ed. D. Coleman, Cambridge: Cambridge University Press.

Long, A. A. and Sedley, D. N. (1987), *The Hellenistic Philosophers*, vol. 1, Cambridge: Cambridge University Press.

Schofield, M. (2007), 'Aenesidemus: Pyrrhonist and 'Heraclitean', in A. M. Ioppolo and D. N. Sedley (eds), *Pyrrhonists, Patricians, Platonizers: Hellenistic Philosophy in the Period 155–86 BC*, Napoli: Bibliopolis.

Woodruff, P. (1988), 'Aporetic Pyrrhonism', *Oxford Studies in Ancient Philosophy*, VI: 139–68.

Woodruff, P. (2010), 'Pyrrhonian Modes', in Richard Bett (ed.), *Cambridge Companion to Ancient Scepticism*, Cambridge: Cambridge University Press.

12

Epistemologies in Neoplatonism

Péter Lautner

1. Introduction

Neoplatonist views on acquiring and retaining knowledge varied a great deal. Because of the strong emphasis on the substantial distinction between body and soul, on the one hand, we have theories emphasizing that knowledge is made possible by the kinship of our individual soul to the ordering principles of the intelligible and the physical world. On the other hand, occasionally, we also meet theories which lay great emphasis on the acquisition of empirical knowledge.

2. Plotinus

Due to the general Neoplatonic commitment to the unaffected character of the soul Plotinus endorsed a theory of sense-perception which stresses that the sense itself cannot be affected by external objects. His approach can be interpreted as an answer to the sceptical challenge.[1] The principal thesis is that the cognitive process in general cannot be described in terms of reception of the external forms. Instead, it is a process generated from within, as it were, instigated by the intellect. As a consequence, the sense also must be active in the perceptual process. Its primary task is not to receive sensory impressions but to judge them (*Ennead* III.6.1, IV.6). Sense-perceptions are not affections but activities concerned with the affections and judgements; this judgement belongs to the perceiving soul, not to the body which contains affections only (III.6.1). Sometimes, however, we find explanations that are not so elaborate. In clarifying the relation between body and soul in the sensory process he uses the metaphor of weaving, with the soul representing the craftsman and the body his tool (IV.3.26.1–9). Sensory affections occur in the body whereas the soul receives

224   *Knowledge in Ancient Philosophy*

either the impression of the body or the impression that comes though the body or the judgement which it makes from the affection of the body. It is not clear whether the three options are compatible or not, but so much is obvious that sense-perception cannot be identified with affection. When we see a human being (V.3.3.1, see also IV.7.6.7–8) we are not merely apprehending an aggregate of sensible qualities such as colours and shapes but also identify them as forming a certain compound. Such a conceptual content is what makes sense-perception a genuine cognitive act. Sensory affections alone cannot provide us with that information. As a consequence, sense-perception involves the activation of some cognitive content (*logos*) which is innate to the soul.[2]

The most elaborate discussion of the sensory process is to be found in IV.4.23. Plotinus makes it clear that the perceiving soul needs body. The basic premise is that sense-perception is for the soul an apprehension in which it grasps the quality within the bodies and impresses their forms into itself. If the soul were on its own it would grasp only what it has in itself, a pure thought. In order to grasp something different it has to acquire them either by being assimilated to it or by being together with something so assimilated. Plotinus rules out that the soul as an immaterial entity can be assimilated to the perceptible things while remaining itself. It is just as absurd as the assimilation of a point to a line. Something must be affected by the forms coming from external objects, however, and this something cannot be soul. For this reason, the soul and the external thing cannot be the only participants in sense-perception. There must be a third thing which is affected in the perceptual process, and this is what receives the form as well. It is of the same nature as the external object, and this is why it can be affected by external objects. By contrast, the soul must be aware of the affection without being affected. Thus Plotinus concludes that the only viable position is that sense-perception occurs by means of bodily organs.

The immaterial nature of the sense faculty seems to guarantee the unity of perception as well. In criticizing Stoic theories, Plotinus (IV.7.6–7) argues that the spatial extension of the body provides unity in a loose sense only, as a spatial continuity of non-identical parts. As opposed to the Aristotelian theories his account fails to make mention of the common sense (*koinē aisthēsis*).[3] If the function of the general sense were to collect the data from different sense-modalities and serve as a focal point of the different particular senses, then Plotinus' theory does not require it because the undifferentiated nature of perception makes such a distinct power wholly superfluous.[4] There is, however, a distinct power, the power of representation (*phantasia* or *to phantastikon*) where the various perceptions terminate (IV.3.29–30). Although it is not quite clear whether representation and perception are two distinct faculties or not, Plotinus' formulations tend to confirm that they perform different activities for unlike sense-perception the representational power does not need the body for its operation. They also have different objects. The objects of the representational power are images, whereas the sensory power is directed towards the perceptible forms. However, there is a suggestion based on IV.3.29 that the perceptual act and the primary grasp of the image by the *phantasia* are simultaneous. The suggestion might imply that sense-perception considered as perceptual judgement involves the grasp of the representation that constitutes the judgement.[5] Consequently, there is no sharp divide between sense-perception and representation for the former grasps its object by means of a judgement that itself is simultaneously grasped by the representational faculty. Moreover, sense-perception produces contents that are without extensions and can be described as intelligible impressions, forms, or representational images (*phantasmata*). They provide the basic material for the acquisition of empirical concepts. Both memory and discursive reason draw on such images, which implies that the representational power is active when we are remembering or reasoning discursively. In this sense, its range extends to all sorts of apprehension below the level of intellection. Memory is not a simple conservation of sense data. Rather, it is an active force working with images that are not impressions coming from without but contents residing there (IV.6.3).[6] They must be activated in due time. Thus Plotinus' theory of memory is based on a conception of the soul according to which it is active both in perception and thinking. For this reason, memory has both perceptible and intelligible objects, the latter being through innate ideas which do not have to be acquired by the soul since they are inherent in it. This being said, he distinguishes two types of memory, one which deals with an acquired object and another which neither relies on an acquired object nor involves time (IV.3.26).[7] The type of memory involving time cannot belong to the undescended part of the soul. Recollection (*anamnēsis*) is much less important than either in Plato or in Aristotle. Because in Plotinus' view memory is not a sheer conservation of sense impressions but an active force, much of the work which Plato and Aristotle attributed to recollection can be done by memory just as well.[8]

The criteria in perceptual judgements are called *logoi*. They are notions residing in discursive reason and responsible for judging the data coming from sense-perceptions. They constitute the innate knowledge of the soul and serve as the epistemological principles for empirical cognition. They are called standards (*kanōnes*) (V.3.3–4) as well, with a term recalling Hellenistic theories.[9] Knowledge of this innate content implies self-knowledge; the soul knows itself

226 *Knowledge in Ancient Philosophy*

by knowing its innate content which belongs to its substance. This kind of knowledge meets all the criteria for certain knowledge and is safe from sceptical attacks.[10] The soul owes its innate content to the Intellect on which it depends. The Intellect never errs because there is no external object against which the content of its knowledge, the ideas, could be tested and the relation of the Intellect to the objects of knowledge is so intimate that nothing can be inserted between them (V.3.5, V.5.2). For this reason, the Intellect knows its objects in a strictly direct way which makes its knowledge infallible. The constant presence of these intelligible principles in the soul is one of the essential theses of Plotinus' epistemology. Using a metaphorical language Plotinus says that the truth here is not the truth of something else but it is what it says (V.3.5.26), implying that the thought of the intellect coincides with its being; at this level, reality and thought converge.

There is a debate whether Plotinus' theory involves a direct realism which means that there are no mental entities mediating our apprehension of the physical world, or it is rather a kind of representational approach implying either that our mental states are also objects of inquiry or that reason examines only and exclusively the content of sensory representations.[11] It seems to be quite clear that in the case of the Intellect we can talk about direct realism only; the intelligible objects of knowledge are given to the knower directly. As for the possibility of a perceptual realism is concerned, however, we have to see that Plotinus' notion of sense-perception is fairly complex. It seems that one of the key notions of Plotinus' theory of the perceptual process is 'assimilation' (*homoiōsis*) (IV.4.23.6), which means that there must be a formal kinship between the sense and the sense object in sense-perception.[12] In fact, the affection becomes a form when sense-perception occurs. In order for the sense-perception to occur, however, there must be something intermediate between soul and body (IV.4.23.25–30), but this something is a quality which is a proportional mean which links the extremes to one another. The intermediate status enables the qualities to bridge the gap between the external physical entities that are judged and the perceiving soul which judges them.[13] Discursive reason (*dianoia*) does not only receive the perceptual content (V.3.2.7–9, V.3.3.2–6) but also activates its characteristic power to identify it as an instance of the form 'human being'. The process unfolds in three steps. First, the discursive soul realizes that a human being has been perceived.[14] Realization is a conscious activity which coincides with a threshold of activity in the individual human soul (V.3.3). The second step is a kind of conversation of the soul with itself (V.3.3.3–4). In using the memory of previous perceptions in order to identify the person, reason asks itself 'Who is this?', to which the answer may be 'Socrates'. In the third step the discursive soul unfolds the perceptual form and examines the internalized sense-perceptions (V.3.3.5–6).[15] For the perceptual images are complexes and stored in the representational capacity in this way discursive reason is able to break them down into their ingredients. This is how discursive reason can handle empirical material. Of course, one might ask how innate notions come into the play. It seems that only a very limited number of them have the status of a priori standards in us, most important of them being the 'norm of the good' (*kanona agathou*, V.3.3.9) which serves as a general condition for the activities of discursive reason. Furthermore, we also have to see that discursive reason is where different types of cognitive activities meet; it works not only with content of perceptual origin but also with the concepts derived from the Intellect and, in a process called recollection, it matches the two different contents to one another (V.3.2.7–14).

3. Porphyry

Porphyry modifies the Plotinian picture in many points. First of all, in accounting for the arousal of empirical universals he seems to endorse a four-step model (*Commentary on Ptolemy's* Harmonics 13.21–14.6 Döring).[16]

The first stage is, then, sense-perception. It grasps the form of the perceptible object by grabbing it from the matter. Porphyry stresses the formal character of sense-perception, but he does not draw the conclusion that it is conceptual. It is also unclear whether sense-perception involves a kind of judgement. Porphyry does not say it here and it may well be that judgement occurs at a later stage.

Second, the form received by the senses is apprehended by the belief-making capacity (*doxa*) which gives it a verbal expression. Porphyry uses two verbs to explain how this verbalization takes place, *prosagoreuein* and *anagraphein*. It seems that *anagraphein* signifies the description of the properties making up the whole perceptible form. The description may well be nothing but a list of them. The properties can be different in kind, since on Aristotle's model with which Porphyry was familiar red and smooth are primary objects of sense-perception, whereas spherical belongs to the so-called common sensibles (*koina aisthēta*), the perception of which requires cooperation of two particular senses at least. In this commentary, however, Porphyry does not pay attention to the divergence. We have, then, a list of the properties that make up the perceptible form of the external object. It is like an inventory by the aid of which we can identify the object. It may need memory even if it is not mentioned here. The verb *prosagoreuein* may refer to the act of recognition. The belief-making capacity gives name to the perceived object, which enables us to classify it properly.

The next stage in the transmission of perceptible forms is characterized by the image-making, or representational, capacity. The primary function of this capacity is to produce images. As the text indicates, it functions like a painter or a sculptor. But it is not producing mere fantasies in the modern sense. Here Porphyry is clearly not interested in this aspect of *phantasia*. Rather he insists that *phantasia* is not content with the purely verbal description provided by *doxa*, but will make images that fit the perceptible form, and by the aid of which we can identify the perceptible form. The precise mechanism of the image-making capacity is formulated by means of analogies. It is like the activity of those who try to descry persons sailing into port, or by way of those who attend to features to match them, and work out details of resemblance. It seems both procedures aim at pictorial identification. When the image-making activity has reached its goal, the image thus produced can be stored in the soul.[17] This stored content is called *ennoia*, and in all likelihood it is a mental image, a kind of pictorial representation of the sensible forms. Porphyry does not mention any other factor in this process that could modify or further transmute this product of the image-making capacity, and he calls this content *ennoia*. For the image-making capacity works like a painter, the psychic contents it produces are pictorial. But these images cannot be equated with memory images or with the impressions in the sensory faculty for both memory images and the impressions in the sensory faculty are images of individuals. By contrast, *ennoia* seems to be a kind of universal insofar as it represents types.

The final step is characterized by the emergence of the universal concept (*to katholou*). It is not pictorial and Porphyry does not call it image in a metaphorical sense either. At the end of the cognitive process, the intellect confirms the content so acquired. Just like in Plotinus, the intellect cannot err for it apprehends the objects directly without any interfering factor. The theory has two important features. The first is that there is an alternation of pictorial and conceptual phases. Sense-perception and *phantasia* produce pictorial content, whereas *doxa* and the intellect work with names and concepts. The second is that intellect is linked to the image-making capacity, which implies that it works with pictorial content as well.

The confirming activity is made possible by the specific connection between the rational soul and the world of nature. The only fragment we have from Porphyry's *On sense-perception* (fr. 264 Smith) says that it holds together everything that exists and everything is the soul insofar as it holds together various bodies. For this reason, the text goes on, it is reasonable to say that the soul recognizes itself in all that exists. As the noblest kind of perception, sight is tied to a certain self-knowledge. By encountering visual objects, the soul comes to know itself; it recognizes itself as being in the visible objects. Unfortunately, the fragment does not inform us about the way the soul deals with the perceptual input. We might have to turn to other fragments for explanation. Porphyry have a more detailed explanation of the relation between sense-perception and the rational soul. As we have seen, the commentary on Ptolemy's *Harmonics* links sense-perception to the intellect by saying that just like the judgement made by the intellect perceptual judgement does not involve matter either. From this point of view sense-perception resembles the material intellect (*hulikos nous*), for both receive forms. More evidence for the relation between sense-perception and intellect can be found in a fragment from his commentary on the *Timaeus* (fr. LXIV Sodano). Although the fragment deals with the world soul primarily it turns out very quickly that Porphyry posits a substantial identity between the world soul and the individual human soul. It implies that what he says about the basic activities of the former may apply to the latter, too. The text testifies to Porphyry's thesis of the unity of every soul; it speaks about a single power, called *logos*, which is present in them. It is a power which provides every soul with a unique structure, thereby making each of them a single entity. If the soul turns to the sensible world, it engenders beliefs which cannot be at the level of true knowledge. In *Sentence* 16 we find further information. We read that the soul possesses the notions (*logoi*) of everything. On the one hand, the thesis may be a version of Plato's theory of recollection. On the other hand, however, the notions pertain both to the Ideas directly, and to the forms of the physical bodies that acquire these forms from the Ideas. It the first case the soul turns inward to examine them, in the second case it turns outward and draws on sense-perception to get acquainted with the sensible forms. The link between self-knowledge and sense-perception is not discussed in the passage but Porphyry makes another interesting point. He claims that thinking does not occur without *phantasia*.[18] The claim is blatantly Aristotelian (*De anima* 427b15–16) although Porphyry adds that it applies to living beings only. Immaterial beings are able to think without the representational faculty. If the individual human soul must rely on representational images in order to think, then perceptual content must be present in a form in the human intellect, too. For this reason, self-knowledge of the intellect involves knowledge of a content originated in sense-perception.

230   *Knowledge in Ancient Philosophy*

Intellect contains concepts of different origin. We have evidence both that he uses abstractionist language (*Commentary on Ptolemy's* Harmonics, referred to above) and that he accepts the existence of transcendent Forms (*Sentences* 1–4, 34–9). From these passages it emerges that he did try to harmonize Plato and Aristotle even if harmonizing their theories in this field was not an easy task. The use of abstractionist language might give the impression that he was a conceptualist when it came to universals.[19] In his short commentary on Aristotle *Categories* (90.12–91.5) he seems to claim that particulars (e.g. individual horse) are prior to the concept of horse insofar as if there are no individual cows then no one would be capable of having the concept of horse, whereas there might have been individual horses without anyone having the concept of horse. Of course, it does not rule out the existence of Ideas since Porphyry does not say that particulars are naturally prior to the species they belong to; rather, he claims only that particulars are prior in another way to the species.[20] It seems to be a kind of epistemological priority because we have to perceive the particular thing in order that a possibly innate concept in us becomes activated. In order to think of the horse in general we have already had to encounter some instances of the species. Similarly, in order to think of the genus 'animal' we have already had to have in mind some of the species belonging to the genus. Such kind of epistemological priority, however, may not be explained in terms of abstractionism. Furthermore, if abstractionism may not be the proper description of Porphyry's position, then we may not be allowed to call it conceptualism either. It is true that the *Isagoge* seems to announce a conceptualist approach but the work also shows that Porphyry declines to discuss these matters.[21] It does not mean, however, that he did not express firm beliefs about the nature of universals. He simply claims that as an introduction to Aristotle's logical works the *Isagoge* may not be the proper place to discuss the issue at length.[22] Even when Porphyry uses the term for abstraction (*Commentary on Ptolemy's* Harmonics 11.21; 13.22) he insists that the soul possesses the notions (*logoi*) that serve also as the structural elements of the physical world. It is true that the process of recognition requires our cognitive power to tear away the sensible forms from their matter but the soul can judge the perceptible particulars because it is endowed with all the forms as *logoi* beforehand.

4. Proclus

Unfortunately, Porphyry's account has survived in a fragmentary form only, which does not allow us to draw very far-reaching consequences. In Syrianus,

Epistemologies in Neoplatonism   231

Proclus' teacher, we find a similar and more elaborated model. In his commentary on books *M* and *N* of Aristotle's *Metaphysics* he distinguishes four types of *logoi*. There are the so-called emmattered or physical *logoi* which are sent by the Intellect to provide structure to the sensible world. They do not reside in the individual human soul although they are perceived when we perceive physical objects. Sense-perception produces the so-called *doxastikoi logoi*, notions based on sense-experience. As their name shows, they constitute belief (*doxa*) which is the kind of knowledge concerning the sensible world. The non-empirical sources of knowledge are called substantial *logoi*; they belong to the very essence of the soul. They are the outcome of the soul's original existence in the intellect from which it has been emanated. A projected version of substantial *logoi* is to be found in discursive reason (*dianoia*); they are called *dianoētikoi logoi*. They coexist with the representational form in *phantasia*, but they are not empirically acquired. The link between *doxastikoi logoi* and *dianoētikoi logoi* represents the link between empirical and innate knowledge. They can be matched because all of them originate in the Intellect.

Proclus' theory of sense-perception is notoriously complex which may be due to his commitment to a broad use of the term *aisthēsis*. In the commentary of the *Timaeus* he distinguishes between four types (II 83.16–84.5). The first is the most genuine and has nothing to do with the bodily senses directly. It imitates the activity of the intellect and contains in itself the object of sense-perception. It does not proceed from one object to another for that activity would characterize a divided power. Furthermore, it does not operate externally for that kind of activity implies that the power is incomplete. In sum, it contains the whole of what is subject to sense-perception and is a kind of *sunaisthēsis*, a kind of joint perception involving consciousness. The second type operates externally, but does so in a special way. Its activity is complete and its object of cognition is always grasped in an unchanging way, from every point of view and as a whole. Moreover, no affection can reach it from the outer world. It is also free from all the infirmities due to the partial sense organs residing in matter. The third is a capacity which is affected by external objects and a combination of two elements: it is subject to affections and at the same time is a kind of cognition. It starts with an affection and results in cognition. This is what most philosophers in antiquity would call ordinary sense-perception. The last type is an activity which can only lead to the most obscure form of cognition. It is for the most part an affection and close to the interactions between physical bodies. It does not know the forms of sensible objects, for example, it remains ignorant as to whether the object affecting the sense is warm or cold. All that it grasps is whether the

232   *Knowledge in Ancient Philosophy*

stimulus falling under the particular senses is pleasant or painful. Proclus relates it to the perception of plants and refers to *Timaeus* 77 b where we read that the third, lowest class of living beings has a share in the appetitive part of the soul only, and as a consequence they can have pleasures, pains, and desires. It seems that due to the complexity of human nature we are endowed all the four types.[23]

This complexity may help us understand the structure and role of the two other important cognitive capacities that are linked to perception, belief, and *phantasia*. Proclus credits both capacities with new roles. Belief (*doxa*) is linked to sense-perception directly. In the *Timaeus*-commentary I.248-22-9 we are told that sense-perception is in a way lodged in the belief-making capacity. It recognizes the whole before the parts and studies the form of sensible things indivisibly (I.249.25). It can say not only that this is red and this is sweet, but also that all these qualities pertain to one and the same thing, and see these qualities as forming a unity. This is how belief can reveal the essence (*ousia*) of the sensible things. It does not know the causes, however. It comprehends sense-perception and projects *logoi* in order to know the nature of sensible things.[24] The projecting activity of belief is made possible by the fact that it takes on scientific distinctions from the discursive reason.[25] The representational capacity is the highest form of the non-rational cognitive activities. It can correct the mistakes made by sense-perception which, for example, presents the sun as a foot wide. However, it is functioning by the aid of imprints and shapes and therefore it needs to be tested by *doxa* which is the superior capacity. It contains not only imprints of perceptual origin, however, for it has an important role in geometrical reasoning as well. In his commentary on Book I of Euclid's *Elements* (48.1-57.8 Friedlein) Proclus argues that the concept of circle or triangle cannot be derived from sense-perception. In attacking abstractionism, he claims that they are contained in the soul's *logoi* as definitions. However, because geometrical objects must have an extension by definition images of these *logoi* must be projected from the discursive reason into *phantasia* where they become extended. The geometer deals with the *logoi*, forms, in the discursive reason but does so by projecting images into the *phantasia*.[26] These images are perfect embodiments of geometric definitions because they are originated in the forms. If they were put together out of sense-perceptions they could not be perfect representations of geometrical definitions.[27]

Proclus' theory of scientific understanding in general is based on his rejection of abstractionism. For this reason, his approach can be understood as a response to Aristotle's views on demonstrative science His ontological account, in which mathematical objects are projections onto the imagination

Epistemologies in Neoplatonism   233

of forms that preexist in discursive reason, secures the status of mathematics as an explanatory science, hence as a science in the strict sense. When we see the various references to demonstrative explanation scattered throughout Proclus' commentary on the *Elements* in light of the ancient interpretation of Aristotle's *Posterior Analytics* and Proclus' notion of causality, they supply us with arguments that the abstractionist conception of mathematical objects is inconsistent with the theory of demonstration. Thus we can understand his contention that the forms in discursive reason are the causes of demonstration, presuppose a consistent alternative to Aristotle's theory of demonstration, which rests on the assumptions that causes necessarily bring about their effects by being active and that logical relations are images of causal relations.[28] He used a model according to which science works on the basis of some elementary concepts and propositions – among them a kind of definitions of the elementary concepts themselves. The explanation of definitions provides epistemic connection between a rational and an empirical approach to the natural world. A crucial task in establishing the connection is performed by the belief-making capacity and by geometrical conversion. The model allowed Proclus to study the physical reality in a scientific way, thus making physics a true science. On this account, physics starts from universal, necessary, and known concepts and propositions.[29]

Proclus' views on innate notions are connected to his interpretation of Plato's theory of recollection. In his commentary on Plato's *Alcibiades I* he connects projection of *logoi* to recollection (15.11–12 Segonds). Self-knowledge also presupposes that the soul turns inwards and grasps the innate intelligible structure. This process is nothing but recollection.[30] The innate, but latent knowledge that we grasp by the aid of recollection differs from the awareness of them, which exists as a mere notion (*ennoia psilē, in Alc. I.* 191.12–13) or preconception. The distinction between the innate knowledge of the soul and the awareness of it is made possible by the application of Aristotle's theory of two kinds of *energeia* (*De anima* II 5, 417a21-b28). It can be applied to process of the acquisition of knowledge. On the Aristotelian model, the first step consists of our potentiality of being knowable; as human being we are capable of acquiring knowledge. In the second step, the first phase of actuality, we have already acquired knowledge but are not practicing it. This phase may be illustrated with the example of the sleeping geometer. The final step is the actual exercise of the knowledge in question. Proclus uses Aristotle's model but we have to see that he makes an important change. Knowledge is not acquired in any phase of the process, it is always there, even if we are not aware of it.

5. Alexandrian Neoplatonists

The Neoplatonists in Alexandria may share the overall metaphysical framework with their colleagues at Athens but in some respects – which are relevant for present purposes – they held markedly different theories. Due to the contact with the flourishing medical school at Alexandria they showed much more interest in the physiological aspect of sense-perception. In his commentary on Aristotle's *De anima* John Philoponus insists that perceptual, that is, formal alteration goes hand in hand with a kind of physiological change (309.15–29; 438.6–15). Because the medical school followed Galen's doctrines, which stressed the role of *pneuma* in cognitive processes in general, philosophers in Alexandria laid strong emphasis on the physiological side in many activities of the soul. As a consequence, Philoponus' theory of sense-perception does not fit in with the claim that the sensory process does not involve an extra material change in the sense organ. Both the specific sense organs (like the vitreous liquid and choroid or corneal membrane in the eyes) and the primary sense organ (like the optic *pneuma*) contract or expand in the perceptual process (395.15–16), a claim repeated in his *De intellectu* as well (18.2–3 Verbeke). The physiological explanation applies also to second-order perception – perception of the perceptive activity itself – not only to the first one. Philoponus elaborates a theory that contains elements of both literalist and spiritualist positions. On the one hand he claims that sense-perception necessarily involves bodily processes, either in the particular sense organs, such as the acoustic membrane or the tongue, or in the primary sense organ, the *pneuma*. On the other hand, we cannot say either that the activities of the senses are to be reduced to bodily activities. Bodily and cognitive changes are changes of the same substrate from different perspectives, and we cannot establish a primacy between them in terms of efficient causality. Efficient causality can only be established in the way the external objects affect the specific sense organs.

Another important achievement in epistemology is tied to the theory of science. Again, we have to turn to Philoponus. His commentaries on Aristotle's *Prior* and *Posterior Analytics* are witnesses of the effort to accommodate Aristotle's philosophy of science to Neoplatonic metaphysics. One of the key terms to be reinterpreted is sensory experience (*empeiria*) as a link connecting sense-perception and scientific understanding (*epistēmē*). In the commentary on the *Posterior Analytics* Philoponus suggests that experience can be of general facts but fails to be the knowledge of universals in a special sense, explained in *An. Post.* I 4–5, which means that sensory experience involves a kind of general knowledge which, however, fails to establish necessity. For this reason, he may subscribe to the thesis that experience is knowledge of the particulars; due to his views on the nature of sense-perception this knowledge contains elements of the knowledge of universals right from the start.[31] Even if he allows, however, that sense-perception involves concepts he insists in his commentary on the *Prior Analytics* (214.19ff.), that sense-perception alone does not produce scientific understanding. To explain it he uses a narrative which is somewhat similar to the description we find in the *Timaeus*. The individual soul is possessed by drowsiness at birth, as it were, and needs the senses to wake up and rouse up the spark of knowledge hidden within us. Perceptible objects stimulate the soul to project the notions of paradigms that belong to its essence. Without the stimuli coming from sense objects there is no projective activity in the soul and, consequently, there is no scientific understanding of universals either. Sensory experience plays a crucial role in this process of awakening the soul.

6. The final period of the Academy at Athens

The last period of the school witnesses a resolute effort to provide a projectivist theory of sense-perception. In his commentary on Aristotle's *De anima* Pseudo-Simplicius, Priscian of Lydia (?)[32] insists that perceptual process is a projection of *logoi* onto the sense. The projection itself does not require time. The soul comes to be in a cognitive state all of a sudden (121.33), even if this occurs from time to time. One may liken the complex cognitive processes as a series of indivisible units. The cognitive act itself is instantaneous. The agenda behind the approach may be that the commentator wished to deprive the soul in general of all sorts of physical characteristics. Because sense-perception needs body, however, he has to argue that bodily changes in the organ do not undermine the approach. He claims that the sense organ does not need to be altered in any way in order to be cognitively active, whereas it needs to be altered in order to be sensibly active (122.10–20). It means that the organ must undergo changes that are prerequisite for cognitive activities, but cognition itself is not a change. The perceptible object has to act on the sense organ and upon its being acted the perceptual power projects the *logoi* within it of the perceptible things in a way appropriate to the affect in the sense organ and recognizes the perceptible object through its own activity. Sense-perception occurs by formal assimilation since by projecting the proper *logos* the perceptual power comes to be in a state of accord with the form of the perceptible object. The theory has been repeated by Priscian of Lydia in

236 *Knowledge in Ancient Philosophy*

his *Metaphrasis* with the note that the representational capacity plays a central role in arranging these *logoi* (23.13–24.1).[33]

Damascius followed the projectionist theory and raised important questions about the structure of our knowledge. In the first version of his commentary on the *Phaedo* (I 269 Westerink) he cast doubt on the reliability of a certain kind of reflection. As he says, we do not have any internal criteria on the basis of which we could be certain whether we are recollection or inventing something new. Recollection is a specific cognitive activity, just like thinking or perceiving.[34] On Damascius' account, when we recollect we activate a latent knowledge, either an information coming from sense-perception or a knowledge of the Forms. But, just as in many other cognitive activities, we have to reckon with a kind of incertitude for recollection often appears as a newly acquired knowledge. For this reason, at the moment of recollection we cannot be sure whether we are recalling a previously acquired knowledge or we are acquiring a new knowledge now. The simple fact that a previously unnoticed notion pops up in our soul does not guarantee that we become clear about the cognitive process leading to the arousal of that notion. We cannot identify the process on the basis of the content alone. It looks, therefore, as if reflection were an unreliable guide; it does not inform us about the kind of cognitive activity we are engulfed with. We are aware that something cognitive is going on in the soul but we are not in the position to qualify it precisely. The uncertainty gives rise to a series of sceptical remarks (II.19). If our reflexive activity does not always reveal the true nature of our cognitive life in such everyday circumstances, then what happens if it is more seriously affected? In dreams or in sickness our awareness is much heavily affected, which results in our inability to realize that something is false or impossible. It leads us back to the sceptical problems with which Plotinus was struggling three centuries earlier.

Notes

Nick Smith suggested many improvements. I am very grateful to him for his help.

1 The sceptical challenge was interpreted as directed against the distinctly empirical theories of Hellenistic schools; see Kühn (2009).

2 See Emilsson (1988: 133–4).

3 But we also have to see that Plotinus was drawing on Aristotle's views, which led him to the assumption that *phantasia* is not simply a faculty of images. See King (2009: 183–4).

4 See Emilsson (1988: 107).

5 As has been suggested in ibid., 111.

6 See Chiaradonna (2009: 14–15). See also Sheppard (1991: 170) who stresses that *phantasma* is a mental image, a notion which can be seen in the *De anima* commentary of Pseudo-Simplicius, Priscian of Lydia (?), as well.

7 See Chiaradonna (2015).

8 However, D'Ancona (2007: 87ff.) suggests that recollection retains its Platonic role in the undescended soul insofar as it refers to the intelligibles.

9 See Brisson (1999: 91–3).

10 See Kühn (2009: 193–9) with reference to V.3.5.28–31.

11 See Emilsson (1988: 133; 2007: 127–9) and Magrin (2010: 290).

12 As has been emphasized by Gerson (1994: 168).

13 See Chiaradonna (2011: 193).

14 See ibid., 202. Of course, it implies that sense-perception itself is unconscious which may make the act of judgement somewhat obscure.

15 See Remes (2007: 145) and Chiaradonna (2011: 203).

16 The account may come from Thrasyllus, a Platonist philosopher in the age of Augustus; see Tarrant (1993: 108–47). He claims that the theory is by Thrasyllus. It may well be true; but even in that case Porphyry paraphrases it with approval, for nowhere in the commentary does he make any objection to it.

17 This also explains how memory is connected to *phantasia* (Sheppard 2007: 73).

18 As Jean Pépin (in Brisson [2005: II 448]) makes clear, Porphyry was following Plotinus in narrowing the applicability of Aristotle's thesis.

19 See, for example, *Isagoge* sec. 10, 16.20–18.9.

20 See Barnes (2003: 274–5).

21 See *Isagoge* (Preface: 1.9–14) with the comments in Helmig (2012: 172).

22 Furthermore, the whole approach and content of the *Isagoge* make it necessary that it should be discussed in a more logical way (*logikōteron*), which means that – if only for present purposes – Porphyry disregards the ontological framework behind such theories (Chiaradonna 2008: 2–20).

23 This is how I present Proclus' argument in Lautner (2004) against Blumenthal (1982), but see Baltzly (2009: 268–9) who argues that the two higher modes of perception which Proclus ascribes to the universe and to the heavenly bodies, respectively, may not occur in us.

24 Thus, *doxa* exerts its function by forming a so-called later-born concept (*husterogenēs logos*), an image of its innate *logos*, triggered by an impression derived from sense-perception – in its turn an image of the *universale in re*, to use later terminology. For an analysis of this role of *doxa*, see Martijn (2010b: 147–52).

25 On Proclus' views on *doxa*, see the detailed analysis in Helmig (2012: 239–61).

26 See Mueller (1990: 473–4).

238   *Knowledge in Ancient Philosophy*

27 For the function of *phantasia* as a mirror, see Sheppard (2003: 210–12) and Helmig (2012: 229). For a possible origin of Proclus' theory in Iamblichus, see Sheppard (1997).

28 For a useful examination of the issue, see Harari (2006, 2008).

29 See Martijn (2010a). This kind of axiomatic structure can be discovered in Proclus' *Elements of Physics*.

30 For a detailed explanation, see Steel (1997a: 23–5) and Helmig (2012: 301–17).

31 It may be a Neoplatonic element in his thought (Tuominen 2010: 124).

32 The authorship of this commentary is very much disputed. For a useful survey of the different approaches, see Steel (1997b), who argues for Priscian's authorship.

33 On the implications of the projection theory on the soul's structure and activity, see Steel (1978: 137–8) and Sorabji (2006: 120).

34 In this context, Damascius also criticized Proclus for defending the ability of non-rational animals to recollect. For more on this, see Gertz (2011: 120–1).

References

Baltzly, D. (2009), 'Gaia Gets to Know Herself: Proclus on the World's Self-Perception', *Phronesis*, 54: 261–85.

Barnes, J. (trans. and comm.) (2003), *Porphyry: Introduction*, Oxford: Oxford University Press.

Blumenthal, H. J. (1982), 'Proclus on Perception', *Bulletin of the Institute of Classical Studies*, 29: 1–11.

Brisson, L. (1999), '*Logos* et *logoi* chez Plotin. Leur nature et leur rôle', *Cahiers philosophiques de Strasbourg*, 8: 87–108.

Brisson, L. (ed.) (2005), Porphyry: *Sentences* T. I–II, Paris: J. Vrin.

Chiaradonna, R. (2008), 'What Is Porphyry's *Isagoge*?' *Documenti e studi sulla tradizione filosofica medieval*, 19: 1–30.

Chiaradonna, R. (2009), 'Plotin: La mémoire et la connaissance des intelligibles', *Philosophie antique*, 9: 5–33.

Chiaradonna, R. (2011), 'Plotinus' Account of the Cognitive Powers of the Soul: Sense-Perception and Discursive Thought', *Topoi*, 31: 191–207.

Chiaradonna, R. (2015), 'Plotinus on Memory, Recollection and Discursive Thought', in L. Castagnoli and P. Ceccarelli (eds), *Greek Memories: Theories and Practices*, Cambridge: Cambridge University Press.

D'Ancona, C. (2007), 'Plotino: memoria di eventi e anamnesi di intelligibili', in M. M. Sassi (ed.), *Tracce della mente. Teoria delle memorie da Platone ai moderni*, Pisa: Edizioni della Scuola Normale.

Emilsson, E. K. (1988), *Plotinus on Sense-Perception: A Philosophical Study*, Cambridge: Cambridge University Press.

Emilsson, E. K. (2007), *Plotinus on Intellect*, Oxford: Oxford University Press.

Gerson, L. P. (1994), *Plotinus*, London: Routledge.

Gertz, S. R. P. (2011), *Death and Immortality in Late Neoplatonism: Studies on the Ancient Commentaries on Plato's* Phaedo, Leiden: Brill.

Harari, O. (2006), '*Methexis* and Geometrical Reasoning in Proclus' Commentary on Euclid's *Elements*', *Oxford Studies in Ancient Philosophy*, 30: 361–89.

Harari, O. (2008), 'Proclus' Account of Explanatory Demonstrations in Mathematics and Its Context', *Archiv für Geschichte der Philosophie*, 90: 137–64.

Helmig, C. (2012), *Forms and Concepts. Concept Formation in the Platonic Tradition*, Berlin: Walter de Gruyter.

King, R. A. H. (2009), *Aristotle and Plotinus on Memory*, Berlin: Walter de Gruyter.

Kühn, W. (2009), *Quel savoir après le scepticisme? Plotin et ses prédecesseurs sur la connaissance de soi*, Paris: J. Vrin.

Lautner, P. (2004), 'Some Clarifications on Proclus' Fourfold Division of Sense-Perception in the *Timaeus* Commentary', in M. Perkams and R. M. Piccione (eds), *Proklos. Methode, Seelenlehre, Metaphysik*, Leiden: Brill.

Magrin, S. (2010), 'Sensation and Scepticism in Plotinus', *Oxford Studies in Ancient Philosophy*, XXXIX: 249–98.

Martijn, M. (2010a), 'Proclus on the Order of Philosophy of Nature', *Synthese*, 174: 205–23.

Martijn, M. (2010b), *Proclus on Nature: Philosophy of Nature and Its Methods in Proclus' Commentary on Plato's* Timaeus, Leiden: Brill.

Mueller, I. (1990), 'Aristotle's Doctrine of Abstraction in the Commentators', in R. Sorabji (ed.), *Aristotle Transformed: The Ancient Commentators and Their Influence*, London-Ithaca: Duckworth-Cornell University Press.

Remes, P. (2007), *Plotinus on Self: The Philosophy of the 'We'*, Cambridge: Cambridge University Press.

Sheppard, A. (1991), '*Phantasia* and Mental Images. Neoplatonist Interpretations of *De anima* 3.3', in H. J. Blumenthal and H. Robinson (eds), *Aristotle and the Later Tradition*, Oxford: Clarendon Press.

Sheppard, A. (1997), '*Phantasia* and Mathematical Projection in Iamblichus', in H. J. Blumenthal and J. F. Finamore (eds), *Iamblichus: The Philosopher* (= *Syllecta Classica* 8), Iowa City: University of Iowa Press.

Sheppard, A. (2003), 'The Mirror of Imagination: The Influence of *Timaeus* 70e ff.', in R. W. Sharples and A. Sheppard (eds), *Ancient Approaches to Plato's* Timaeus (*BICS Supplement 78*), London: ICS.

Sheppard, A. (2007), 'Porphyry's Views on *Phantasia*', in G. Karamanolis and A. Sheppard (eds), *Studies on Porphyry*, London: ICS.

Sorabji, R. R. K. (2006), 'Universals Transformed. The First Thousand Years after Plato', in P. F. Strawson and A. Chakrabarty (eds), *Universals, Concepts and Qualities: New Essays on the Meaning of Predicates*, Aldershot: Ashgate.

Steel, C. (1978), *The Changing Self. A Study on the Soul in Later Neoplatonism: Iamblichus, Damascius and Priscianus*, Brussels: Paleïs der Academien.

240 *Knowledge in Ancient Philosophy*

Steel, C. (1997a), 'Breathing Thought: Proclus on the Innate Knowledge of the Soul', in J. J. Cleary (ed.), *The Perennial Tradition of Neoplatonism*, Leuven: Leuven University Press.

Steel, C. (1997b), 'Introduction to *"Simplicius", On Aristotle On the Soul 2.5–12'*, in *Priscian, On Theophrastus On Sense-Perception with 'Simplicius', On Aristotle On the Soul 2.5–12*, London: Duckworth.

Tarrant, H. (1993), *Thrasyllan Platonism*, Ithaca, NY: Cornell University Press.

Tuominen, M. (2010), 'Back to *Posterior Analytics* II 19: Aristotle on the Knowledge of Principles', in J. H. Lesher (ed.), *From Inquiry to Demonstrative Knowledge: New Essays on Aristotle's* Posterior Analytics, *Apeiron*, 43, 115–45. Kelowna, BC: Academic Printing and Publishing.

13

Roman Epistemology

Walter Englert

1. Introduction

Unlike the ancient Greeks, the Romans had no indigenous philosophical tradition. *Philosophia* was a Greek word, and as the Romans came in contact with Greek culture, they were initially suspicious of Greek philosophy. Romans who wanted to study philosophy did so in Greek, with Greek philosophers as teachers and interlocutors. In the first century BCE and first century CE, Roman writers began to bring philosophy into Latin. Rather than doing philosophy in Greek, or simply producing literal Latin translations of Greek philosophical texts, they created original works of philosophy in Latin. As part of this process of writing philosophy in Latin, Roman writers faced the problem of how to integrate epistemology, central to the Greek philosophical schools they were championing, into their own philosophical and literary works.

This chapter explores the epistemological aspects of the works of Lucretius, a Roman Epicurean poet; Cicero, a member of the sceptical New Academy; and Seneca, a Roman Stoic who wrote almost a hundred years after Lucretius and Cicero. In their works, the three authors deploy the epistemological views of their philosophical schools carefully as part of their efforts to persuade them of their respective philosophical positions. They do so, however, in different ways. Lucretius focuses almost exclusively on Epicurean physics, and reserves epistemological arguments for grounding particular arguments and refuting the views of other philosophers. In contrast, Cicero writes one of his most important philosophical works, the *Academica*, specifically on epistemology and argues that studying epistemology is crucial to picking which philosophical school to follow and determining how to live. Seneca, finally, focuses primarily on Stoic ethics, but is well-versed in Stoic epistemology and brings aspects of it in as needed to support the ethical arguments he is making.

2. Lucretius and Epicurean epistemology

Lucretius' *De Rerum Natura*, or *On the Nature of Things*, is an astounding literary and philosophical achievement. In six books of Latin verse, Lucretius sets out for his Roman readers the philosophical system of the Greek philosopher Epicurus. The poem shows that Lucretius, writing in the 50s BCE, was fully versed in Greek and Latin literature, and had studied the works of Epicurus in depth. In an illuminating study, David Sedley (1998: 92) has described Lucretius as an 'Epicurean fundamentalist' who worked almost exclusively from Epicurus' own writings, especially his major work *On Nature*, and largely ignored contemporary philosophical debates. As far as we can tell, Lucretius did not consider himself a philosopher, and perhaps the best way to describe him is as a Roman poet who attempts to present the main features of Epicurus' philosophy in an epic poem, using the Greek philosopher/poet Empedocles and the Roman epic poet Ennius as his poetic models to bring Epicureanism to his fellow Romans.

Lucretius' poem sets out Epicurus' atomic view of reality in six books, focusing almost exclusively on Epicurean physics. Books 1 and 2 treat the nature of the atom, Books 3 and 4 the nature of the soul and perception, and Books 5 and 6 the nature of the world. The poem is designed to take Lucretius' Roman readers from the world of their own perceptions, beliefs, and emotions to a philosophical understanding of the nature of reality. Lucretius tries to show his readers that many of their most important views about the world are mistaken, but that if they embrace the tenets of Epicureanism they will be able to understand the way the world works, order their lives accordingly, and obtain happiness.

The main thrust of Epicureanism was ethical. Epicurus had argued that there is no sense in doing philosophy if it does not help one live one's life well and bring one happiness, and Lucretius endorses this view. His purpose is to reveal how the world works, and what this means about how best to live one's life.

Before examining Lucretius' use of Epicurean epistemology, it will be helpful to have a brief overview of Epicurean epistemology to see how Lucretius adapts it in his poem.[1] Epicurus notoriously shunned logic as traditionally practiced, preferring instead to discuss what he called 'canonic' (from the Greek word *kanōn*, 'rule, standard'), his term for his theory of knowledge which he connected closely to physics. Epicurus was an empiricist, arguing that knowledge was possible and derived from sensation. He held that there are three criteria of truth: sensation, general concepts, and feelings (Diogenes Laertius 10.31).[2]

Epicurus held that sensations were the primary criterion of truth. He taught that 'all sensations are true', a claim which at first sight appears implausible.

Epicurus, though, carefully distinguished sensations themselves from the judgements that people make about them. In the case of an optical illusion like an oar that appears bent in water, Epicurus would say that the image of the oar our eyes receive is true: we see an image made up of certain sizes, shapes, colours, and so on. Where we may get into trouble is when we add judgements to our perceptions, such as 'this is an oar', or 'this oar is bent'. The former statement is true, but in the case of an oar half-submerged in water, the latter is not. It is not sensation that has fooled us, but our interpretation of the sensation. Our knowledge of the world is ultimately based on sensations, and the judgements we make on the basis of sensation must be scrutinized for the many errors our minds may introduce.

One of the most important ways people can avoid making errors of judgement and attain knowledge is by attending to 'preconceptions'.[3] Epicurus maintained that 'preconceptions' or 'general concepts' (in Greek, *prolēpseis*) could function as one of the criteria of truth. He believed that all humans from childhood form 'preconceptions' by generalizing from their sensations. After seeing a number of examples of a certain type of sensation, and hearing people refer to them as, for example, 'birds', a child gradually builds up a general concept of what a bird is. From such general concepts, people make statements that are true and false about objects in the world.

Epicurus' third criterion of truth was feelings (*pathē*). He taught that all of our actions must be judged by the primary feelings of pleasure and pain, and took them to be the criterion of ethical truth. All our actions must be directed to maximizing our pleasure and minimizing our pain in the long run.

Relying on these criteria of truth, Epicurus argued that we could gain knowledge not only of the visible world around us, but also of the microscopic world of atoms and the movements of the heavens above us. On the one hand, when investigating the visible world directly accessible to us, Epicurus taught that we should accept as true things that could be verified by direct and clear observation, and false those things that could not. On the other hand, when investigating 'non-evident things' (*adēla*, *Letter to Herodotus* 10. 38)[4] like the underlying principles of matter (e.g. atoms and the void), the workings of the heavens, and other things we do not have direct access to, he argued that we must make use of analogies with the physical world around us, and accept as true those views that are 'uncontested' and as false those views that are 'contested'.[5] For example, Epicurus argues that the only view that can explain the origins and workings of the physical world around us is atomism, because it alone accounts for and does not conflict with the facts of the world as we

244 *Knowledge in Ancient Philosophy*

experience them. Similarly, when discussing the movements of the heavens, Epicurus posits explanations that are not contradicted by the evidence. Unlike at the microscopic level, though, where he held that the *only* theory that fits all the facts is atomism, in astronomy and meteorology there are often multiple explanations possible which do not contradict the phenomena. For example, Epicurus posited a number of possible explanations for why the moon waxes and wanes. All of these explanations may be true, and he notes it would be a mistake to argue for one to the exclusion of the others (*Letter to Pythocles* 94–5).

It is also clear from Epicurus' *Letter to Herodotus* 37–8 and from what remains of *On Nature*[6] that he thought it important to preface his account of physics with a section on canonic and epistemology.[7] This prefatory section lays particular stress on the need to start from the three criteria of truth (preconceptions, perceptions, and feelings) as the foundation for the physical system he goes on to expound in the rest of his work.

Turning back to Lucretius, we can explore how Lucretius presents Epicurus' epistemological system in *On the Nature of Things*. Tellingly, Lucretius does not follow Epicurus' example of beginning his work with a discussion of canonic and epistemology. Instead, he begins his poem by directing his reader's attention to the goddess Venus and the beauty of a spring day:

> Mother of the descendants of Aeneas, pleasure of humans and gods,
> life-giving Venus, it is you who beneath the gliding signs
> of heaven makes the ship-bearing sea and the fruitful earth
> teem with life, since through you the whole race of living creatures
> is conceived, born, and gazes on the light of the sun.
> You, goddess, you the winds flee, you the clouds
> of the sky flee at your coming, for you earth the artificer
> sends up her sweet flowers, for you the expanses of the sea smile,
> and the heavens, now peaceful, shine with diffused light. (1.1–9)[8]

It is a lovely picture, describing the Roman goddess Venus and activities of the natural world. But it is a picture that Lucretius goes on to dismantle in the rest of the poem, arguing as he proceeds that in order to understand the world, and how to be happy in it, one must reject this and other views of the gods and the nature of reality and see that everything around us is made up of atoms and void.[9]

Lucretius, following Epicurus' lead, argues that knowledge of the world is possible, but does not start as Epicurus had by discussing basic principles of canonic and epistemology upon which his system rests. Instead, he has his readers gaze at the world and think about what the causes are of everything they see around them. As we will see, this is characteristic of Lucretius' method throughout the poem.

In the opening of book 1, following his invocation of Venus quoted above, Lucretius invokes his addressee, Memmius (50–61), praises Epicurus' attack on traditional religion and sets out the many evils religion brings to humans (62–135), and describes the difficulty of his poetic task (136–48). Two things particularly stand out. The first is terminological, and the second epistemological.

First, Lucretius lets his readers know that he will not be using technical philosophical vocabulary like Epicurus and other Greek philosophers did. In lines 54–61 he writes,

> For I am beginning to set out for you the deepest workings
> of the heavens and the gods, and to reveal the first beginnings of things
> out of which nature creates all things, and increases and maintains them,
> and into which nature dissolves them again once they have perished.
> These we are accustomed, in setting forth our account, to call
> 'matter' and 'the generating bodies of things' and to name them
> 'the seeds of things', and to use the term 'first bodies' for them,
> because all things exist from these first beginnings.

Anticipating arguments about the atomic nature of reality he will make later in the book, Lucretius lets his readers know that he will be using various non-technical terms for 'atoms'. Rather than simply transliterating the Epicurean term *atomos* directly from Greek, as other Roman authors did (Sedley 1998: 38), Lucretius uses a number of terms, each designed to bring out aspects of the nature of atoms. This is not an isolated case.[10] Lucretius proceeds in the same way with his rendering of other Greek technical vocabulary throughout the work, preferring to use non-technical language whenever possible. Given this preference, it is not surprising that Lucretius did not give knotty and technical discussions of epistemological issues as much prominence as he does other less philosophically specialized issues.

Second, Lucretius concludes this section of Book 1 with a striking phrase:

> Therefore this fear and darkness of the mind must be shattered
> apart not by the rays of the sun and the clear shafts
> of the day but by the external appearance and inner law of nature. (lines 146–8)

The final phrase of this sentence, 'the external appearance and inner law of nature' (*naturae species ratioque*), is an important one. Lucretius uses the

246 *Knowledge in Ancient Philosophy*

phrase in the opening sections of three other books (2.61, 3.93, 6.41), and it is a productively ambiguous expression. As Sedley (1998: 37) points out, the phrase *naturae species ratioque* can be translated either as 'looking at nature and reasoning about it', or as 'the appearance and rationale of nature'. Taken in the first way, the phrase emphasizes how humans must use both perception and reason to figure out the nature of the world. Construed in the second way, it stresses that nature reveals itself to us both in the appearance of the world around us, and in its regular inner workings that produce the appearances that we see. In either case, Lucretius seems to be introducing, without yet fully explaining, two of Epicurus' criteria of truth, perception (which attends to the external appearances of things), and reason (which makes use of preconceptions or general concepts to get at the nature of reality).

Thus, in place of the formal methodological section on canonic and epistemology that begins Epicurus' *Letter to Herodotus* and (probably) his *On Nature*, Lucretius substituted lines 1.1–148. There are probably many reasons he did so, but one of the most important was his belief that his project must meet his readers where they are. Launching the poem with a section on methodology and epistemology would have risked alienating his Roman readers. Instead, he brings his readers into the poem by focusing their attention on features of the world around them and some of the traditional ways Romans have understood them, and delays the explanation of the epistemology that clarifies why we should have confidence in the new system he is proposing. He hints at this with the phrase *naturae species ratioque*, but waits until later in the poem to make clear how we are to understand the significance of the phrase. The methodological points that Epicurus felt it necessary to preface his accounts with are ones Lucretius introduces later in his account.

After this opening section, Lucretius launches in Book 1 directly into the foundational principles of Epicurean atomism, and in general follows the order of Epicurus' *Letter to Herodotus*, and his *On Nature*.[11] Lucretius deviates from Epicurus' account in three significant ways.

First, in setting out his first principle in lines 1.149–214, 'Nothing is created out of nothing through divine intervention', Lucretius has added a word to Epicurus' formulation: *divinitus* ('through divine intervention'). Lucretius argues, following Epicurus, that things cannot just spring up spontaneously, but goes beyond Epicurus to keep his readers' eyes on what this means about the gods' role in nature: they have none. The way the world works must be explained not by the gods, but by the atomic system he is beginning to expound.

Second, Lucretius, in line with the vivid description of the natural world with which he begins the poem, makes greater use throughout the poem than Epicurus did of specific evidence from the senses about the world around us. For example, in support of the first principle, Lucretius argues:

> For if things came to be from nothing, every kind of thing
> could be born from all things, and nothing would need a seed.
> Men might sprout from the sea and the scaly race
> of fishes from the earth, and birds might hatch from the sky.
> Cattle and other livestock, and every kind of beast,
> with uncertain birth would inhabit farms and wilderness alike. (1.159–64)

Lucretius uses evidence from perception in support of his argument that 'Nothing is created out of nothing through divine intervention', arguing that if it were not true, we would see things randomly coming to be from other things, and we would not be able to explain the orderliness that is so apparent around us.

Third, Lucretius does not foreground the major tenets of Epicurean canonic and epistemology in Book 1, but he does not leave them out altogether. For example, at 1.422–5, in his proof of the existence of body and void, he explains that we must trust our perception that body exists and base our reasoning about the ultimate principles upon it:

> For ordinary perception declares by itself that body exists.
> Unless trust in perception is firmly founded and flourishes,
> in the case of hidden things there will be nothing to which we can refer
> to prove anything at all with the reasoning power of the mind.

Similarly, in another section later in Book I, arguing against Heraclitus' view that the ultimate principle of the world is fire, he writes,

> For [Heraclitus] believes that the senses truly perceive fire,
> but not other things, which are no less clear.
> This seems to me to be both silly and crazy.
> What other criterion can we use? What can be more certain to us
> than our senses themselves, by which we distinguish true and false? (1.696–700)

In both passages, Lucretius grounds his argument in Epicurean canonic and epistemology, invoking the view that our only access to truth is through one of the criteria of truth: sensation.

After Book 1, Lucretius continues to roll out the major doctrines of Epicurean physics. It is not until Book 4, however, that Lucretius again returns explicitly to

248   *Knowledge in Ancient Philosophy*

Epicurean canonic and epistemology, in a famous section in which he discusses vision and optical illusions. At 4.462–8 he writes,

> We see an amazing number of other things of this type,
> all of which seek to shatter one's trust, so to speak, in the senses,
> but in vain, since by far the largest part of these deceive
> because of the inferences of the mind, which we ourselves contribute
> so that things not seen by the senses are taken as things seen.
> For nothing is more difficult than to distinguish clear things
> from doubtful ones which the mind adds immediately on its own.

In this passage, Lucretius clearly alludes to Epicurus' principle that all perceptions are true, and that error only arises when the mind misinterprets the evidence of the senses. Immediately following this passage, Lucretius launches into an attack on scepticism (4. 469–521).[12] It is the longest sustained defence in Lucretius of the truth of perception. He argues that we need to recognize that all knowledge ultimately derives from perception, and realize that the belief that we can reject the senses and still reason correctly about anything is self-defeating. How, Lucretius asks, could the sceptic even know what true and false are if he denies that sensations are true, and if it is from the sensations that the preconception (*notities*, Lucretius' Latin translation of *prolēpsis*) of the truth comes? Lucretius vividly illustrates how precarious any system of knowledge is which is based on the incorrect interpretation of sensation by using the analogy of a house that is constructed with a carpenter's warped measuring tools. Just as a house whose foundation is not laid accurately can bulge, sway, and even collapse, so also a philosophical system whose reasoning is not based on the firm foundation of the senses must turn out to be wrong: 'So too your reasoning about things must be / warped and false, when it has arisen from false senses' (4. 520–1). There are several other passages where Lucretius discusses aspects of canonic as he sets out Epicurean physics,[13] and the same holds true for them as the passages we have just discussed. Lucretius does not single out canonic and epistemology for his reader in a sustained way in the poem. It is not that he thinks epistemological issues are unimportant. He brings them up as he needs to support his argument, but the main thrust of his argument is clearly on physics and explaining the atomic nature of the universe.

Rather than explaining canonic as a prelude to setting out physics as Epicurus had done, Lucretius right from the beginning keeps his focus on the physical world around us and the physical theories that ultimately explain it. By the end of the poem, Lucretius' readers are able to grasp the main tenets of Epicurean physics, and to understand how this knowledge could help them attain happiness. The poem argues that given the atomic nature of the world and the way it works, it is clear that the gods are not to be feared, death is nothing to us, and happiness is easy to attain. If Lucretius had started off his account in Book 1 with canonic and epistemology, he would have run the risk of alienating his readers. Instead, he starts with the goddess Venus, calls his readers' attention to the beauty of the world around them, and then begins to show how the Epicurean account of nature is a superior one to the traditional Roman mythological view: it accounts for the complexity and beauty of the world around us better, and enables us to live without fear. Lucretius only highlights Epicurean canonic and epistemology insofar as it buttresses his poetic account of how things are, showing us a glimpse of the epistemological foundation of Epicurus' philosophy.

3. Cicero and Academic Scepticism

Cicero, an older contemporary of Lucretius, was born in 106 BCE and was one of Rome's most famous orators and politicians. He had a brilliant political career, attaining the consulship, Rome's highest office, in 63 BCE. Cicero had received an excellent rhetorical and philosophical education when he was young, and he studied both in Rome and in Athens with some of the leading Epicurean, Stoic, and Academic philosophers of his day. Cicero's political fortunes suffered significant setbacks after his consulship, including exile from Rome in 58–57 BCE. He continued to serve the state, but in the 50s and 40s BCE he wrote a series of rhetorical and philosophical works to bring Greek philosophy to Rome. In the mid-to-late 50s, about the same time Lucretius composed *On the Nature of Things*, Cicero wrote the philosophical dialogues *On the Orator*, *On the Republic*, and *On the Laws*. In the 40s he wrote a series of philosophical works, including the *Hortensius*, the *Academica*, *On the Ends of Good and Evil*, *On the Nature of the Gods*, the *Tusculan Disputations*, *On Divination*, *On Fate*, and *On Duties*.

In his works in the 50s, he was more concerned with oratorical, political, and ethical issues, but in the 40s epistemology was central to his philosophical writing project. The *Hortensius*, now lost except for fragments,[14] was a protreptic work that laid out the case for its Roman audience of the importance and value of doing philosophy. The work he wrote next, the *Academica*, focused on epistemology and the question of whether knowledge is possible. Cicero also discussed epistemology in shorter passages in works he wrote after the *Academica*,[15] but we will focus on the *Academica*, his major treatment of the topic.

The *Academica* has a complicated textual history (Griffin 1997). Cicero wrote the first version in two books, entitled the *Catulus* and the *Lucullus*, in the spring of 45 BCE. The dramatic date, setting, and imagined speakers were the same as those in the *Hortensius*: the *Catulus* and *Lucullus* were set in 62–61 BCE, in villas around the Bay of Naples, and the interlocutors included Hortensius (a leading orator of his day), Catulus (a former Roman consul and politician), Lucullus (a famous Roman general and politician), and Cicero himself. Before the first version was widely circulated, Cicero changed his mind about its speakers. Worried that the philosophical arguments he had put in the mouth of Lucullus would seem too sophisticated for a Roman general, he rewrote the work in four books and apparently renamed them the *Academic Books* (*Academici Libri*). He kept the setting in the Bay of Naples, but changed the dramatic date to 45 BCE and reduced the interlocutors to three[16]: Varro (a Roman writer, scholar, and adherent of the New Academy), Atticus (a close friend of Cicero's), and Cicero. To make matters even more complex, neither version of the *Academica* has survived intact. What remains are (1) part of the first book of the original four from the second version of the *Academica* (with Varro and Cicero as the chief speakers), and (2) all of the *Lucullus*, the second half of the original two book version, with Lucullus and Cicero as the main speakers.

Given the work's fragmentary survival, it is hard to get a handle on Cicero's main purpose in writing the work. I want to explore two main issues. First, although modern scholars have questioned Cicero's choice of some of the Latin terms to translate Greek philosophical vocabulary, and the cogency of some of the individual arguments in the work, there is general agreement that the *Academica* demonstrates Cicero's ability to understand sophisticated epistemological arguments and set them out clearly for his readers. Second, and related to this, is the question of why Cicero would produce a dialogue that contains so many intricate and philosophically sophisticated arguments focusing on epistemology for a general Roman audience. Let us turn to look at both of these issues in more detail.

In the *Academica*, Cicero sets out the epistemological theories of the sceptical New Academy of Arcesilaus, Carneades, Clitomachus, Metrodorus of Stratonicea, and Philo of Larissa, and juxtaposes them with the views of the revived Old Academy promoted by Antiochus of Ascalon. Cicero had studied with both Philo and Antiochus, and he viewed the schools they represented, the New Academy and the Old Academy, along with Epicureanism and Stoicism, as the main philosophical schools of his day.

Arcesilaus was the first member of Plato's Academy who took a turn from dogmatism to scepticism. He argued in particular against the epistemological views of Zeno, the founder of Stoicism, and initiated a back and forth exchange between members of the two schools that continued down to Cicero's time two centuries later. As Charles Brittain (2006: xiii–xix) has helpfully noted, readers of the *Academica* must keep three layers of arguments straight: (1) the epistemological debates between the Stoics (including Zeno, Chrysippus, Diogenes of Babylon, and Antipater) and New Academics (Arcesilaus, Carneades, Clitomachus, and Metrodorus of Stratonicea) in the third to second century BCE; (2) the epistemological debate in the second to first century between the New Academic views of Philo and the Old Academic views of Antiochus; and (3) the arguments between the interlocutors in the two versions of Cicero's *Academica*, set, respectively, in 62 BCE and 45 BCE.

The main point at issue in the *Academica* is that of whether knowledge is possible. The Stoics argued that knowledge is attainable, and members of the sceptical New Academy presented counterarguments to show that it was not. Antiochus, who claimed he was reviving the Old Academy, argued that there was a single unified philosophical tradition that included Plato, Aristotle, and the Stoics. He saw Stoic doctrines as refinements of the earlier teachings of Plato and Aristotle, and took over Stoic doctrines, including their epistemology, into the doctrines of his revived Old Academy.[17] In the *Lucullus*, the part of the first version of the *Academica* that survives, Lucullus speaks for Antiochus' dogmatic position and Cicero for Philo's sceptical position. In the part of Book 1 of the second version of the *Academica* that survives, Varro defends Antiochus' position, and Cicero again takes Philo's side.

The Stoic account of perception and knowledge presented in the *Academica* are complex but can be briefly summarized.[18] The Stoics were empiricists who held that knowledge was gradually built up in human beings from sensations. Key terms in Stoic epistemology were (1) impression, (2) assent, (3) apprehension or cognition, and (4) knowledge. (1) Adult human beings have an impression (*phantasia* in Greek, *visum* in Latin) when a sensation is impressed on the soul from outside through the sense organs. These impressions are propositional in form, for example, 'this is white', 'this is a human being'. (Long and Sedley 1987: 240). (2) Humans either assent (*sunkatathesis* in Greek, *adsentiri/approbare* in Latin) or withhold assent from the propositional content (*lekta*) of impressions. When they assent to *lekta* (e.g. assenting to the impression 'this is a human being'), they come to hold opinions, which can be either true or false. (3) Apprehension or cognition (*katalēpsis* in Greek, *perceptio/comprehensio/cognitio* in Latin) results from assenting to a particular type of impression, called a 'cognitive impression' (*phantasia katalēptikē*), which 'arises from what is, of such a kind as could not arise from what is not' (Sextus Empiricus, *Against the Professors* 7.247–52 = Long and Sedley 1987: 243). The Stoics held that cognitive impressions were always true, and that when we assent to them we have a true apprehension or cognition. (4) Knowledge (also often translated 'scientific knowledge': *epistēmē* in Greek, *scientia* in Latin) develops out of apprehensions/cognitions: 'Scientific knowledge [*epistēmē*] is a cognition [*katalēpsis*] which is secure and unchangeable by reason' (Stobaeus 2.73,16 = Long and Sedley 1987: 256). To further clarify the relationship of the four terms, Cicero cites a vivid story about how Zeno used to represent the difference and relationship among impressions, assent, apprehension, and knowledge (*Academica* 2.145: tr. Brittain 2006: 84):

> Zeno used to demonstrate this with gestures. When he had put his hand out flat in front of him with fingers straight, he would say: 'An impression is like this.' Next, after contracting his fingers a bit: 'Assent is like this.' Then, when he had bunched his hand up to make a fist, he would say that this was an 'apprehension' or 'grasp'. (This image also suggested the name he gave to it, *katalēpsis* [lit. 'grasp'], which hadn't been used before.) Finally, when he had put his left hand on top, squeezing his fist tight with some force, he would say that scientific knowledge was like that: a state none but the wise enjoyed.

The Stoic belief that knowledge was possible was directly challenged by the sceptical Academy beginning with Arcesilaus and Carneades. As is clear in the *Academica*, Academic philosophers attacked Stoic epistemology primarily by questioning the status of *katalēpsis*, or apprehension/cognition. Cicero sets out the Academic case concisely at *Academica* 2.83:

> But, to narrow down our debate, please note how small our disagreement is. There are four premises to the conclusion that nothing can be known or apprehended, which is the only subject at question here. They are that
>
> [1] there are some false impressions;
> [2] those [scil. false] impressions aren't apprehensible;
> [3] when two impressions don't differ at all, it's not possible that one is apprehensible, while the other isn't;
> [4] there is no true impression derived from the senses that may not be paired with another impression that doesn't differ from it at all but isn't apprehensible.
>
> Everyone concedes the second and third of these four premises. Epicurus doesn't grant the first; but you, our current opponents, concede that one, too. So the battle is entirely over the fourth premise. (Trans. Brittain 2006: 48–9)

Roman Epistemology 253

This argument lays out the main difference between the Stoics and Antiochus on the one side, and the New Academics on the other. As Cicero notes at the beginning of this passage, the conclusion of this argument is that nothing can be known or apprehended. Cicero points out that the New Academics accept all of the premises (1–4) that lead to the conclusion, while the Stoics and Antiochus do not accept the fourth premise. On the Stoic view, there are impressions that are true and apprehensible, that is, cognitive impressions, that differ from other sorts of impressions that are not cognitive, are assented to by the Stoic sage, and allow us to have cognitions/apprehensions. If the Stoics were to agree that there were no cognitive impressions that could not be distinguished from non-apprehensible impressions, their definition of a cognitive apprehension would collapse.

The Stoics put forward a number of arguments to show that cognitive impressions exist and can be distinguished from non-cognitive impressions, including the metaphysical claim that no two things are exactly alike (and thus one impression could always be distinguished from another), and a claim, based on experience, that people can develop expertise in distinguishing things that at first glance seem indistinguishable (Brittain 2006: xxii). An important part of the Stoic response to the Academic attack was to argue that if there were no cognitive impressions, no one, including the Stoic sage, could be sure that they were assenting to a true proposition, and thus should never assent to any impressions at all. The Stoics argued that if this were true, one would not be able to act at all.

The Academics responded to the Stoics by arguing that action was possible even without the existence of cognitive impressions. All Academics agreed that there are not cognitive impressions that humans beings can assent to in the Stoic sense, and thus that knowledge is unattainable. They developed a system that allowed for holding views and acting, however, although there were differences in emphasis among members of the New Academy.

Cicero (*Academica* 2.99–104) describes one of Carneades' views as interpreted by his student Clitomachus as follows. While Clitomachus denied that there were cognitive impressions, and said one should not assent to impressions, he believed that some impressions are more persuasive (*pithanon* in Greek, *probabile* in Latin) than others, and that one could give 'approval' (*probatio*) to persuasive impressions, hold them as persuasive, and act upon them. Charles Brittain (2008: 9–13) has labelled this Academic view 'radical scepticism', and points out that radical sceptics would not hold these views as beliefs, in the Stoic sense, because they would not take them as true, but merely persuasive

254   *Knowledge in Ancient Philosophy*

and subject to change. Cicero seems to adopt this position as his own in the *Academica*.

A second type of Academic scepticism that Cicero describes, labelled by Brittain (2008:13–16) as 'mitigated scepticism', is one that appears to have been adopted, again developing arguments of Carneades, by Philo of Larissa, Cicero's teacher.[19] Rather than reject assent altogether as the Clitomachus had done, Philo argued that assent is possible, not to cognitive impressions as the Stoics had thought, but to non-cognitive impressions that were 'persuasive'. Philo thus held, unlike Clitomachus, that it was rational to form beliefs on the basis of persuasive impressions that, although one could never be certain they are true, might provide evidence for the truth.

Given the depth and complexity of Cicero's discussion of the epistemological theories of the sceptical New Academy and the revived Old Academy of Antiochus, it is important to turn to the second question raised earlier: why would Cicero write such a technical work on epistemology for his Roman readers immediately after he had written the more accessible *Hortensius*?

There are many possible reasons, but I think a crucial one is directly related to the main topic of the *Hortensius*. Once Cicero's readers have read his account in the *Hortensius* of why one should do philosophy, an important next question is which philosophy would be the best to follow. In the *Academica*, Cicero presents his own answer to the question: the sceptical New Academy. But he presents his case in a way that allows his readers to weigh the evidence themselves and make their own choice about which epistemological theory and philosophical school to adopt. At the end of the *Lucullus* (*Academica* 2. 147–8) Cicero asks his fellow interlocutors what their final views are on the issues they have discussed. Lucullus remains committed to the views of Antiochus, Cicero to the sceptical views of Clitomachus, Catulus to the mitigated sceptical views of Philo, and Hortensius to Cicero's sceptical view. By ending the work in this way, Cicero shows what he thinks the most persuasive view is, but also indicates that each participant in the dialogue, and by extension his readers, need to think through the material on their own and make up their own minds about how best to pursue the study of philosophy.

Given this goal, Cicero must take his readers deeply enough into questions of epistemology to get them to see the differences between the leading philosophical schools of his day: the Stoics, Antiochus' Old Academy, the various sceptical New Academics, and to a more limited degree, the Epicureans.[20] He does this not just with the philosophical arguments he presents, but also with the way he embeds many of the arguments in Roman life and the natural world. In the

Academica, the discussion takes place sitting in the open colonnade (*xystus*) of a villa (2.9), involves stories of Roman administrative and military service (2.11, 2.61), makes use of an analogy based on an intimate knowledge of the Roman Forum (2.70), discusses the relative sharpness of human vision by using examples of gazing at villas at lesser and greater distances from where they are seated at Cumae (2.80), references a well-known example of identical Roman twins (2.84), and refers effectively in two passages to the lovely waters in the area where they are speaking. In one instance (2.100) Cicero discusses how the sage would weigh factors like the distance of the voyage, the seaworthiness of the boat, the experience of the helmsman, and the weather in judging the likelihood of successfully completing a voyage across the bay where they are located. In another vivid section (2.105), Cicero notes the constantly changing colours of the sea that glitters before them to challenge the truth of any individual visual perception. The passage is an excellent example of how Cicero brings his readers into the conversation, making them visualize, along with the interlocutors, the vivid details of a Mediterranean seascape and its philosophical significance. It shows how even everyday sights can be opened up by exploring their epistemological significance.

In short, Cicero takes his Roman reader through a number of technical epistemological discussions, but also succeeds in helping his reader grasp why studying epistemology matters. Not only does he help his readers see that understanding the strengths and weaknesses of the epistemological views of different philosophical schools will help them choose which philosophical school to follow, but also why this is important to their lives. 'Since the order structuring one's whole life is implied by the definition of the highest good, a disagreement about that is a disagreement about the order structuring one's whole life' (*Academica* 2.132, trans. Brittain 2006: 78). And since each philosophical school argues for its view of the highest good based on its epistemology, it is clear that Romans who want to figure out which school to follow must look at their epistemological views.

4. Roman epistemology under the Roman Empire: Seneca

Seneca,[21] born about 100 years after Cicero and Lucretius, wrote philosophy in Latin under different circumstances than either of his predecessors. He was born between 4 and 1 BCE in Corduba, Spain, and was brought to Rome at an early age where he was thoroughly educated in rhetoric and Stoic philosophy. Apart from

256 *Knowledge in Ancient Philosophy*

his philosophical works, he is most famous for being the tutor and advisor of the emperor Nero. His position under Nero became increasingly precarious, and he was forced by Nero to commit suicide in 65 CE.

Seneca is the author of a number of philosophical essays, philosophical letters, and plays, written in a characteristically pointed and memorable style. Brad Inwood (2005: 13) has argued that Seneca's engagement in philosophy was different from Lucretius' and Cicero's, since he had to do less 'missionary work' than his predecessors, and could engage more directly in 'primary philosophy'. His prose works focus primarily on Stoic ethics, and are designed to help his readers live a life consistent with Stoic principles and make progress towards virtue. Some of his works (the *Natural Questions*,[22] *On Providence*, and some of his letters) discuss Stoic physics, especially as it relates to understanding nature and learning to live in accordance with it, but the majority of his essays and letters focus on Stoic ethics. Although Seneca had a deep understanding of all aspects of Stoic philosophy, he chose to downplay Stoic logic and epistemology except as it would help his readers live better. He was not afraid to warn his readers against pursuing the study of logic unnecessarily (Asmis 2015: 226; Seal 2015: 214), and on the few occasions when he explores aspects of Stoic epistemology, he does so only insofar as it helps his readers understand the moral points he is making better. Seneca does not devote any of his philosophical essays or letters to a systematic exposition of the main features of Stoic epistemology. To see how Seneca incorporates aspects of Stoic epistemology in his works, however, it will help to look briefly at the *Letters to Lucilius* which were written towards the end of Seneca's life. (I omit discussion of the details of Stoic epistemology here since they are outlined in the section on Cicero above.)

The *Letters to Lucilius* are considered Seneca's crowning literary and philosophical achievement. A total of 124 letters have survived arranged in twenty books. They treat a variety of topics, and focus primarily on learning how to make moral progress and achieve happiness. In the letters, Seneca plays the role of a Stoic moral advisor to the slightly younger Lucilius and gives advice about how to deal with particular problems facing Lucilius or Seneca. Few letters engage epistemology directly, but a number of them touch on epistemological issues in the service of advancing the discussion of ethical issues. For example, *Letter* 89 focuses on the parts of philosophy and philosophy's relationship to knowledge (*sapientia*),[23] *Letter* 120 explores how human beings come to have a conception (*notitia*) of the good (*bonum*) and the honourable (*honestum*), and *Letter* 124 discusses whether the good (*bonum*) is grasped (*conprendatur*) by perception (*sensus*) or the intellect (*intellectus*).[24] In each of these discussions, Seneca demonstrates command of the relevant details of Stoic epistemology, but always sets them out in the service of broader ethical goals. For example, in *Letter* 89.18 he reminds Lucilius that he is going into such detail about the parts of Stoic philosophy so that it will directly relate to ethics (*mores*); in *Letter* 120 he keeps the question of how we acquire the conception of the good and honourable focused on ethics throughout; and *Letter* 124 ends with a call to Lucilius, once he sees that the good is ultimately grasped by our reason and intellect, to apply this knowledge to seeing what is really valuable in life.

Although Seneca avoids discussing Stoic epistemology for its own sake, it would be wrong to think it is peripheral to his project. It is the ultimate foundation that his ethical arguments rest on, and he deploys it as needed in his works. Indeed, Jula Wildberger (2006: 94–102) has made the interesting suggestion that features of Stoic epistemology help explain some of the striking features of Seneca's letters, including his emphatic use of rhetoric. Seneca's constant and vivid repetitions of key terms and themes may be designed to drive out false impressions and to substitute true beliefs in their place, and then even gradually transform true beliefs into true concepts in the mind of the reader.

5. Conclusion

The three Roman authors we have looked at, Lucretius, Cicero, and Seneca, succeeded over the course of a century to make the doctrines of the schools they represented (Epicureanism, the Sceptical New Academy, and Stoicism) available to their fellow Romans in Latin. They crafted a philosophical vocabulary in Latin, helped their readers think and express philosophical thoughts in their native language, and argued that the philosophies they promoted could make an important contribution to the lives of their readers. They also demonstrated mastery of the epistemological doctrines of their schools and showed how epistemology could buttress the arguments they were making about how best to live one's life. Lucretius uses epistemology to undergird the major claims of Epicurean physics, Cicero argues that studying epistemology is central to choosing which philosophical school to follow and how to lead one's life, and Seneca called on aspects of Stoic epistemology to help his readers make moral progress.

Notes

1 This brief overview of Epicurean canonic is adapted in part from a section of the Introduction to my translation of Lucretius (Lucretius 2003: xvi–xviii). For a more detailed analysis of Epicurean epistemology, see Pierre-Marie Morel's chapter in this volume.

2 Diogenes Laertius lists a fourth criterion of truth, introduced by other Epicureans as 'focusing of thoughts into an impression'. For more on this term, see Long and Sedley (1987: 90).

3 For more on the Epicurean concept of *prolēpsis* ('preconception'), see, most recently, Tsouna (2016). Earlier important accounts include Asmis (1984: 19–80; 2009) and Long and Sedley (1987: 87–90).

4 Epicurus' three letters (*Letter to Herodotus*, *Letter to Pythocles*, and *Letter to Menoeceus*) are found in Diogenes Laertius Book 10. Translations of Epicurus' letters can be found in Inwood and Gerson (1994, 1998).

5 For more on Epicurus' scientific methodology, see Asmis (1984 and 2009), Long and Sedley (1987: 90–7), and Gerson (2009).

6 Book I of the *On Nature* is lost, but Sedley (1998: 113) writes, 'Book I no doubt started with the methodological preliminaries echoed at *Letter to Herodotus* 37–8.'

7 Diogenes Laertius' (10.30–4) account of Epicurus' doctrines proceeds in the same way, prefacing his presentation of the *Letter to Herodotus*, *Letter to Pythocles*, and *Letter to Menoeceus* with his summary of Epicurean canonic and epistemology.

8 All translations of Lucretius are from Lucretius (2003).

9 Gale (1994: 208–28) presents a nuanced and insightful reading of the opening and closing of the poem.

10 For a clear and persuasive account of Lucretius' general avoidance of employing technical Latin terms to translate technical Greek terms, see Sedley (1998: 35–61).

11 For more on the relationship of Lucretius' account in Book 1 to Epicurus, see ibid., 186–202.

12 For more on this passage, see Burnyeat (1978) and Sedley (1998: 85–90).

13 These passages include 4.379–406 (the relationship between perceiving the motion of shadows and the mind's role in interpreting them), 4.802–17 (the role that the 'focusing of the mind' and 'focusing of the senses' play in thinking and in perception), and 5.1028–90 (the development of language and the role that preconceptions play in this development).

14 On the *Hortensius*, see Grilli (2010).

15 Cicero briefly touches on Epicurean epistemology, at *On the Ends of Good and Evil* 1.22, 29–33, 63–4, and *On the Nature of the Gods* 1.43–45, 62–4; on Stoic epistemology, at *On the Ends of Good and Evil* 3. 17–18, 72–3, and *On the Nature of the Gods* 2.5, 13–15; 3.10–11.

Roman Epistemology

16 There was also a brief intermediate stage of composition, when Cicero was contemplating changing the interlocutors to Cato and Brutus. See Griffin (1997: 20–7).

17 For a recent examination of Antiochus' adoption of Stoic epistemology, see Brittain (2012).

18 My account follows those in Long and Sedley (1987: 236–59) and Brittain (2006: xix–xxxviii; 2012). For a fuller account of Stoic epistemology, see the chapter by Marcelo Boeri in this volume.

19 I leave out here what seems to have been Philo's later adoption of a form of fallibilism in his *Roman Books*. Cicero mentions Philo's later views and Antiochus' reaction to them at *Academica* 2.11–12 and 2.18. For more on Philo's views in his *Roman Books*, see Striker (1997) and Brittain (2001: 129–68; 2008: 16–20).

20 Although Cicero does not include an interlocutor who presents Epicurean epistemology, he does comment on aspects of Epicurean philosophy and epistemology, in the *Academica*: 1.5–7, 2.19, 2.45, 2.79–83, 2.97, 2.101, 2.106, 2.115, 2.123, 2.131, 2.139–40, 2.142.

21 Vogt (2016) provides a helpful introduction to Seneca and his writings.

22 The *Natural Questions* raises some epistemological issues that are not treated in this chapter. For more on the topic, see Inwood (2005: 157–200).

23 For a recent analysis of *Letter* 89, see Armisen-Marchetti (2014: 233–8).

24 For discussion and analysis of *Letters* 120 and 124, see Inwood (2007: 322–32, 361–77).

References

Armisen-Marchetti, M. (2014), 'Ontology and Epistemology', in G. Damschen and A. Heil (eds), *Brill's Companion to Seneca, Philosopher and Dramatist*, Leiden: Boston.

Asmis, E. (1984), *Epicurus' Scientific Method*, Ithaca, NY: Cornell University Press.

Asmis, E. (2009), 'Epicurean Empiricism', in J. Warren (ed.), *The Cambridge Companion to Epicureanism*, Cambridge: Cambridge University Press.

Asmis, E. (2015), 'Seneca's Originality', in S. Bartsch and A. Schiesaro (eds), *The Cambridge Companion to Seneca*, Cambridge: Cambridge University Press.

Brittain, C. (2001), *Philo of Larissa: The Last of the Academic Sceptics*, Oxford: Oxford University Press.

Brittain, C. (ed.) (2006), *On Academic Scepticism*, Indianapolis: Hackett.

Brittain, C. (2008), *Philo of Larissa*, in E. N. Zalta (ed.), *The Stanford Encyclopedia of Philosophy* (Fall 2008), http://plato.stanford.edu/archives/fall2008/entries/philo-larissa/.

Brittain, C. (2012), 'Antiochus' Epistemology', in D. N. Sedley (ed.), *The Philosophy of Antiochus*, Cambridge; New York: Cambridge University Press.

Burnyeat, M. F. (1978), 'The Upside-Down Back-to-Front Sceptic of Lucretius IV 472', *Philologus*, 122: 197–206.

Gale, M. (1994), *Myth and Poetry in Lucretius*, Cambridge: Cambridge University Press.

Gerson, L. P. (2009), *Ancient Epistemology*, Cambridge: Cambridge University Press.

Griffin, M. (1997), 'The Composition of the *Academica*: Motives and Versions', in B. Inwood and J. Mansfeld (eds), *Assent and Argument: Studies in Cicero's Academic Books: Proceedings of the 7th Symposium Hellenisticum (Utrecht, August 21–25, 1995)*, Leiden-New York: Brill.

Grilli, A. (ed.) (2010), *Ortensio: Testo Critico, Introduzione, Versione e Commento*, Bologna: Pàtron.

Inwood, B. (2005), *Reading Seneca: Stoic Philosophy at Rome*, Oxford: Oxford University Press.

Inwood, B. (2007), *Seneca: Selected Philosophical Letters*, Oxford: Oxford University Press.

Inwood, B. and Gerson, L. P. (eds) (1994), *The Epicurus Reader: Selected Writings and Testimonia*, Indianapolis: Hackett.

Inwood, B. and Gerson, L. P. (eds) (1998), *Hellenistic Philosophy: Introductory Readings*, Indianapolis: Hackett.

Long, A. A. and Sedley, D. N. (1987), *The Hellenistic Philosophers*, Cambridge: Cambridge University Press.

Lucretius (2003), *On the Nature of Things*, trans. W. G. Englert, Newburyport, MA: Focus Publishing.

Seal, C. (2015), 'Theory and Practice in Seneca's Writings', in S. Bartsch and A. Schiesaro (eds), *The Cambridge Companion to Seneca*, Cambridge: Cambridge University Press.

Sedley, D. N. (1998), *Lucretius and the Transformation of Greek Wisdom*, Cambridge: Cambridge University Press.

Striker, G. (1997), 'Academics Fighting Academics', in B. Inwood and J. Mansfeld (eds), *Assent and Argument: Studies in Cicero's Academic Books: Proceedings of the 7th Symposium Hellenisticum (Utrecht, August 21–25, 1995)*, Leiden-New York: Brill.

Tsouna, V. (2016), 'Epicurean Preconceptions', *Phronesis*, 61: 160–221.

Vogt, K. (2016), 'Seneca', in E. N. Zalta (ed.), *The Stanford Encyclopedia of Philosophy* (Spring 2016), http://plato.stanford.edu/archives/spr2016/entries/seneca/.

Wildberger, J. (2006), 'Seneca and the Stoic Theory of Cognition: Some Preliminary Remarks', in K. Volk and G. D. Williams (eds), *Seeing Seneca Whole*, Leiden-Boston: Brill.

Index

absence of disturbance (see *ataraxia*)

abstractionism 230, 232, 233

Academica (Cicero) 192, 194, 196, 197, 198, 199, 201, 241, 249–55, 259 (see also *Catulus, Lucullus*)

Academic Scepticism 175, 206, 207, 210, 211–13, 217

  debate with Stoics 213–24

Academy, Academic 241, 249–55, 257

account (see *logos*)

Achilles 32

Ackrill, J. 102

action theory 215

activity 147, 150, 152–7, 162–3, 164, 165, 166, 224 (*see also* actuality)

actuality 233 (*see also* activity)

adēla, (*see* non-evident things)

adsentiri (*see* assent)

Aenesidemus 210, 217–20

Aeschylus 16

Aeschines 21

Aëtius 187, 189, 190, 191, 194, 195

affections 224

Against Colotes (Plutarch) 61

Against the Professors (Sextus Empiricus) 57, 61, 62, 64, 189, 192, 195, 196, 197, 198, 201, 252

agnōsia 103 (*see also* ignorance)

agnosticism 56, 57, 59

Agrippa 210, 21, 219

aisthēsis 108–12, 116–17, 119, 121, 122, 231 (*see also* perception)

aitia 22, 25, 113 (*see also* cause, reason)

Alcman of Croton 12, 34, 45

Allen, J. 189

Anacreon 13

Anaxagoras 19, 42–3, 50

Anaxarchus 209

Anaximander 33, 37, 55

Anaximenes 33

Andocides 1

Annas, J. 104, 188

anonymous commentary of Plato's *Theaetetus* 63, 181

Anonymus Iamblichi 19

antilogic 53

Antiochus of Ascalon 210, 213, 250, 251, 253, 254, 259

Antipater 251

Antiphon 16, 19, 50, 51, 52, 56, 63

Antisthenes 21

apodeixis 174, 182–3, 185

Apollo 32

Apology (Plato) 24, 75, 79, 80, 81, 82, 100

aporia (perplexity) 86, 92

appearances 44 (see also *phantasia*)

apprehension 251, 252, 253

approbare (*see* assent)

approval (*probatio*) 253

apraxia 215

Arcesilaus 197, 198, 208, 210–12, 214, 215, 250, 251, 252

Archelaus 50

Archilochus 12

Archytas 26, 27

aretē 13, 24, 50, 52, 61 (*see also* virtue, excellence)

Aristophanes 16

Aristotle 2, 6–8, 10, 11, 20, 23, 25, 43, 45, 51, 61, 62, 63, 64, 65, 125–41, 188, 208, 215, 225, 229, 230, 231, 232, 233, 234, 235, 251

arithmetic 108, 119–20 (*see also* mathematics)

Armisen-Marchetti, M. 259

Arnim von, H. 200

Asclepius (commentator on Aristotle) 61

Asmis, E. 179, 182, 185, 256, 258

assent 189, 194, 197, 198, 216, 251–4

assimilation 224, 226

astronomy 41, 108

ataraxia 8, 170, 184, 206 (*see also* tranquility)

Atomists 42–4

262   *Index*

atoms 42–4
Atticus 250

Bacchylides 16, 17
Barnes, J. 28, 39, 42, 47, 164
Beere, J. 165
being 41, 46, 108, 111, 119, 121 (*see also*
    what is/what is not)
  degrees of 94
belief 1, 3, 68, 69, 72, 74, 80, 135–6,
    148–53, 187, 189, 242, 248, 253,
    254, 257 (see also *doxa, hupolēpsis,*
    opinion, *pistis*)
  and action 215–17
  suspension of (see also *epochē*)
belief-making capacity (see *doxa*)
Benson, H. 5–6, 87, 101, 102, 103
Bett, R. 59, 61
Blood 44
Bluck, R. 101, 102
Boeri, M. 8, 259
Bonhöffer, A. 201
bonum 256 (*see also* good)
Bostock, D. 90, 101, 121, 123
boulēsis (*see* rational desire)
Brancacci, A. 21
Brickhouse, T. 72, 82, 83
Brittain, C. 251, 252, 253, 254, 255, 259
Brown, L. 121, 123
Brunschwig, J. 47
Brutus 259
Buchheim, T. 52
Burnyeat, M. 61, 121, 122, 123, 125, 132,
    145, 164, 258

calculating part (of the soul) 127,
    134–6, 140–1
canonic 242, 244, 246, 247, 248, 249, 258
    (see also *kanōn*)
capacity (*dunamis*) 128, 147, 149–50,
    154–6, 158–9, 165, 166 (*see also*
    potentiality)
Capizzi, A. 64
Carneades 196, 210–12, 217, 250, 251,
    252, 253, 254
Carpenter, A. 122, 123, 124
Carpenter, M. 82
Castagnoli, L. 61
Categories (Aristotle) 230

Cato the elder 212
Cato the younger 259
Catulus 250, 254
Catulus (Cicero) 250 (see also *Academica*)
causal modes 219–20 (*see also*
    Eight Modes)
cause 67, 130, 132, 233, 234, 245 (see also
    aitia, reason)
Cave (Allegory of) 85, 99
certainty 7
Chappell, T. 121, 124
Charmides (Plato) 72, 75–6, 82
Cherniss, H. 123, 124
Chrysippus 192, 251
Cicero 9, 170, 172, 180, 182, 187, 188, 192,
    194, 196, 197, 198, 201, 208, 210–11,
    212, 241, 249–55, 258, 259
Clement of Alexandria 179
Clitomachus 250, 251, 253, 254
cognition 44, 197, 198, 199, 201, 224,
    251, 252, 253 (see also *comprehensio,*
    katalēpsis, logos, perceptio)
cognitive (or graspable) impression 188,
    195, 196, 197, 252, 253, 254 (see also
    phantasia katalēptikē)
Colotes 171
commanding faculty (*hegemonikon*) 189,
    190, 194
Commentary on Alcibiades *I* (Proclus) 233
Commentary on Aristotle's Analytica
    Priora (John Philoponus) 234, 235
Commentary on Aristotle's Analytica
    Posteriora (John Philoponus) 234
Commentary on Aristotle's De anima (John
    Philoponus) 234
Commentary on Aristotle's De anima
    (Pseudo-Simplicus, Priscian of
    Lydia(?)) 235, 237
Commentary on Euclid's Elements *I*
    (Proclus) 232, 233
Commentary on Ptolemy's Harmonics
    (Porphyry) 227, 228, 229, 230
Commentary on the Phaedo
    (Damascius) 236
Commentary on the Timaeus
    (Porphyry) 229
Commentary on the Timaeus (Proclus)
    231, 232
common sense 224

Index

common sensibles 227
comprehensio 252 (*see also* cognition)
comprehension (see *nous*)
concept 188, 189, 190, 191, 192, 193, 198, 227, 230, 233, 242, 243, 246, 257
  general 242, 243, 246
contemplation 23 (see also *theoria*)
convention 43, 44
Cooper, J. 112, 123, 124
Corax 52
Corduba (Spain) 255
Cornford, F. 121, 124
cosmology 4, 21, 27, 41
cosmos/*kosmos* 37, 38, 42, 43, 46
Critias (Plato) 121
craft/craft-knowledge 67, 75, 79, 126–7, 137 (*see also* expertise, skill, *technē*)
Craik, E. 16
Cratylus (Plato) 65
criterion 169, 171–6, 179–83, 205, 213, 214–15
  of truth 188, 196, 242, 243, 244, 246, 258
  for action 216
Critias 19, 55
Cumae 255
custom (as a guide to the sceptic) 217
Cynics 27
Cyrenaics 27

Damascius 236
Dancy, R. 121, 124
De anima (Aristotle) 149, 150, 156, 164, 165, 229, 233
Defense of Palamedes (Gorgias) 51, 53, 57–8
definition/definitional knowledge 76–80, 172, 174, 177, 179, 181–2, 232, 233
De intellectu (John Philoponus) 234
De interpretatione (Aristotle) 149–50
deliberation 127, 133–6, 138, 140
Democritus 19, 20, 42–4, 61, 62, 171, 175, 206, 209
demonstration 129, 131–3, 145–6, 162–3, 232, 233 (see also *apodeixis*)
demonstrative science 232
De Rerum Natura (Lucretius) 242 (see also *On the Nature of Things*)
Descartes 69, 213, 215

description 227
determinism 212
dialectics 187, 199
dialegesthai (*see also* dialectics) 118
dialogue (see *dialegesthai*)
dianoētikoi logoi 231
dianoia 96–9, 118 (*see also* discursive reason, discursive soul)
Diels, H. and Kranz, W. 47, 49, 64
Diogenes of Apollonia 19
Diogenes of Babylon 251
Diogenes Laertius 49, 52, 53, 64, 175–8, 182–3, 188, 195, 198, 201, 242, 258
Diogenes of Oenoanda 171–2, 178, 186
discursive reason 226, 227, 231, 232, 233 (see also *dianoia*)
discursive soul 226, 227 (see also *dianoia*)
Dissoi Logoi 19, 20
dissonance (as a mode) 219–20
divided line 85, 96–7, 104, 120
dogmatism 205, 214, 216, 219
  negative dogmatism 208, 211, 215, 217
Donellan, K. 103
doxa 21, 22, 94–6, 98, 103, 112–13, 117–18, 122, 123, 148–53, 169, 174–7, 179–80, 183–4, 187, 227, 228, 231, 232, 233 (*see also* belief, opinion)
doxastikos logos 231
dream theory 113–16
dunamis (*see* capacity)

eidōla 173, 175 (*see also* images)
Eight Modes 218–20 (*see also* Modes, Five Modes, Ten Modes)
eikasia (imaging or imagination) 96
Elea, Eleatic 38
Eleatic properties 40, 42
Eleatic Stranger 22
elements 41, 42–3
Elements of Physics (Proclus) 238
Elenchos/elenchus (Socratic) 21, 72–81
Emotion 242
Empedocles 18–19, 21, 27, 43, 44, 55, 242
empeiria 119, 234, 235 (*see also* experience)
empiricism 6, 8, 9, 169–70, 173, 183–5, 190, 242, 251 (*see also* proto-empiricism)
Encomium of Helen (Gorgias) 51, 53, 54, 57

264 *Index*

end (*see* teleology)
energeia 233
Englert, W. 9
Enneads (Plotinus) 223, 224, 225, 226
Ennius 242
ennoia 227, 228
Ephesus 36
epi (set over) 95
Epictetus 188, 192
Epicurus/Epicurean 8, 9, 14–15, 27, 62,
    169–76, 175–86, 190, 201, 209, 241–9,
    250, 257, 258
Epinomis (Ps.-Plato) 27
epistēmē 2, 4, 11–28, 68, 94–6, 103,
    107–9, 111–16, 117–18, 118–20, 121,
    123, 125, 128, 131, 145–8, 148–53,
    158–63, 232, 234, 235, 252 (*see also*
    understanding
epistēmē haplōs (*see* unqualified
    knowledge, understanding, science)
epistēmonikon (*see* understanding part)
epistemological methods in Plato 96
epistemological priority 230
epochē 9, 205, 209, 211, 218 (*see also* belief)
equipollence (see *isosthenia*)
eristic 53
essence 232, 235
ethics 1, 10, 14–15, 20, 24, 67, 69, 71, 79,
    81, 199
Euclid 232
eudaimonia 14 (*see also* happiness)
Eudemian Ethics (Aristotle) 25, 125,
    127–8, 135–6
Euripides 16–17
Eusebius 64
Euthydemus 50
Euthydemus (Plato) 4, 53, 65, 68,
    70–1, 75, 92
Euthyphro (Plato) 77–9, 82
evening star 41
Everson, S. 165, 166
excellence (see *aretē*)
Excerpts (Stobaeus) 188, 194, 197, 198, 199
exercise (*see* activity)
experience 169–71, 174, 176, 178, 183 (see
    also *empeiria*)
expertise 55, 67, 74 (*see also* craft, skill,
    technē)
explanation 126, 128, 130, 132, 136, 244

multiple 244
    (see also *aitia*, *logos*)
externalism 7, 148–9, 153, 165
eye 43

fallibilism/infallibilism 62, 200, 226, 259
farming 119, 120
feeling 242, 244
    as a guide to the sceptic 217
    (see also *pathē*)
Ferejohn, M. 104
Ferrari, G., and Griffith, T. 103
Fine, G. 68, 88, 92, 95, 101, 103, 122, 124
fire 37
Five Modes 219–20 (*see also* Modes,
    Eight Modes, Ten Modes)
flux 110
focusing of the mind 258
focusing of the senses 258
forms 6, 25, 26, 85, 90–100, 102, 103, 109,
    111, 112, 116, 117–18, 121, 123, 229,
    230, 236
Franklin, L. 91, 102, 103
Frede, D. 120
Frede, M. 188, 196, 198, 199
function (*see* teleology)

Gagarin, M. 64
Gale, M. 258
Galen 175, 234
Gansen, T. 122, 124
Garden (Epicurean) 170–2
Gartner, C. 7
Geddes, W. 101
general concepts (*see* concept)
generalship 119–20
Generation of Animals (Aristotle) 148
genus 230
geometrical conversion 233
geometry 108, 125–6, 137 (*see also*
    mathematics)
Gerson, L. 121, 189, 197, 258
Giannopoulou, Z. 121
gignōskein (see *gnosis*)
Glidden, D. 178–85
gnomē 36, 44
gnōsis 68, 96, 103, 104, 108, 127, 131, 135,
    145–6, 148–53 (see also *epistēmē*,
    knowledge)

Index

gods 31–5
gold 37
Goldschmidt, V. 178, 180, 185
Gonzalez, F. 103
good 256 (see also *bonum*, happiness)
Gorgias 19, 20, 49, 50, 51, 52, 53, 54, 57–9, 207
Gorgias (Plato) 50, 54, 74, 76, 80, 81, 82, 199
Gosling, J. 123, 124
Gourinat, J.-B. 199, 202
Graham, D. 3–4, 28, 47, 64
graspability (see *katalēpsis*)
Griffin, M. 250, 259
Grilli, A. 258
Grube, D. 97, 103
Gulley, N. 101, 102
Guthrie, W. 59, 64
gymnosophists 209

Hackforth, R. 101, 102, 123, 124
Hammerstaedt, J. 178, 185
Hankinson, R. 188, 189
harmony 45
happiness 67, 68, 70, 71, 128–9, 138, 242, 249, 256 (see also *eudaimonia*)
Harte, V. 102, 104, 122, 124
Hecataeus of Miletus 36
Heinimann, F. 64
Hellenistic 225, 229
Henry, D. 129–30
Heraclitus 18–19, 20, 21, 27, 28, 35–8, 39, 46, 54, 55, 100, 109, 206
Hermarchus 171
Herodotus 16, 55
Hesiod 31–2, 36, 38, 50
Hetherington, S. 10
Hippias 50
Hippias Major (Plato) 24, 82
Hippocrates/Hippocratic 16
hodos (see road)
Homer 12, 13, 32, 36, 38, 50, 64, 109
honourable (*honestum*) 256
Hortensius 250, 254
Hortensius (Cicero) 249, 254, 258
housebuilding 119–20
Huffman, C. 26
Hume, D. 201, 206
hupolēpsis 148–53 (*see also* belief)

Hussey, E. 47, 64
hypothesis, method of 85, 94, 97–9, 100, 104
    as a mode 219–20

ideas (*see* forms)
ignorance 4, 5, 67–82, 85, 92–5, 100, 104
    (see also *agnosia*)
images 43, 225, 228, 229, 233 (see also *eidōla*)
impression 188, 189, 190, 192, 193, 194, 195, 196, 198, 224, 251, 252, 253, 254, 257 (see also *phantasia, tupos*)
impressor (*phantaston*) 188
impulsive impression 194
inactivity (see *apraxia*)
incorrigibility 90
indeterminability 209
induction 162–3, 166
infallibilism (*see* fallibilism)
inference 34, 45, 172, 174, 182–4
information 2, 3, 6
innateness 191, 224, 225, 226, 227, 230, 233
intellect 226, 228, 230, 257
intellectualism (Socratic) 71–2, 80
intelligence 126, 134 (see also *noēsis, nous, phronēsis*)
intelligible object 226
intelligible principles 226
intelligible structure 233
Inwood, B. 194, 200, 256, 259
Inwood, B., and Gerson, L. 258
Ionia, Ionian 33–8, 46
Irwin, T. 92–3
Isagōgē (Porphyry) 237
isosthenia 211

Johansen, T. 122, 124
John Philoponus 234
judgement 224, 225, 243
justification 1, 2, 3, 7, 147, 150 (see also *logos*)

Kahn, C. 122, 124
kanōn 242 (*see also* canonic)
Kant, I. 46
katalēpsis 214, 252 (*see also* cognition, perceptio, comprehensio)
kathartic argument 208

266   *Index*

Kelsey, S. 91, 102, 103
Kerferd, G. 49
knowledge vii, viii 1–10, 32, 45–6, 94–6,
     125, 127–8, 130–2, 134–5, 137, 139,
     169, 170–1, 174, 175, 176, 177, 179,
     180, 181, 183, 184, 185, 187, 188,
     190, 191, 192, 193, 194, 197, 242,
     243, 244, 248, 249, 251, 252, 253,
     255, 256, 257
    divine and human 32–8, 45–6
    knowing that vs. knowing why 147
    (see also *epistēmē, gnōsis,* science,
     understanding)
kosmos (*see* cosmos/*kosmos*)
kratein (to have power) 43
Kripke, S. 103
krisis (separation) 39

Laches (Plato) 77, 82
Laks, A. 47
Laks, A. and Most, G. 57
language 192, 193, 201
Larisa 113
Lautner, P. 9
Laws (Plato) 27, 60, 121
Lee, M.-K. 59, 61
lekta (*see* proposition)
Lesher, J. 47, 64
Letter to Herodotus (Epicurus) 243, 244,
     246, 258
Letter to Menoeceus (Epicurus) 258
Letter to Pythocles (Epicurus) 244, 258
Letters to Lucilius 256, 259
Leucippus 42, 57
light and night 41, 42
limiters and unlimiteds 45–6
Lloyd, G. 33–4, 47
Locke J. 169
logic 187, 242, 256
logistikon (*see* calculating part)
logos/logoi 36–7, 112–16, 117–18, 122,
     231, 232, 233, 235, 236 (*see also*
     explanation, justification)
Lombardo, S. 27
Long, A. 174, 177, 179, 185–6, 199
Long, A. and Sedley, D. 200, 251, 252, 258
lookouts (see *tēresis*)
Lorenz, H. 112
Lourenço, J. 4–5, 81

Lucilius 256
Lucretius 9, 170, 172–3, 175, 180, 183–5,
     241, 242–9, 255, 258
Lucullus 250
Lucullus (Cicero) 250, 251, 254 (see also
     Academica)
Lysis (Plato) 82

man-measure thesis (Protagoras) 52, 53,
     59–63 (*see also* relativism)
Manuwald, A. 181, 186
Marmadoro, A. 165, 166
materialism 190 (*see also* physicalism)
material intellect 229
mathematics 23, 119, 123, 131 (*see also*
     arithmetic, geometry)
May, H. 83
McDowell, J. 121, 124
McPartland, K. 7
measurement 119–20
medicine 16, 19, 119–20
Meditations (Descartes) 69
Megarians 213
Melissus 19, 57
Memmius 245
membrane 234
Memorabilia (Xenophon) 64
memory 32, 45, 191, 192, 193,
     225, 226
Menexenus (Plato) 63
Meno (Plato) 5, 10, 22, 70, 77, 82, 96–8,
     92–3, 95, 102, 104, 113, 120, 122,
     165, 191
Meno's paradox 86–8, 90, 93
mental image 228
mere notion (*ennoia psilē*) 233
Metaphrasis (Priscian of Lydia) 235
Metaphysics (Aristotle) 25, 26, 45, 62, 63,
     65, 156, 159, 165, 166, 231
Metrodorus of Lampsacus 171
Metrodorus of Stratonicea 250, 251
Mignucci, M. 196
Miletus 33, 36
Milesians 33–4
mind 43–4, 191, 192, 193, 194, 196, 197,
     198, 201
misperception 156, 157, 166
mnemosunē 32
Modrak, D. 112, 124

Index

Modes 217–20 (*see also* Eight Modes, Five Modes, Ten Modes)
monism 40
moon 41
moral 187 (*see also* ethics)
Moravcsik, J. 93
Morel, P.-M. 8, 179, 184–6, 258
morning star 41
Moss, J. 82, 164
Most, G. 64
multiple explanations (*see* explanation)
Musaeus 50
Muses 32
music 108, 119, 120
Musonius Rufus 188

naturalism 7
Natural Questions (Seneca) 256, 259
nature 45
   as a guide to the sceptic 217
natures 38 (*see also* nature)
Nehamas, A. 92–3, 102
Nemesius 190
Neo-Ionians 41–6
Neoplatonism 9
Nero 256
Nicomachean Ethics (Aristotle) 26, 125–41, 151, 164
Nielsen, K. 133
noēsis (intelligence or understanding) 96
non-evident things 243
non-identity of discernibles 89
norm 227
notions 225, 229, 230 (see also *logos/logoi*)
notitia 248, 256 (*see also* preconception)
Notomi, N. 3, 49, 51, 64
nous (comprehension) 25, 108, 117, 119, 146, 158–63 (*see also* intelligence, knowledge, *comprehensio, katalēpsis*), thought, understanding)

Obbink D. 185–6
Olfert, C. 134
On Common Notions (Plutarch) 189, 199
On Divination (Cicero) 249
On Duties (Cicero) 249
On the Ends of Good and Evil (Cicero) 249, 258
On Fate (Cicero) 201, 249

On Gods (Protagoras) 52, 56, 64
On the Laws (Cicero) 249
On Nature (Epicurus) 244, 246, 258
On the Nature of the Gods 249, 258
On the Orator (Cicero) 249
On Providence (Seneca) 256
On Plato's *Parmenides* (Proclus) 65
On Sense-Perception (Porphyry) 228
On the Republic (Cicero) 249
On Stoic Self-Contradictions (Plutarch) 192
On the Senses (Theophrastus) 43
On the Soul (Aristotle) 43
On What Is Not (Gorgias) 57
ontology 40, 41, 43, 45
opinion 5, 8, 38, 45, 54, 94, 95, 97, 100, 103, 104, 187, 188, 197, 198, 199, 251 (*see also* belief, *doxa*)
Orpheus 50
ouden mallon (no more this than that) 218–19
ousia (see essence, being)
Outlines of Pyrrhonism (Sextus Empiricus) 62, 64
Owen, G. 101, 123, 124

pain 243
paradox (inquiry *vs.* discovery) 102
Parmenides 19, 38–41, 45, 46, 54, 55, 57, 63, 100, 103, 171
Parmenides (Plato) 107, 115, 118, 121, 123
particulars 132–3, 135, 138
pathē 243 (*see also* feeling)
Peck, A. 164
Pendrick, G. 64
Penner, T. 72, 96, 101, 103
perceptio 252 (*see also* cognition
perception 8, 43, 44, 45, 68, 71, 80, 150, 152, 153–8, 159, 165, 166, 188, 189, 190, 191, 193, 194, 195, 198, 199, 202, 225, 228, 229, 234, 235, 242, 243, 244, 246, 247, 248, 255, 256, 258 (see also *aisthēsis, sensus*)
perceptible/sensible form 225, 227, 228, 232
perceptual content 226
perceptual experience 193
perceptual images 227
perceptual power 235

268   *Index*

perceptual realism 226
presocratic questioning of 206–7
Pericles 50, 60
peritrope argument 110
persuasive 253, 254
Phaedo (Plato) 5, 10, 21, 45, 86–9, 90–2,
 101, 102, 107, 111, 120, 121, 122, 191
Phaedrus (Plato) 56, 101, 119, 121
phantasia 173, 189, 251 (*see also*
 appearance, impression,
 representation, *visum*)
phantasia kataleptikē 188, 213,
 215, 252 (*see also* cognitive
 impression)
phantasma (figment) 195
phantaston (*see* impressor)
Philebus (Plato) 23, 107, 108, 114, 115,
 118–20, 121, 122, 123
Philip of Opus 27
Philo of Larissa 210, 213, 250, 251,
 254, 259
Philodemus 172, 180–1, 183, 185–6
Philolaus of Croton 19, 45–6
philosophia 241
phronēsis 20, 21, 24, 26, 68, 108, 119, 147,
 148, 151, 164 (*see also* intelligence,
 practical wisdom)
physicalism 189 (*see also* materialism)
physics 241, 242, 244, 247, 248, 249,
 256, 257
Physics (Aristotle) 165, 166
physis (*see* nature, natures)
pictorial content 228, 229
Pindar 12
pistis (belief or trust) 96
pithanon (*see* persuasive)
Plato 5–6, 20, 21, 23, 27, 28, 41, 45, 50, 51,
 58, 59, 60, 63, 64, 73, 81, 107–23, 165,
 169, 171, 179, 181, 183, 187, 188, 206,
 225, 229, 230, 233, 251
 and Academics 207–8, 212–13
 the Platonic Principle 218–19
pleasure 118, 120, 243
Plotinus 27, 223–7, 236
pluralists 42, 46
Plutarch 61, 170–1, 189, 192
pneuma 234
Polansky, R. 82
Politicus (Plato; see *Statesman)*

political science (*politikē epistēmē*) 125,
 128, 131, 133, 138–41
politics 128
Politics (Aristotle) 139, 166
Polus 50
Polystratus 171
Porphyry 227–30
Poseidon 33
Posterior Analytics (Aristotle) 7, 23, 25, 45,
 122, 126, 128–33, 145, 146, 147,
 150–1, 158–9, 233
potentiality (see capacity)
practical/theoretical 1, 23–4 (see also
 phronēsis)
practical truth 134, 136
practical wisdom 133, 135–41 (see also
 phronēsis)
preconception 170–2, 176–82, 184–6, 192,
 201, 243, 244, 246, 248, 253, 258 (see
 also *notitia*)
Preparation for the Gospel (Eudebius) 64
Priscian of Lydia 235
probabile (*see* persuasive)
probatio (*see* approval)
Proclus 65, 230–3
Prodicus 53, 55, 56
project 232
projective activity 235
projectionist 236
prolēpsis (*see* preconception)
proper function 149–53, 153–8 (*see also*
 teleology)
propositions/propositional attitudes 6, 85,
 95, 96, 99, 103, 194, 197, 233
 propositional content (*lekta*) 251
Protagoras 28, 49, 50, 52, 53, 54, 56,
 59–61, 62, 63, 64, 108, 109, 207,
 215, 217
Protagoras (Plato) 28, 49, 50, 82
Protagoreanism 109, 110, 112
 contra 94
proto-dualism 43
proto-empiricism 40, 45–6 (*see also*
 empiricism)
proto-rationalism 40, 45–6 (*see also*
 rationalism)
Ps. Galen 190, 201
Pseudo-Simplicius 235
Ptolemy 229

Index

269

Pyrrho of Elis and Pyrrhonism 205,
208–9, 214, 215, 206, 220
  Pyrrhonian revival 217–19
Pythagoras/Pythagorean 18, 26, 36, 45, 86

qualities 42

rational desire 136
rational soul 228, 229
rationalism 6, 8 (*see also*
  proto-rationalism)
reality 242, 246
reason/reasoning 22, 39–40, 194, 199,
  200, 246, 248, 252, 257 (see also
  aitia, logos)
reciprocity (as a mode) 219–20
recognition 228, 230
recollection (*anamnēsis*) 5, 8, 9, 10, 85–8,
  90–2, 94, 96, 99, 103, 225, 227, 229,
  233, 236
Reeve, C. 103, 133
regress (as a mode) 219–20
relativism 59–63, 65, 207, 218–19 (*see also*
  man-measure thesis)
relativity (as a mode) 219–20
reliability 1, 3, 72, 80
religion, ancient Greek 35, 245
representation 224, 225, 226, 232 (see also
  phantasia)
representational power/capacity 225, 228,
  229, 231, 232 (see also *phantasia*)
Republic (Plato) 6, 82, 86, 92, 94, 95, 97,
  103, 104, 109, 111, 120, 121, 122,
  165, 187
Reshotko, N. 5–6, 8, 82, 95, 102
rhetoric 52, 53, 54, 57, 58, 207
river 37
road 37
Robinson, T. 53
Roman Books (Philo) 259
Rome 255
Romilly de, J. 51
Ross, W. 121, 124, 164
routine (see *tribē*)

sailing 119–20
Sandbach, F. 191
Sanderman, D. 82
Santana, A. 82

saphēs 35, 46
Sappho 12
sceptics, scepticism 7, 8–9, 68, 69, 170–2,
  175, 249–55
  skeptical argument schemata 217–20
  (*see also* Modes, Eight Modes, Five
  Modes, Ten Modes)
Schiappa, E. 53
Schofield, M. 189
science 7, 8, 125–6, 128–30, 133, 135,
  137–8, 169, 176, 181, 183–5
  (see also *epistēmē*, knowledge,
  understanding)
scientia 252, 256 (see also *epistēmē*,
  knowledge)
scientific part (of the soul) (see
  understanding part of the soul)
Scolnicov, S. 93
Scott, D. 86–7, 90–1, 101, 102, 201
Seal, C. 256
second-order perception 234
secret doctrine 109–10
Sedley, D. 122, 123, 124, 174, 177, 186,
  242, 245, 246, 248
self-knowledge 225, 229
Semonides 31
Seneca 9, 241, 255–7
sensation 169–79, 182–4, 242, 243, 247,
  248, 251
sense organ 190, 194, 198
sense perception (*see* perception)
sensible form (*see* perceptible/
  sensible form)
sensory experience (see *empeiria*)
sensus 257 (*see also* perception)
Sentences (Porphyry) 229, 230
Sextus Empiricus 53, 57, 58, 59, 61, 62, 64,
  175–6, 183, 189, 192, 196, 197, 198,
  201, 210, 216, 220, 252
ship-building 119–20
skill 2–3, 5, 11–28 (*see also* craft, expertise,
  technē)
Simonides 15, 50
Smith, M. 178, 186
Smith, N. 4–5, 72, 82, 83, 103, 104, 202
Snell, B. 64
Socrates 20, 21, 23, 50, 51, 63, 67–82, 112,
  113, 116, 118, 171
  and Academics 207

and modes 208
as proto-sceptic 209
Solon 12, 15, 17
sophia 2, 4, 5, 11–28, 68, 108,
 126, 134–5, 139, 145, 147 (*see also*
 wisdom)
sophist (*sophistēs*) 49–65
Sophist (Plato) 58, 107, 114, 115,
 119, 121
Sophistical Refutations (Aristotle) 51
Sophist (Plato) 58, 102
Sophistical Refutations 51
Sophocles 16
Sorabji, R. 194
Sosa, E. 2–3
soul 117, 188, 189, 190, 191, 193, 194, 195,
 198, 199, 201
species 230
Sprague, R. 49, 64
standard 225
Statesman (Plato) 22, 107, 114, 118,
 119, 121
Stobaeus 188, 194, 197, 198
Stoics, Stoicism 8–9, 27, 62, 170, 172,
 175–6, 205, 210, 212, 217, 224, 241,
 249, 250–7
Stoic-sceptic debate 213–14
Striker, G. 178, 186, 259
stuffs 42
subjectivism 62
substantial *logoi* 231
Suda 49
sun 41
sunaisthēsis (joint perception involving
 consciousness) 231
sunkatathesis (see assent)
Symposium (Plato) 121, 122
Syrianus 230

technē 6, 19, 52, 53, 54, 68, 70, 119,
 123, 147, 159, 164 (*see also* craft,
 expertise, skill)
as a guide to the sceptic 217
teleology 148–9, 153–8 (*see also* proper
 function)
Ten Modes 210, 218, 220
tēresis 217
Thales 33–4

Theaetetus 108, 109, 111–13, 118
Theaetetus (Plato) 6, 24, 28, 52, 58, 59, 60,
 62, 63, 64, 92, 95, 100, 102, 107,
 108–16, 117, 118, 120, 121, 122,
 123, 165
Theognis/Theognidea 12–13, 31–2
Theophrastus 43
theoretical vii (*see also* practical/
 theoretical)
theoretical wisdom (see *Sophia*)
theoria 147, *see* contemplation
Thomas, J. 93
thought 226
Thrasyllus 212
Thrasymachus 50, 52
Thucydides 17
Timaeus 116–17, 120, 123, 235
Timaeus (Plato) 41, 107, 115, 116–18,
 121, 122
time 117
Timon 64, 209
Tisias 52, 65
Topics (Aristotle) 157
tranquility 206, 217–18, 220 (see also
 ataraxia)
tribē (routine) 119
truth (and falsehood) 2–3, 4, 23, 38, 41,
 42, 52–55, 68, 73, 108, 109, 111, 112,
 117–18, 119–20, 123, 126, 132,
 134–7, 140, 188, 195, 197, 242, 243,
 246, 247, 248, 251, 254, 255
Truth (Protagoras) 52, 59
Tsouna, V. 172, 178–9, 186, 258
tupos 173, 178 (*see also* impression)
Tusculan Disputations (Cicero) 201, 249
two world theory 94

understanding 3, 5, 6–8, 9, 125–41 (see also
 epistēmē, knowledge, *nous*, science)
part of the soul (*epistēmonikon*) 127,
 134–6, 140–1
theoretical 125–8, 133, 135–7, 141
unqualified (*epistēmē haplōs*)
 126–33, 140
unfold 227
universe 117 (see also *cosmos/kosmos*)
universals/universal concept 126–7, 129–31,
 133–7, 139–40, 228, 230, 233

Varro 250
Velleius 180
Venus 244, 245, 249
verbalization 227
virtue 67, 125–8, 133–6, 140–1, 199 (see also *aretē*)
visum (*see* impression, *phantasia*)
Vlastos, G. 73, 82, 95, 101, 103
Vogt, K. 259
void 42
vortex 44

warrant 1, 2, 7, 147, 152–3, 156–7, 165
wax tablet model 111
weighing 119–20
West, M. 23
what-is/what-is-not 39–40, 41 (*see also* being)
White, N. 92

Wildberger, J. 257
Williams, T 102
Williamson, T. 196
wisdom 2–3, 4, 11, 36, 67, 69, 71, 80, 187, 199, 200 (see also *phronēsis*, *sophia*)
Wolfsdorf, D. 2, 3, 22, 23, 82
Woodruff, P. 9, 82
world, world-order (*see* cosmos/*kosmos*)

Xeniades 62
Xenophanes 17–18, 34–6, 54, 55, 64
Xenophon 64

Zeno of Citium 190, 194, 199, 210, 251, 252
Zeno of Elea 19, 57
Zeus 31, 33
Zilioli, U. 61